Principles of Addictions and the Law

Applications in Forensic, Mental Health, and Medical Practice

Principles of Addictions and the Law

Applications in Forensic, Mental Health, and Medical Practice

Edited by
Norman S. Miller

AMSTERDAM • BOSTON • HEIDELBERG • LONDON
NEW YORK • OXFORD • PARIS • SAN DIEGO
SAN FRANCISCO • SINGAPORE • SYDNEY • TOKYO

Academic Press is an imprint of Elsevier

BP 45

Academic Press is an imprint of Elsevier
32 Jamestown Road, London NW1 7BY, UK
30 Corporate Drive, Suite 400, Burlington, MA 01803, USA
525 B Street, Suite 1900, San Diego, CA 92101-4495, USA

First edition 2010

British Library Cataloguing-in-Publication Data
A catalogue record for this book is available from the British Library

Library of Congress Cataloging-in-Publication Data
A catalog record for this book is available from the Library of Congress

ISBN: 978-0-12-496736-6

For information on all Academic Press publications
visit our website at www.elsevierdirect.com

Typeset by Macmillan Publishing Solutions
www.macmillansolutions.com

Printed and bound in United States of America

10 11 12 13   10 9 8 7 6 5 4 3 2 1

Working together to grow
libraries in developing countries

www.elsevier.com | www.bookaid.org | www.sabre.org

ELSEVIER   BOOK AID International   Sabre Foundation

Contents

Contributors

Anna Baumgras (1), Midland, MI, USA

Maureen Beasley-Greenwood (4), Cherry Street Health Services, Grand Rapids, MI, USA

Roy G. Beran (5), South Western Clinical School, University of New South Wales: School of Medicine, Griffith University; and Strategic Health Evaluators, Chatswood, NSW, Australia

Mark Cooney (9), Thomas M. Cooley Law School, Lansing, MI, USA

Adair Crosley (14), Northwestern University, Chicago, IL, USA

Mark S. Gold (12), School of Law Department of Psychiatry, University of Florida College of Medicine & McKnight Brain Institute, Depts of Psychiatry, Neuroscience, Anesthesiology, Community Health & Family Medicine, Gainsville, FL, USA

Bruce A. Goldberger (13), Department of Pathology, Immunology and Laboratory Medicine, University of Florida College of Medicine, Gainesville, FL, USA

Mark J. Greenwood (4), Aero Med Spectrum Health, Grand Rapids, MI, USA

Richard A. Greer (12), Division of Forensic Psychiatry, University of Florida, College of Medicine, Department of Psychiatry, Gainsville, FL, USA

Peter J. Hammer (8), Wayne State University Law School, Detroit, MI, USA

Kavita Kalidas (18), Headache Fellow, Department of Neurology, University of South Florida College of Medicine, FL, USA

Susan C. Kim (7), O'Neill Institute for National and Global Health Law, Georgetown University, Washington, DC, USA

Janine Kremling (16), Department of Criminal Justice, California State University at San Bernardino, CA, USA

Woodburne O. Levy (18), Department of Mental Health and Behavioral Sciences, University of South Florida College of Medicine, James A Haley Veteran Affairs Medical Center, Tampa, FL, USA

Sana Loue (6), Case Western Reserve University, School of Medicine, Department of Epidemiology and Biostatistics, Cleveland, OH, USA

Michele L. Merves (13), Department of Pathology, Immunology and Laboratory Medicine, University of Florida College of Medicine, Gainesville, FL, USA

Norman S. Miller (2, 3, 10, 17, 19), Department of Medicine, College of Human Medicine, Michigan State University, East Lansing, MI, USA

Roger H. Peters (16), Department of Mental Health Law and Policy, Louis de la Parte, Florida Mental Health Institute, University of South Florida, FL, USA

John M. Ray (16), Department of Psychology, University of South Florida, FL, USA

Joel M. Silberberg (14), Division of Psychiatry and Law, Feinberg School of Medicine, Northwestern University, Chicago, IL, USA

Werner U. Spitz (11), Wayne State University School of Medicine, University of Windsor, Ontario, Canada

Sara Spratt (2), Private Practice, Chicago, IL, USA

Lesley Stone (7), Georgetown University School of Foreign Service, Washington, DC, USA

Frank E. Vandervort (15), University of Michigan, Ann Arbor, MI, USA

Drug and alcohol addictions and the law are historically well acquainted in the American legal system. The pervasive presence of legal consequences from alcohol and drug disorders is evidence in medical-legal populations. The identification and treatment of addictive diseases are increasingly important in forensic practice, particularly in cases pertaining to criminal conduct, malpractice, employment, disability, child custody, and correctional psychiatry.

Courts make legal decisions that have direct bearing on the fate of those with addictive disorders. The legislative branches of federal and state governments create significant and far-reaching laws that affect large numbers of addicted individuals. The constitutional amendments, particularly the 14th Amendment, provide due process and equal protection of the law for individuals with drug and alcohol addictions. Governmental administrative agencies create policies, rules, codes, and regulations to execute legislative statutes that govern the deterrence, treatment, prosecution, and diversion of offenders with addictive diseases.

Alcohol and drug addiction occupy a paradoxical place within medicine and the law. On the one hand, addiction is considered a disabling illness. As early as 1925 the United States Supreme Court stated that addicts "are diseased and proper subjects for ... treatment." On the other hand, addiction is considered willful misconduct. Although court decisions, the Rehabilitation Act of 1973, and the Americans with Disabilities Act of 1990 have provided protection for addiction treatment and rehabilitation, other court decisions and laws have provided punishment for those with alcohol and drug addiction who commit crimes.

Addiction to drugs and alcohol is a mental illness that can reduce the capacity of the individual to resist the use of these substances and hence avoid the resulting adverse consequences. The addictive drive can compel the individual to relapse to the adverse effects of alcohol and drugs despite the initially intact capacity to form intent in the legal sense in the abstinent state. Once the compulsive use of drugs and alcohol is initiated, the capacity to form intent is further compromised by the intoxicating effects of these substances acting directly on the brain.

Addiction is a disease that is defined by a preoccupation with acquiring alcohol and drugs, compulsively using them, and patterns of relapse to alcohol and drugs. Preoccupation is demonstrated by a high priority for the use of alcohol and drugs in an individual's life. Compulsivity is demonstrated by continued use despite recurring adverse consequences, including legal consequences. Addicted individuals often relapse, returning to drug use despite adverse consequences.

Legal decisions have acknowledged that addiction to drugs and alcohol is not willful misconduct in a legal sense. Court cases have emphasized that being a drug addict or an alcoholic is a status and not a crime.

Principles of Addictions and the Law is a book for mental health professionals, health practitioners, and legal professionals wanting to better understand how the science of addiction may be relevant to the law, and how laws and legal practices pertain to clients with addiction problems. Information in this book will assist psychologists and physicians with understanding the process and statutes that may apply to their client/patient, as well as information to improve their knowledge in serving as an expert witness. Information in this book will similarly assist legal professionals in understanding statutes and case law pertaining to addiction.

The book begins with an overview of how addictions are treated within the law, and moves on to privacy of medical records, bioethical decisions that relate to substance abuse and addiction, drug testing – what it can and can't show, forensic toxicology, epidemiology, co-morbidity, the general biology of addiction, and then the effects of substance abuse and addiction on special populations.

As an introduction to some of the material covered later in the book, it may be useful to know legal precedents relating to addiction and the law. In Robinson v California, the U.S. Supreme Court ruled that the California law against being a drug addict was unconstitutional. The Court said that the law could not make "status" a crime, and the treatment and punishment represented different goals. In Powell v State of Texas, the U.S. Supreme Court ruled that public drunkenness was a crime, but that being an alcoholic (status) was not.

In Foucha v Louisiana, the U.S. Supreme Court ruled that Foucha was not suffering from a mental illness, and that due process required that he could be held only as long as he was both mentally ill and dangerous. He had committed his crime while in a drug-induced psychosis. In the abstinent state, he was not considered mentally ill, although he probably did suffer from a drug addiction.

Addiction is highly correlated with violence and criminal behavior. According to the MacArthur study, substance abuse tripled the rate of violence among individuals in the community who were not patients and increased the rate of violence among discharged patients by up to five times. Patients discharged from psychiatric hospitals who had symptoms of alcohol or drug use were as violent as their neighbors who were not patients. In a study of self-reported violence among 10,000 individuals within a community, alcohol and drug abuse or dependence accounted for more than half of the incidences of violence among those individuals who had psychiatric diagnoses. According to another study, substance abuse is a much greater risk factor for violence than is mental illness. Alcohol or drug dependence is the leading psychiatric diagnoses in studies of completed suicides, and is a leading risk factor in those who attempt and complete suicide.

Alcohol and drug addiction are highly prevalent in criminal acts. All drugs, including alcohol, are associated with crime. At least 35% of convicted offenders were under the influence of alcohol at the time of their offense. An additional significant proportion of offenders were using other drugs at the time of their offense. More than 50% of murderers were using alcohol, drugs, or both at the time of their crime. Alcohol, cocaine, amphetamine and derivatives, phencyclidine hydrochloride, and heroin drugs are particularly linked to violent behavior toward others.

In other studies, violence due to alcohol and drugs was attributed to crimes to gain access to these substances and to resolve disputes over them, as well as to the effects of these substances on the individual's mind and behavior. Drugs diminish control, impair insight and judgment, induce grandiosity and paranoia, disinhibit, and provoke and stimulate uncontrollable behaviors. Alcohol intoxication was responsible for most violent crimes, including murders, assaults, sexual assaults and family violence. Sixty-two percent of violence offenders were drinking at the time of their crime. Among individuals with psychotic disorders, those with substance-related co-morbidity and a history of violent behavior are more likely to be hospitalized repeatedly and least likely to comply with medications after discharge.

Alcohol and drug disorders are highly prevalent in incarcerated populations. Lockups contain large numbers of individuals with alcohol and drug intoxication withdrawal. The suicide rate is higher in lockups than in jails or prisons. Eighty-two percent of all jail inmates said they had used an illegal drug, and 25% stated they had received treatment for a mental or emotional disorder. Sixty-one percent of the men and 70% of the women in jail had a lifetime prevalence of substance use disorder. Sixty-two percent of prison inmates reported regular drug use of a drug at sometime in their lives. Half of all prison inmates in 1991 had used cocaine in some form. More than 80% of the women in prison had a lifetime prevalence of a substance use disorder. According to the National Institute of Mental Health Epidemiologic Catchment Area program study, 72% of prison inmates had a lifetime prevalence of substance abuse.

There is legal precedent in how to appropriately treat this population. The 8th Amendment prohibits cruel and unusual punishments. It applies to those who are convicted of a crime, but not to the pretrial detainees. Convicted prisoners, therefore have a constitutional right to medical care. In Estelle v Gamble, the U.S. Supreme Court set the "deliberate indifference" to serious medical need as the standard that constitutes "unnecessary and wonton infliction of pain" proscribed by the 8th Amendment.

In Ruiz v Estelle, prisoners brought forth a class action suit regarding conditions of confinement. Six essential elements from the district court ruling provided guidelines for planning mental health services: systemic screening and evaluation; treatment that was more than mere seclusion or close supervision; participation by trained mental health professionals; accurate, complete and confidential records; safeguards against psychotropic medication prescribed in dangerous amounts, without adequate supervision, or otherwise inappropriately administered; and a suicide prevention program.

This gives a flavor of some of the issues relating to addiction and the law discussed further in this book. Chapters here further discuss privacy issues of the addicted patient, drug testing, forensic toxicology, epidemiology, co-morbidity, the general biology of addiction, and the effects of substance abuse and addiction on special populations. Written by experts in law and psychiatry, with case law, clinical vignettes, and landmark cases to illustrate material, we believe this book will be an important reference to those needing to better understand the principles of addiction and the law.

Chapter 1

The Basic Legal Structure and Organization

Anna Baumgras
Midland, MI, USA

INTRODUCTION: SOURCES OF LAW

The United States legal system is structured to protect individual rights and prevent overpowering government officials from violating those rights. The United States Constitution is the supreme source of law. It establishes and controls the legal system structure. All other laws are measured against, and must be consistent with, the Constitution. The Constitution establishes two basic levels of law: the state and the federal. At the federal level, the Constitution establishes three sources of law: the Executive Branch, the Legislative Branch, and the Judicial Branch (the Legislative Branch is governed by Article I; the Executive Branch is governed by Article II; the Judicial Branch is governed by Article III). All states have enacted a state constitution, which establishes the structure of the state government. Often the state constitution resembles the United States Constitution, and therefore establishes a state executive branch, legislative branch and judicial branch. However, the state constitution details vary by state. State law also establishes and regulates local law, including county, city, township and village law.

Each branch of government serves a distinct purpose in governing the country and provides a "check" on another branch to keep the government balanced. The Executive Branch is responsible for "tak[ing] Care that the Laws be faithfully executed …"(U.S. Const. art. II, § 3). In other words, the main purpose of the Executive Branch is to execute the laws enacted by the Legislature. To execute these laws, the President appoints the heads of federal agencies. Agencies are responsible for the day-to-day enforcement of laws and for supplementing broad statutory language by promulgating rules and regulations. Examples of agencies are the Environmental Protection Agency (EPA) and the Food and Drug Administration (FDA). The Executive Branch also has the power to create law by issuing Executive Orders and entering into treaties (U.S. Const. art. II, § 2). The Legislative Branch is responsible for drafting and enacting statutes (U.S. Const. art. I, § 8). The Judicial Branch is responsible for interpreting

Principles of Addictions and the Law: Applications in Forensic, Mental Health, and Medical Practice laws, ensuring they are constitutional and applying them to the facts of a case to facilitate an impartial outcome (U.S. Const. art. III, § 2). This chapter will focus on the federal system, including the Judicial Branch, basic constitutional rights and the Legislative Branch. It will also address how addictions interact with the law.

THE JUDICIAL BRANCH

Article III, section 1 of the Constitution establishes the Judicial Branch by stating, "The judicial Power of the United States shall be vested in one supreme Court, and in such inferior Courts as the Congress may from time to time ordain and establish" (*Idem* at § 1). Article III, section 2 provides the Judicial Branch with authority over cases and controversies arising under the Constitution or the laws of the United States (*Idem* at § 2).

The United States has two basic court systems: the state and the federal. In each of these systems there is a hierarchy of courts (see Figure 1.1). At the state level, the lowest levels of courts are the Trial Courts, followed by the Appellate Courts and finally the State Supreme Courts. At the federal level, the country is divided into ninety-four districts and thirteen circuits. Each section represents a court's jurisdiction. The lowest levels of courts are the United States District Courts, followed by the United States Courts of Appeals (Circuit Courts) and finally the Supreme Court of the United States. Each lower level court is bound by higher level court decisions within the same jurisdiction. The state courts are also bound by the United States Supreme Court's decisions. Additionally, each court is bound by its prior decisions under the principle of *stare decisis et non quieta movere*, which means "to stand by things decided, and not to disturb settled points" (Garner, 2004). These principles allow relative consistency in law.

The different levels of courts serve different functions. The trial court first determines the facts involved in the case and establishes the record. The record may consist of written memoranda of law (briefs) written by each party, oral

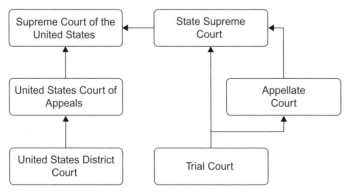

FIGURE 1.1 Diagram of the Court System.

arguments, testimony and exhibits. Then the trier of fact, either a judge or a jury in the trial court, will apply the law to the established facts and make a decision.

If either party is unhappy with the outcome, it may appeal the case. However, only matters of law can be appealed. The appellate court reviews the trial court's decision for reversible error. The appellate court will neither hear new testimony on the issue, nor review new evidence; it must base its decision on the record, the written appellate briefs and the appellate oral arguments. Typically, the intermediate appellate court must hear a case because the parties have a right to appeal; conversely, the Supreme Court (state or federal) can use discretion when deciding whether to hear a case.

Currently there are over 2,000 special courts dedicated solely to presiding over nonviolent drug and alcohol offenses (Office of National Drug Control Policy). These courts, called "drug courts," focus on the defendant's treatment and recovery, rather than his or her guilt. Offenders are placed in treatment programs that involve counseling, frequent drug testing and frequent court appearances, rather than jail or prison. Participants in the drug court programs who complete their treatment may have their charges dropped or their penalties reduced (National Criminal Justice Reference Service). Research has shown that participating in treatment rather than jail reduces the chance of future criminal behavior (National Criminal Justice Reference Service).

CIVIL LAW VERSUS CRIMINAL LAW

There are two basic types of cases: civil and criminal. In a civil case, an individual(s) (the plaintiff) files suit against another individual(s) (the defendant). In a criminal case, the government, acting on behalf of the victim, files a suit against the defendant. Each type of case has a different standard of proof that the proponent of the case must satisfy to prevail. Generally, in a civil case involving solely monetary interests, the plaintiff must prove his or her claim by a "preponderance of the evidence" (more likely than not). If the civil case involves a social policy interest, the plaintiff has a slightly higher standard of proof. He or she must prove his or her claim by "clear and convincing evidence."

Because the consequences for criminal cases are more severe, the burden of proof is higher than in civil cases. The state must prove that the defendant is guilty of every element of the alleged crime "beyond a reasonable doubt." Although there is no standard definition for beyond a "reasonable doubt," the Ohio Legislature has provided one definition:

> "Reasonable doubt" is present when the jurors, after they have carefully considered and compared all the evidence, cannot say they are firmly convinced of the truth of the charge. It is a doubt based on reason and common sense. Reasonable doubt is not mere possible doubt, because everything relating to human affairs or depending on moral evidence is open to some possible or imaginary doubt. "Proof beyond a reasonable doubt" is proof of

such character that an ordinary person would be willing to rely and act upon it in the most important of the person's own affairs.

(Ohio Rev. Code Ann. § 2901.05(E) (West 2008))

Criminal Law

Elements of Crimes

Most crimes consist of two elements: the *actus reus*, which is Latin for "guilty act" (Garner, 2004); and the *mens rea*, which is Latin for "guilty mind" (*Idem*). In other words, to be convicted the defendant must have intended to commit a crime and must have physically acted in furtherance of that crime. According to the Model Penal Code (MPC) a failure to act may be considered an act. One limitation of the act requirement is that the act must be a voluntary act. MPC section 2.01(1) states: "A person is not guilty of an offense unless his liability is based on conduct that includes a voluntary act or the omission to perform an act of which he is physically capable."

There are two forms of criminal intent (*mens rea*); general intent and specific intent. General intent is associated with criminal recklessness (conscious disregard for a known risk) and criminal negligence (should have been aware of a risk). Crimes that typically involve general intent include battery, rape, or involuntary manslaughter. Specific intent is associated with purpose (conscious object) and knowledge (aware that a result will occur). Crimes that typically involve specific intent include assault, voluntary manslaughter and intent to kill.

There are two levels of punishment, depending on the severity of the crime. The first is a misdemeanor, which is generally punishable by less than a year in jail or a monetary fine. The second is a felony, which is generally punishable by at least one year in prison or possibly death. The defendant's state of mind at the time of the crime may also significantly impact on the level of punishment. For example, as discussed *infra*, diminished capacity may affect the defendant's ability to form the requisite intent.

Defenses to Crimes

Intoxication

Whether a defendant can claim intoxication as a defense to a crime often depends on whether it was voluntary or involuntary intoxication. Voluntary intoxication occurs when the defendant intentionally consumes a substance known to be intoxicating without any duress. The defendant does not have to intend to become intoxicated. Voluntary intoxication may be a defense to specific intent crimes if the defendant can prove it precluded him or her from forming the requisite intent; it is never a defense to general intent crimes. Involuntary intoxication occurs when the defendant consumes an intoxicating substance under duress, or when the defendant does not know the substance is intoxicating. Involuntary intoxication may be a defense to both general intent and specific intent crimes.

Model Penal Code § 2.08

Intoxication

1. Except as provided in Subsection (4), intoxication of the actor is not a defense unless it opposes an element of the offense.
2. When recklessness establishes an element of the offense if the actor, due to self-induced intoxication, is unaware of a risk of which he would have been aware had he been sober, such unawareness is immaterial.
3. Intoxication does not, in itself, constitute mental disease within the meaning of the Model Penal Code.
4. Intoxication that: (a) is not self-induced; or (b) is pathological is an affirmative defense if by reason of such intoxication the actor at the time of his conduct lacks substantial capacity either to appreciate its criminality (wrongfulness) or to conform his conduct to the requirements of law.
5. Definitions:
   a. "intoxication" means a disturbance of mental or physical capabilities resulting from the introduction of substances into the body;
   b. "self-induced intoxication" means intoxication caused by substances that the actor knowingly introduces into his body, the tendency of which to cause intoxication he knows or ought to know, unless he introduces them pursuant to medical advice or under such circumstances as would afford a defense to a charge of crime;
   c. "pathological intoxication" means intoxication grossly excessive in degree, given the amount of intoxicant, to which the actor does now know he is susceptible.

   It is important to note that intoxication may be caused by any substance, including alcohol, drugs, or medication.

Insanity

Generally, drug addiction and intoxication do not qualify for an insanity defense. However, prolonged drug use or excessive alcohol use may cause delirium tremens, which is a form of insanity. Therefore, the defendant may be permitted to claim both an insanity defense and an intoxication defense. Additionally, a few jurisdictions have permitted an addicted defendant to raise an insanity defense because the addiction impaired criminal responsibility. Whether a jurisdiction permits addiction to qualify for an insanity defense may depend on the insanity test it has adopted.

There are four tests courts use to determine whether a person is legally insane. The first is the M'Naghten Rule, which states that a defendant is not guilty when a disease of the mind caused a defect of reason such that the defendant lacked the ability at the time of his or her actions either: (1) to know the wrongfulness of his or her actions; or (2) to understand the nature and quality of his or her actions. The second is the Irresistible Impulse Test, which states that a defendant is not guilty if a mental illness rendered him or her unable to control his or her actions, or to conform his or her conduct to the law. The third is the Durham Test, which states that the defendant is not guilty if his or her crime was the product of mental disease or defect. The last is the American Law Institute or Model Penal Code Test, which states that the defendant is not guilty if he or she suffered from a mental disease and therefore lacked substantial capacity either: (1) to appreciate the criminality of his or her conduct; or (2) to conform his or her conduct to the law.

The legislature has codified the insanity defense at 18 U.S.C. § 17.

1. *Affirmative defense*: it is an affirmative defense to a prosecution under any federal statute that, at the time of the commission of the acts constituting the offense, the defendant, as a result of a severe mental disease or defect, was unable to appreciate the nature and quality or the wrongfulness of his acts. Mental disease or defect does not otherwise constitute a defense.
2. *Burden of proof*: the defendant has the burden of proving the defense of insanity by clear and convincing evidence.

Civil Law

A civil offense is termed a tort. The goal of tort law is to make the injured party whole again, usually by requiring the opposing party to pay damages. Two common types of torts are intentional torts and unintentional torts.

Intentional Torts

Intentional torts generally require that the plaintiff establish three elements: (1) the defendant acted; (2) the defendant intended the consequences of his or her act; and (3) the defendant's actions caused the injury. As in criminal law, intent can be specific or general. Examples of intentional torts include civil assault and civil battery. Battery occurs when the defendant acts intending to cause harmful or offensive contact to the plaintiff, or apprehension of such contact, and such contact results. Assault occurs when the defendant acts intending to cause imminent apprehension of harmful or offensive contact to the plaintiff and such imminent apprehension results.

Unintentional Torts

Unintentional torts fall under the category of negligence. To establish a case of negligence, the plaintiff must prove four elements: duty; breach; causation; and damages. Duty arises when the defendant must act with a certain standard of care to avoid injury to the plaintiff. Breach occurs when the defendant fails to exercise that duty of care. Causation requires the plaintiff to connect the defendant's actions with his or her injury. The plaintiff must prove two forms of causation: actual cause and proximate cause. Actual cause means that the defendant's act was in fact the cause of the injury. Proximate cause means that the defendant's act was sufficiently connected with the plaintiff's injury to hold the defendant liable for the injury. Therefore, certain intervening forces that produce unforeseeable injuries may sever the defendant's liability, despite his or her negligent actions actually causing the plaintiff's injuries. Finally, damages occur when the plaintiff suffers actual harm, either to his or her person or property.

Malpractice is a form of professional negligence. Professionals are held to a standard of care as measured by others within that profession. Therefore, professionals such as doctors and lawyers are required to exercise their superior knowledge when acting on or with patients or clients.

Offenses Related to Addictions

Clearly, addictions and the law are intertwined. For example, addiction may cause a person to commit a theft crime such as larceny, robbery, or burglary when he or she needs money to buy the intoxicating substance. Additionally, addiction may cause a person to commit an offense because of the intoxication. Driving under the influence, public intoxication and possession are common offenses an addict may commit. Because states generally regulate these offenses, the elements of the offense and the penalties vary by state. Below are examples of how states define and punish these offenses.

Driving Under the Influence (DUI) or Driving While Intoxicated (DWI)
Florida Statute Annotated § 316.193

1. A person is guilty of the offense of driving under the influence and is subject to punishment as provided in subsection (2) if the person is driving or in actual physical control of a vehicle within this state and:
    a. the person is under the influence of alcoholic beverages, any chemical substance …, or any substance controlled under [the statute], when affected to the extent that the person's normal faculties are impaired;
    b. the person has a blood-alcohol level of 0.08 or more grams of alcohol per 100 milliliters of blood; or
    c. the person has a breath-alcohol level of 0.08 or more grams of alcohol per 210 liters of breath.

2a. Except as provided [in the statute], any person who is convicted of a violation of subsection (1) shall be punished:
    1. By a fine of:
        a. not less than $500 or more than $1,000 for a first conviction.
        b. not less than $1,000 or more than $2,000 for a second conviction; and
    2. By imprisonment for:
        a. not more than six months for a first conviction.
        b. Not more than nine months for a second conviction.

West Virginia Code § 17C–5–2(d)

Any person who:

1. Drives a vehicle in this state while he or she:
   a. is under the influence of alcohol;
   b. is under the influence of any controlled substance;
   c. is under the influence of any other drug;
   d. is under the combined influence of alcohol and any controlled substance or any other drug; or
   e. has an alcohol concentration in his or her blood of eight hundredths of 1% or more, by weight, but less than fifteen hundredths of 1%, by weight;
2. Is guilty of a misdemeanor and, upon conviction thereof, shall be confined in jail for up to six months and shall be fined not less than $100 nor more than $500. A person sentenced pursuant to this subdivision shall receive credit for any period of actual confinement he or she served upon arrest for the subject offense.

Public Drunkenness or Public Intoxication

Arkansas Code Annotated § 5–71–212

1. A person commits the offense of public intoxication if he or she appears in a public place manifestly under the influence of alcohol or a controlled substance to the degree and under circumstances such that:
   a. the person is likely to endanger himself or herself or another person or property; or
   b. the person unreasonably annoys a person in his or her vicinity.
2. Public intoxication is a … misdemeanor.

Georgia Code Annotated § 16–11–41

1. A person who shall be and appear in an intoxicated condition in any public place or within the curtilage of any private residence not his own other than by invitation of the owner or lawful occupant, which condition is made manifest by boisterousness, by indecent condition or act, or by vulgar, profane, loud, or unbecoming language, is guilty of a misdemeanor.

Possession

21 United States Code § 844

It shall be unlawful for any person knowingly or intentionally to possess a controlled substance unless such substance was obtained directly, or pursuant to a valid prescription or order, from a practitioner, while acting in the course of his professional practice, or except as otherwise authorized by this [statute].

Alabama Code 1975 § 13A–12–212

1. A person commits the crime of unlawful possession of controlled substance if:
   a. except as otherwise authorized, he possesses a controlled substance;
   b. he obtains by fraud, deceit, misrepresentation or subterfuge or by the alteration of a prescription or written order or by the concealment of a material fact or by the use of a false name or giving a false address, a controlled substance;
2. Unlawful possession of a controlled substance is a … felony.

BASIC CONSTITUTIONAL RIGHTS

The Bill of Rights

The United States Constitution is the source of law that trumps all other laws. Article VI declares, "This Constitution, and the Laws of the United States which shall be made in Pursuance thereof … shall be the supreme Law of the Land; and the Judges in every State shall be bound thereby …" (U.S. Const. art. VI). The Constitution includes seven Articles and twenty-seven Amendments. The first ten Amendments are the Bill of Rights, which establish the fundamental rights of Americans. For example, the First Amendment protects the freedom of speech and religion. It states, "Congress shall make no law respecting an establishment of religion, or prohibiting the free exercise thereof; or abridging the freedom of speech …" (U.S. Const. amend. I). The Fourth Amendment protects against unreasonable searches and seizures. It states:

> The right of the people to be secure in their persons, houses, papers, and effects, against unreasonable searches and seizures, shall not be violated, and no Warrants shall issue, but upon probable cause, supported by Oath or affirmation, and particularly describing the place to be searched, and the persons or things to be seized.
>
> (U.S. Const. amend. IV)

The Sixth Amendment establishes the right of a criminal defendant to have a speedy trial and the assistance of counsel. It states:

> In all criminal prosecutions, the accused shall enjoy the right to a speedy and public trial, by an impartial jury of the state and district wherein the crime shall have been committed, which district shall have been previously ascertained by law, and to be informed of the nature and cause of the accusation; to be confronted with the witnesses against him; to have compulsory process for obtaining witnesses in his favor, and to have the assistance of counsel for his defense.
>
> (U.S. Const. amend. VI)

The Eighth Amendment prohibits cruel and unusual punishment. It states: "Excessive bail shall not be required, nor excessive fines imposed, nor cruel and unusual punishments inflicted" (U.S. Const. amend. VIII). The Eighth Amendment has been used to strike down laws that made addiction a crime. For example, in *Robinson v. California*, the Supreme Court determined that a

California statute making addiction to narcotics a criminal offense was unconstitutional under the Eighth and Fourteenth Amendment. The Court reasoned that punishing people merely for their "status" as an addict constituted cruel and unusual punishment (*Robinson v. California*, 1962). However, in *Powell v. Texas* (1968) the Supreme Court determined that a conviction for public drunkenness was not cruel and unusual punishment because the conviction was not based on the defendant's status as an alcoholic, but rather on being drunk in public, which is a health and safety hazard.

The Fifth Amendment establishes the right against compelled self-incrimination. It states: "No person shall be ... compelled in any criminal case to be a witness against himself ..." (U.S. Const. amend. V). The Supreme Court has decided that this privilege only protects testimonial or communicative evidence. Therefore, the government may compel a defendant to produce blood samples for the purpose of determining his or her blood-alcohol level without violating the Fifth Amendment (*Schmerber v. California*, 1966).

Substantive Due Process, Procedural Due Process and Equal Protection

The Fifth and Fourteenth Amendments warrant additional attention. The Fifth Amendment also states: "No person shall be ... deprived of life, liberty, or property, without due process of law ..." (U.S. Const. amend. V). The Fourteenth Amendment states: "No state shall ... deprive any person of life, liberty, or property, without due process of law" (U.S. Const. amend. XIV § 1). They both require the government to provide a person with due process before depriving him or her of life, liberty or property. The difference between the two amendments is that the Fifth Amendment applies to the federal government and the Fourteenth Amendment applies to the state governments.

There are two forms of due process: substantive and procedural. Procedural due process requires the government to provide a fair procedure to a person before depriving him or her of life, liberty, or property. A person may be deprived of liberty when he or she loses significant freedom or is denied a constitutional or statutory freedom. For example, committing a person to a mental institution without consent is a deprivation of liberty (see *Jones v. United States*, 1983). Property includes personal and real property, as well as an entitlement to a state or federal benefit (see *Board of Regents v. Roth*, 1972). For example, the Supreme Court has decided that a person has a property interest in welfare benefits when he or she satisfies all statutory requirements entitling him or her to receive those benefits (*Goldberg v. Kelly*, 1970).

The procedure that the government must provide depends on the circumstances of the deprivation. Generally, the deprived person is entitled to notice of the deprivation and a hearing. During the hearing, the government will explain its reason for deprivation and the deprived person will have an opportunity to respond.

Substantive due process protects certain rights from unreasonable government regulation. In contrast to procedural due process, which concerns the procedural rights guaranteed by the due process clauses, substantive due process is concerned with the substantive rights guaranteed by the clauses. The Supreme Court has determined that certain fundamental rights are part of the liberty rights guaranteed by the due process clauses. Therefore, if legislation invades these rights, the legislation may be unconstitutional. Examples of these rights include the right to travel, the right to privacy, the right to vote and First Amendment rights.

Related to substantive due process doctrine is the equal protection doctrine, which prohibits the government from treating a person or classes of people differently than others. The Equal Protection Clause states, "No state shall deny to any person within its jurisdiction the equal protection of the laws" (U.S. Const. amend. XIV § 1). The Supreme Court has created three classifications of people under the Equal Protection Clause: suspect classes; quasi-suspect classes; and non-suspect/quasi-suspect classes. Suspect classes include race, national origin, or alienage. The quasi-suspect classes include gender, illegitimacy and illegal alien children. All other classifications (i.e., sexual orientation, disability, political affiliation) are considered non-suspect/quasi-suspect classes.

The court will use one of three tests when someone challenges a law under substantive due process or equal protection.

1. Strict scrutiny, the highest level of scrutiny, is used when a suspect class or a fundamental right is implicated. The government must prove: (1) a compelling purpose in enacting the law; and (2) that the law is necessary or the least restrictive means to achieve that purpose. In other words, the law must be narrowly tailored to achieve the compelling purpose.
2. Intermediate scrutiny is used when a law implicates a quasi-suspect class. The government must prove: (1) an important purpose in enacting the law; and (2) that the law is substantially related to that purpose.
3. Rational relationship, the lowest level of scrutiny, is used when neither strict scrutiny nor intermediate scrutiny applies. The government must prove: (1) a legitimate state purpose in enacting the law; and (2) that the law is rationally related to that purpose.

THE LEGISLATIVE BRANCH

The Legislative Branch is responsible for enacting laws. Article I, section 1 of the Constitution states: "All legislative Powers herein granted shall be vested in a Congress of the United States, which shall consist of a Senate and House of Representatives" (U.S. Const. art. I, § 1). As the constitution makes clear, the United States Congress is a bicameral legislature, meaning it consists of two houses: the House of Representatives and the Senate. The House of Representatives consists of 435 representatives, apportioned among the states by population. Each representative serves a two-year term. The Senate consists of 100 senators, with each of the 50 states contributing two senators. Each senator serves a six-year term.

The Legislative Branch enacts laws by passing bills. Anyone can draft a bill, but only a member of Congress can introduce a bill. The general legislative process is as follows: after a bill is introduced by either a representative or a senator, it is sent to a committee within that house (see Figure 1.2). The committee may hold hearings on the bill to collect more information. During the hearing, the bill's sponsors will appear. Witnesses and representatives of interest group may also appear. The committee may also recommend amendments to the bill.

After the committee has finished reviewing the bill, it will decide whether to report the bill to the entire house. If the committee decides to not report the bill, the bill is rejected. If the committee decides to report the bill to the entire house, the bill is then debated on the floor of the house. Members of the house may argue for or against the bill and may offer amendments. Finally, the house will vote on the bill.

After one house has passed a bill, it is sent to the other house and the process is repeated in that house. If the second house amends the bill in any manner, it must be sent again to the first house to approve the amendments. For example, if a bill originated in the Senate, the Senate must approve of the bill. After the Senate approves the bill, the Senate's version is sent to the House. If the House amends the Senate's version of the bill, it must send its version back to the Senate for approval. If the two houses are unable to agree on the bill's language, they may request a conference committee, consisting of both senators and representatives, to resolve the differences. For a bill to become a law, both houses must agree on the same version of the bill.

After both houses agree on a version of the bill, it is sent to the President to review. The President may sign the bill, veto it, or take no action. The bill becomes law upon the President's signing. If the President vetoes the bill, it is returned to Congress where it dies unless two-thirds of each house votes to override the veto. If the President takes no action within ten days and Congress is still in session, the bill becomes law without the President's signature. However, if the President takes no action and Congress is no longer in session, the bill dies through the "pocket veto."

Statutes Regulating Addictions

Summarized below are five statutes that relate to addictions. The first three specifically relate to drug and alcohol abuse. The Americans with Disabilities Act and the Rehabilitation Act are more general statutes that may or may not regulate addictions, depending on the circumstances.

Narcotic Addict Rehabilitation Act (42 U.S.C. § 3401 et seq.)

In 1966, Congress enacted the Narcotic Addict Rehabilitation Act with the purpose of rehabilitating addicts through civil commitment, rather than punishing them. Although most of the Act was subsequently repealed, Congress' policy remains in effect.

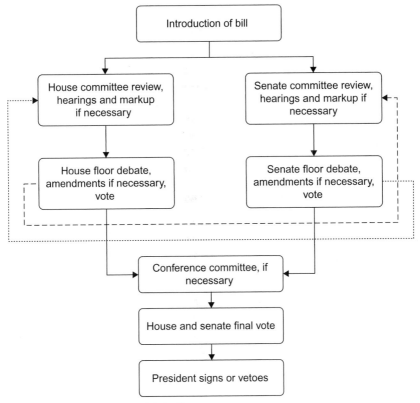

FIGURE 1.2 Diagram of the Legislative Process.

It is the policy of the Congress that certain persons charged with or convicted of violating Federal criminal laws, who are determined to be addicted to narcotic drugs, and likely to be rehabilitated through treatment, should, in lieu of prosecution or sentencing, be civilly committed for confinement and treatment designed to effect their restoration to health, and return to society as useful members.

It is the further policy of the Congress that certain persons addicted to narcotic drugs who are not charged with the commission of any offense should be afforded the opportunity, through civil commitment, for treatment in order that they may be rehabilitated and be returned to society as useful members and in order that society may be protected more effectively from crime and delinquency which result from narcotic addiction (§ 3401).

Drug Abuse Prevention, Treatment and Rehabilitaiton Act (21 U.S.C. § 1101 et seq.)

In 1979 Congress passed the Drug Abuse Prevention, Treatment and Rehabilitation Act because it found: "drug abuse is rapidly increasing in the United States

(§ 1101(1)) … and drug abuse seriously impairs individual, as well as societal, health and well-being" (§ 1101(2)). The goal of the Act was to coordinate the use of federal resources to combat drug use by creating preventative and treatment programs, and to increase research on the potential consequences of drug abuse (§ 1102). Most of the Act's provisions have been repealed.

Comprehensive Alcohol Abuse and Alcoholism Prevention, Treatment and Rehabilitation Program Act (42 U.S.C. § 4541 et seq.)

The counterpart to the Drug Abuse Prevention, Treatment and Rehabilitation Act is the Comprehensive Alcohol Abuse and Alcoholism Prevention, Treatment and Rehabilitation Program Act of 1979. Congress enacted the law because: "alcohol is one of the most dangerous drugs and the drug most frequently abused in the United States (§ 4541(1)) … [and] alcohol abuse and alcoholism, together with abuse of other legal and illegal drugs, present a need for prevention and intervention programs designed to reach the general population …" (§ 4541(7)). Like the goal of the Drug Abuse Prevention, Treatment and Rehabilitation Act, the goal of this Act was to initiate prevention and treatment programs, and to increase research on the potential consequences of alcohol abuse and alcoholism. Most of the Act's provisions have also been repealed.

The Americans with Disabilities Act (42 U.S.C. § 12101 et seq.)

In 1990 Congress enacted the Americans with Disabilities Act (ADA), which prohibits discrimination against a: "qualified individual with a disability because of the disability of such individual …" (§ 12112(a)). The Act is divided into four subchapters: Employment (I); Public Services (II); Public Accommodations and Services Operated by Private Entities (III); and Miscellaneous (IV). Protections provided by the ADA are similar to those provided by the Civil Rights Act of 1964. For example, the ADA states:

> "No covered entity shall discriminate against a qualified individual with a disability because of the disability of such individual in regard to job application procedures, the hiring, advancement, or discharge of employees, employee compensation, job training, and other terms, conditions and privileges of employment."
>
> (§ 12112)

Under the ADA, the term "disability" is defined as: (1) a physical or mental impairment that substantially limits one or more major life activities of such individual; (2) a record of such an impairment; or (3) being regarded as having such an impairment (§ 12102). Courts have held that alcoholism or drug addiction *may* constitute a disability under the ADA, depending on the circumstances. For example, a heroin addiction did constitute a disability under the ADA when it: "impaire[d] the major life activities of … working and parenting" (*MX Group, Inc. v. City of Covington*, 2000). Conversely, alcoholism did not constitute a disability under the ADA when it did not: "substantially impair [the plaintiff] from participating in any major life activity … [including] his ability to care for himself, perform manual tasks, walk, see, hear, speak properly, breath, or work in some specifically identified class of jobs" (*Roig v. Miami Federal Credit Union*, 2005).

Additionally, courts have held that alcoholism or drug abuse may affect a person's status as a "qualified individual" under the ADA. The ADA defines "qualified individual with a disability" as "an individual with a disability who … can perform the essential functions of the employment position that such individual holds or desires …" (§ 12111(8)). For example, an individual was a "qualified individual" under the ADA when he was able to perform his job as a police dispatcher competently, despite his alcoholism affecting his ability to regularly report to work and to comply with his employer's rule for requesting leave (*Office of Senate Sergeant at Arms v. Office of Senate Fair Employment Practices*, 1996). Conversely, a doctor was not a "qualified individual" under the ADA when he was a recovering alcoholic and was visibly drunk while treating a patient, thereby rendering him unable to perform his duties as a hospital's chief of internal medicine (*Altman v. New York City Health and Hospitals Corp.*, 1996).

The ADA also specifies that a person who is currently using illegal drugs is not a "qualified individual with a disability" when the regulated entity (i.e., an employer) acts on the basis of the illegal use (42 U.S.C. § 12114(a)). The ADA is careful to express that only *current* users are not covered. If an individual has completed rehabilitation and no longer uses illegal drugs, or if an individual is currently in rehabilitation and no longer uses illegal drugs, they are not excluded. Regulated entities are permitted to administer policies and procedures, including drug tests, to ensure that individuals are no longer using illegal drugs (§ 12114(d)).

The Rehabilitation Act (29 U.S.C. § 701 et seq.)

In 1973 Congress enacted the Rehabilitation Act to "empower individuals with disabilities to maximize employment, economic self-sufficiency, independence, and inclusion and integration into society" (§ 701). The Act prohibits discrimination based on disability in programs receiving federal funding, in programs conducted by federal agencies, and in the employment practices of the federal government or federal contractors. For example, the Act states:

> " … no otherwise qualified individual with a disability … shall, solely by reason of her or his disability, be excluded from the participation in, be denied the benefit of, or be subjected to discrimination under any program or activity receiving federal financial assistance or any program or activity conducted by any executive agency …."
>
> (§ 794(a))

Generally, the Act adopts the ADA's definition of disability (§ 705(9)). Like the ADA, certain sections (subchapter V) of the Rehabilitation Act do not cover people who are currently using illegal drugs (§ 705(c)(i)). Additionally, under certain sections (government contracts, federal agency programs and federally financed programs), "person with a disability" does not include a person whose current alcohol use prevents him or her from performing his or her job or constitutes a threat to the property or safety of others (§ 793; § 794). For example, in *Newland v. Dalton* (1996), the court determined the Navy did not violate the Rehabilitation Act when terminating an employee who fired a weapon at a tavern's employees during a drunken rampage because the employee was terminated for his conduct, rather than his alcoholism. Additionally, in *Heron v. McGuire* (1986), the court determined a police officer who was addicted to heroin was not a "handicapped individual" under the Rehabilitation Act because his current use rendered him unfit for duty as a police officer.

CONCLUSION

This chapter provided an overview of the basic legal structure and organization, including a synopsis of the Constitution, the Judicial Branch, and the Legislative Branch. Each source of law plays an essential and important role in the governmental and legal organization. The chapter provided examples of how the law regards addictions. Clearly, addictions are linked with the law. Addictions often accompany or cause a person's legal problems. Addictions may also absolve legal problems. Both the courts and the legislature have addressed, and continue to address, how addictions may affect a person's life. The next chapters will provide greater detail on how the legal system and the medical field treat specific issues relating to addictions.

REFERENCES

Altman v. New York City Health and Hospitals Corp., 100 F.3d 1054 (2d Cir. 1996).
Board of Regents v. Roth, 408 U.S. 564 (1972).
Garner, B. A. (Ed.). (2004). *Black's Law Dictionary* (8th ed.). Eagan, MN: West Group.
Goldberg v. Kelly, 397 U.S. 254 (1970).
Heron v. McGuire, 803 F.2d 67 (C.A. 2 1986).
Jones v. United States (1983).
MX Group, Inc. v. City of Covington, 106 F.Supp.2d 914 (E.D. Ky. 2000).
National Criminal Justice Reference Service. Available at: http://www.ncjrs.gov/spotlight/drug_courts/summary.html.
Newland v. Dalton, 81 F.3d 904 (C.A. 9 1996).
Office of National Drug Control Policy Website. Available at: http://www.whitehousedrugpolicy.gov/enforce/drugcourt.html.
Office of Senate Sergeant at Arms v. Office of Senate Fair Employment Practices, 95 F.3d 1102 (Fed. Cir. 1996).
Powell v. Texas, 392 U.S. 514 (1968).
Robinson v. California, 370 U.S. 660 (1962).
Roig v. Miami Federal Credit Union, 353 F.Supp.2d 1213 (S.D. Fla. 2005).
Schmerber v. California, 384 U.S. 757 (1966).

Chapter 2

Addictions and the Law

Norman S. Miller, MD, JD, PLLC
Department of Medicine, College of Human Medicine, Michigan State University,
East Lansing, MI, USA

Sara Spratt, JD
Private Practice, Chicago, IL, USA

Drug and alcohol addictions and the law are historically well-acquainted in the American legal system. The pervasive presence of legal consequences from alcohol and drug disorders is evidence in medical-legal populations. The forensic psychiatrist performs a variety of consultative functions, treatment roles and evaluation determinations pertaining to individuals with a history of alcohol and drug disorders. The identification and treatment of addictive diseases are increasingly important in forensic practice, particularly in cases pertaining to criminal conduct, malpractice, employment, disability, child custody and correctional psychiatry (Goldsmith & Miller, 1994).

The forensic psychiatrist has many avenues for interaction with clients and professionals in the legal system in state and federal courts. These courts make legal decisions that have a direct bearing on the fate of those with addictive disorders. The legislative branches of the federal government and state governments create a number of significant and far-reaching laws that affect large numbers of addicted individuals. The constitutional amendments, particularly the Fourteenth Amendment, provide due process and equal protection of the law for individuals with drug and alcohol addictions. Governmental administrative agencies create policies, rules, codes and regulations to execute legislative statutes that govern the deterrence, treatment, prosecution and diversion of offenders with addictive diseases (Committee on Psychiatry and Law, 1991; Ciccone, 1999).

Alcohol and drug addiction occupy a paradoxical place within medicine and the law. On the one hand, addiction is considered a disabling illness. As early as 1925 the United States Supreme Court stated that addicts "are diseased and proper subjects for ... treatment" (*Linder v. US*, 1925). On the other hand, addiction is considered willful misconduct. Although court decisions, the Rehabilitation Act of 1973 and the Americans with Disabilities Act of 1990 have provided protection for addiction treatment and rehabilitation, other court decisions and laws have provided punishment for those with alcohol and drug addiction who commit crimes.

MENS REA AND CAPACITY

Definition and Relevance to Addictions

Mens rea is central to legal consequences and ethical decisions regarding individuals who have drug and alcohol addictions and violate laws, particularly as a result of their addiction. The application of *mens rea* in criminal cases involving alcohol and drug disorders depends in part on the acceptance of addiction as a disease. Whether conduct influenced by alcohol and drugs arises from a disease, or whether the conduct is willful misconduct, will have significant and fundamental implications for intent to commit a crime or failure to conform to a law and subsequent charges, convictions and sentencing (Waterson, 1991).

Mens rea is defined as "guilty mind" and encompasses specific and general intent. Specific intent is the intent to accomplish the precise criminal act that one is later charged with. At common law, the specific-intent crimes were robbery, assault, larceny, burglary, forgery, false pretenses, embezzlement, attempt, solicitation and conspiracy (Black's Law Dictionary, 2004). General intent is the intent to perform an act even though the actor does not desire the consequences that result. This is the state of mind required for the commission of certain common-law crimes not requiring a specific intent or not imposing strict liability. General intent usually takes the form of recklessness, which involves actual awareness of a risk and the culpable taking of that risk or negligence, which involves blameworthy inadvertence (Black's Law Dictionary, 2004). Negligence is not criminal unless considered so by statute, as there is no intent to do harm and it was unreasonable to be unaware (Resnick, 1998).

In criminal cases where specific intent is necessary, the specific intent must be proven by the prosecution beyond a reasonable doubt. If there is no intent, then there is no crime or a lesser offense is charged. Diminished capacity is the impaired ability or the total lack of ability to form the requisite intent to purposely or knowingly commit a criminal act. Many states allow forensic testimony for diminished capacity; however, several states bar or restrict such testimony. Medical and scientific evidence may show that the intoxicating effects of alcohol and drugs can reduce or block an individual's ability to form requisite intent to commit a crime. The principal sites of actions of alcohol and drugs are located in the frontal lobe (insight and judgment) and in the temporal lobe (memory). Diminished capacity from alcohol and drugs can be due to impaired insight and judgment and faulty memory (Miller, 1991; Adams & Victor, 1993; Lande, 1993; Berman, 1997).

Forensic testimony is often crucial to understanding the role of drugs or alcohol in the formation of specific intent or lack thereof; the influence of drugs or alcohol on insight, judgment and memory, and the role of other mental aspects contributing to the act. The testimony often revolves around the responsibility of the individual beyond the intent to commit the crime. Because the individual is suffering from an addictive disease, the charges may be excused or lessened or the sentence mitigated because of the lack of specific intent.

However, the individual may be held responsible for accepting treatment to prevent or reduce the probability of recurrence of criminal acts. The implication is that treatment that leads to abstinence from alcohol and drugs will deter future episodes of crime that are related to the acquisition, compulsive use of and relapse to drugs (addiction) (Goldsmith & Miller, 1994).

Legal Precedent

In *People of California v. Saille*, the California Supreme Court ruled that the trial court did not err in its jury instruction in view of Senate Bill 54 abolishing the defense of diminished capacity in 1981. However, a defendant is still free to show that, due to mental illness or intoxication, he or she did not form the intent to kill unlawfully. In other words, diminished capacity depended on the proof that voluntary intoxication affected the ability to form intent (*People of the State of California v. Saille*, 1991).

Voluntary intoxication, which is the voluntary use of alcohol and drugs to the point of intoxication, does not qualify for diminished capacity. Historically, mere drunkenness from alcohol or drugs has not been an excuse for a criminal act. Involuntary intoxication can be an insanity defense in instances of becoming intoxicated by the external actions of others or through furtive methods. Other states or conditions that qualify for a diminished capacity defense are idiosyncratic (pathological) intoxication, delirium tremens and permanent psychosis secondary to alcoholism (e.g., Wernicke–Korsakoff syndrome) (Waterson, 1991; Resnick, 1998).

ADDICTIVE DISEASE

Intoxication and Addiction

Intoxication, in addition to or originating from a mental illness such as alcohol and drug addiction, can preclude specific intent. Addiction to drugs and alcohol is a mental illness that can reduce the capacity of the individual to resist the use of these substances, and hence avoid the resulting adverse consequences. The addictive drive can compel the individual to relapse to the adverse effects of alcohol and drugs despite the initially intact capacity to form intent in the legal sense in the abstinent state. Once the compulsive use of drugs and alcohol is initiated, the capacity to form intent is further compromised by the intoxicating effects of these substances acting directly on the brain (Miller, 1991).

Addiction is a disease that is defined by a preoccupation with acquiring alcohol and drugs and compulsively using them, and patterns of relapse to alcohol and drugs. Preoccupation is demonstrated by a high priority for the use of alcohol and drugs in an individual's life. Compulsivity is continued use despite recurring adverse consequences, including legal consequences. Relapse is a return to use despite adverse consequences. Pervasive to preoccupation, compulsivity and relapse, is a loss of control over alcohol and drug use that renders the individual incapable of resisting the urges to use these substances. The loss of control is largely unconscious and persistent, similar to drive states such as hunger or sex. As with most drive states, conscious control is possible, the loss of control for use of alcohol and drugs is ultimately expressed in some way (Koob, 1999; Leshner, 1999).

Legal decisions have acknowledged that addiction to drugs and alcohol is not willful misconduct in a legal sense. Court cases have emphasized that being a drug addict or an alcoholic is a status and not a crime (Miller, 1991).

Legal Precedent

In *Robinson v. California*, the United States Supreme Court ruled that the California law against being a drug addict was unconstitutional. The court said that the law could not make "status" a crime, and the treatment and punishment represented different goals (*Robinson v. California*, 1962). In *Powell v. State of Texas*, the United States Supreme Court ruled that public drunkenness was a crime, but that being an alcoholic (status) was not (*Powell v. State of Texas*, 1968).

CRIMINAL LAW

Insanity Defense

Intoxication from alcohol and drugs does not qualify for an insanity defense because the individual is otherwise sane by legal standards in the abstinent state. Voluntary intoxication from alcohol and drugs does not equate to insanity in the legal sense, despite the use of these substances rendering the defendant "unable to appreciate the nature and quality of the acts or to know right from wrong, or conform to the requirements of the law" (*People v. Free*, 1988; *State v. Hartfield*, 388 SE2d 802 (SC 1990); *United States v. Knott*, 1990). The intoxicated state is considered legally preventable by refraining from or resisting the use of alcohol and drugs to appreciate the criminality of this conduct or to conform to the requirements of the law. Court decisions would suggest that an individual who commits a crime under the influence of alcohol or drugs may not be legally dangerous or mentally ill in the abstinent state.

Legal Precedent

In *Foucha v. Louisiana*, the United States Supreme Court ruled that Foucha was not suffering from a mental illness, and that due process required that he could be held only as long as he was both mentally ill and dangerous. He had committed his crime while in a drug-induced psychosis. In the abstinent state, he was not considered mentally ill, although he probably did suffer from a drug addiction (*Foucha v. Louisiana*, 1992).

CRIMINAL COMPETENCE

In the landmark case for the precedent for criminal competence, *Dusky v. United States*, the United States Supreme Court ruled that the test for whether or not a defendant is competent to stand trial is whether he or she has sufficient present ability to consult with his or her lawyer with a reasonable degree of rational understanding, and whether he or she has rational as well as factual understanding of proceedings against him or her. It is not enough that he or she is oriented to time and place and has some recollection of events. Dusky was accused of kidnapping a 15-year-old girl. He and two boys had been drinking vodka prior to offering to drive the girl home. Instead of taking the girl home, they drove to a back road where the two boys raped her. Dusky tried but was unable to rape her. Although Dusky was also schizophrenic, he was not grossly impaired if he took proper amounts of Thorazine (*Dusky v. United States*, 1960).

Generally, alcoholics and drug addicts in the abstinent or sober state show the ability to understand legal charges and proceedings against them, particularly at the time of trial. Despite gross impairment of mental capacity while under the influence of alcohol and drugs, alcoholics and drug addicts alone do not show sufficient difficulty in grasping the nature of the offense in assisting the attorney in their defense during the legal proceedings for the specific charges in question (Wild et al., 1998).

CIVIL COMPETENCE

Civil competence is a capacity or a potential of mental functioning required, in a decision-specific manner, to understand and perform certain tasks of decision-making. Competence is presumed to be present unless there is an active and affirmative finding by a court that it is not present. Incompetence means that a mental illness is causing a defect in judgment in the specific area in question. Individuals suffering from addictive diseases generally satisfy the legal criteria for civil competence, unless a mental illness or state such as intoxication can be shown to produce a lack of understanding and judgment for the specific decisions or tasks in question (Gutheil, 1998).

ALCOHOL AND DRUG USE AND ADDICTION AS RISK FACTORS IN CRIME AND CRIMINAL INTENT

According to the MacArthur study, substance abuse tripled the rate of violence among individuals in the community who were not patients and increased the rate of violence among discharged patients by up to five times. Patients discharged from psychiatric hospitals who had symptoms of alcohol or drug use were as violent as their neighbors who were not patients (Steadman et al., 1998).

In a study of self-reported violence among 10,000 individuals within a community, alcohol and drug abuse or dependence accounted for more than half of the incidences of violence among those individuals who had psychiatric diagnoses. According to another study, substance abuse is a much greater risk factor for violence than mental illness. Alcohol or drug dependence is the leading psychiatric diagnosis in studies of completed suicides, and is a leading risk factor in those who attempt and complete suicide (Swanson et al., 1990).

Alcohol and drug addiction are highly prevalent in criminal acts. All drugs, including alcohol, are associated with crime (Bureau of Justice Statistics, 1998). At least 35% of convicted offenders were under the influence of alcohol at the time of their offense (Guze et al., 1968). An additional significant proportion of offenders were using other drugs at the time of their offense (Hood et al., 1990). More than 50% of murderers were using alcohol, drugs, or both, at the time of their crime. Alcohol, cocaine, amphetamine and derivatives, phencyclidine hydrochloride and heroin are drugs that are particularly linked to violent behaviors toward others (Swanson et al., 1990; Pihl & Hoaken, 1997).

In other studies, violence due to alcohol and drugs was attributed to crimes to gain access to these substances and to resolve disputes over them, as well as to the effects of these substances on the individual's mind and behavior (Bureau of Justice Statistics, 1998). Drugs diminish control, impair insight and judgment, induce grandiosity and paranoia, disinhibit and provoke and stimulate uncontrollable behaviors (Brecher et al., 1988). Alcohol intoxication was responsible for most violent crimes, including murders, assaults, sexual assaults and family violence (Braun, 1986; Murdoch et al., 1990). Sixty-two percent of violent offenders were drinking at the time of their crime (Murdoch et al., 1990). Among individuals with psychotic disorders, those with substance-related co-morbidity and a history of violent behavior are more likely to be hospitalized repeatedly and least likely to comply with medications after discharge (Drake et al., 1993; Resnick, 1998).

CIVIL LAW IN SELECTED POPULATIONS

Child Abuse and Custody

The Child Abuse Prevention and Treatment Act of 1974 defines child neglect and abuse as: "the physical and mental injuring, sexual abuse, negligent treatment, or maltreatment of a child under the age of 18." Alcohol and drug use and addiction are commonly associated with physical and sexual abuse and neglect. The common form of maltreatment is physical neglect. Head trauma is the leading cause of child abuse fatalities (Quinn, 1998). Statutes requiring child abuse to be reported are an affirmative duty for professionals related to acts required to protect third parties (e.g., *Tarasoff*) (Quinn, 1998).

Courts consider addictive disease a treatable cause of child abuse in those who have responsibility for a child's welfare but commit acts of abuse as a result of an alcohol or drug problem, or while under the influence of these substances. Courts may offer the parent the alternative to comply with treatment and monitoring in lieu of termination of parental rights. Termination of parental rights, either voluntary or involuntary, can result from not satisfying the stipulations of addiction treatment and monitoring by the court, because the condition was viewed as not likely to change within the foreseeable future (Schoettle, 1984).

Decisions for child custody disputes rely on the standard of the "best interest" of the child. Predictors of negative outcome for custodial care of a child include a history of alcohol or drug problems in the parent. Of crucial importance to a positive outcome is the custodial parent–child relationship, which can be impaired in those with alcohol and drug disorders. The need for evaluation of addictive disease in both parents and referral for treatment is evidence for the welfare of the child and the ability of the parent to meet requirements for the best interest of the child (Ash & Guyer, 1984).

Sexual Offenders

Most sex crimes involve the influence of, or complications due to, the presence of alcohol and drug disorders. Substance abuse was the most common diagnosis in murderers (34.6%), rapists (29.4%) and rapist–murderers (40%). A common, if not *the* most common, reason given for recidivism due to violation of parole is relapse to alcohol and drug use (Yarvis, 1995). Despite the glaring presence of addiction, the need for treatment of it to improve compliance with other treatments for sexual offenders and to prevent relapse to alcohol and drugs has not been established. More clinical programs, and studies to document their efficacy, are needed to show the effectiveness of addiction treatment in this population. Studies indicate that addiction treatment is effective in achieving reduced drug and alcohol use and abstinence in other psychiatric and nonpsychiatric populations.

Malingering

The clinical characteristic of addictive disease includes denial, minimization and rationalization. As a result, alcoholics and drug addicts regularly deny and minimize their use. Other motivating factors for denial may be to avoid prosecution, to avoid loss of a job or child custody and social stigma. On the other hand, the notion that alcoholics and drug addicts, or normal individuals, exaggerate their suicidal tendencies or make contingent suicide threats for nonmedical or nonpsychiatric reasons (e.g., hospital admission) is simply not supported by studies or reasonableness. The addict who is out of control and at risk for danger to self or others, or who is incapable of caring for himself or herself is most likely using complaints of suicide to emphasize feelings of helplessness and hopelessness arising out of sickness and a sense of being out of control (Miller et al., 1992).

One study compared veterans who exaggerated their suicidal tendencies or made contingent suicide threats for the purpose of being admitted to a hospital with "genuinely" suicidal patients. Those who threatened suicide had more substance abuse, but no statistical difference in the incidence of completed suicide at the six-month follow-up (Lambert & Bonner, 1996). Active drug addicts and alcoholics may seek addiction treatment under duress of threat of legal prosecution, but alcohol and drugs are central problems in these individuals' lives and are often the cause of the legal predicament. Coerced addiction treatment can be an effective means of removing the drug factor from criminal recidivism (Miller & Flaherty, 2000).

CORRECTIONS AND COERCED TREATMENT

Goals of Treatment

The purposes of punishment are deterrence of future crimes, incapacitation to prevent individuals from committing further crimes, rehabilitation to correct the underlying problems of criminal conduct and retribution because they deserve it. The correctional system provides an opportunity to intervene for those individuals with alcohol and drug disorders, particularly when these disorders are implicated with the crimes causing their incarceration. Until recently, criminals did not receive attention for their addictive diseases. Programs are gradually being introduced into the criminal justice system to provide addiction treatment services (Scott, 1998).

Studies of recidivism have shown that untreated alcohol and drug addiction lead to a high rate of relapse and repeated criminal offenses. Because of the strong association of criminal conduct with alcohol and drug disorders, the need for treatment during incarceration to correct the underlying problems and to deter further criminal conduct is obvious. It is important that addiction treatment continues as a condition of parole and release into the community.

Diversion

Diversion is the evaluating of detainees for the presence of a mental disorder and negotiating with the legal system and mental health providers, including addiction treatment, to offer a disposition in lieu of prosecution or as a condition of reduction in charges (Steadman et al., 1994). Factors in determining diversion of a mentally ill offender at the pretrial stage include the seriousness of the crime and the area of jurisdiction (Davis, 1994). Traditional diversion programs to reduce recidivism of repeat violations of driving while intoxicated have been operating successfully for decades. Drug courts are examples of a growing trend of attempts at diverting alcoholics and drug addicts to treatment programs to correct the underlying problems of their crimes (Miller & Flaherty, 2000).

Prevalence of Alcohol and Drug Disorders during Incarceration

Lockups contain large numbers of individuals with alcohol and drug intoxication withdrawal. The suicide rate is higher in lockups than in jails or prisons (Scott, 1998). Eighty-two percent of all jail inmates said they had used an illegal drug and 25% stated that they had received treatment for a mental or emotional disorder (Harlin, 1998). Sixty-one percent of the men and 70% of the women in jail had a lifetime prevalence of substance use disorder (Teplin, 1994; Teplin et al., 1996). Sixty-two percent of prison inmates reported regular use of a drug at some time in their lives. Half of all prison inmates in 1991 had used cocaine in some form (Beck et al., 1993). More than 80% of the women in prison had a lifetime prevalence of a substance use disorder (Jordan et al., 1996). According to the National Institute of Mental Health Epidemiologic Catchment Area program study, 72% of prison inmates had a lifetime prevalence of substance abuse (Regier et al., 1990).

Prevalence of Suicide and Alcohol and Drug Disorders during Incarceration

In lockups, 60% of the suicide victims were under the influence of alcohol, drugs, or both, at the time of arrest and booking. Fifty percent of the suicides occurred within the first 24 hours and 27% occurred within the first three hours (Hayes, 1989). Suicides occurred three to eight times more often in jails than in the general population (Durand et al., 1995). The rate of suicide in prisons was approximately twice that in the general population (Lester, 1987).

Legal Precedent

The Eighth Amendment prohibits cruel and unusual punishments. It applies to those who are convicted of a crime, but not to the pretrial detainees. Convicted prisoners, therefore, have a constitutional right to medical care. In *Estelle v. Gamble*, the United States Supreme Court set the "deliberate indifference" to serious medical need as the standard that constitutes "unnecessary and wonton infliction of pain" proscribed by the Eighth Amendment (*Estelle v. Gamble*, 1976).

In *Ruiz v. Estelle*, prisoners brought forth a class action suit regarding conditions of confinement. Six essential elements from the district court ruling provided guidelines for planning mental health services: systemic screening and evaluation; treatment that was more than mere seclusion or close supervision; participation by trained mental health professionals; accurate, complete and confidential records; safeguards against psychotropic medication prescribed in dangerous amounts, without adequate supervision, or otherwise inappropriately administered; and a suicide prevention program (Scott, 1998).

THE DEATH PENALTY AND ADDICTIONS

A psychiatric and medical examination often finds a history of alcohol and drug disorders among individuals sentenced for capital punishment. Substance-related disorders are the most common psychiatric diagnoses in prisoners sentenced to death. Studies show that between 70% and 80% of prisoners have had a lifetime prevalence of substance-related disorders.

In *Eddings v. Oklahoma*, a 16-year-old boy was sentenced to death for killing a police officer. The case was appealed to the United States Supreme Court based on the argument that the trial court had not sufficiently considered the mitigating evidence. The United States Supreme Court agreed, reversing the decision and remanding the case for the sentencing judge to give fuller consideration to the mitigating evidence. This decision can open the doors to providing evidence of the role of alcohol and drug disorders in a capital crime. Ultimately, mitigating evidence could save the life of an individual who otherwise may not have formed the intent to commit a crime if not under the influence of alcohol and drugs (*Eddings v. Oklahoma*, 1981).

INVOLUNTARY HOSPITALIZATION

Civil commitment statutes generally require components of mental illness, dangerousness (to self or others), grave disability (unable to care for self), treatability and the least restrictive alternative. Civil commitment is common for those suffering from the complications of alcohol and drug disorders. Suicidal behavior is strongly associated with intoxication from alcohol and drugs. The availability of treatment for withdrawal and the addictive disorder itself makes involuntary hospitalization an important potential step in reducing dangerousness and introducing individuals to sustained recovery (Miller et al., 1992).

Unfortunately, there are no legal precedents to hold an alcoholic or a drug addict who, in the abstinent state, appears to be at high risk for relapse to alcohol or drugs. Despite the effectiveness of coerced treatment in promoting sustained abstinence and reducing complications from alcohol and drug disorders, courts do not allow clinicians to hold individuals against their will to initiate addiction treatment. Coerced treatment is effective in confronting the denial of the addictive illness and motivating individuals to comply with treatment, and ultimately find sustained abstinence and recovery (Miller & Flaherty, 2000).

MALPRACTICE

In a malpractice case, the plaintiff must prove negligence by a preponderance of the evidence, that negligence occurred more likely than not, and that the care did not meet the standard of practice. Negligence is defined as dereliction or breach of a duty directly causing actual damage. Cases of malpractice that involve alcohol and drugs, including prescription of addicting medications, are increasingly common. There are several major areas of case law that hold the physician liable for negligence when treating patients with alcohol and drug disorders (Resnick, 1998).

Competence to Sign into an Institution

Voluntary patients must be competent to sign into an institution and must understand the implications of doing so. The importance of assessing the capacity of an intoxicated patient to make decisions and understand their consequences is highlighted by legal precedent.

In *Zinermon v. Burch*, the United States Supreme Court held that in states such as Florida, which requires a patient to be competent before voluntarily signing into an institution, the failure to screen out incompetent patients violates those patients' constitutional rights. The implication was that the court suggested that all voluntary patients should be screened for competence before voluntary hospitalization is allowed (*Zinermon v. Burch*, 1990).

Informed Consent

The essential requirements of informed consent are that the patient understands the nature and extent of his or her addiction problems, the risks and benefits of proposed treatment, and alternative courses of treatment. The patient must be competent to give informed consent to accept or reject treatment. The implications from legal decisions pose challenges for clinicians who treat patients with addictions.

In 1960, *Natanson v. Kline* was the first court requirement of informed consent (*Natanson v. Kline*, Kan 1960). In 1972, the United States Court of Appeals' ruling in *Canterbury v. Spence* was for the court to require that information include inherent and potential risks of the proposed treatment, the alternatives to treatment, if any, and the likely result if the patient remained untreated (*Canterbury v. Spence*, 1972).

Although many clinicians, including physicians, are not aware of the effectiveness of addiction treatment, their lack of sufficient skill and knowledge may not protect them against liability if a patient is to be informed about his or her addictive disease and the risks and benefits of treatment versus no treatment. Given recent court cases, the possibility of malpractice may be increased in clinical cases of nicotine dependence if physicians do not explain the nature and extent of complications from continued smoking, the benefits of treatment and the risks of refusing treatment. The liability for malpractice may be extended to other addictive drugs, including alcohol and medications, if sufficient attempts are not made to inform the patient of the nature and extent of the addictive disease, particularly the adverse consequences, the need for treatment, and the outcomes with and without treatment.

Injury to a Third Party by Alcoholics and Drug Addicts

The *Tarasoff* principle imposes the duty to protect others from patients who are likely to harm themselves or others, as established in legal cases involving alcohol and drugs. Prosenjit Poddar, an Indian graduate student at the University of California, Berkeley, started to date a fellow student named Tatiana Tarasoff. He kissed her a few times and believed they had a special relationship. When Tarasoff learned of Poddar's feelings, she told him that she was involved with other men and did not want to pursue an intimate relationship with him. Subsequently, Poddar became severely depressed and neglected his appearance, studies and health. The condition persisted so Poddar went to a psychologist, Dr Moore, at the University Health Service. He revealed his intention to get a gun and shoot Tarasoff. Dr Moore sent a letter to the campus police requesting them to take Poddar to a psychiatric hospital. The campus police interviewed Mr Poddar, but he convinced them that he was not dangerous. They released him on the promise that he would stay away from Ms Tarasoff. When the Health Service psychiatrist in charge returned from vacation, he directed that the letter to the police be destroyed and no further action taken.

On 27 October 1969, the defendant went to Tarasoff's home to speak with her. She was not at home, and her mother told him to leave. The defendant returned later, armed with a pellet gun and a kitchen knife, and found Tarasoff alone. She refused to speak with him, and when he persisted, she screamed. At this point the defendant shot her with the pellet gun. She ran from the house, was pursued, caught and repeatedly and fatally stabbed by the defendant (*People v. Poddar*, 1974).

In deciding that psychiatrists have a duty to protect an ascertainable victim against foreseeable danger, the court took many factors into consideration: the foreseeability of harm to the plaintiff; the degree of certainty that the plaintiff suffered injury; the closeness of the connection between the defendant's conduct and the injury suffered; the moral blame attached to the defendant's conduct; the policy of preventing future harm; the extent of the burden to the defendant and consequences to the community of imposing a duty to exercise care with resulting liability for breach; and the availability, cost and prevalence of insurance for the risk involved.

Relying primarily on forseeability of harm to the plaintiff, the court held that: "[w]hen a therapist determines, or pursuant to the standards of his profession should determine, that his patient presents a serious danger of violence to another, he incurs an obligation to use reasonable care to protect the intended victim against such danger. The discharge of this duty may require the therapist to take one or more of various steps, depending upon the nature of the case. Thus, it may call for him to warn the intended victim or others likely to apprise the victim of the danger, to notify the police, or to take whatever other steps are reasonably necessary under the circumstances." Even though no relationship existed between Tarasoff and the therapist, there was a relationship between

Poddar and the therapist, which supported an affirmative duty for the benefit of third persons, namely Tarasoff (*Tarasoff v. Regents of University of California*, 1976).

Other court decisions have not always supported the *Tarasoff* decision; the precedent is clearly available for plaintiffs' cases (*Boynton v. Burglass*, 1991; *Santa Cruz v. Northwest, Dade County Community Health Center*, 1991; *Nasser v. Parker*, 1995; *Thapar v. Zezulka*, 1999). In *Petersen v. Washington State*, the Washington Supreme Court ruled that the hospital was liable for not extending the involuntary stay of a patient who, in a psychosis induced by phencyclidine hydrochloride, struck the plaintiff's car five days after release. The patient was a known drug addict who was seen driving recklessly on hospital grounds one day before discharge (*Petersen v. State*, 1983).

ADOLESCENTS AND JUVENILE COURT AND ADDICTIONS

Prevalence of Alcohol and Drug Use and Disorders in Juvenile Populations

The onset of alcohol and drug use and disorders is often during the adolescent years (younger than 18 years). Ninety percent of high school seniors consume alcohol and 5% do so daily (Miller, 1998). According to the Epidemiologic Catchment Area study, the mean age at onset of alcohol dependence is 22 years for men and 25 years for women. The mean duration of alcohol dependence is nine years to diagnosis. Significant drug use is discernible as early as the fourth, fifth and sixth grades. Although alcohol is the most common drug used, younger individuals typically consume other drugs, including nicotine, marijuana, cocaine, organic solvents, heroin, hallucinogens and tranquilizers (PRIDE, 1999).

As with adults, assessing the future dangerousness of adolescents includes an evaluation for alcohol and drug use. In a study of 72 adolescents charged with murder at the Michigan Center for Forensic Psychiatry between 1977 and 1985, 75% of the crime group (defined as killing during another crime such as robbery) and 33% of the conflict group (defined as involved in an interpersonal conflict with the victim) were intoxicated at the time of the offense (Cornell et al., 1987).

From 1992 to 1994, 25% of those who perpetrated school deaths had a history of being previously involved with alcohol and drugs to a significant degree, and 35% were involved in drug-related gangs (National Center for Education Statistics, 1998). In general, studies show a strong association of drug and alcohol disorders with delinquency, truancy, violent crimes, property crimes and other legal problems (National Center for Education Statistics, 1998). Diversion is a common practice in juvenile court. The court can order to divert the case out of the legal system, often to alternative programs for the assessment and treatment of alcohol and drug disorders.

Legal Precedents

In *Kent v. United States* and *In re Gault*, the United States Supreme Court held that a juvenile is entitled to a hearing, access to counsel, a written statement by the judge for reasons of waiver (*Kent v. United States*, 1966), notice of charges, counsel, confrontation, cross-examination of witnesses and privilege against self-incrimination (*In re Gault*, 1967). These safeguards allow for evaluations for identifying the underlying problem of addictive disease and diverting to alternative programs to provide education, intervention and treatment for alcohol and drug related offenses.

The Juvenile Justice and Delinquency Prevention Act emphasized community-based treatment and prevention. It established the Office of Juvenile Justice and Delinquency Prevention, deinstitutionalized status offenders and limited placement of juveniles in adult institutions (Scott, 1998).

FORENSIC PATHOLOGY AND DRUG TESTING

Forensic Pathology

Knowledge of the role of forensic pathology can be important to determinations made by a forensic psychiatrist. Factors of potential importance in identifying the role of alcohol and drugs are time of death, time of injury, manner of death and manner of abuse (as in child abuse, rape or penetration). Virtually any interface between the law and medicine may call for the expertise of a forensic pathologist (Spitz, 1993).

Drug Testing

Toxicology determinations on urine, blood, hair and other body fluids or tissues are crucial to ascertaining the influence of alcohol and drugs on a particular individual or crime. Drug testing is also used to monitor compliance with diversion, probation, or stipulation of release from incarceration. Drug testing is one measure of treatment compliance and can be motivation for continued participation in monitoring programs (Wecht, 1998; Miller & Flaherty, 2000).

MEDICAL RECORDS

Federal and state statutes limit access to medical information (45 C.F.R. §164.501 *et seq.* (2000)). Federal confidentiality laws (45 C.F.R. §2.1 *et seq.* (2009)) and state licensing and confidentiality laws protect the identity, diagnosis and treatment episodes of those who have alcohol and drug problems. Special federal rules pertain to the confidentiality of information concerning patients treated for or referred for treatment for alcoholism or drug addiction. The rules apply to any facility receiving federal funds for any purpose, including Medicare or Medicaid reimbursement. The rules pre-empt any state law that purports to authorize disclosures contrary to them, but states are permitted to impose tighter confidentiality requirements.

Methadone treatment programs must maintain records traceable to specific patients, showing dates, quantities and batch or code marks of the drug dispensed for three years after the date of dispensing. When narcotics are administered for the treatment of hospitalized patients who are dependent on narcotics, the hospital must maintain accurate records, showing dates, quantities and batch or code marks of the drug administered for at least three years (Hirsh, 1998).

REHABILITATION ACTS

The Rehabilitation Act of 1973 and the Americans with Disabilities Act of 1990 have provided broad protection for individuals with physical and mental impairments. These acts provide precedent for inclusion of alcohol and drug addiction as a disability. An employee with an alcohol problem, drug problem, or both (which can apply to illegal drugs if in treatment and not using them) can be offered accommodation in the form of addiction treatment before losing his or her employment. An alcoholic is entitled to the option of addiction treatment to perform the essential functions of a particular job. An alcoholic who refuses treatment can be terminated from his or her position, especially if unable to perform his or her functions due to continued alcohol use. However, court decisions have made some distinctions as to how these acts can be applied to individual cases (*Treadwell v. Alexander*, 1983; *Whitlock v. Donovan*, 1984; *Crewe v. US Office of Personnel Management*, 1987; *Callicotte v. Carrlucci*, 1988; *Traynor v. Turnage* and *McKelvey v. Turnage*, 1988; *Greater Cleveland Regional Transit Authority v. Ohio Civil Rights Commission*, 1989; *Rodgers v. Lehman*, 1989; Parry, 1993).

In *Traynor v. Turnage* and *McKelvey v. Turnage*, two veterans sued the Veterans Administration for violation of the Rehabilitation Act, which prohibits discrimination against disability. The United States Supreme Court stated that Traynor and McKelvey, who claimed that alcoholism created a disabling condition, were denied benefits "because they engaged with some degree of willfulness in the conduct that caused them to become disabled." The historic dichotomy is illustrated in this case, in which alcoholism is considered a disabling condition, but willful misconduct can be present in the individual with alcoholism (*Traynor v. Turnage* and *McKelvey v. Turnage*, 1988).

CONCLUSION

Addictions and the law are interwoven in court cases, legislative actions, constitutional law and administrative policy. In general, the law views alcohol and drug addiction as an illness in an individual who bears responsibility for its consequences, including punishment and therapeutic treatments. The individual is not completely guilty or absolved from criminal or civil responsibilities because of addictive disease. Increasingly, alcohol and drug disorders are considered the root causes of criminal and civil violations that can be ameliorated or eliminated through therapeutic actions sanctioned and monitored by the courts.

The forensic psychiatrist and the generalist should acquaint themselves with the efficacy of addictions treatment and the importance and advantages of identifying addictive diseases in their patients. They must also consider the legal consequences for not informing patients of the treatment options for their addictions. If addiction treatment is viewed as an alternative consequence of addictive disease in legal cases, the psychiatrist can cooperate with the legal system to improve clinical care and reduce harm to self and others by those suffering from alcohol and drug disorders. In this model, addiction treatment becomes the "carrot" in mitigation and the legal consequences for not complying with the alternative are the "stick" to induce the individual to exercise personal responsibility in his or her decisions.

REFERENCES

Adams, R. D., & Victor, M. (1993). *Principles of Neurology*. New York, NY: McGraw-Hill.

Ash, P., & Guyer, M. (1984). Court implementation of mental health professionals' recommendations in contested child custody and visitation cases. *Bull Am Acad Psychiatry Law, 12,* 137–147.

Beck, A., Gilliard, D., Greenfeld, L., et al. (1993). *Survey of State Prisoner Inmates,* NCJ Publication No. 136949. Washington, DC: U.S. Department of Justice, National Institute of Justice.

Berman, B. (1997). Responsibility for crime and injury when drunk. *Addiction, 92,* 1183–1188.

Boynton v. Burglass, 590 So2d 446 (Fla App 1991).

Braun, P. F. (1986). *Alcohol and Aggression*. London, UK: Croom Helm.

Brecher, M., Wang, B. W., Wong, H., & Morgan, J. P. (1988). Phencyclidine and violence: clinical and legal issues. *J Clin Psychopharmacol., 8,* 397–401.

Bureau of Justice Statistics. (1998). *Criminal Victimization*. Washington, DC: U.S. Department of Justice.

Callicotte v. Carrlucci, 698 F Supp 944 (DCDC 1988).

Canterbury v. Spence, 464 F2d 772 (DC Cir 1972).

Ciccone, T. R. (1999). The United States Supreme Court and psychiatry in the 1990s. *Psychiatr Clin North Am., 22,* 197–211.

Committee on Psychiatry and Law, Groups for the Advancement of Psychiatry. (1991). The law and the legal process. In: *Mental Health Professional and the Legal System*. New York, NY: Brunner, Mazel.

Cornell, D. G., Benedek, E. P., & Benedek, D. M. (1987). Juvenile homicide: prior adjustment and a proposed typology. *Am J Orthopsychiatry, 57,* 383–393.

Crewe v. US Office of Personnel Management, 834 F2d 140 (8th Cir 1987).

Davis, S. (1994). Factors associated with the diversion of mentally disordered offenders. *Bull Am Acad Psychiatry Law, 22,* 389–397.

Drake, R. E., McHugo, G. J., & Noordsy, D. L. (1993). Treatment of alcoholism among schizophrenic outpatients: 4-year outcomes. *Am J Psychiatry, 150,* 328–329.

DuRand, C. J., Burtka, G. J., Federman, E. J., Haycox, J. A., & Smith, J. W. (1995). A quarter century of suicide in a major urban jail: implications for community psychiatry. *Am J Psychiatry*, *152*, 1077–1080.

Dusky v. United States, 362 US 402, 80 SCt 788 (1960).

Eddings v. Oklahoma, 455 US 104 (1981).

Estelle v. Gamble, 429 US 97 (1976).

Foucha v. Louisiana, 504 US 71 (1992).

Garner, B. A. (Ed.). (2004). *Black's Law Dictionary* (8th ed.). Eagan, MN: West Group.

Goldsmith, R. J., & Miller, N. S. (1994). Training psychiatric residents in the addictions. *Psychiatric Annals*, *24*, 432–439.

Greater Cleveland Regional Transit Authority v. Ohio Civil Rights Commission, 567 NE2d 1325 (Ohio Ct App 1989).

Gutheil, T. G. (1998). *Civil competencies*. Forensic Psychiatry Review Course. Bloomfield, CT: American Academy of Psychiatry and the Law.

Guze, S. B., Wolfgram, E. D., McKinney, J. K., & Cantwell, D. P. (1968). Delinquency, social maladjustment, and crime: the role of alcoholism (a study of first-degree relatives of convicted criminals). *Diseases of the Nervous System*, *29*, 238–243.

Harlin, C. W. (1998). *Profile of Jail Inmates, 1996*, NCJ Publication No. 164620. Washington, DC: U.S. Department of Justice, Bureau of Justice Statistics.

Hayes, L. M. (1989). National study of jail suicides: seven years later. *Psychiatr Q*, *60*, 7–30.

Hirsh, H. L. (1998). *Medical Records in Legal Medicine* (4th ed.). St. Louis, MO: Mosby (pp. 280–298).

Hood, I., Ryan, D., Monforte, J., & Valentour, J. (1990). Cocaine in Wayne County Medical Examiner's cases. *J Forensic Sci.*, *35*, 591–600.

In re Gault, 387 US 1 (1967).

Jordan, B. K., Schlenger, W. E., Fairbank, J. A., & Caddell, J. M. (1996). Prevalence of psychiatric disorders among incarcerated women: II. Convicted felons entering prison. *Arch Gen Psychiatry*, *53*, 513–519.

Kent v. United States, 383 US 541 (1966).

Koob, G. F., & Caine, S. B. (1999). Cocaine addiction therapy: are we partially there? *Nat Med.*, *5*, 993–995.

Lambert, M. T., & Bonner, J. (1996). Characteristics and six-month outcome of patients who are suicide threats to seek hospital admission. *Psychiatr Serv.*, *47*, 871–873.

Lande, R. G. (1993). Alcohol: the clinician's role in evaluating legal responsibility. *Mil Med.*, *158*, 748–751.

Leshner, A. I. (1999). Science-based views of drug addiction and its treatment. *JAMA*, *282*, 1314–1316.

Lester, D. (1987). Suicide and homicide in USA prisons. *Psychol Rep.*, *61*, 126.

Linder v. US, 268 US 5, 18 (1925).

Miller, N. S. (1991). *Comprehensive Handbook of Drug and Alcohol Addiction*. New York, NY: Marcel Dekker.

Miller, N. S. (1998). Special problems of the alcohol and drug dependent: clinical interactions and detoxification. In R. J. Frances & S. I. Miller (Eds.), *Clinical Textbook of Addictive Disorders* (2nd ed.) (pp. 262–290). New York, NY: Guildford Press.

Miller, N. S., & Flaherty, J. A. (2000). Effectiveness of coerced addiction treatment (alternative consequences): a review of the clinical research. *J Subst Abuse Treat.*, *18*, 9–16.

Miller, N. S., Giannini, A. J., & Gold, M. (1992). Suicide risk associated with drug and alcohol addiction. *Cleve Clin J Med.*, *59*, 535–538.

Murdoch, D., Pihl, R. O., & Ross, D. (1990). Alcohol and crimes of violence: present issues. *International Journal of Addictions*, 25, 1065–1081.

Nasser v. Parker, 249 Va 172 (1995).

Natanson v. Kline, 350 P2d 1093 (Kan 1960).

National Center for Education Statistics. (1998). *Violence and Discipline Problems in US Public Schools, 1996–1997*. Washington, DC: National Center for Education Statistics.

National Parents Resource Institute for Drug Education (PRIDE). (1999). Study shows nine-year-olds already involved in drugs and alcohol: transition from fifth to sixth grade seen as a vulnerable time. *Pride News Releases, April 7*.

Parry, J. W. (1993). Mental disabilities under the ADA: a difficult path to follow. *Mental and Physical Diseases and the Law Report, 10*, 100–112.

People of the State of California v. Saille, 54 Cal3d 1103 (Cal 1991).

People v. Free, 122 Ill2d 367 (1988).

People v. Poddar, 10 Cal3d 750 (1974).

Petersen v. State, 100 Wash2d 421 (Wash 1983).

Pihl, O., & Hoaken, P. (1997). Clinical correlates and predictions of violence in patients with substance abuse disorders. *Psychiatric Annals*, 27, 735–740.

Powell v. State of Texas, 392 US 514 (1968).

Quinn, K. M. (1998). *Child abuse,* Forensic Psychiatry Review Course. Bloomfield, CT: American Academy of Psychiatry and the Law.

Regier, D. A., Farmer, M. E., Rae, D. S., Locke, B. Z., Keith, S. J., Judd, L. L., & Goodwin, F. K. (1990). Comorbidity of mental disorders with alcohol and other drug abuse: results from the Epidemiologic Catchment Area (ECA) study. *JAMA, 264*, 2511–2518.

Resnick, P. J. (1998). *Basic law for psychiatrists,* Forensic Psychiatry Review Course. Bloomfield, CT: American Academy of Psychiatry and the Law.

Resnick, P. J. (1998). *Outline of psychiatric malpractice,* Forensic Psychiatry Review Course. Bloomfield, CT: American Academy of Psychiatry and the Law.

Resnick, P. J. (1998). *Risk assessment of the mentally ill individual,* Forensic Psychiatry Review Course. Bloomfield, CT: American Academy of Psychiatry and the Law.

Robinson v. California, 370 US 660 (1962).

Rodgers v. Lehman, 869 F2d 253 (4th Cir 1989).

Santa Cruz v. Northwest, Dade County Community Health Center, 590 So2d 444 (Fla App 1991).

Schoettle, U. D. (1984). Termination of parental rights – ethical issues and value conflict. *J Am Acad Child Adolesc Psychiatry, 23*, 629–632.

Scott, C. L. (1998). *Correctional psychiatry,* Forensic Psychiatry Review Course. Bloomfield, CT: American Academy of Psychiatry and the Law.

Scott, C. L. (1998). *Juvenile court assessment,* Forensic Psychiatry Review Course. Bloomfield, CT: American Academy of Psychiatry and the Law.

Spitz, W. U. (Ed.). (1993). *Medicolegal Investigation of Death* (3rd ed.). Springfield, IL: Charles C. Thomas.

State v. Hartfield, 388 SE2d 802 (SC 1990).

Steadman, J. H., Barbera, S. S., & Dennis, D. L. (1994). A national survey of jail diversion programs for mentally ill detainees. *Hospital and Community Psychiatry, 45*, 1109–1113.

Steadman, H. J., Mulvey, E. P., Monahan, J., Robbins, P. C., Appelbaum, P. S., Grisso, T., Roth, L. H., & Silver, E. (1998). Violence by people discharged from acute psychiatric inpatient facility and by others in the same neighborhoods. *Arch Gen Psychiatry, 55*, 393–401.

Swanson, J. W., Holzer, C. E. III, Ganju, V. K., & Jono, R. T. (1990). Violence and psychiatric disorders in the community: evidence from the Epidemiologic Catchment Area surveys. *Hospital and Community Psychiatry, 41*, 761–770.

Tarasoff v. Regents of University of California, 17 Cal3d 425 (1976).

Teplin, L. A. (1994). Psychiatric and substance abuse disorders among male urban jail detainees. *Am J Public Health, 84,* 290–293.

Teplin, L. A., Abram, K. M., & McClelland, G. M. (1996). Prevalence of psychiatric disorders among incarcerated women: Pretrial jail detainees. *Arch Gen Psychiatry, 53,* 505–512.

Thapar v. Zezulka, 994 SW2d 635 (Tex 1999).

Traynor v. Turnage and *McKelvey v. Turnage*, 485 US 539 (1988).

Treadwell v. Alexander, 707 F2d 473 (11th Cir 1983).

United States v. Knott, 894 F2d 1119 (9th Cir 1990).

Waterson, R. T. (1991). Just say no to the charges against you: alcohol intoxication, mental capacity, and criminal responsibility. *Bull Am Acad Psychiatry Law, 19,* 277–290.

Wecht, C. H. (1998). *Forensic Pathology in Legal Medicine* (4th ed.). St. Louis, MO: Mosby (pp. 280–298).

Whitlock v. Donovan, 598 FSupp 126 (DCDC 1984).

Wild, T. C., Graham, K., & Rehm, J. (1998). Blame and punishment for intoxicated aggression: when is the perpetrator culpable? *Addiction, 93,* 677–687.

Yarvis, D. M. (1995). Diagnostic patterns among three violent offender types. *Bull Am Acad Psychiatry Law, 23,* 411–419.

Zinermon v. Burch, 494 US 113 (1990).

Chapter 3

Physician Practice of Addictions in Medical Practice

Norman S. Miller, MD, JD, PLLC

Department of Medicine, College of Human Medicine, Michigan State University, East Lansing, MI, USA

INTRODUCTION

The role of physicians in the prevention and treatment of addictive disorders is growing in importance and magnitude. The public and managed care organizations are increasingly looking to physicians for leadership and advocacy for patients who have drug and alcohol addictions. The political climate and enormous need combine to make the role of physicians essential to prevention and treatment strategies for addiction diseases. Efforts by physicians in the past have been slow and obstructionist, because of moral views and lack of training in alcohol and drug problems and disorders. Physicians who were not prepared to confront patients about their addictions, and nonphysicians who could treat but not communicate with the physicians, competed for the overall care of the patients. Frequently, patients had to bridge the gap at the expensive cost of delay in prevention and diagnosis of problematic use of alcohol and drugs.

Until now, physicians played a supporting role or no role at all in fostering and developing effective prevention and treatment methods for addictive disorders. The attitude of "see no evil, hear no evil, do no evil" no longer allows physicians to ignore common alcohol and drug problems in their patients. Increasingly, generalists are called on to screen, detect, prevent and treat alcohol and drug disorders in their populations.

The challenge to medical schools and training programs to provide education and clinical experience in addiction has never been greater and more pressing for addicted patients. Despite the presence and affects of alcohol related disorders, medical schools and residency programs fail to teach such disorders to their students competently. Although alcohol disorders cause over 100,000 deaths each year, the medical education community has yet to incorporate alcohol disorder education sufficiently into their curricula (Miller, 2001). Increasingly, medical students and residents are aware of the need and demonstrate interest in becoming knowledgeable and skilled in the prevention and treatment of alcohol and drug addiction. Both residency directors and curriculum deans affirmatively endorsed that assessment of deficiencies in training and education for alcohol disorders would lead to significant improvements in medical education for residents and medical students (Miller, 2001).

We have a large body of knowledge and basic skills in the prevention and treatment of addictive disorders. Considerable resources have been spent on research and development of clinic methods for prevention and treatment. The next step is to implement what is effective and useful to patients. The role of physicians will become apparent if they concentrate on what is effective in preventing and treating addictive disease (Lewis, 1997).

After reading this chapter you will be better able to understand:

1. The clinical prevalence of addictive disorders in the general, as well as special circumstance, populations;
2. The role of the physician in the prevention and treatment of addictive disorders;
3. Methods to improve prevention and treatment of addictive disorders primarily through improving medical school education.

CLINICAL PREVALENCE

Prevalence of Alcohol and Drug Dependence in the General Population

Alcohol and drug dependence are among the most prevalent illnesses in American society. The Epidemiological Catchment Area study, which is a survey of mental health and substance-related disorders in nearly 20,000 adult Americans, found a 13.5% lifetime prevalence of alcohol abuse or dependence and 7% drug dependence (Regier et al., 1990). Alcoholism and related illnesses are major causes of morbidity and mortality in patients in the United States throughout the world. More than half of all accidental deaths, suicides and homicides are alcohol- or drug-related (SAMHSA, 1992). A significant proportion of fetal anomalies can be attributed to the use of drugs or alcohol during pregnancy, with an estimated rate of 11% of illicit drug use among pregnant women (Chasnoff et al., 1989). The use of intravenous methods of administering illicit drugs has contributed to the increasing number of deaths from AIDS, according to data from the Centers for Disease Control and Prevention (Miller, 1994).

Prevalence of Multiple Drug Use and Dependence in Treatment

The use of multiple drugs and alcohol is extraordinarily common (e.g., alcohol and cocaine, heroin and cocaine, marijuana with alcohol or cocaine). The large overlap in the use of drugs and alcohol has had significant ramifications for diagnosis and treatment as they are traditionally practiced (Grant, 1996; Martin et al., 1996; Wiseman & McMillan, 1996; Kandel et al., 1997; Miller, 1997).

Research models for dependence on alcohol and drugs are affected by multiple use and dependence. In practice, one drug is frequently substituted for another, and the majority of individuals develop combined alcohol and multiple-drug dependence. The concurrent and simultaneous occurrences of multiple drug and alcohol dependence suggest a generalized susceptibility to the various types of dependence (Miller et al., 1990; Kasselbaum & Chandler, 1994; Patton, 1995; Denison et al., 1997).

Prevalence in the Medical Population

Drug and alcohol addiction are among the most common disorders seen in medical practice. They are at least as common as hypertension (Fleming & Barry, 1992). Addiction is associated with a wide range of problems, including pancreatitis, liver disease, accidents, suicide, depression and anxiety. Twenty to fifty percent of inpatient hospitalizations may be attributed to substance use and addiction, and 25% to 50% of emergency room visits are alcohol use and addiction related (Beresford, 1979; Hold et al., 1980; McIntosh, 1982; Ward et al., 1982; Cherpitel, 1988; Moore et al., 1989).

Although addiction is an extremely common disorder, it remains inadequately diagnosed and treated by physicians. Of the 20% of patients seen in ambulatory care settings who are estimated to be addicted to substances, only 5% of these patients are diagnosed (Cyr & Wartman, 1988). Physicians do not diagnose or treat substance use and addiction with the same frequency, accuracy, or effectiveness as they do other chronic medical diseases (Kamerow et al., 1986; Cleary et al., 1988). In a recent study, resident physicians correctly identified less than half of the patients with positive scores on a CAGE questionnaire, 22% of patients with an alcohol abuse history and 23% of patients with a history of substance abuse (Buchsbaum et al., 1991; Schmidt et al., 1995).

Prevalence in Family and Workplace Populations

The psychological and social costs of alcoholism and drug addiction are considerable to patients in medical practice. Alcoholism is a major cause of family dysfunction, including domestic violence and child abuse. Over 40% of adults report exposure to problem drinkers in their families (Schoenborn, 1988). Alcoholism is a major contributor to poor job performance and loss of productivity. Data show that 15% of heavy alcohol users missed work because of illness or injury in the past 30 days and 12% of heavy users skipped work because of drinking in the past 30 days (NIDA, 1997).

CLINICAL DIAGNOSIS

Physicians must make the diagnosis of alcohol and drug dependence to develop an integrated approach to medical education about addiction. Physicians must diagnose patients who present with abnormal alcohol and drug use (Fleming et al., 1997; Klamen & Miller, 1997; Parish, 1997). Physicians must ask routine screening questions to all patients they see and maintain a high index of suspicion for addictive diseases, especially in light of the extreme levels of denial often present in addicted patients. Physicians seeing patients in high-risk populations, such as emergency departments, prisons and trauma units must have an especially high index of suspicion. A family history is the best predictor of addiction in patients; therefore, questions about family history take on special importance in the detection of substance abuse or addiction. In addition, patients with chief or presenting complaints such as sleep disorders, "stress," chronic dyspepsia, recurrent peptic ulcers, or recurrent trauma should also raise a physician's index of suspicion. Physicians must be taught to listen carefully for rationalization, minimization and denial in patient's responses while observing their affective component associated with these complaints and responses (Miller et al., 1997).

Risk Assessment by Physicians

Physicians should be able to detect patients in environments that pose a risk for the development of substance dependence. Categories of vulnerability to the use of alcohol, tobacco and other drugs should be learned by every physician. Family environment includes family conflict, poor discipline style, parental rejection of the child, lack of adult supervision or family rituals, poor family management or communication, sexual and physical abuse and parental or sibling modeling for use of alcohol, tobacco, and other drugs. The school environment involves lack of school bonding and opportunities for involvement and reward, unfair rules, norms conducive to use of drugs and school failure because of poor school climate. Community environment pertains to poor community bonding; community norms that condone alcohol, tobacco and other drug abuse; disorganized neighborhoods; lack of opportunities for positive youth involvement; high levels of crime and drug use; endemic poverty; and lack of employment opportunities. Peer factors include bonding to peer groups whose members use alcohol, tobacco and other drugs or engage in other delinquent behaviors (Wmick & Larson, 1997).

Physical Examination and Laboratory Testing

The physical examination may be helpful in detecting alcohol or drug dependence. Information about intoxication, withdrawal, or alcohol- or drug-related organ damage and disease may yield important information about the adverse complications of addictive illness. Although no specific finding is pathognomonic of alcoholism, a physician's use of physical findings may be valuable in penetrating denial and convincing patients of the significant extent of their alcohol and drug use. Laboratory tests, such as urine toxicology screen, macrocytic red cell indices, or serum glutamic-oxabacetic transaminase and serum glutamic-pyruvic transaminase, may also be helpful. None of these, however, is of the same degree of importance and specificity as a thorough history for addiction with every patient (Miller et al., 1997).

CLINICAL COURSE AND PATHOPHYSIOLOGY

Clinical Comorbidity

Substance abuse disorders have been associated with serious problems including violence, injury, disease and death. It has been estimated that one in every four deaths can be attributed to the use of alcohol, tobacco, or some other form of drug. For example, tobacco use alone has been linked to 90% of lung cancer cases, 75% of emphysema cases and 25% of ischemic heart disease cases (Wyatt & Decker, 2007).

TREATMENT OF MEDICAL DISORDERS ASSOCIATED WITH ALCOHOL AND DRUG USE AND ADDICTION

Physician Intervention

Physicians should know how to provide simple interventions to eliminate or decrease substance abuse before it becomes dependence or addiction. Studies have shown that brief, empathic interventions by physicians can decrease the consumption and adverse effects of addictive substances by 20% to 50% (Chick et al., 1985; Wallace et al., 1988; Babor & Grant, 1990; Wmick & Larson, 1997). Physicians should be taught that messages that state that the attainment of the goal of reducing alcohol-related problems is the patients' responsibility and the encouragement of abstinence is a powerful modifier of patients' behavior toward alcohol and drugs.

Physicians should be well-versed in using prevention strategies for those patients at risk for substance abuse or dependence. Counseling patients about the health risks and dangers of substance abuse or addiction can be extremely effective in reducing their occurrence. The education of patients about the long-term and short-term consequences of substance abuse and addiction, including the severe risks encountered by drinking and driving, is fundamental to interventions by physicians. Physicians should be aware that many patients' peers probably do not approve of substance abuse and addiction, including the severe risks encountered by drinking and driving, and this is fundamental to interventions by physicians. Physicians should also be aware that many patients' peers probably do not approve of substance use as a healthy activity, which may prove to be an effective deterrent. Physician communication and physician availability as a source of confidential information about addictions are key to successful interventions. Open discussion between patient and physician of issues relating to the health effects of alcohol and drugs can be extremely helpful (Fleming et al., 1997; Parish, 1997).

Requirements of Physicians for Diagnosing and Treating Addictive Disease

A physician specialist in the treatment of alcoholism and other drug addictions must:

- Possess a current MD or DO license;
- Be able to recognize and diagnose alcoholism or other drug dependencies at both early and late stages and possess sufficient knowledge and communication skills to prescribe a full range of treatment services for alcohol and other drug addiction patients, their families, or significant others;
- Demonstrate a functionally positive attitude toward addicted patients, their families, and indicated significant others;
- Be knowledgeable in addiction treatment and be able to intervene to get patients and their families or significant others into treatment for their needs;
- Be able to provide, refer and support standard addiction treatment methods for alcohol and drug addictions;
- Be able to recognize and manage the medical and psychiatric complications of alcohol and other drug addictions;
- Be able to recognize and manage the signs and symptoms of withdrawal from alcohol and other drugs of addiction;
- Possess sufficient knowledge and communication skills concerning alcohol and other drug addictions to provide consultation, teach lay and professional people, and provide continuing education in this field.

General physicians must possess:

- The ability to competently obtain a history and perform a physical examination on patients with addictive disease (this presumes an ability and willingness to hospitalize patients if necessary);
- An understanding of the medical, psychiatric and social complications of addictive disease (this presumes a knowledge of self-help groups, such as AA, Narcotics Anonymous and Al-Anon, and presumes a knowledge of special groups for professionals);
- A positive attitude which is essential in establishing a relationship with patients in the treatment of alcoholism and drug addiction;
- A knowledge of the spectrum of this disease and the natural progression if untreated;
- A knowledge of the medical and psychiatric effects and organ damage attributable to alcoholism or other drug addictions (this presumes a knowledge of, and ability to prescribe, treatment);
- A knowledge of the classifications of drugs of addiction and their pharmacology and biochemistry (this presumes maintenance of current knowledge in this field and knowledge and skill in one or more methods of teaching and learning);
- A knowledge and skill in standard addiction treatment to prevent relapse and recurrence of adverse consequences of addictive diseases (ASAM, 1991).

Abstinence-Based Method

Controlled studies have found significant results in treatment outcomes in abstinence-based programs, particularly when combined with referral to Alcoholics Anonymous (AA). The first randomized clinical trial of abstinence-based treatment showed significant improvement in drinking behavior compared with that of a more traditional form of treatment (Durfee et al., 1994). A total of 141 employed alcoholics were randomized to the abstinence-based program (Hazelden type) (n = 74) or to traditional-type treatment (n = 67). The abstinence-based treatment was significantly more involving, supportive, encouraging to spontaneity and oriented to personal problems than the traditional-type treatment. The one-year abstinence rate was significantly greater for the abstinence-based treatment; in addition, dropout rates were 7.9% for the abstinence treatment group and 25.9% for the traditional treatment group, respectively (Keso & Salaspuro, 1990).

In another controlled study, 227 workers newly-identified as alcoholics and cocaine addicts were randomly assigned to one of three treatment regimens: compulsory inpatient treatment and compulsory attendance at regimens; compulsory inpatient treatment and compulsory attendance at AA meetings; and a choice of options (i.e., inpatient, outpatient, or AA meetings). Inpatient back-up was provided if needed (Walsh et al., 1991). On seven measures of drinking and drug use, the hospital group had significantly greater abstinence at one-year and two-year follow-up. Those assigned to AA had the lowest abstinence rates, and those allowed to choose either an inpatient or outpatient program or AA had intermediate results. The programs for inpatient and outpatient treatment were abstinence-based with eventual referrals to AA at discharge (Walsh et al., 1991).

Previous evaluation studies of large populations of patients (>9,750 subjects) enrolled for abstinence-based methods have shown favorable outcomes for addiction treatment. The populations consisted of multiple dependent patients, including those with alcohol, prescription drug, cannabis, stimulant, cocaine and opiate dependence (DSM-III-R Substance Dependence). The overall abstinence rates at one year were 60% for inpatients and 68% for outpatients (57% of the cases were contacted for inpatients, 62% for outpatients) (Harrison et al., 1991; Hoffmann & Miller, 1992); however, abstinence rates were increased to 88% for inpatients and 93% for outpatients who participated in continuing care following discharge. At one-year follow-up only 8% were attending continuing care after discharge in the inpatient treatment programs and 17% were attending the outpatient programs. Moreover, abstinence rates after discharge were 75% for inpatients and 82% for outpatients who were regular attendees at AA. Accordingly, 46% and 51% of those discharged from the inpatient and outpatient programs, respectively, were attending AA at least once per week. Abstinence rates at one year for non-attendees at AA were 49% and 57%, respectively. Significant outcomes on other variables were reported, such as improved psychosocial functioning and employment and legal histories for those completing the treatment programs in these studies (Harrison et al., 1991; Hoffmann & Miller, 1992; Miller, 1995).

According to survey results (1992) conducted by AA (Chappel, 1993), recovery rates achieved in the AA fellowship were:

1. Of those sober in AA less than a year, 41% remain in the AA fellowship for an additional year (Chappel, 1993).
2. Of those sober more than one year and less than five years, 83% remain in the AA fellowship for an additional year.
3. Of those sober five years or more, 91% remain in the AA fellowship for an additional year. Attendance in abstinence-based treatment programs can increase the recovery rates in AA, such as 80% from 41% with referral to AA following the treatment program (Miller, 1995).

Improving Treatment for Alcoholism

Although treatment for alcoholism and drug addiction is clearly and significantly effective, treatment is not always as successful as physicians would wish it to be, nor is it sufficiently available to those who need it. Current data show 35% to 40% of alcoholics undergoing outpatient treatment relapse within three months. Improving alcoholism treatment and its availability are important priorities. The Institute of Medicine (IOM) of the national Academy of Sciences conducted a comprehensive study of the alcohol treatment process and system, titled *Broadening the Basis of Treatment for Alcohol Problems* (IOM, 1989). The conclusions in their report emphasized that alcohol treatment was effective, but that improvement of the current alcohol treatment system in a cost-effective manner was needed. The IOM report identified several areas of treatment that needed improvement. These included: (1) the need for improvements and standardization in the diagnosis and assessment of alcoholism; (2) the need for more community-based assessment and interventions; (3) the need to base treatment referrals and level of treatment on the assessments; (4) the need for improved linkages between primary care, community-based treatment and specialized treatment services; (5) a treatment system that provides better continuity of care; (6) the need for adequate financing for a spectrum of treatment modalities and sites to match the diversity of the population; and (7) the elimination of organizational, personal and regulatory barriers to the diagnosis and treatment of alcohol problems.

In response to the IOM report, several groups have developed guidelines for the development of model treatment systems to meet the diverse needs of patients with substance-related disorders. In 1993, the American Society of Addiction Medicine developed core benefit requirements for addiction treatment. These include: (1) the need for and level of treatment must be a clinical judgment based on established criteria (e.g., the American Society of Addiction Medicine Patient Placement Criteria) (ASAM, 1992) with quality of care assured by appropriate review; (2) the concept that treatment for substance-related disorders should be included in any basic health benefit; (3) the concept that coverage should include a continuum of primary care and specialty services;

(4) that ongoing treatment evaluation, case management and outcome studies should be an integral part of the ongoing evaluation of services; (5) that eligibility should be based on competent diagnosis using objective criteria (DSM-IV, ICD-9/10) (Buchsbaum et al., 1991); (6) that coverage should be nondiscriminatory on the same basis as other medical care; and (7) that caps or limits on treatment should be applied on the same basis as other medical care. The need for a comprehensive treatment benefit package was also affirmed at a researcher's recent consensus conference (Institute of Medicine, 1989).

WHY PHYSICIANS ARE UNPREPARED TO TREAT DRUG- AND ALCOHOL-RELATED DISORDERS

Despite the enormous cost to individuals and society from alcohol- and drug-related disorders, medical schools only spend an average of 12 hours of curricular time on these disorders in an entire four years of training. Studies conducted a decade apart showed a consistent pattern of increasingly negative attitudes toward such disorders on the part of medical students and residents as their levels of training and clinical experience increased. Studies show that physicians generally have negative and pessimistic views about these disorders and do not routinely screen patients in general practice for them. In general, physicians do not feel competent treating alcohol-related disorders, do not like working with patients who have these disorders, and do not find treating these patients rewarding. Essential role models are lacking for future physicians to develop attitudes and skills to treat patients with addictive diseases, resulting in an endless loop of physician ignorance and neglect regarding addictions.

Physician education and training in addictions has long been ignored, although it has recently begun to increase selectively in medical schools and continuing medical education. A study that examined changes in alcohol and drug education in United States medical schools between 1976 and 1992 (Fleming et al., 1994) found positive changes in education about drug and alcohol addictions. The number of teaching units in addictions had increased two-fold in medical schools. More opportunities existed for required and elective experiences in addiction treatment and more teaching activities were based in alcohol-treatment and drug-treatment settings. Faculty members who were teaching in this area had increased, and medical school graduates reported greater satisfaction with the medical school curriculum in substance abuse and addiction education. The number of fellowship positions in addictions had increased and more primary care physicians were participating in advanced training; however, although promising, these results also showed only eight medical schools to have required courses in substance abuse and addiction treatment. In addition, with the exception of the departments of family medicine and psychiatry, less than one third of the departments in the specialties had even a single identified faculty member teaching in this area (Gopalan et al., 1992). Medical educators do not spend anywhere near the same amount of time teaching in the area of addictions as they do in other areas of chronic disease, such as hypertension or cardiac disease, although these diseases are no more common than the addictive disorders.

Clearly, given the poor rates of diagnosis and treatment of substance abuse and addiction by physicians, significant changes must continue to be made in our medical educational and training system to combat this problem. As has been previously mentioned, training in addictions has begun to increase, but whether these new measures have been wholly successful is unclear.

Recommendations for Improving Education Training

A 1996 survey concerning alcohol- and drug-related disorders showed that little change had occurred in the way of increasing curriculum coverage in this area. Family medicine residency directors, internal medicine residency directors and medical school curriculum deans from randomly-selected medical programs were invited to participate in this survey. Deans affirmed the general lack of medical education on addictive diseases provided to prepare physicians to treat patients properly. Survey directors developed a three-item instrument to assess the need for integrated curricula for drug- and alcohol-related disorders in United States medical schools and to identify barriers to implementing such a curriculum. These questions were e-mailed to the curriculum deans at 30 randomly selected medical schools. Seventy-three percent of the deans responded. The overwhelming majority of the responding curriculum deans (96%) reported that an integrated curriculum in drug and alcohol disorders would be at least somewhat helpful.

Based on these 1996 results, survey directors are proposing the development of an assessment toolbox, in order to evaluate core competencies for medical students and residents to care for patients with alcohol disorders. Assessment tools would be consistent with the general competencies that have been established by the Accreditation Council for Graduate Medical Education (ACGME) and the Medical School Objectives Project (MSOP). This toolbox would provide an easy and efficient way for program directors to obtain standardized information on their students' competency levels and progression in the area of alcoholic disorder prevention, diagnoses and treatment. This toolbox would consist of multiple choice questions, a performance assessment, and record review and patient surveys that would meet ACGME accreditation requirements. Survey directors are seeking grant money in order to develop, test and distribute this toolbox, as well as an implementation plan to medical schools and residency programs (Miller, 2001).

Although programs have not seen many changes in terms of the amount of the curriculum dedicated to substance use disorder education, a spotlight has been placed on the program, and action plans to improve medical education in this area have been implemented. In both 2004 and 2006, the Office of National Drug Control Policy had a leadership conference on Medical Education in Substance Abuse. The 2004 conference had representatives from more than 60 different federal agencies, medical groups and certification boards in attendance to discuss ways to increase physicians' motivation and ability to prevent, diagnose and treat various substance abuse disorders (Wyatt et al., 2005). The 2006 conference's main purpose was to provide a framework to improve the education and practice of addiction medicine. During this conference, attendees divided into work groups to address improvements needed in various areas, including undergraduate, graduate and continuing medical education in the area. Following this meeting, the AOAAM (American Osteopathic Academy of Addiction Medicine) attempted to get a consistent core curriculum in addiction medicine for all osteopathic medical schools passed by the AOA House of Delegates at a 2007 meeting. Unfortunately, despite a large amount of support, this effort was unsuccessful. At the time of this publication, the AOAAM intended to present a revised version of the plan in 2008 (Wyatt et al., 2005).

The implementation of national conferences and web-based educational programs has shown that the importance of addiction medicine education in the medical school curriculum has been recognized. Unfortunately, no supplemental conference or web-based program can take the place of direct core curriculum integration on this topic. Due to the great percentage of the patient population affected by substance abuse disorders, it is imperative that medical educators make implementation of substance use education a part of their core curriculum as quickly as possible. Following is some additional information on research studies on integration of addictive disorder information into medical school education.

Research Studies on Medical Education in the Area of Addictive Medicine

Increases in technology and online learning have greatly contributed to additional medical student exposure in this area. Distance learning by the way of online courses has been added to many university options and is increasingly shaping parts of medical school education. Noted as a traditionally neglected field, addiction education was tested in this format at New York University Medical School. An interactive web module was designed to improve students' competence in the area of alcohol abuse screening and intervention techniques. This online module was offered as an alternative choice to attending a lecture on the same topic. Traditionally, first year medical students at New York University were given three chronological sessions on this topic, a lecture, a small group seminar and then an OSCE case. The lecture and web module shared the same format outlines; however, researchers hypothesized that the online module would be more effective than a traditional lecture in teaching medical students how to interview and screen their patients for suspected alcohol abuse effectively. Students were assigned to the lecture or module group based on class schedule. One to three weeks after participating in one of these sessions, both groups of students participated in seminars in which the methods of alcohol screening and interventions were reviewed. Three to five weeks following the module or lecture exposure, students were rated on their performance in dealing with an OSCE alcohol case. The case presented to each student was that of an adult woman with hazardous drinking tendencies in need of cutting down on her alcohol consumption or stopping altogether. Student performance was assessed using the AUDIT-C, CAGE and six brief intervention components. Those who completed the web-based module performed better on average than their lecture-based counterparts on both performance and intervention ratings on this standardized OSCE Case (Lee et al., 2008).

Computerized learning in this area has not been limited to undergraduate medical education. A study investigating the effectiveness of a CD-ROM and web-based training program to provide formal tobacco intervention training in pediatric residency programs was started in 2004. A study conducted prior to this at the New Jersey Medical School confirmed that formal training in addressing tobacco increased resident tobacco intervention activities (Hymowitz et al., 2004). However, a 1991–1992 survey evaluating 116 of the 124 accredited United States allopathic medical schools found that there were only 0.28 faculty members per school responsible for substance abuse training in pediatrics (Miller et al., 2001). The lack of professionals available to train pediatric residents in this area led researchers to develop the *Solutions for Smoking* program, consisting of a chapter-based educational website and a CD-ROM containing examples of interview, counsel and intervention skills necessary for prevention and detection of tobacco usage in the pediatric patient population. The CD-ROM included 32 role-played scenarios ranging from 2 to 12 minutes in length, modeling state-of-the-art approaches to tobacco intervention. The online chapters focused on providing knowledge while the CD-ROM focused on helping students develop effective how-to approaches in tobacco intervention and treatment. Fifteen residency programs throughout New York and New Jersey were taking part in this four-year randomized study evaluating the efficacy of this training tool at the time of Hymnowitz's publication. The 15 schools were randomly assigned to one of two groups, the special training versus the standard training group. In the special training group, *Solutions for Smoking* was the primary training tool. This group also received clinic mobilization assistance in the form of informative tobacco posters and brochures for the waiting areas and examining rooms of their clinics. The standard training group received reading material on clinical tobacco use interventions and did not receive any help with clinic mobilization. Baseline surveys were taken on resident tobacco knowledge at the beginning of the study. These surveys were planned to take place yearly through the remainder of the study. In addition, Observed Structured Clinical Examinations (OCSEs) were going to be used to determine the difference in resident tobacco intervention skills between the special and standard training groups. This study planned to publish a final report on the efficacy of this training program in tobacco intervention at the completion of the study (Lee et al., 2008).

CONCLUSION

With increasing pressure on general physicians by managed care organizations and the public to treat and advocate for drug and alcohol addicted patients, it is more necessary than ever that physicians have the knowledge and skills to address this segment of the population appropriately.

Specifically, physicians need a better understanding of the prevalence of alcohol and drug dependence in a variety of populations, along with increased awareness of the economic impact of addictive illnesses on our society. Routine screening questions should be incorporated into patient encounters, and physicians should be able to identify environments that may pose a risk for the development of addiction. Physicians need training and practice in referring patients to treatment teams, monitoring patients in recovery and providing interventions that will eliminate or reduce substance abuse before it becomes addiction.

The treatment outcomes in abstinence-based programs, particularly those combined with referral to AA, have been encouraging, demonstrating that addiction is a treatable illness and not a character defect. In addition, several studies provide evidence that addiction treatment is cost-beneficial, resulting in reduced medical costs, lowered absenteeism and increased productivity.

Despite these encouraging results, there is still room for improvement. Treatment is not always effective and it is not sufficiently available to everyone who needs it. Addicted individuals are both stigmatized and marginalized, and many are too ill to advocate for themselves.

Widespread recognition in the medical community of addiction as a treatable illness will contribute to a greater understanding of addictive disorders and reduce the stigma attached to the diagnosis and treatment of addiction. For this to occur, better training for physicians in the recognition and management of addictive disorders, starting at the medical school level, is necessary. The approval of addiction medicine as a clinical specialty by the American Medical Association has also helped to advance the legitimacy of addiction as a treatable illness, and provides a focal point for the synthesis and integration of clinical, teaching and research activities central to addiction medicine. The combination of knowledge, skills and attitudes outlined in the article will go a long way toward increasing physicians' abilities to assist their patients with recovery from addiction.

REFERENCES

Adams, W. L., Yuan, Z., Barboriak, J. J., & Rimm, A. A. (1993). Alcohol-related hospitalizations of elderly people: Prevalence and geographic variation in the United States. *Journal of the American Medical Association, 270*, 1222–1225.

American Academy of Pediatrics Committee on Substance Abuse. (1995). Alcohol use and abuse: A pediatric concern. *Pediatrics, 95*, 439–442.

American Society of Addiction Medicine. (1991). *Physicians in Addiction Medicine Policy Statement*. Washington, DC: American Society of Addiction Medicine.

American Society of Addiction Medicine (ASAM). (1992). *ASAM Patient Placement Criteria, Psychoactive Substance Use Disorders.* Washington, DC: American Society of Addiction Medicine.

Babor, T., & Grant, M. (1990). *Project on Identification and Management of Alcohol Related Problems: Report on Phase II: A Randomized Clinical Trial of Brief Interventions in Primary Health Care.* Geneva, Switzerland: World Health Organization.

Beresford, T. P. (1979). Alcoholism consultation and general hospital psychiatry. *General Hospital Psychiatry, 1,* 293–300.

Buchsbaum, D. G., Buchanan, R. G., Lawton, M. J., & Schnoll, S. H. (1991). Alcohol consumption patterns in a primary care population. *Alcohol, 26,* 215–220.

Burner, S. T., Waldo, D. R., & McKusick, D. R. (1992). National health expenditures projections through 2030. *Health Care Financial Review, 14,* 1–15.

Chappel, J. N. (1993). Long-term recovery from alcoholism. *Psychiatric Clinics of North America, 16,* 177–187.

Chasnoff, I. J., Griffith, D. R., MacGregor, S., Dirkes, K., & Burns, K. A. (1989). Temporal patterns of cocaine use in pregnancy: Perinatal outcome. *Journal of the American Medical Association, 261,* 1741–1744.

Cherpitel, C. J. S. (1988). Alcohol consumption and casualties: A comparison of two emergency room populations. *British Journal of Addiction, 83,* 1299–1307.

Chick, J., Lloyd, G., & Crombie, E. (1985). Counseling problem drinkers in medical wards: A controlled study. *BMJ, 290,* 965–967.

Cleary, P. D., Miller, M., Bush, B. T., Warburg, M. M., Delbanco, T. L., & Aronson, M. D. (1988). Prevalence and recognition of alcohol abuse in a primary care population. *American Journal of Medicine, 85,* 466–471.

Cyr, M. G., & Wartman, S. A. (1988). The effectiveness of routine screening questions in the detection of alcoholism. *Journal of the American Medical Association, 259,* 51–54.

Denison, M. E., Parades, A., & Booth, J. B. (1997). Alcohol and cocaine interaction and aggressive behaviors. *Recent Developments in Alcohol, 13,* 283–303.

Durfee, M. F., Warren, D. G., & Sdao-Javier, K. (1994). A model for answering the substance abuse educational needs of health professionals: The North Carolina Governors Institute on Alcohol and Substance abuse. *Alcohol, 11,* 483–487.

Ershoff, D., Radcliffe, A., & Gregory, M. (1996). The Southern California Kaiser-Permanent Chemical Dependency Recovery Program evaluation: Results of a treatment outcome study in an HMO setting. *Journal of Addictive Diseases, 15,* 1–25.

Fleming, M. F., & Barry, K. L. (1992). *Addictive Disorders.* St. Louis, MI: Mosby-Year Book.

Fleming, M. F., Barry, K. L., Johnson, K., & London, R. (1997). Brief physician advice for problem alcohol and drug use: A randomized controlled study in community-based primary care practices. *Journal of the American Medical Association, 277,* 1039–1045.

Fleming, M. F., Barry, K. L., Davis, A., Kropp, S., Kahn, R., & Rivo, M. (1994). Medical education about substance abuse: Changes in curriculum and faculty between 1976 and 1992. *Academic Medicine, 69,* 362–369.

Gerstein, D. R., Johnson, R. A., Harwood, H., Suter, N., & Malloy, K. (1994). *Evaluating recovery services: The California Drug and Alcohol Treatment Assessment* (CALDATA). Sacramento, CA: State of California Department of Drug and Alcohol Programs.

Gopalan, R., Santora, P., Stokes, E. J., Moore, R. D., & Levine, D. M. (1992). Evaluation of a model curriculum on substance abuse at the Johns Hopkins University School of Medicine. *Academic Medicine, 67,* 260–266.

Grant, B. F. (1996). DSM-I, DSM-III R, and ICD-10 alcohol and drug abuse/harmful use and dependence, United States, 1992: A nonsociological comparison. *Alcoholism – Clinical and Experimental Research, 20*, 1481–1488.

Harrison, P. A., Hoffmann, N. G., & Streed, S. G. (1991). Drug and alcohol addiction treatment outcome. In N. S. Miller (Ed.), *Comprehensive Handbook of Drug and Alcohol Addiction* (pp. 1163–1200). New York, NY: Marcel Dekker.

Hoffmann, N. G., & Miller, N. S. (1992). Treatment outcomes for abstinence-based programs. *Psychiatric Annals, 22*, 402–408.

Hoffmann, N. G., DeHart, S. S., & Fulkerson, J. A. (1993). Medical care utilization as a function of recovery status following chemical addictions treatment. *Journal of Addictive Diseases, 12*, 97–108.

Hold, S., Stewart, I. C., Dixon, J. M., Elton, R. A., Taylor, T. V., & Little, K. (1980). Alcohol and the emergency service patient. *British Medical Journal, 281*, 638–640.

Holden, C. (1985). The neglected disease in medical education. *Science, 229*, 741–742.

Holder, H. D., & Blose, J. O. (1992). The reduction of health care costs associated with alcoholism treatment: A 14-year longitudinal study. *Journal of Studies Alcohol, 53*, 293–302.

Hymowitz, N., Schwab, J., Haddock, C., Burd, K. M., & Pyle, S. (2004). The pediatric residency training on tobacco project: baseline findings from the resident tobacco survey and observed structured clinical examinations. *Preventive Medicine, 39*, 507–516.

Institute of Medicine. (1989). *Broadening the Base of Treatment for Alcohol Problems*. Washington, DC: National Academy Press.

Kamerow, D. B., Pincus, H. A., & MacDonald, D. I. (1986). Alcohol abuse, other drug abuse, and mental disorders in medical practice: Prevalence, costs, recognition, and treatment. *Journal of the American Medical Association, 255*, 2054–2057.

Kandel, D., Chen, K., Warner, L. A., Kessler, R. C., & Grant, B. (1997). Prevalence and demographic correlates of symptoms of last year dependence on alcohol, nicotine, marijuana, and cocaine in the US population. *Drug Alcohol Depend, 44*, 11–29.

Kasselbaum, G., & Chandler, S. M. (1994). Polydrugs use and self control among men and women in prisons. *Journal of Drug Education, 24*, 333–350.

Keso, L., & Salaspuro, M. (1990). Inpatient treatment of employed alcoholics: A randomized clinical trial on Hazelden-type and traditional treatment. *Alcoholism – Clinical and Experimental Research, 14*, 584–589.

Klamen, D. L., & Miller, N. S. (1997). Integration in education for addiction medicine. *Journal Psychoactive Drugs, 29*, 263–268.

Lee, J., Triola, M., Gillespie, C., Gourevitch, M. N., Hanley, K., Truncali, A., Zabar, S., & Kalet, A. (2008). Working with patients with alcohol problems: a controlled trial of the impact of a rich media web module on medical student performance. *Journal of General Internal Medicine, 23*(7), 1006–1009.

Lewis, D. C. (1997). The role of the generalist in the care of substance-abusing patient. *Medical Journal North America, 814*, 831–844.

Martin, C. S., Clifford, P. R., Maisto, S. A., Earleywine, M., Kirisci, L., & Longabaugh, R. (1996). Polydrug use in an inpatient treatment sample of problem drinkers. *Alcoholism – Clinical and Experimental Research, 20*, 413–417.

McIntosh, I. D. (1982). Alcohol-related disabilities in general hospital patients: A critical assessment of the evidence. *International Journal of the Addictions, 17*, 609–639.

Miller, N. S. (1994). *Principles of Addiction Medicine*. Washington, DC: American Society of Addiction Medicine.

Miller, N. S. (1995). *Treatment of Addictions: Applications of Outcome Research for Clinical Management*. New York, NY: Haworth Press.

Miller, N. S. (1997). Generalized vulnerability to drug and alcohol addiction. In N. S. Miller (Ed.), *The Principles and Practice of Addictions in Psychiatry* (pp. 18–25). Philadelphia, PA: WB Saunders.

Miller, N. S., Gold, M. S., & Smith, D. B. (1990). *Manual of Therapeutics for Addictions*. New York, NY: Wiley-Liss.

Miller, N., Sheppard, L., Colenda, C., & Magen, J. (2001). Why physicians are unprepared to treat patients who have alcohol- and drug-related disorders. *Academic Medicine, 76*(5), 410–418.

Miller, N. (2001). Research Plan Proposal for NIAAA. pp. 47–76.

Moore, R. D., Bone, L. R., Geller, G., Mamon, J. A., Stokes, E. J., & Levine, D. M. (1989). Prevalence, detection, and treatment of alcoholism in hospitalized patients. *Journal of the American Medical Association, 261*, 403–407.

NIDA. (1997). *Preliminary Results from the National Household Survey on Drug Abuse: 1991*. Rockville, MD: US Department of Health and Human Services, Substance Abuse and Mental Heath Services Administration, Office of Applied Studies.

Parish, D. C. (1997). Another indication for screening and early intervention problems. *Journal of the American Medical Association, 277*, 1079–1080.

Patton, L. H. (1995). Adolescent substance abuse: Risk factors and protective factors. *Pediatric Clinics of North America, 42*, 283–293.

Pols, R. G., Sellman, D., Jurd, S., Baigent, M., Waddy, N., Sacks, T., Tucker, P., Fowler, J., & White, A. (1996). What is the psychiatrist's role in drugs and alcohol? *Australian and New Zealand Journal of Psychiatry, 30*, 540–548.

Regier, D. A., Farmer, M. E., Rae, D. S., Locke, B. Z., Keith, S. J., Judd, L. L., & Goodwin, F. K. (1990). Comorbidity of mental disorders with alcohol and other drug abuse. *Journal of the American Medical Association, 268*, 1012–1014.

Rice, D. P., Kelman, S., Miller, L. S., et al. (1985). *The Economic Costs of Alcohol and Drug Abuse and Mental Illness* DHHS Publication # (ADM) 90-1649. Rockville, MD: US Department of Health and Human Services, Public Health Service, Alcohol, Drug Abuse, and Mental Health Administration.

Schmidt, A., Barry, K. L., & Fleming, M. F. (1995). Detection of problem drinkers: The Alcohol Use Disorders Identification Test (AUDIT). *Southern Medical Journal, 88*, 52–59.

Schoenborn, C. A. (1988). *Exposure to alcoholism in the family: U.S. Advance Data from Vital and Health Statistics*. National Center for Health Statistics, No. 205.

Substance Abuse and Mental Health Services Administration (SAMHSA). (1992). *Highlights from the 1991 N DATUS Survey*. Rockville, MD: SAMHSA.

Turnure, C. (1993). *Minnesota Consolidated Fund, Annual Cost Offsets*. Minneapolis, MN: Minnesota Department of Human Services.

Wallace, P., Cutler, S., & Haines, A. (1988). Randomized controlled trial of general practitioner intervention in patients with excessive alcohol consumption. *British Medical Journal, 297*, 663–668.

Walsh, D. C., Hingson, R. W., Merrigan, D. M., Levenson, S. M., Cupples, L. A., Heeren, T., Coffman, G. A., Becker, C. A., Barker, T. A., Hamilton, S. K., et al. (1991). A randomized trial of treatment options for alcohol-abusing workers. *New England Journal of Medicine, 325*, 775–782.

Ward, R. E., Flynn, T. C., Miller, P. W., & Blaisdell, W. F. (1982). Effects of ethanol ingestion on the severity and outcome of trauma. *American Journal of Surgery, 144*, 153–157.

Wiseman, E. J., & McMillan, D. E. (1996). Combined use of cocaine with alcohol or cigarettes. *American Journal of Drug and Alcohol Abuse, 22*, 577–587.

Wmick, C., & Larson, M. J. (1997). Community action programs. In J. H. Lowenson, P. Ruiz & R. B. Millman et al. (Eds.), *Substance Abuse: A Comprehensive Textbook,* (3rd ed.) (pp. 755–763). Baltimore, MD: Williams & Wilkins.

Wyatt, A., & Dekker, M. (2007). Improving physician and medical education in substance use disorders. *Journal of the American Osteopathic Association, 107*(9), ES27–ES38.

Wyatt, A., Vilensky, W., Manlandro, J. J., Jr, & Dekker, M. A., II (2005). Medical education in substance abuse: from student to practicing physician. *Journal of the American Osteopathic Association, 105*(6), S18–S24.

Chapter 4

Medical Licensure and Credentialing

Mark J. Greenwood, DO, JD, FAAEM, FCLM
Aero Med Spectrum Health, Grand Rapids, MI, USA

Maureen Beasley-Greenwood, MS, PA-C
Cherry Street Health Services, Grand Rapids, MI, USA

INTRODUCTION

Medicine is a regulated profession because of the potential harm to the public if an incompetent or impaired physician is licensed to practice. After medical school education, postgraduate training and passing examinations a physician undergoes certification, licensure and credentialing (Table 4.1). To protect the public from the unprofessional, unlawful, fraudulent or incompetent practice of medicine, each of the fifty states, the District of Columbia and the United States territories have a medical practice act that defines the practice of medicine and delegates the authority to enforce the law to a state medical board. Raising the subject of the incompetent or impaired physician (Table 4.2) also raises the question of the extent to which patients in particular, and the public in general, have the right to be informed of the risk that comes from the compromised condition. Further, how can this right be delineated in light of the conflict between the need to hold persons accountable only when appropriate, and on the other hand, the need for open reporting systems required if the healthcare system is to become increasingly safe?

Of the entities that play important roles in balancing the interests and rights of the physician, patients and the public this chapter will survey both peer review organizations and databases that compile information on various indicators of a physician's ability to practice medicine. It will also survey the topic of medical licensing boards, because whether by peer review actions, hospital credentialing actions, or criminal and civil proceedings evidence of significant compromise on the part of a physician will inevitably lead to the medical licensing board. Finally, because part and parcel of any evidence of abuse of alcohol or drugs by a physician is the inference that his or her medical practice is also compromised, we discuss ways in which actions on the part of all parties involved can proceed with appropriate care and deliberation.

Principles of Addictions and the Law: Applications in Forensic, Mental Health, and Medical Practice

TABLE 4.1 Definitions

Professional certification: implies that a person has obtained a certain level of knowledge and ability (through education and training) to competently complete a job or task, usually by passing an examination, earned from a professional society. Certification in general is valid for a specific period of time, renewed periodically and commonly shows evidence of continued learning (CME – continuing medical education).

Board certification: the process by which a person is tested and approved to practice in a specialty field after successfully completing the requirements of a board of specialists in that field. Certification is through a professional association: by allopathic boards (MD); members of the American Board of Medical Specialties (ABMS); by osteopathic boards (DO); and by members of the American Osteopathic Association (AOA).

Licensure: refers to the state or condition of having a license granted by official or legal authority to perform medical acts and procedures after demonstration of a certain level of knowledge and ability. Licensure is issued, regulated and administered by a state government agency for public protection purposes (the state medical board).

Credentialing: the process of assessing the qualifications of licensed professionals; the process generally is an objective evaluation of a subject's current licensure, training or experience, competence and ability to provide particular services or perform particular procedures. Credentialing may include granting and review of specific clinical privileges, and granting medical or allied health staff membership.

TABLE 4.2 Definitions

Competence means possessing the requisite abilities and qualities (cognitive, noncognitive, and communicative) to perform effectively in the scope of professional physician practice while adhering to professional ethical standards.

Dyscompetence means failing to maintain acceptable standards of one or more areas of professional physician practice.

Incompetence means lacking the requisite abilities and qualities (cognitive, noncognitive and communicative) to perform effectively in the scope of professional physician practice.

Impairment means the inability of a licensee to practice medicine with reasonable skill and safety by reason of: (1) mental illness; (2) physical illness or condition including, but not limited to, those illnesses or conditions that would adversely affect cognitive, motor or perceptive skills; or (3) habitual or excessive use or abuse of drugs defined by law as controlled substances, of alcohol, or of other substances that impair ability.

(Federation of State Medical Boards of the United States, Inc. (2006). Essentials of a Modern Medical Practice Act, (11th ed.), [Electronic version], pp. 26 and 28. Available at http://www.fsmb. org/pdf/GPROL_essentials_eleventh_edition.pdf Accessed 5 November 2008)

PEER REVIEW

The person most likely to be in a position to both witness the harmful (or potentially harmful) actions or behavior of a compromised physician and to form an opinion on extent of culpability in light of the degree and nature of that compromise, is one of his or her professional colleagues. Yet, in a survey of physicians on medical professionalism reported in the *Annals of Internal Medicine*, 96% of respondents said physicians who are significantly impaired or incompetent should be reported to authorities, but 45% of respondents said they were aware of bad behavior by doctors that they did not report (Campbell et al., 2007, p. 795). This, of course, is not surprising, given that physicians themselves who report problems have been sued, ostracized, or punished in some way. That nearly half of physicians fail to report other physicians who are compromised by significant impairment or incompetence is evidence that policing the profession cannot be the responsibility of individual physicians, but must be achieved by more formal means. One means of policing is by way of peer review.

The Healthcare Quality Improvement Act (HCQIA) of 1986 was the principal legislation that created the peer review system used in the United States today. The HCQIA was enacted by Congress to reduce the number of medical malpractice suits against hospitals by eliminating incompetent physicians. The intent of the Act was multifaceted: to improve the quality of medical peer review; to encourage physician participation in identifying and disciplining their incompetent or unprofessional peers; and to prevent incompetent physicians from moving from state to state without disclosure or discovery of their previous damaging or incompetent performance (HCQIA, 42 U.S.C. § 11101 (1–5)). A peer review body that conducts a professional review, such as a hospital review committee, must file a report to the agency having jurisdiction over a healthcare practitioner if certain actions are taken by a healthcare facility including the denial, rejection, termination or revocation of staff privileges of a healthcare practitioner (HCQIA, 42 U.S.C. § 11132(a)(1)), because such actions raise concerns about the competency of the practitioner to be investigated by the state agency as authorized by the HCQIA.

The HCQIA has two important safeguards: it offers immunity to participants who engage in professional peer review actions; and it has provisions for maintaining the confidentiality of information.

Immunity

The HCQIA: "provide[s] qualified immunity from damages for actions of hospitals, doctors and others who participate in professional peer review proceedings" (*Brown v. Presbyterian Healthcare Serv.*, 1996, p. 1333), but for the act to provide immunity to claims for monetary damages arising from peer review actions several statutory requirements must be met. First, it must be a professional review action, defined as "an action or recommendation by a professional review body taken in the conduct of professional review activity concerning the competence or professional conduct of an individual physician [and the] conduct must affect or have the potential to affect the health of a patient, as well as either the physician's membership in a professional society, or clinical privileges" (HCQIA, 42 U.S.C. § 11151(9)). A professional review activity is further defined as: "an activity of a healthcare provider entity to determine whether a physician can have privileges with respect to a healthcare entity, the scope of these privileges, or whether the privileges should be modified" (HCQIA, 42 U.S.C. § 11151(10)).

Peer review actions are often challenged in court, based on arguments that the action did not meet the statutory required elements and as so was not a professional review action. For example, the issue in *Wojewski v. Rapid City Regional Hosp.* (2007) was whether a "meeting" between physicians must be a "formal" event, or merely be one that has the effect of determining the scope of a physician's privileges to qualify under the immunity provisions of the HCQIA. The court held that the "informal" meeting qualified as a professional peer review activity (an activity of a healthcare provider entity to determine a physician's scope of privileges with respect to the healthcare entity), because the doctors in the meeting were engaged in a professional review activity that related to the professional review action of revoking a physician's surgical privileges. As such, this met the requirements of the statute and therefore they were entitled to immunity (American College of Legal Medicine, 2007, p. 69). This holding is important because it extends HCQIA's immunization to more informal meetings of physicians provided that they are working in the capacity for a healthcare entity and that they have the power to limit or modify some privilege of the physician (American College of Legal Medicine, 2007, p. 69).

Second, beyond satisfying the requirements for a qualified peer review action, for immunity to apply the professional review action must also meet four provisions. The review action must be taken: (1) in furtherance of quality healthcare; (2) after a reasonable effort to obtain the facts of the matter; (3) after adequate notice and hearing procedures are afforded to the physician involved; and (4) in the reasonable belief that the action was warranted by the known facts (HCQIA, 42 U.S.C. § 11112(a)(1–4)).

Courts have interpreted this language quite strictly and often in ways that work against physicians that are targeted by the peer review process, including physicians who wish to show that review proceedings were in bad faith. These physicians are confronted with the HCQIA provision that professional review actions: "shall be presumed to have met the statutory standards unless the presumption is rebutted by a preponderance of the evidence" (HCQIA, 42 U.S.C. § 11112(b)). Because the result is that the physician-plaintiff bears the burden of proving that the peer review process was not reasonable, this: "may encourage abuse by effectively shielding peer review participants from legal liability" (Kinney, 2008, p. 793). Some authorities claim there is much evidence to suggest that rather than identify and eliminate incompetent physicians through "good faith" professional review activities as intended, hospital peer review proceedings (known as "sham" reviews) "have been used to punish competitor physicians or physicians who have objected to hospital policies on grounds of safety and quality concerns" (Kinney, 2008, p. 794).

Confidentiality

The second important function of the HCQIA is to provide confidentiality of peer review proceedings. In general, information reported is considered confidential and shall not be disclosed except with respect to professional review activity as necessary and in accordance with the regulations for disclosure to authorized parties (HCQIA, 42 U.S.C. § 11137(b)). Thus, in order to evaluate adverse or potentially adverse events in healthcare, and to credential healthcare providers appropriately, discussions must be frank, open and complete, and must be undertaken in an environment that supports such discussions. The American College of Medical Quality (ACMQ) provides professional policies and guidelines on medical professionalism with standards for the peer review physician (Table 4.3). The ACMQ endorses the confidentiality of peer review proceedings "provided that peer review is performed in good faith and by qualified experts, and peer review deliberation, including information divulged either orally or in written form, is confidential" (ACMQ, 2008a).

TABLE 4.3 The Peer Review Physician

- Reviews and critiques the medical decision-making or other medical activities of other physicians.

- Is in the same or similar specialty as the physician whose work is under review.

- Applies the medical standard of care.

- Has immunity from lawsuits that may arise from the review activities provided they perform the review reasonably and in good faith.

- Must be similarly credentialed and qualified as the subject physician.

- Must possess the appropriate clinical judgment based on training, education and experience.

- Should be subject to the same licensing and regulatory control as the subject physician.

- Must understand that peer review may be considered to constitute the practice of medicine.

(American College of Medical Quality (ACMQ), Professional Policies: Peer Review, Policy 19, adopted 4/21/01. Retrieved 30 November 2008 from http://www.acmq.org/policies)

PHYSICIAN PROFILE DATABASES

Physician profile databases play an increasingly important role in medical licensure and credentialing. There are questions central to the development and implementation of these databases. To what extent can, and should, state and federal government agencies discover, compile and disseminate information? What level of scrutiny of physicians is justified against the background of an ever-increasing demand by consumers for public reporting of information on physicians in professional databases?

Two separate programs established by Congress, the National Practitioner Data Bank (NPDB) and the Healthcare Integrity and Protection Data Bank (HIPDB), are designed to encourage the peer review process, to improve the quality of healthcare and to combat fraud and abuse in healthcare delivery. These data banks are primarily alert or "flagging" systems, in essence, a national tracking system of practitioner profile information, intended to help facilitate a comprehensive review of a healthcare practitioners' professional credentials and past adverse actions (Practitioner Data Banks, 2008). The information contained in these databases is confidential and protected under The Privacy Act of 1974 (5 U.S.C. § 552a), which protects contents of the federal system of records by allowing disclosure only to eligible entities that meet requirements under the act (NPDB and HIPDB, 2008).

The National Practitioner Data Bank was established by the Healthcare Quality Improvement Act (HCQ IA) of 1986 and began operations in 1990 (National Practitioner Data Bank, 2008a). The intent of the NPDB is to improve the quality of healthcare by encouraging state licensing boards, hospitals and other healthcare entities to identify and discipline those who engage in unprofessional behavior. A primary effect is to prevent individual unprofessional or incompetent practitioners from moving from state to state without disclosure or discovery of previous medical malpractice payment and adverse action history (National Practitioner Data Bank, 2008b). The NPDB is a program reported to, and maintained by, the federal government. The primary focus is on adverse actions taken against physicians to assist hospital, state licensing boards and other healthcare entities in conducting investigations of the qualifications of the healthcare practitioner they wish either to hire, license, grant membership, or grant clinical privileges. It contains information on: (1) adverse licensure actions (e.g., revocations, suspensions, censures, probation and surrenders for quality purposes); (2) adverse clinical privileges actions (e.g., reduction, revocation or non-renewal); and (3) adverse professional society membership actions (Table 4.4) In addition, the NPDB contains actions against physicians, dentist and other healthcare practitioners including: (4) paid medical malpractice judgments and settlements; (5) exclusions from participation in Medicare/Medicaid programs; and (6) registration actions taken by the US Drug Enforcement Administration (DEA) (National Practitioner Data Bank, 2008a) (see Table 4.5).

TABLE 4.4 Actions Reportable to the NPDB

Adverse actions reportable to the NPDB, if based on professional competence or conduct, include:

- denial of an initial application for clinical privileges;

- reduction or revocation of clinical privileges, even without demotion or dismissal;

- non-renewal of clinical privileges;

- summary suspension if lasting more than 30 days;

- granting of clinical privileges that are more limited than those requested;

- failure to renew clinical privileges while under investigation; and

- any kind of medical malpractice payment.

(Fact Sheet on the National Practitioner Data Bank, July 2008, pp. 2–3. Retrieved 29 November 2008 from www.npdb-hipdb.hrsa.gov/pubs/fs/Fact_Sheet-National_Practitioner_Data_Bank.pdf)

For the NPDB to function properly, health entities must comply with both requirements, to report and to query physician information. Hospitals, healthcare entities with formal peer review, professional societies with formal peer review and state licensing medical boards are required to report information to the NPDB, and the information in turn is made available to hospitals, healthcare entities with formal peer review, professional societies with formal peer review, state licensing medical boards and practitioner self-queries. The NPDB is prohibited from disclosing specific information on practitioners to the general public. Hospitals are required to query the NPBD whenever a physician applies for initial privileges and medical staff membership, and thereafter every two years for information on each physician on the medical staff (HCQIA, 42 U.S.C. § 11135(a)(1–2)). Thus, hospitals and other healthcare entities rely heavily on information from the NPDB in making physician staffing and credentialing decisions. All reports remain on file with the NPDB permanently unless they are either voided or corrected by the reporting entity or by the Secretary of the United States Department of Health and Human Services.

The Healthcare Integrity and Protection Data Bank was established under the Health Insurance Portability and Accountability Act (HIPAA) of 1996 as part of a program to combat fraud and abuse in healthcare insurance and healthcare delivery. The databank catalogs and reports certain final adverse actions against healthcare providers, suppliers, or practitioners. It became operational in March 2000 (Practitioner Data Banks, 2008). The database contains information on: (1) civil judgments against healthcare providers and suppliers; (2) federal or state criminal convictions against healthcare providers, suppliers related to the delivery of a healthcare item or service; (3) actions by federal or

---

TABLE 4.5 Controlled Substances

State licensure includes the authority to prescribe regular prescription drugs, but drugs that are seen as having potential for abuse, called "controlled substances," are regulated by the Controlled Substance Act of 1970 which classifies them into five categories (or schedules) according to the potential for abuse. These drugs cannot be prescribed or dispensed by a licensed healthcare provider without a Federal Drug Enforcement Administration (DEA) registration number, called a "Certificate of Registration." Some states themselves also require an additional form of licensure, called "Controlled Substance Registration," separate from the medical license for controlled substance authority.

Report to the Federal Register

The DEA is required to report to the NPDB healthcare practitioners who have had their Controlled Substance Act registration number revoked or suspended because of violations of this law (e.g., improperly selling controlled drugs), but it does not report such actions to other authorities, such as state medical licensing boards. However, suspensions or revocations are published in the *Federal Register*, the daily publication for rules and notices of federal agencies and organizations, so state medical boards, hospitals and other healthcare entities can obtain this information through this publication.

(Department of Health and Human Services, Office of Inspector General, DEA Reporting to the National Practitioner Data Bank, March 1997, pp. 1–2. Available at http://www.oig.hhs.gov/oei/reports/oei-12-96-00160.pdf Accessed 29 December 2008)

---

state agencies responsible for the licensing and certification of healthcare providers; (4) exclusions of healthcare providers from participation in federal or state healthcare programs; and (5) any other adjudicated actions against healthcare providers (HIPDB, 2008, p. 1). The HIPDB information is available to federal and state government agencies, health plans and through self query by health practitioners or suppliers. The HIPDB is prohibited from disclosing specific information on a practitioners or suppliers to the general public (HIPDB, 2008, pp. 1–2).

Like the NPDB and the HIPDB, other databases have been designed to assist eligible entities in investigating qualifications and credentials of healthcare providers. The Federation Physician Data Center (FPDC) is a central repository for formal actions taken against physicians by all state licensing and disciplinary boards, Canadian licensing authorities, the United States armed forces, the United States Department of Health and Human Services, and other national and international regulatory bodies, and is compiled and maintained by the Federation of State Medical Boards (FSMB, 2008a). The FPDC contains more than 156,000 board actions related to approximately 46,000 physicians dating to the 1960s. This information is available to licensing and disciplinary boards, the military, governmental and private agencies, and organizations involved in the employment and credentialing of physicians (FSMB, 2008a). A fee is required to access these services. The FSMB receives reports of actions by state medical boards daily. "The Federation maintains comprehensive quality control procedures to enhance accuracy and integrity of the FPDC. Actions reported are verified in writing and accompanied by supporting documentation, and each action is reviewed before it is added to the bank" (FPDC, 2008b). Permanent files of supporting documentation are maintained.

The FPDC offers two services frequently used in performing credentialing functions or pre-employment background checks: (1) the board action data bank search; and (2) the disciplinary alert service. Both of these services are considered primary source equivalent by National Committee for Quality Assurance (NCQA) and Joint Commission on Accreditation of Healthcare Organizations (JCAHO).

A board action data bank search allows entities to query the database to identify actions reported on specific practitioners. The service provides entities with information pertaining to any actions contained in FSMB's board action data bank (BADB), a database that maintains records on medical licensure and collects and reports on disciplinary actions against physicians taken by medical boards, hospitals and other authorities. This service also provides a historical view of disciplinary actions taken by the reporting entities (FPDC, 2008c).

The disciplinary alert service is a continuous monitoring service that alerts the subscriber to adjudicated cases. It is a mechanism that regularly screens practitioners against reporting entities on an ongoing basis. This service assists subscribers in meeting the needs of organizations and agencies responsible for evaluating physician applications for licensure, employment, or specific privileges (FPDC, 2008c).

The NPDB, HIPDB and FPDC are testament to federal and state government agencies considerable ability to discover and compile information. They also have considerable ability to limit dissemination of the information and have done so to the exclusion of the public, who have traditionally found it difficult to obtain information about physicians regarding adverse actions on licenses. However, with the advent of the Internet, and with the increasingly widespread availability of records in electronic format, consumers are gaining access to ever-expanding types of information, and some agencies have become more forthcoming with information. The Federation of State Medical Boards, using its comprehensive, nationally-consolidated data bank of United States licensed physicians, for example, responded to the increase in demand for public access to detailed physician information by allowing consumers to access physician profile data including information on disciplinary sanctions, education, medical specialty, licensure history and practice locations, through the DocInfo website (www.docinfo.org). There is a per-profile fee for this service.

In addition, all states now have physician profile information regarding licensure status provided through a state entity (such as the state medical board or health department) and made available to consumers for free via mail, telephone, fax or the Internet. These state-sponsored databases all provide licensure status; however, some states also include board actions and disciplinary history and other states have extended information and report malpractice actions and criminal actions involving a felony (FSMB, 2008b).

Representing the newest foray into consumer-to-consumer profiling of physicians is Angie's list (www.angieslist.com). Angie's list began as an online service that allows consumers to rate the quality and price of services they received for home maintenance and repair. The database recently extended its mission to allow consumers to rate, and other consumers to obtain reports on, physicians according to various categories: price; quality; responsiveness; punctuality; and professionalism. Aside from the issues of accuracy, validity, and reliability, there may be concerns about the possibility that reports can be made in bad faith (see Table 4.6).

MEDICAL LICENSING BOARDS

As most of the regulation of healthcare occurs at the state level, any evidence that comes to light – actions on hospital privileges, malpractice actions, competence, and matters both civil and criminal – that a physician is compromised in a significant way will eventually reach the state medical board through the peer review process, or from databases that compile and disseminate information on the widest of ranges of activity. But how must these regulatory agencies, both charged with the duty to maintain the well-being of the public by ensuring that its physicians are competent, and holding in the form of electronic databases,

---

TABLE 4.6 Physician Profile Databases

ChoiceTrust (www.ChoiceTrust.com) provides a limited national database of physician information including disciplinary actions. Searches are free. Sanction reports cost $9.95. Credential history reports cost $7.95 (accessed 2 January 2009).

Consumer Info Central (www.ConsumerInfoCentral.com) (formerly SearchPointe) a free database of more than 650,000 MDs and DOs with active licenses in the United States Provides information on education, training, specialties, license status and disciplinary actions. For a fee of $9.95, a person can receive a report containing information on all states where the physician is licensed, National Test information, ABMS certification, sanctions and disciplinary actions (accessed 2 January 2009).

HealthGrades.com (www.healthgrades.com) provides free ratings of physicians, hospitals, health plans and HMOs. Website includes an easily accessible basic physician profile including information on board certification, education/training, disciplinary actions and patient opinions (accessed 2 January 2009).

extensive and easily transferable information, balance this duty with the right of a physician to privacy and due process?

Physicians traditionally have been in charge of regulating their own profession. As recently as in the early 1900s there was no formal system to monitor physicians and no effective way to ensure that a physician was qualified to practice medicine. Rather, each practitioner was likely the sole monitor of his or her own qualifications to practice general medicine or a given specialty. With time, there has been increasing professional oversight through professional societies, and more formal oversight through regulations administered by state licensing agencies broadly charged with protecting the public from all varieties of healthcare providers. With recent efforts to improve patient safety by preventing medical errors, and to protect the public by increasing the quality of healthcare, medical boards are under increasing pressure to protect the public against "bad doctors" by measuring competency and capacity to practice medicine and surgery.

The Tenth Amendment of the United States Constitution authorizes states to establish laws and regulations protecting the health, safety and general welfare of their citizens. In response to the Tenth Amendment, each state legislature has enacted a Medical Practice Act (FSMB, 2006) that defines the proper practice of medicine and gives responsibility to the medical board to regulate that practice. The State Medical Board is the state regulatory body that maintains and enforces standards of training and ethics for physicians (FSMB, 2008c). It is the regulatory agency authority to license and certify healthcare professionals (oversight of initial licensure and then maintenance of active licensure of healthcare providers) and implements state regulations regarding medical licensure. The state medical board is charged with the duty to discipline providers for repeated lapses in quality or bad behavior, such as prescribing violations (Table 4.7). The Board is responsible for complaint intake, investigation and adjudication of disciplinary actions (FSMB, 2008a). Boards also facilitate rehabilitation of physicians where appropriate. Beyond these duties, boards are now beginning to focus on requiring that physicians, in order to maintain licensure, demonstrate continued medical competence through assessment of practice performance.

Parallel to the expanding roles and responsibilities of state medical boards is the importance of two entities: courts for judicial review; and the Federation of State Medical Boards (particularly, its model policies) for guidance and standards.

Judicial Oversight

What is the role of the court in ensuring that a physician's peers, hospitals and government entities, especially state medical boards, discharge their duties appropriately given a physician's constitutional right to due process? With boards acting as investigator, prosecutor and decision-maker, their role is

TABLE 4.7 Prescribing Practices Warranting Action

- overprescribing;
- failure to obtain history and physical exam;
- failure to keep accurate records;
- failure to evaluate/monitor patients;
- prescribing for themselves or immediate family;
- prescribing to drug-dependent persons;
- being a "source" of drug diversion.

(Federation of State Medical Boards. Retrieved 17 December 2008 from http://www.fsmb. org/smb)

significant. This role, governed by provisions of the Administrative Procedure Act, is subject to review by the courts.

When courts review medical disciplinary proceedings against physicians they distinguish the constitutional right to be applied from the interest to be protected. The Due Process Clause of the Fourteenth Amendment to the United States Constitution precludes states from depriving any person of "life, liberty, or property, without due process of law." Those holding a license, regardless of type, have a "right" to due process; they have an "interest" in their property, their liberty, or both (*Nguyen v. State of Washington*, 2001, p. 5). When adjudicating claims, courts will focus on the nature of the interest at stake, such that the more important the interest, the more process will be required. The distinction between interest and right is important, because it is the nature and importance of the interest – an interest subject to the potentially erroneous deprivation – which determines the constitutionally-required minimum standard of proof as a function of due process.

The issue in *Nguyen v. State of Washington*, Department of Health Medical Quality Assurance Commission, was the process due an accused physician by the state before it could deprive him of his interest in the property and liberty represented by his medical license (*Nguyen v. State of Washington*, 2001, p. 5). The court held that the Due Process Clause requires proof neither by the lowest standard, "preponderance of the evidence," where mere money is involved; nor by the highest standard, evidence that is "beyond-a-reasonable-doubt," as required in criminal proceedings. Rather the court held that evidence is subject by the intermediate standard; that is, requiring that it be "clear and convincing." The courts reasoning for the intermediate standard is that medical disciplinary hearings: (1) involve much more than a mere money judgment; (2) are quasi-criminal; and (3) also potentially tarnish one's reputation (*Nguyen v. State of Washington*, 2001, p. 8).

Contrast *Nguyen* to the court in *Ongom, App. v. Dept. of Health*, Office of Professional Standards, Res., who, while citing *Nguyen* extensively, determined that the registered nursing assistant license, although a significant property interest, is not equivalent to a medical license and so revocation requires only the lowest "preponderance of evidence" standard. In its reasoning, the court noted the significant difference between a physician's license and a registered nursing license in education, training and examination requirements, and the implications for professional reputation and stigma attached to loss (*Ongom v. Dept. of Health*, 2005, p. 944).

Federation of State Medical Boards

For guidance in discharging its varied roles and responsibilities, state boards have an important resource at their disposal. The Federation of State Medical Boards (FSMB) is a non-profit organization, established in 1912, and now representing the 70 allopathic and osteopathic medical boards of the United States and the territories. Its mission is "to continuously improve the quality, safety and integrity of healthcare through developing and promoting high standards for physician licensure and practice" (FSMB, www.fsmb.org). Each member is an independent state agency, has control of local resources and implements state regulations regarding standards for medical licensure.

The Model Policy

Forced to reconcile the many competing priorities held by various, and inevitably adversarial, stakeholders; state medical boards may look to the FSMB for guidance in discharging their duties. In particular, they may look to the FSMB's "Guide to Essentials of a Modern Medical Practice Act," a model policy that serves as a guide to states when adopting new, or amending existing, regulations for medical practices and to encourage the development and use of consistent standards by boards responsible for physician regulation (FSMB, 2006). The model policy contains a wide range of information on the role of the state medical board, and recommends procedures for enforcement and disciplinary action, compulsory reporting and communication, and investigation. Particularly helpful in the "Guide to Essentials of a Modern Medical Practice Act" are provisions specific to the impaired and dyscompetent physicians.

Compulsory Reporting

The following entities should be required to report to the board promptly and in writing any information that indicates a licensee is or may be medically incompetent, guilty of unprofessional conduct, or mentally or physically unable to engage safely in the practice of medicine, any restriction, limitation, loss or denial of licensee's staff privileges or membership: all licensed healthcare providers; state medical associations; all hospitals and other healthcare organizations in the state; all peer review bodies in the state (FSMB, 2006, pp. 30–31).

Examination/Evaluation

The board should be authorized to require a licensee to submit to a mental or physical examination or a chemical dependency evaluation conducted by an independent evaluator designated by the board, including withdrawal and laboratory examination of bodily fluids (FSMB, 2006, p. 20).

Grounds for Action

The board should be authorized to take disciplinary action for unprofessional conduct, defined to mean, but not limited to, the following: practice or other behavior that demonstrates an incapacity or incompetence to practice medicine; prescribing, selling, administering, distributing, ordering or giving any drug legally classified as a controlled substance or recognized as an addictive or dangerous drug for other than medically accepted therapeutic purposes; prescribing, selling, administering, distributing, ordering or giving any drug legally classified as a controlled substance or recognized as an addictive or dangerous drug to a family member or to himself or herself; violating any state or federal law or regulation relating to controlled substances (FSMB, 2006, pp. 20–22).

Disciplinary Action against Licensees

A range of disciplinary actions should be available and include, but are not limited to the following: revocation of the medical license; suspension of the medical license; probation restrictions and conditions relating to practice; satisfactory completion of an educational, training and/or treatment program or programs (FSMB, 2006, p. 19).

Impaired Physicians

The board should be authorized to require a licensee to submit to a mental or physical examination or chemical dependency evaluation. The licensee should be deemed to have given consent and to have waived all objections to the admissibility of the results in any hearing before the board (FSMB, 2006, p. 26).

The board should be authorized to establish rules and regulations for the review and approval of a medically-directed impaired physician program (IPP). Those in a treatment program should be exempt from the mandatory reporting requirements relating to an impaired physician who is participating satisfactorily in the program and should require that any impaired physician whose participation is unsatisfactory be reported to the board (FSMB, 2006, p. 27).

THE IMPAIRED HEALTHCARE PROFESSIONAL

A physician compromised by alcohol or substance abuse may practice substandard medical care and put patients at risk of harm. Because a physician impaired in this way presents perhaps the greatest risk to a patient's health; because allegations of such impairment will harm a physician in ways possibly devastating to both social and professional reputation; because hospitals are charged with ensuring that its staff physicians are competent but may have financial reasons for ignoring incompetence; and because regulatory agencies are charged with the well-being of the public, but must balance this duty with the right of physician to privacy and due process, it is in cases where there are allegations of compromise by alcohol or substance abuse, when the stakes for physician and patient are highest, and when the interactions between many of the parties involved, including attorneys and administrators, are the most contentious.

Identifying the Problem

In the United States, approximately 8% to 15% of the population has a problem with substance and alcohol abuse – more specifically, studies show that about 10% of Americans have an alcohol dependency problem and about 5% have a drug problem. Statistics are about the same within the physician population (Leape (Congress), 2007, p. 12). Other experts report higher estimates – about 6% of physicians have a drug problem and 14% have problems with alcohol (Redling, 2008, p. 65). An alcohol or drug impaired healthcare provider can be recognized by co-workers because they often exhibit aberrant behavior: changes in reliability; efficiency; prescribing patterns; work patterns; physical appearance; and behavior (Table 4.8).

Ethical Responsibility and Legal Risk

The duty to disclose complete and accurate information about an impaired physician can be seen as a matter of patient safety. Further, nondisclosure of an impaired physician represents not only failure to protect the safety of future patients, but also deprives the physician of receiving needed treatment for substance or alcohol abuse. There is an obligation, for example, under federal law to report to the NPDB (HCQIA, 42 U.S.C. §§ 11131–11133), and failure to disclose imposes a liability risk for tort claims. In *Kadlec Medical Center v. Lakeview Anesthesia Associates* (2008), a previous employer failed to inform a potential employer of a physician's dismissal from a group practice due to personal use of narcotics. The physician was no longer permitted to practice

TABLE 4.8 How to Recognize a Drug Impaired Co-worker

- Work absenteeism, absences without notification and an excessive number of sick days used;

- Frequent disappearances from the work site, long unexplained absences, making improbable excuses, taking frequent or long trips to the bathroom or to the stockroom where drugs are kept;

- Excessive amounts of time spent near a drug supply, volunteer for overtime and at work when not scheduled to be there;

- Work performance which alternates between periods of high and low productivity and may suffer from mistakes made due to inattention, poor judgment and bad decisions;

- Confusion, memory loss, and difficulty concentrating or recalling details and instructions; ordinary tasks require greater effort and consume more time;

- Heavy "wastage" of drugs, insistence on personal administration of injected narcotics to patients;

- Sloppy record-keeping, suspect ledger entries and drug shortages;

- Progressive deterioration in personal appearance and hygiene;

- Uncharacteristic deterioration of handwriting and charting;

- Personality change: mood swings, anxiety, depression, lack of impulse control;

- Patient and staff complaints about healthcare providers changing attitude/behavior.

(Drug Enforcement Administration, Office of Diversion Control, Drug Addiction in Health Care Professionals, pp. 2–3. Available at http://www.deadiversion.usdoj.gov/pubs/brochures/drug_hc Accessed 15 December 2008)

at Lakeview, and he was dismissed from the anesthesiology practice. Nothing was reported to the hospital executive committee, the state Board of Medical Examiners, or the NPDB (NPDB, 2008, p. 1). Two of the physician partners, in fact, wrote favorable referral letters and the physician was ultimately credentialed by Kadlec Medical Center.

While impaired by narcotics at the new position, the physician caused a patient to sustain extensive brain damage during a routine surgery. The physician and Kadlec were sued for medical negligence, and then Kadlec and its insurer filed suit against Lakeview and the anesthesiology partners who wrote the positive letters. The jury awarded a large judgment in favor of Kadlec, based on theory that the defendants had a duty to disclose the physician's addiction, and that they intentionally and negligently misrepresented the physician's qualifications (NPDB, 2008, p. 1). The appeals court, affirming in part, ruled that the defendants did not have a duty to disclose (except in the context

---

TABLE 4.9 Medical Board Actions

Common board actions on licensure (if a violation has occurred) include:

- Reprimand or censure: physician receives a public admonishment;

- Administrative fine/monetary penalty: physician must pay a civil penalty fee imposed by the board;

- Restitution: physician must reimburse a patient or entity for monies improperly earned;

- Probation: physician's license is monitored for a period of time;

- Limitation or restriction: physician's license is restricted in some way (e.g., a physician is prohibited from performing specific procedures or prescribing certain drugs);

- Suspension: physician may not practice for a period of time;

- Summary suspension: physician's license is suspended immediately, with evidence that their medical practice presents a threat to public health and safety;

- Voluntary surrender of license: physician surrenders license to avoid further disciplinary action;

- Denial: physician isn't granted a license to practice or license isn't renewed;

- Revocation: physician's license is terminated; physician can no longer practice medicine.

(Federation of State Medical Boards, Investigatory and Disciplinary Powers. Available at http:// www.fsmb.org/smb_protecting_public. Accessed 17 December 2008)

---

of fiduciary relationships), but that they did have a duty to not misrepresent the physician's qualifications (ACLM, 2008).

Confidentiality versus Disclosure

Impaired physicians may, under some circumstances, be required to disclose their status to licensing boards and health facility authorities. Although generally they remain entitled to opportunities for employment that are nondiscriminatory, their licenses are restricted and they may be allowed to practice only under certain conditions (e.g., with restrictions on procedures or prescribing certain drugs) (Table 4.9). However, physicians who fail to disclose their impaired health status appropriately to the medical board are at risk of disciplinary action by the professional regulatory body and potential loss of license. And what of disclosure to patients of the restrictions on a physician's license: "When impaired physicians practice under such conditions, courts may hold that they have no legal duty to voluntarily disclose their status to patients"

(Veerapen, 2007, p. 480)? Further, patients injured by impaired physicians only have a remedy through the courts "as professional regulatory bodies can only offer the public a means of registering a complaint but are unable to provide financial compensation for an injured patient" (Veerapen, 2007, p. 480).

Physician Health Program (PHP)

All states have a physician health program (PHP) for treatment of doctors for alcoholism or drug abuse (Leape & Fromson, 2006, p. 113). Programs may be administered by the state medical society, the state medical board, or an independent agency. Programs provide assessment, recommendations for treatment, follow-up and monitoring (Thayer, 2007, p. 1). Questions arise about whether a licensing board that allows a physician to enter a rehabilitation program without public knowledge is fulfilling its role as a consumer protection agency: can the medical board advocate for physician's rights and still provide a mechanism to protect the public? Most state boards achieve a balance by offering the means for a physician to enter a program (e.g., by self-referral) to obtain confidential help and rehabilitation provided that it is before the impairment becomes a safety risk, and before there is a case opened with the board. On the other hand, when necessary to implement non-confidential disciplinary action, boards may mandate that an impaired physician participate in the PHP. In this way the PHP, while positioned to help ensure public safety, is nonetheless subject to oversight such that in the event of a physician's non-compliance with the PHP regimen, the board can step in and take further action (Thayer, 2007, pp. 1–2).

REFERENCES

American College of Legal Medicine. (2007). Peer review. *Legal Medicine Perspectives*, *16*(4), 68–69.

American College of Legal Medicine. (2008). Physician references. *Legal Medicine Q & A*, *7*(3), 1–2.

American College of Medical Quality (ACMQ). (2008a). *Professional policies: Confidentiality of peer review information*, Policy 20, adopted 21 April 2001. Retrieved 30 November 2008 from <http://www.acmq.org/policies/>.

Brown v. Presbyterian Healthcare Serv., 101 F.3d 1324, 1333 (10th Cir. 1996).

Campbell, E. G., Regan, S., Gruen, R. L., Ferris, T. G., Rao, S. R., Cleary, P. D., & Blumenthal, D. (2007). Professionalism in medicine: Results of a national survey of physicians. *Annals of Internal Medicine*, *147*, 795–802.

Health Care Quality Improvement Act of 1986 (HCQIA), Title IV of Public Law 99–660, Sec. 402, 1986, 100 Stat. 3784 codified at 42 U.S.C. § 11101, *et seq.*

Kadlec Medical Center v. Lakeview Anesthesia Associates, No. 06–30745 (5th Cir. May 8, 2008).

Kinney, E. D. (2008). The corporate transformation of medical specialty care: The exemplary case of neonatology. *Journal of Law, Medicine & Ethics*, *36*(4), 790–802.

Leape, L. L. (2007). Problem doctors: Is there a system-level solution? *Congress Review*, *3*, 12–13.

Leape, L. L., & Fromson, J. A. (2006). Problem doctors: Is there a system-level solution? *Annals of Internal Medicine*, *144*, 107–115.

Nguyen v. State of Washington, Dep't of Health Medical Quality Assurance Commission, 144, Wn.2d 516, 29 P.3d 689 (2001), [Electronic version] pp. 1–58.

Ongom, App. v. Dept. of Health, Office of Professional Standards, Res., 124 Wn.App. 935, 104 P.3d 29 (2005).

Redling, B. (2008). Is your partner impaired? *Physicians Practice*, 65–68.

Thayer, J. (2007). The future of physician/professional health programs. *The Monitor*, *7*(2), 1–2.

The Privacy Act of 1974, Public Law 93–579, 88 Stat. 1897 (1974), codified 5 U.S.C. § 552a.

Veerapen, R. J. (2007). Informed consent: physician inexperience is a material risk for patients. *Journal of Law, Medicine & Ethics*, *35*(3), 478–485.

Wojewski v. Rapid City Regional Hosp., Inc., 730 N.W.2d 625 (S.D. 2007).

PROFESSIONAL DATABASES

Angie's List. (1995). Angie's List at <http://www.angieslist.com/> Accessed 27.12.08.

Bureau of Health Professionals. (2007). *Health Resources and Services Administration*: *Practitioner Data Banks*. Retrieved 6 December 2008 from <http://www.bhpr.hrsa.gov/dqa/>.

Federation Physician Data Center. (2008a). *Protecting the Public*. Retrieved 17 December 2008 from <http://www.fsmb.org/smb_protecting_public/>.

Federation Physician Data Center. (2008b). *Data Collection*. Retrieved 16 December 2008 from <www.fsmb.org/fpdc_data/>.

Federation Physician Data Center. (2008c). *Services*. Retrieved 16 December 2008 from <www.fsmb.org/fpdc_services/>.

Health Resources and Service Administration: Healthcare Integrity and Protection Data Bank. Retrieved 16 December 2008 from: <http://www.npdb-hipdb.hrsa.gov/hipdb/>.

Health Resources and Services Administration: National Practitioner Data Bank and Healthcare Integrity and Protection Data Bank. Retrieved 6 December 2008 from <http://www.npdb-hipdb.hrsa.gov/>.

Health Resources and Services Administration: National Practitioner Data Bank. Retrieved 6 December 2008 from <http://www.npdb-hipdb.hrsa.gov/npdb/>.

Healthcare Integrity and Protection Data Bank (HIPDB) under Section 1128E of the Social Security Act as added by Section 221(a) of the Health Insurance Portability and Accountability Act (HIPAA) of 1996, Title XI of Public Law 104–191, codified 42 U.S.C. § 1301, *et seq*.

Healthcare Integrity and Protection Data Bank (HIPDB). (2008). *Fact Sheet on the Healthcare Integrity and Protection Data Bank*, (July), (pp.1–4). Retrieved 6 December 2008 from <http://www.npdb-ipdb.hrsa.gov/pubs/fs/Fact_Sheet-Healthcare_Integrity_and_Protection_ Data_Bank.pdf/>.

National Practitioner Data Bank (NPDB). (2008a). *Physician References*. Retrieved 16 December 2008 from <www.bhpr.hrsa.gov/dqa/>.

National Practitioner Data Bank (NPDB). (2008b). *Physician References*. Retrieved 16 December 2008 from <www.npdb-hipdb.hrsa.gov/npdb NPDB/>.

Practitioner Data Banks. (2008). Practitioner Data Banks. Retrieved 16 December 2008 from <www.bhpr.hrsa.gov/dqa/>.

STATE MEDICAL BOARDS

Federation of State Medical Boards (FSMB). (2008c). *About State Medical Boards – Overview of State Medical Boards.* Retrieved 17 December 2008 from <http://www.fsmb. org/smb_overview/>.

Federation of State Medical Boards of the United States, Inc. (2006). *Essentials of a Modern Medical Practice Act* (11th ed.), (Electronic version), (pp. 1–40). Dallas, TX: Federation of State Medical Boards of the United States, Inc. Available at <http://www.fsmb.org/pdf/ GPROL_essentials_eleventh_edition.pdf/> Accessed 05.11.08.

Federation of State Medical Boards. (2008). *Federation of State Medical Boards (Home Page).* Retrieved 17 December 2008 from <http://www.fsmb.org/m_fpdc/>.

Federation of State Medical Boards. (2008a). *Federation Physician Data Center (Home Page).* Retrieved 16 December 2008 from <http://www.fsmb.org/m_fpdc/>.

Federation of State Medical Boards. (2008b). *Physician Profile Overview by State,* (updated 1 July 2008). Retrieved December 16, 2008 from <http://www.fsmb.org/pdf/GPROL_Physician_ Profiling.pdf/>.

Chapter 5

Privacy within the First Decade of the Twenty-First Century

Roy G. Beran

South Western Clinical School, University of New South Wales: School of Medicine, Griffith University; and Strategic Health Evaluators, Chatswood, NSW, Australia

INTRODUCTION

With the advent of the "age of technology" has come the age of information sharing. One can "google" almost anything or anyone. Failing "google," other search engines include "yahoo" or "wikipedia," just to name a couple, so that absolute privacy for individuals is no longer a reality.

The use of mobile phones means that all one's movements and activities can be pinpointed to within centimeters for location. Credit card expenditure can facilitate personality profiling and give those who are interested an overall impression of who the subject is, what activities they enjoy, where they spend their time and money, as well as their hobbies and recreational pursuits. Were this not enough, the ubiquitous nature of closed circuit television (CCTV) can track a person, in real-time, across a whole city the size of greater London. Traffic cameras and speed cameras can capture where one is driving and with whom.

Thus, any illusion concerning privacy has long evaporated before one even contemplates a medical history, the doctor–patient relationship and medical records. Even within that domain of medicine, the use of restricted medications requiring governmental authority, prescriptions in general and use of a medicare card (within the Australian context of universal insurance) makes a mockery of anyone claiming, or insisting, on privacy. Universal insurance allows tracking of which doctors were seen, the type and length of a consultation, the name and specialty of any consultant involved, the treatment and hence diagnosis of the patient, and also the degree of disability or mobility (concerning transportation subsidy and disability supports or special parking arrangements) and need for extra assistance that may be required.

It follows that anyone who truly wishes to invade one's privacy can do so with relative ease, yet we have enacted statutes to cover privacy and govern the behavior of the doctor and his or her use, or abuse, of medical knowledge. What follows will be an overview of the legal position regarding privacy with particular reference to Australian jurisdiction. In general terms, the Australian experience is not vastly different to that existing in the rest of the world. It is indisputable that the surveillance methods cited above have universal application, the relevance of which cannot be ignored and which invade any concept of individual privacy.

CODES OF CONDUCT FOR PRIVACY

The concept of confidentiality, within the medical model, is not a novel development. As far back as the Hippocratic Oath, circa 460 BC, the oath included the words:

"... what I may see or hear in the course of treatment ... I will keep to myself, holding such things shameful to be spoken about ..."

(Edelstein, 1987)

Even in the 1990s, significantly predating current privacy legislation, the Royal Australasian College of Physicians (RACP) offered, within its code of conduct, the following excerpt:

"... The principle of confidentiality is fundamental to the relationship between doctor and patient. Respect for confidentiality as with consent, gives expression to the patient's autonomy by acknowledging that it is the patient who controls any information relating to his or her medical condition or treatment. Medical information should not be divulged by a physician except with consent of the patient ..."

(RACP, 1992)

Despite this respect for privacy the RACP recognized that there were circumstances in which there may be "... an overriding public interest in disclosing confidential patient information to a third party ..." (RACP, 1992) as is the case with driver licensing authorities. Other situations which take priority over respect for confidentiality between doctor and patient include court ordered disclosure (accepting that there is no legally binding doctor–patient privilege to protect confidentiality), statutory provision for disclosure (as with communicable and notifiable diseases) or where there exists "... an overriding legal, moral or social duty ..." (Beran, 2004).

PATIENT ACCESS TO MEDICAL RECORDS

The collection and retention of medical information on patients is the fundamental starting point when considering privacy in medical practice. There was a fundamental change in dealing with patient information in Australia with the publication of the National Privacy Principles, which were contained within the Privacy Act 1988 (Cth), which governed how patient information should be collected, managed and transferred. The Federal Privacy Commissioner published a set of guidelines to assist those in private practice (Federal Privacy Commissioner, 2001), and in the same year the federal government extended the relevance of the Privacy Act 1988 (Cth) to the private sector. This impacted on the integrity of patient information and gave patients access to their records to correct content if they felt there was inaccuracy.

Several Australian states also passed privacy legislation (Health Records Act 2001 (Vic); Information Privacy Act 2001 (Vic); Health Records (Privacy and Access) Act 1997 (ACT); Health Records and Information Privacy Act 2002 (NSW)) thereby reinforcing legal obligations in the handling of sensitive medical information by a range of health professionals, not restricted to doctors and medical practitioners. While disclosure of such confidential information is largely precluded, exceptions exist, such as: consequent to patient consent to disclosure; subsequent to requisite disclosure enforced by the courts; or as a necessary act in the seeking of consent from next of kin to provide medical intervention.

Privacy, within the context of mental health, is also protected by various state acts in Australia (Mental Health Act 1990 (NSW); Mental Health Act 2000 (Qld); Mental Health Act 1993 (SA); Mental Health Act 1996 (Tas); Mental Health Act 1986 (Vic); Mental Health Act 1996 (WA)). This must be tempered with the recognition that family members may play a necessary role within the therapeutic process, prompting a 2004 amendment to the Mental Health Act 1986 (Vic).

When trying to define the application of the changes to the Privacy Act 1988 (Cth) a survey was conducted (Beran, 2003), with a less than 50% response rate, in which medical defence organizations (MDOs) were more helpful than governmental agencies. It was months after conducting of the study that a response was received from the federal privacy commissioner (Beran, 2003). The major finding of the survey was that a "one size fits all" approach to privacy has significant flaws when applying generic privacy legislation to the medical environment (Beran, 2003).

The question of access and correction of medical records was recognized as "the most difficult principles ..." (Beran, 2003), and was accepted as "not absolute." Records prepared prior to 21 December 2001 were beyond the scope of the act unless "relied upon after that date ..." (Beran, 2003). Allowance was made in the area of psychological or psychiatric management when access to medical records may be deemed detrimental to the patient's well-being, depending on the view of the therapist (Beran, 2003).

ELECTRONIC HEALTH RECORDS

Within the introduction the lack of privacy, in the present electronic environment, has been exposed. Federal efforts to bring in electronic records to capture a patient's personal health data over a lifetime have the capacity to completely undermine what is left of the doctor–patient relationship (Iacovino et al., 2006).

The *Australian Doctor*, an Australian medical broadsheet newspaper, revealed: "Government unveils blueprint for e-health records" (Smith, 2008a). It suggested that electronic records: "... will allow clinicians immediate access to a patient's health summary ..." (Smith, 2008a). The information will offer: "... past and present medications to details of health conditions, immunization histories and histories of clinical procedures..." (Smith, 2008a). Other data would reveal discharge summaries, test results, care plans and specialists' letters. The suggestion is that patients would: "... have to opt in to join the system ..." with a right: "to add their own information or prevent certain information from being added ..." (Smith, 2008a), but this assumes a level of sophistication not necessarily available to the patient, and a level of integrity to the system which fails to accept reality. Reality may result in subtle coercion forcing patients to "opt in," which may be exploited by potential insurers or even government agencies.

It was argued in the *Medical Observer*, another Australian medical broadsheet newspaper, that the national e-data collection will be a reality by 2012 and Ms Susan Killion, head of the Australia Institute of Health and Welfare's Health Group, stated that the available data would explore: "... demographics, workforce issues ..., outcomes, whether best practice is being followed, patterns of care and patient's perception of their care ..." (Bracey, 2008).

Kramer (2008a) has investigated the position of e-mail within electronic medicine and recognized the potential abuse of privacy within this mode of medical management. She wrote: "... Never assume an e-mail will remain confidential – even 'deleted' e-mails may still be recoverable – and remember it is not always possible to verify the sender's identity ..." (Kramer, 2008a). The article suggested the use of encryption for electronic communication and the need for defined transparent standard operating procedures, but forensic technology can usually overcome such "crude" protection thereby accessing the most private of information.

Fears relating to e-mail communications and potential breaches of confidentiality are not merely hypothetical, with the Victorian Health Services Commission investigating how sensitive psychiatric information could be transmitted inadvertently to an independent person (Ferguson, 2008). The use of facsimile transmission of information may also corrupt privacy with the potential for causing great embarrassment, and possibly litigation for breach of confidence and hence negligence (Ferguson, 2008).

Iacovino et al. (2006) acknowledge that different jurisdictions, be they in Australia, Canada, the United States or Europe, have similar legal principles regarding confidentiality and privacy relating to electronic health records. Nevertheless, differences in judicial systems, medical traditions and government policy impede the transposition of effective models to different environments.

UPDATE FROM THE PRIVACY COMMISSIONER

There has been an update to advise doctors of the impact of the Australian Privacy Act 1988 (Cth) (Federal Privacy Commissioner, 2001; Beran, 2004). The advice allows doctors to disclose information about patients who are injured and unconscious if it is needed to help with the patients care, or for compassionate reasons. Only necessary information should be revealed and in general terms a doctor can share health information for treatment-related purposes if it is reasonable to assume the patient would not object.

It is accepted that the person who created medical records owns them, while patients can access them unless this would negatively impact on either the patient or someone else in a significant way. Access may result in generation of a fee for the patient to cover "reasonable costs" of both staff, and where applicable, copying. MDOs advocate that where a doctor has any doubt about obligations or restrictions, relevant to any privacy issue, it is prudent to seek advice from the MDO to ensure appropriate compliance (Kramer, 2008b).

PRACTICE AUDITS

The role of health insurance was acknowledged within the introduction with the potential to track a patient's passage through the healthcare system. What was not considered was the potential for practice audits, implemented to monitor compliance with the insurance requirements, to jeopardize doctor–patient relationships (Wilson and McKenzie, 2008). Proposed legislation is being developed in consultation with the Privacy Commissioner, but the Australia Medical Association (AMA) has expressed concerns regarding issues of confidentiality and the need for patient consent (Wilson & McKenzie, 2008).

Medicare Australia, as part of its audit capacity: "… will be able to compel GPs to give it access to patient medical records as part of a new crackdown on fraud …" (Smith, 2008b). The president of the AMA expressed fear regarding the intrusion of "big bureaucracy" into the therapeutic relationship.

Such audits are not restricted to investigation of potential fraud and may be used: "… to 'fish' for evidence based on youngsters' sexual history …" (Colyer, 2008). GPs from two health clinics have objected to federal investigators demands to gain access to sensitive patient records which would undermine confidence and the integrity of the doctor–patient relationship. The doctors have suggested that representatives from the Medical Board, namely fellow doctors, rather than non-medical investigators, conduct the suggested audit while the Crime Commission's executive endorsed the coercive power as a useful tool (Colyer, 2008).

CONCLUSION

Privacy has been the subject of much legislative protection which, upon superficial scrutiny, ensures protection of confidential, sensitive information. Reality, as discussed within this paper, suggests that such protection is far from perfect. So long as the person inappropriately seeking access to confidential information has some competence within information technology, or has access to someone with such expertise, then privacy is, more likely than not, a victim of the explosions of information sharing, and will become widely available irrespective of the patient's wishes.

REFERENCES

Beran, R. G. (2003). Application of amendments to the Privacy Act (Cth) as they affect private clinical practice. *Med Law, 22*(4), 599–612.

Beran, R. G. (2004). Privacy. In S. Sandy Sanbar (Ed.), *Legal Medicine* (6th ed.) (pp. 697–702). Philadelphia, PA: American College of Legal Medicine Mosby Inc.

Bracey, A. (2008). National e-data collection by 2013. *Medical Observer, 4 July,* 9.

Colyer, S. (2008). Fight to protect teens' records – GPs in court battle with crime squad over medical notes. *Australian Doctor, 1 August,* 1–2.

Edelstein, L. (1987). Ancient Medicine. Baltimore, MD: Johns Hopkins University Press, p. 6.

Federal Privacy Commissioner. (2001). *Guidelines on privacy in the private health sector* (November 8). Canberra, Australia: Office of the Privacy Commissioner.

Ferguson, H. (2008). Maximum Security. *Australian Doctor, 9 May,* 45–49.

Iacovino, L., Mendelson, D., & Paterson, M. (2006). Privacy issues, health connect and beyond. In I. Freckelton & K. Peterson (Eds.), *Disputes and Dilemmas in Health Law* (pp. 604–621). Sydney, Australia: Federation Press.

Kramer, K. (2008a). Email consults. *Medical Observer, 25 July,* 36.

Kramer, K. (2008b). Privacy Pitfalls. *Medical Observer, 23 May,* 43–45.

RACP (The Royal Australasian College of Physicians). (1992). *Ethics: A Manual for Consultant Physicians.* Sydney, Australia: RACP pp. 16–17.

Smith, P. (2008a). Government unveils blueprint for e-health records. *Australia Doctor, 11 July,* 4.

Smith, P. (2008b). Medicare to gain access to patient files. *Australia Doctor, 23 May,* 5.

Wilson, P., & McKenzie, S. (2008). New audit laws – a privacy minefield. *Medical Observer, 1 August,* pp. 1 & 4.

Chapter 6

Bioethical Decisions, Substance Use and Addiction: The Clinical Context

Sana Loue, JD, PhD, MPH, MSSA
Case Western Reserve University, School of Medicine, Department of Epidemiology and Biostatistics, Cleveland, OH, USA

INTRODUCTION

Many substances that were once viewed as therapeutically beneficial, such as alcohol, heroin and cocaine, have been found to have the potential to cause harm to users and, in some cases, also to other parties. The provision of treatment to substance users raises serious ethical issues. These include the capacity of the user to provide informed consent, the legal and ethical obligations owed by the healthcare provider in providing treatment to a pregnant woman and in the treatment of pain, and the provision of transplant organs to chronic substance users. Conflicts may arise between providers' legal obligations and perceived ethical obligations, in some such instances. Physicians remain obligated to act in the best interest of the patient and to provide care without bias or prejudice.

Reliance on substances such as alcohol, heroin and marijuana was once viewed as therapeutic. As an example, evidence suggests that alcohol, which was brought to the English colonies by the very first settlers, was used as a medicinal remedy for such ailments as headaches and infections (Murdock, 1998), and was regarded as an essential part of one's daily diet in terms of its caloric and nutritional contributions (Heather & Robertson, 2000). Marijuana was used as a medicinal drug in various cultures for thousands of years to treat a wide range of ailments, including cramps, lack of appetite and rheumatism (Bloomquist, 1971). In fact, the 1851 edition of the *United States Dispensatory* identified marijuana as a remedy for neuralgia, gout, rheumatism, tetanus, hydrophobia, epidemic cholera, convulsions, chorea, hysteria, mental depression, delirium tremens, insanity and uterine hemorrhage. Until 1942, it was included in the *United States Pharmacopoeia* as a remedy for poor appetite (Grinspoon & Bakalar, 1995, 1997).

Even harder drugs were once valued for their therapeutic benefits. Coca leaves have been used for centuries in South America to reduce fatigue and increase stamina (Spillane, 2000). During the late 1800s, it was discovered that cocaine could be used as a local anesthetic; this discovery allowed physicians to perform more delicate surgeries without the risks that attended the use of general anesthetic (Spillane, 2000). Cocaine was also used as a treatment for the "nervousness" thought to be prevalent primarily among "brain workers" as a result of their overstimulation and exhausting work habits, as a treatment for depression, as a treatment for debility, exhaustion, neurasthenia, and overwork, and as a treatment for opiate addiction (Spillane, 2000; Streatfield, 2001). Employers in the mining, textile and road construction industries even made cocaine available to their employees for purchase in their company commissaries.

Later, the use of and reliance on these substances was portrayed as a moral lapse or character defect. In the case of alcohol, this perception came about through the warnings of Puritan clerics about the horrors that would befall those who indulged excessively (Mancall, 1995); the rise of the Temperance Movement in the 1820s as a response to the perceived excesses of use and the association of alcohol with poverty, domestic violence and the abandonment of working-class women (Murdock, 1998); and the increasing portrayal of those who exhibited drunkenness as physical and mental degenerates (Murdock, 1998). In the case of marijuana, cocaine and other "harder drugs," the increasing perception of their use by "ethnic minorities" and foreign-born persons prompted efforts to regulate or criminalize the use of the drugs as harbingers of mental deterioration and depravity although, when they had been used primarily by middle- and upper-class white men and women, they had been seen as therapeutic in nature (Bonnie & Whitebread II, 1999; Spillane, 2000; Streatfield, 2001).

Gradually, from the 1830s through the beginning of the twentieth century, psychiatry integrated the concept of inebriety from alcohol as a disease necessitating treatment (Paredes, 1976). By the 1980s, there was an increased emphasis on the public health implications of alcohol use and a de-emphasis on the clinical aspects (Lemmens et al., 1999). A similar pattern can be seen with the use of other substances. Attempts to control the use of tobacco can be traced back to the 1964 Surgeon General's *Report on Smoking and Health*. Thirty years later, the American Psychological Association, the American Psychiatric Association, the United States Food and Drug Administration, and the United States Surgeon General recognized the addictive properties of nicotine.

SUBSTANCE USE, ADDICTION AND INFORMED CONSENT

Informed consent to treatment requires that the individual giving his or her consent has sufficient information with which to make a decision, that the individual understands the information that is provided, that the consent be given voluntarily and that he or she has capacity to give consent. It is the existence of this last element that is often questioned in the case of individuals who are active substance users or substance-dependent. (The words *competence* and *capacity* are often used interchangeably. We use the term *capacity* here to refer to an individual's cognitive ability to make a decision and reserve the term *competence* to refer to judicial decisions relating to an individual's ability to care for his or her own person and property.)

One writer has vigorously asserted that heroin addicts are obsessed with their use of the drug and, by virtue of their status as heroin addicts, they lack a stable set of values and whatever values they espouse are not truly theirs, suggesting that they cannot be held accountable for any decision (Charland, 2002). This perspective has met with harsh criticism.

First, this perspective is premised on a gross misunderstanding of addiction; the fact of a diagnosis of addiction or substance dependence is relevant to, but not determinative of, the issue of capacity. Second, the dismissal of all heroin addicts as lacking decisional capacity ignores both the fluctuating nature of capacity and the varying level of capacity that may be required for decision-making as a function of differing levels of risk associated with differing treatment strategies (cf. Beauchamp & Childress, 1994).

Various standards have been utilized to determine whether an individual lacks capacity to make a decision. These include the inability: (1) to express or communicate a choice; (2) to understand one's situation and its consequences; (3) to understand relevant information; (4) to give a reason; (5) to give what others would consider a rational reason; (6) to give reasons related to the risks and benefits of a course of action; and (7) to reach what would be considered a reasonable decision by an "objective" standard (Beauchamp & Childress, 1994).

PREGNANCY, SUBSTANCE USE AND ADDICTION

Widespread media attention has been focused on the use of both legal and illicit substances by women during the course of their pregnancies and the presumed adverse effects of such use on their unborn children. These alarming reports have prompted legislators to formulate a variety of proposed solutions to the perceived epidemic, which have included the amendment of civil child welfare laws to facilitate the removal of the newborn child from its mother and the promulgation of various criminal provisions that would permit the protective incarceration and/or criminal prosecution of the substance-using mother. A review of the effects of substance use on infant development and all state laws pertaining to substance use during pregnancy is beyond the scope of this chapter. Accordingly, this portion of the chapter provides basic epidemiological information and highlights the issues raised for the clinician in such circumstances.

The Effects of Substance Use on the Fetus

A relatively small proportion of women use substances while they are pregnant. Findings from the National Household Survey on Drug Abuse (NHSDA) conducted by the Substance Abuse and Mental Health Services Agency (SAMHSA) indicate that, for the years 2002 and 2003, 4.3% of pregnant women aged 15 to 44 ingested illicit drugs during the month prior to the study interview, compared to 10.4% of non-pregnant women in the same age range (Office of Applied Statistics, 2005). A substantially smaller proportion of the pregnant women consumed alcohol (9.8%) and engaged in binge drinking (4.1%) compared to their non-pregnant counterparts (53.0% and 23.2%, respectively).

The effects of maternal substance use on the fetus during its development and on the child after its birth vary significantly, depending on the substance used and the timing and extent of that use. Some of the more widely-studied substances include alcohol and tobacco.

Research reports indicate that potential adverse effects resulting from the ingestion of alcohol during pregnancy include spontaneous abortion, stillbirth, low birth weight, fetal alcohol syndrome, fetal alcohol effects, certain congenital anomalies, and delayed or altered neurobehavioral development of the child (Richardson, 1999; Krulewitch, 2001). The brain is particularly vulnerable to the effects of alcohol ingestion; damage to the developing child's brain has been documented in the regions of the cerebellum, the hippocampus, basal ganglia and corpus callosum (Riley et al., 1995; Mattson et al., 1996; Swayze et al., 1997). The offspring of women who drank more heavily during pregnancy may later experience higher levels of negative affect and insecure attachments, and may display signs of depression (Olson et al., 2001).

Smoking may affect the developing fetus through several mechanisms. First, as the metabolites of the cigarette smoke pass from the mother to the fetus through the placenta, they may act as a vasoconstrictor, causing a reduction of blood flow resulting in fetal deprivation of nutrients and oxygen, leading to episodic fetal hypoxia-ischemia and malnutrition (Ganapathy et al., 1999; Suzuki et al., 1980). This is the basis for fetal intrauterine growth retardation. Other potential adverse effects include spontaneous abortion, the delivery of a low birth weight or premature infant, sudden infant death syndrome (Schoendorf & Kiely, 1992; Mitchell et al., 1993; Lewis & Bosque, 1995), later learning and behavioral problems (Button et al., 2007) and respiratory difficulties, including asthma (Floyd et al., 1991; Kilby, 1997; Richardson, 1999).

In contrast to the generally consistent findings with respect to maternal ingestion of alcohol and tobacco during pregnancy, research findings relating to the effects of *in utero* exposure to marijuana have been inconsistent. Studies have reported an association and no association between cannabis use and lower birth weight (Fried & O'Connell, 1987; Zuckerman et al., 1989; Sherwood et al., 1999). Studies have failed to find a statistically-significant association between prenatal marijuana use and either perinatal morbidity or mortality (Fergusson et al., 2002).

It is now believed that the early research reports that portrayed children exposed to cocaine *in utero* as irreparably injured grossly exaggerated the effects of maternal ingestion of cocaine during pregnancy (Lester & Tronick, 1994; Lester et al., 1996; Bauer et al., 2002). Cocaine-exposed children may display small deficits in intelligence, moderate deficits in language, poor organizational skills and difficulties with abstract thinking and maintaining attention (Delaney-Black et al., 1998; Lester et al., 1998; Leech et al., 1999).

Opiate use has been linked to depressed breathing movements in the new-born, preterm delivery, preterm rupture of the membranes, fetal growth restriction, perinatal mortality and sudden infant death (Rayburn, 2007). There are no known teratogenic effects on the fetus. Because opiates can be used by smoking or injecting the drug, the potential for adverse effects on the fetus depends to some degree on how the drug is administered. Injection using shared, uncleaned injection paraphernalia, for instance, carries a risk of contracting HIV infection, hepatitis B or C and bacterial infection (O'Connor & Kosten, 2000).

Legal Responses to Maternal Substance Use during Pregnancy

Legislators and prosecutors reacted to the perceived epidemic of maternal use of substances during pregnancy. As of 2004, approximately 10 states included maternal substance abuse or infant substance exposure within their statutory definitions of abuse, and 15 mandated the reporting of maternal substance use during pregnancy as child abuse or neglect (Lester et al., 2004). The definition of maternal substance use as a form of child abuse or neglect provides the basis for severe criminal and/or civil penalties. These statutory provisions were often punitive in nature, providing for the characterization of substance use during pregnancy as child abuse, with its attendant consequences, and/or proscribing criminal penalties.

Approximately 240 women in 30 states have been criminally prosecuted for their substance use during pregnancy (Lester et al., 2004). These prosecutions have been premised on statutes prohibiting the delivery of a controlled substance to a minor, child abuse or endangerment and fetal murder/manslaughter (Harris & Paltrow, 2003). Prosecutions for the delivery of a controlled substance to a minor focus on the moments following birth that precede the cutting of the umbilical cord. During these moments, the infant is fully born and is therefore considered a person under the Fourteenth Amendment. At the same time, however, the child is attached to his or her mother by the umbilical cord and may continue to receive drugs through the umbilical cord until it is cut (Linden, 1995; Schueller, 1999). Prosecutions have been brought not only for the use of illegal substances during pregnancy, but also for legal substances. South Carolina, for instance, arrested one woman for the use of alcohol during pregnancy (Paltrow, 1999).

States have more frequently utilized civil mechanisms to address the issue of maternal ingestion of substances during pregnancy. As of 2004, 16 states had implemented legislation permitting the removal of a child from its home based on a positive toxicology screen at birth or a confirmed report of substance use in the home (Lester et al., 2004). More than 30 states now permit the civil commitment of a pregnant woman based on her use of alcohol and drugs during pregnancy (Fentiman, 2006), and some state statutes explicitly provide for the involuntary civil commitment of pregnant women who are dependent on illegal drugs and/or alcohol (Wisconsin Statutes, 2006; Minnesota Statutes Annotated, 2007; South Dakota Codified Laws, 2007).

These legislative efforts appear to arise from a concern for the unborn child and a desire to impose punishment on the mother who continues to abuse substances, notwithstanding the potential harm to her fetus. As such, they assume that the interests of the mother and her fetus are in opposition to each other, that resources are readily available to pregnant women for the treatment of their addiction, that positive effects will result to the fetus from the treatment of the mother's addiction, and that, if detained, the care that pregnant women receive during the course of their confinement will be adequate, if not stellar. Unfortunately, these assumptions may not reflect the prevailing situation. Indeed, research suggests that the management of drug and alcohol withdrawal in jails is often inadequate and sometimes fatal (Fiscella et al., 2004), that little or no prenatal care is provided to women who are incarcerated and that prison conditions may actually increase risks to the health of the fetus (Downs, 2002; Krauss, 1991).

Ethical Issues for the Healthcare Provider

The civil and criminal laws raise significant issues for clinicians providing care to pregnant women (Jos et al., 2003). Depending on the wording of the specific state law, the clinician must consider each of the following issues during the course of providing care to a pregnant woman who is using substances:

1. Is the *in utero* exposure of the fetus to substances reportable as child abuse? Is the legal or illegal nature of the substance (alcohol versus cocaine, for instance) relevant in this regard? Is such a report mandated or permissible?
2. How much maternal substance use constitutes abuse? For instance, does a one-time use of cocaine during pregnancy constitute abuse? Will it result in harm to the fetus? As indicated above, every exposure does not lead to harm. How can this be evaluated compared to daily or weekly use of alcohol which, although legal, has been documented to cause significant adverse effects to the fetus?
3. What, if any, resources are available for substance use treatment for the woman, considering her socioeconomic and health insurance resources, the type of substance that she is using and the stage of her pregnancy? Relatively few substance abuse programs accept pregnant women and many of those that do refuse to accept women whose only source of payment is through Medicaid (Chavkin, 1990).
4. What are the potential effects of treatment or lack of treatment on both the woman and her fetus? Relatively little research has examined the effects of various modes of treatment on the fetus.
5. If reporting is permissible, but not mandated, under state law, what advantage will be gained and what risks will occur if the clinician reports the

woman for child abuse? Will she fail to obtain adequate prenatal care out of fear of losing her child? If she is arrested and detained during her pregnancy, will she receive adequate care in prison or jail?

There are no easy answers to these questions. At times, the clinician may believe that his or her legal duty is in direct opposition to his or her ethical responsibility. As an example, research findings indicate that successful treatment of an addiction often occurs as the result of multiple attempts at treatment over an extended period of time; addiction treatment is a process, rather than an event (Valliant, 1988). Depending on the wording of a state's law, a physician may be mandated to report the suspected substance use of his or her pregnant patient (legal duty), but the threat of such reporting may undermine the progress that the patient has up till now made in reducing her substance use, impair the clinician's therapeutic relationship with the patient and/or discourage the pregnant woman from seeking prenatal care out of fear that she may lose her child. In deciding on a course of action, the healthcare provider will want to evaluate the specific situation in the context of the basic ethical principles of respect for persons, beneficence and justice.

The principle of respect for persons encompasses the patient's right to autonomy and the principle of informed consent. Accordingly, a woman's informed consent or informed refusal must be considered in the context of substance use screening. It is not sufficient to present the woman with only the option of screening or refusing screening. Rather, a discussion of the risks and benefits to the woman and the fetus and to the mother's relationship with that child should occur.

The principle of beneficence demands that the clinician act in the best interest of his or her patient, while the corollary principle of nonmaleficence demands that the clinician refrain from doing harm. While the best interest of the patient and avoidance of harm may be difficult to define if it appears to the clinician that the interests of the mother and the unborn child are not congruent, in most cases those interests are consistent – the birth of a healthy child and the preservation of a mother–child relationship.

The American Academy of Pediatrics (2002) does not endorse universal screening of women and their infants for substance use and exposure, but instead recommends a thorough maternal substance use history. Indeed, the selective screening of prospective mothers based on their ethnicity, socioeconomic status, educational level, race or ethnicity, or other demographic characteristics would contravene the principle of justice, which demands the exercise of fairness and equity and proscribes the imposition of harm on one group within a population, which would likely result from selective screening.

LIVER TRANSPLANTATION

The vast literature relating to organ and blood donation and organ and tissue transplantation and an exploration of all relevant ethical issues is beyond the scope of this chapter. Accordingly, this discussion focuses specifically on ethical issues related to donor and recipient substance use in the context of liver transplantation.

There has been considerable public and professional debate regarding the priority to be given to active substance users and substance-dependent persons in the allocation of organs for transplantation. A survey of Oregon residents suggested that a large proportion of the general public is not in favor of transplantation for those with alcoholic liver disease (Dixon & Welch, 1991). Similar findings resulted from studies in the United Kingdom (Neuberger et al., 1998) and Hong Kong (Chan et al., 2006). This view appears to stem from a belief that, unlike other medical conditions, the alcoholic is responsible for his or her own situation and should, therefore, be given lower medical priority in the allocation of a relatively scarce resource (the organ for transplantation) (Glannon, 1998; Martens, 2001).

Indeed, transplant programs similarly appear to assign a lower priority to substance users, whether legal or illicit. The majority of liver transplant programs and many insurers require 6 to 12 months of abstinence from alcohol as a prerequisite to eligibility for liver transplantation (Weinrieb et al., 2000). Active users of illicit drugs are generally excluded from consideration for orthotopic liver transplantation (Trotter et al., 1996; Keeffe, 1999; Neuberger & James, 1999). Even those in treatment for their addiction, and those for whom effective treatment is unavailable, may be excluded from consideration. Slightly more than one-half of transplant programs accept patients on methadone maintenance treatment for orthotopic liver transplantation, and almost one-third of those that do accept them require the patient to discontinue the methadone treatment prior to transplantation (Koch & Banys, 2001), despite evidence that the long-term outcome of transplant recipients utilizing methadone maintenance treatment is similar to those that are not (Kanchana et al., 2002). Some clinicians, despite their acknowledgement of the difficulty in treating cocaine dependence and the relative nonexistence of effective treatments for that disorder, require cocaine-dependent individuals to complete a substance abuse treatment program and to remain drug free for a minimum period of six months before they will be reconsidered for eligibility to transplantation (Weinrieb & Lucey, 2007).

A utilitarian approach to the ethical issue of allocation of this scarce resource would suggest that those patients who will derive the most medical benefit should receive priority for transplantation (Jonsen, 1997). However, research has not adequately identified or assessed all of the various psychosocial, genetic and medical factors that could potentially be relevant to this determination. Even if all of these factors were to be identified, it is unclear how they should be weighed against each other, for example, an individual of healthy older age versus one that is younger and hypertensive.

Random selection, an approach consistent with an egalitarian view (Jonsen, 1997), is also problematic. This approach would mean that every individual needing a liver transplant would have an equal probability of receiving one. This strategy, however, fails to consider both that some individuals may be in more urgent need of a replacement organ than others, and the sudden changes in a patient's medical condition that could contraindicate proceeding with transplantation.

A moral model would seek to allocate organs on the basis of responsibility for having caused the underlying condition; those who are deemed to be more responsible would receive lower priority (Glannon, 1998). As one scholar has suggested, the allocation of organs on the basis of perceived responsibility would likely result in significant discrimination due to the inability to adequately and fairly assess the extent of an individual's responsibility for his or her condition (Martens, 2001). And, it has been suggested, such an approach in the context of organ transplantation would suggest that this same approach be adopted in the context of other diseases and conditions (Martens, 2001) so that, for instance, an individual whose broken leg resulted from his own negligence in driving should be given lesser medical priority than an individual whose broken leg resulted from a car crash caused by another driver, despite equal severity of injury and comparable underlying health status.

Discussion has also focused on the suitability of organ *donation* by individuals who are active substance users, with some suggestion from research that there may be a higher rate of graft loss related to such use (Komokata et al., 2006). Significant ethical issues arise in this context as well. In view of the incomplete state of our knowledge, should a potential recipient be denied organ transplantation because of the possibility of a poorer outcome? How should urgent need for transplantation be balanced against the consumption of time and energy resources needed to effect the transplantation, which could have a poorer outcome? What is society's obligation to expand the base of available organs in view of the lengthy waiting times (United Network for Organ Sharing, 1998) and scarcity of organs, even if such expansion requires suboptimal donations?

TREATING PAIN

Rush Limbaugh made headlines with his admission of addiction to prescription pain medication, specifically, OxyContin and hydrocodone (Vicodin), which he asserted was the result of his continuing need for relief from chronic back pain (CNN, 2003). NFL star Brett Favre also acknowledged his addiction to Vicodin, which he obtained legally with a doctor's prescription (Bass, 2007). Limbaugh was charged by federal authorities with illegally obtaining painkillers, but neither he nor Favre served prison time. In contrast, the Drug Enforcement Agency has prosecuted 108 physicians during the past four years; of these physicians, 83 plead guilty or no contest, 16 were convicted by juries, 8 cases were pending as of August 2007 and one physician was being sought as a fugitive (Bass, 2007). Some, believing that such prosecutions constitute a "witch hunt," have become concerned for themselves, in addition to voicing concern for patients with legitimate need for pain relief. Although this situation raises important clinical issues, a discussion of pain management guidelines is beyond the scope of this chapter and the reader is urged to consult other sources for this information (Rosenblatt & Mekhail, 2005; Højsted & Sjøgren, 2007). We focus here on the relevant ethical issues.

The Declaration of Geneva (World Medical Association, 2006), the modern version of the Hippocratic Oath, provides in pertinent part that: "[a]t the time of being admitted as a member of the medical profession," a physician shall pledge:

- The health of my patient will be my first consideration;
- I will not permit considerations of age, disease or disability, creed, ethnic origin, gender, nationality, political affiliation, race, sexual orientation, social standing or any other factor to intervene between my duty and my patient;
- I will maintain the utmost respect for human life;
- I will not use my medical knowledge to violate human rights and civil liberties, even under threat;
- I make these promises solemnly, freely and upon my honor.

Additionally, the International Code of Medical Ethics (World Medical Association, 2006) requires, in relevant portion, that a physician:

- Always bears in mind the obligation to respect human life;
- Acts in the patient's best interest when providing medical care;
- Owes his or her patients complete loyalty and all the scientific resources available to him or her. Whenever an examination or treatment is beyond the physician's capacity, he or she should consult with or refer to another physician who has the necessary ability;
- Respects a patient's right to confidentiality. It is ethical to disclose confidential information when the patient consents to it or when there is a real and imminent threat of harm to the patient or to others and this threat can be only removed by a breach of confidentiality;
- Will not enter into a sexual relationship with his or her current patient or into any other abusive or exploitative relationship.

One must ask, then, how these provisions relate to and how are they to be applied in situations in which a patient states the need for pain medication and the physician is concerned about the potential harm that may occur to the patient as a result of its use?

Reading these provisions together, three major themes relevant to this issue become apparent: (1) a focus by the physician on the patient's health and the discernment of and actions consistent with the patient's best interests in the context of providing care; (2) the ascertainment and provision to the patient by the physician of all available scientific resources; (3) interaction by the physician with his or her patient in a manner that is nondiscriminatory, nonabusive, nonexploitative and consistent with the principles of civil and human rights.

The discernment of a patient's best interest will clearly depend on the specific circumstances of any given situation. The alleviation of pain is in the patient's best interest, but medication cannot ease all pain, e.g., existential pain. What constitutes the patient's best interest may be difficult to determine in situations in which the frequent administration of large doses of medication are necessary to alleviate the pain but this may, in the longer term, lead to dependence and the patient's need for substance use treatment. A determination of the patient's best interests will require a careful evaluation of the nature and frequency of the patient's pain, an assessment of the patient's potential for developing a substance use disorder with a reliable screening instrument (see Compton et al., 1998; Heit, 2001; Lebovits, 2005; Rosenblatt & Mekhail, 2005), and ongoing monitoring for the development of abuse and addiction during treatment (Sabage et al., 2003). The ascertainment of and provision to the patient of available scientific resources similarly supports such an approach. Unfortunately, research literature suggests that healthcare professionals often under-utilize appropriate medications, such as opioids, in pain management due to unrealistic concerns about the potential for addiction (Marks, 1973) and an inadequate understanding of the patient's pain (Drayer et al., 1999), to the detriment of their patients. Conversely, the failure to monitor the patient carefully during the course of pain treatment for behavioral indicators of addiction, such as adverse consequences, impaired control over use, compulsive use, and/or preoccupation with use due to craving (Sabage, 2002), suggests a lack of respect and, in egregious cases, an abuse, of the patient.

The provision or withholding of pain medication based on patient demographic characteristics, such as socioeconomic status, race, ethnicity, educational level and/or age, would clearly contravene the basic principle of justice and the promise not to let such considerations interfere with one's responsibilities towards one's patients. Indeed, research suggests that it is not such demographic features that are predictive of a patient's likelihood of developing an addiction in the course of opioid treatment for pain, but rather a personal or family history of addiction and a prior psychiatric disorder (Højsted & Sjøgren, 2007).

The issue of medicinal use of marijuana doubtless raises ethical issues for many physicians. As of 2006, Alaska, Arizona, California, Colorado, Hawaii, Maine, Nevada, Oregon, Washington and Vermont permitted the medical use of marijuana under carefully crafted conditions for the alleviation of pain and a variety of symptoms attributable to various chronic diseases (Swan, 2006). California, for instance, allows individuals meeting specified criteria with a physician's prescription to purchase marijuana for their personal medical use from designated sources that were permitted to grow and distribute marijuana within that state only for such use (Compassionate Use Act of 1996, 2005). Various lawsuits made clear that federal authorities could not only prohibit the sale of marijuana, but could also continue to prosecute both the users and the distributors of the marijuana, despite the fact that such use and distribution complied with the state law (*United States v. Oakland Cannabis Buyers' Cooperative*, 2001; *Gonzalez v. Raich*, 2005). In arguing its position, the United States government repeatedly asserted that there is no medical use for marijuana, despite the findings of the Institute of Medicine (Joy et al., 1999) that inadequate research has been conducted and that there is evidence to suggest that marijuana may be an effective treatment for the symptoms of some disorders, and for the alleviation of the pain associated with some conditions.

For physicians who believe that medical decision-making is best left to the doctor and the patient, and that it is the physician's obligation to treat pain when effective relief is available, these decisions may have represented an unacceptable foray by the government into medical practice. One ethicist remarked: "in the war on drugs, we have had a war on patients. This is a tremendous setback … untreated pain is a public health issue" (Sandra Johnson, quoted in Biskupic et al., 2005, p. 2A). The fear of their own prosecution by federal authorities may have created an additional ethical conflict for them. Still other physicians, believing that marijuana should not be legalized under any circumstances, may have experienced an ethical dilemma seeing their colleagues prescribe marijuana for their patients. It is likely that a decision in this regard – to prescribe or not to prescribe to patients' eligible under the state law – was both a personal and professional one.

CONCLUSION

This chapter has presented the various ethical issues that may confront the care provider in the context of providing care to patients who use substances, who suffer from substance dependence and/or who are in need of prescription medication for pain. Key issues for the physician that are common across these issues include:

- Assessment of the patient's capacity to provide informed consent;
- The physician's obligation to act in the best interest of the patient;
- Potential conflict between what one perceives as one's ethical responsibility to the patient and existing legal obligations; and
- The ethical obligation to provide care without bias or prejudice.

This chapter does not attempt to provide legal advice of any kind and, in situations in which a physician may believe a legal issue exists, he or she is urged to consult with an attorney qualified to address the issues raised.

REFERENCES

American Academy of Pediatrics. (2000). *Guidelines for perinatal care,* (5th ed.). Elk Grove Village, IL: American Academy of Pediatrics.
Bass, F. (2007). Analysis finds pain medicine has risen by 90 percent. *The San Diego Union-Tribune,* August 20.
Bauer, C. R., Shankaran, S., Bada, H., & Lester, B. M. (2002). The maternal lifestyle study: Drug exposure during pregnancy and short-term maternal outcomes. *American Journal of Obstetrics and Gynecology, 186,* 487–495.

Beauchamp, T. L., & Childress, J. F. (1994). *Principles of biomedical ethics,* (4th ed.). New York, NY: Oxford University Press.

Biskupic, J., Koch, W., & Ritter, J. (2005). Patients who use marijuana fear worst if forced to stop. *USA Today,* June 7, 1A, 2A.

Bloomquist, E. R. (1971). *Marijuana: the second trip.* Beverly Hills, CA: Glencoe Press.

Bonnie, R. J., & Whitebread, C. H., II (1999). *The marijuana conviction: A history of marijuana prohibition in the United States.* New York, NY: Lindesmith Center.

Button, T. M. M., Maughan, B., & McGuffin, P. (2007). The relationship of maternal smoking to psychological problems in the offspring. *Early Human Development, 83,* 727–732.

Chan, H. M., Cheung, G. M., & Yip, A. K. (2006). Selection criteria for recipients of scarce liver donors: A public opinion survey from Hong Kong. *Hong Kong Medical Journal, 12,* 40–46.

Charland, L. C. (2002). Cynthia's dilemma: Consenting to heroin prescription. *American Journal of Bioethics, 2,* 37–47.

Chavkin, W. (1990). Drug addiction and pregnancy: Policy crossroads. *American Journal of Public Health, 80,* 483–487.

CNN. (2003). Limbaugh admits addiction to pain medication, (October 10). Last accessed 4 February 2008. Available at <http://www.cnn.com/2003/SHOWBIZ/10/10/rush.limbaugh/>.

Compassionate Use Act of 1996, California Health & Safety Code § 11362.5 (West 2005).

Compton, P., Darakjian, J., & Miotto, K. (1998). Screening for addiction in patients with chronic pain and "problematic" substance use: evaluation of a pilot assessment tool. *Journal of Pain and Symptom Management, 16,* 355–363.

Delaney-Black, V., Covington, C., Templin, T., & Ager, J. (1998). Prenatal cocaine exposure and child behaviors. *Pediatrics, 102,* 945–950.

Dixon, J., & Welch, H. G. (1991). Priority setting: lessons from Oregon. *Lancet, 337,* 891–894.

Downs, R. T. (2002). The right to procreate while incarcerated: a look at the "obvious" differences between male and female inmates. *Southern California Law Review of Law & Women's Studies, 12,* 67.

Drayer, R. A., Henderson, J., & Reidenberg, M. (1999). Barriers to better pain control in hospitalized patients. *Journal of Pain and Symptom Management, 17,* 434–440.

Fentiman, L. C. (2006). The new "fetal protection:" The wrong answer to the crisis of inadequate health care for women and children. *Denver University Law Review, 84,* 537–599.

Fergusson, D. M., Horwood, L. J., Northstone, K., & ALSPAC Study Team. (2002). Maternal use of cannabis and pregnancy outcome. *BJOG: An International Journal of Obstetrics and Gynaecology, 109,* 21–27.

Fiscella, K., Pless, N., Meldrum, S., & Fiscella, P. (2004). Benign neglect or neglected abuse: Drug and alcohol withdrawal in U.S. jails. *Journal of Law, Medicine & Ethics, 32,* 129–134.

Floyd, R. L., Zahniser, C., Gunter, E. P., & Kendrick, J. S. (1991). Smoking during pregnancy: Prevalence, effects, and intervention strategies. *Birth, 18,* 48–53.

Fried, P. A., & O'Connell, C. M. (1987). A comparison of the effects of prenatal exposure to tobacco, alcohol, cannabis, and caffeine on birth size and subsequent growth. *Neurotoxicology & Teratology, 9,* 79–85.

Ganapathy, V., Prasad, P. D., Ganapathy, M. E., & Leibach, L. H. (1999). Drugs of abuse and placental transport. *Advances in Drug Delivery Review, 38,* 99–110.

Glannon, W. (1998). Responsibility, alcoholism and liver transplantation. *Journal of Medicine & Philosophy, 23,* 31–49.

Gonzalez v. Raich, 125 S. Ct. 2195 (2005).

Grinspoon, L., & Bakalar, J. B. (1997). *Marihuana: The Forbidden Medicine.* New Haven, CT: Yale University Press.

Grinspoon, L., & Bakalar, J. B. (1995). Marihuana as medicine: a plea for reconsideration. *Journal of the American Medical Association, 273,* 1875–1876.

Harris, L. H., & Paltrow, L. (2003). The status of pregnant women and fetuses in U.S. criminal law. *Journal of the American Medical Association, 289,* 1697–1698.

Heather, N., & Robertson, I. (2000). *Problem Drinking.* Oxford, UK: Oxford University Press.

Heit, H. A. (2001). The truth about pain management: The difference between a pain patient and an addicted patient. *European Journal of Pain, 5,* 27–29.

Højsted, J., & Sjøgren, P. (2007). Addiction to opioids in chronic pain patients: A literature review. *European Journal of Pain, 11,* 490–518.

Jonsen, A. R. (1997). Ethical issues in organ transplantation. In R. M. Veatch (Ed.), *Medical Ethics* (2nd ed.) (pp. 239–274). Sudbury, MA: Jones and Bartlett.

Jos, P. H., Perlmutter, M., & Marshall, M. F. (2003). Substance abuse during pregnancy: Clinical and public health approaches. *Journal of Law Medicine & Ethics, 31,* 340–347.

Joy, J. E., Watson, S. E., Jr, & Benson, J. A., Jr (Eds.). (1999). *Marijuana and Medicine: Assessing the Scientific Base.* Washington, DC: National Academy Press.

Kanchana, T. P., Kaul, V., Manzarbeitia, C., Reich, D. J., Hails, K. C., Munoz, S. J., & Rothstein, K. D. (2002). Liver transplantation for patients on methadone maintenance. *Liver Transplantation, 8,* 778–782.

Keeffe, E. B. (1999). Patient selection and listing policies for liver transplantation. *Journal of Gastroenterology & Hepatology, 14,* S42–S47.

Kilby, J. W. (1997). A smoking cessation plan for pregnant women. *Journal of Obstetrical, Gynecological and Neonatal Nursing, 26,* 397–402.

Koch, M., & Banys, P. (2001). Liver transplantation and opioid dependence. *Journal of the American Medical Association, 285,* 1056–1058.

Komokata, T., Nishida, S., Ganz, S., Levi, D. M., Fulumori, T., & Tzakis, A. G. (2006). The impact of donor cocaine use on the outcome of adult liver transplantation. *Clinical Transplantation, 20,* 295–300.

Krauss, D. J. (1991). Note, regulating women's bodies: The adverse effect of fetal rights theory on child birth decisions and women of color. *Harvard Civil Rights – Civil Liberties Law Review, 26,* 523–548.

Krulewitch, C. J. (2001). Science update: Alcohol use and pregnancy. *Journal of Midwifery & Women's Health, 46,* 394.

Lebovits, A. (2005). The psychological assessment of the chronic pain patient with a suspected substance use disorder. *Techniques in Regional Anesthesia and Pain Management, 9,* 195–199.

Leech, S. L., Richardson, G. A., Goldschmidt, L., & Day, D. L. (1999). Prenatal substance exposure: Effects on attention and impulsivity of 6-year-olds. *Neurotoxicology and Teratology, 21,* 109–118.

Lemmens, P. H. A., Vaeth, P. A. C., & Greenfield, T. K. (1999). Coverage of beverage alcohol issues in the print media in the United States, 1985–1991. *American Journal of Public Health, 89,* 1555–1560.

Lester, B. M., & Tronick, E. Z. (1994). The effects of prenatal cocaine exposure and child outcome: Lessons from the past. *Infant Mental Health Journal, 15,* 107–120.

Lester, B. M., LaGasse, L., & Seifer, R. (1998). Cocaine exposure and children: The meaning of subtle effects. *Science, 282,* 633–634.

Lester, B. M., Andreozzi, L., & Appiah, L. (2004). Substance use during pregnancy: Time for policy to catch up with research. *Harm Reduction Journal, 1*(1), 5. Last accessed 17 January 2008. Available at http://www.harmreductionjournal.com/content/1/1/5.

Lester, B. M., LaGasse, L., Freier, C., & Brunner, S. (1996). Human studies of cocaine exposed infants. In *NIDA Monograph series: Behavioral studies of Drug-Exposed Offspring: Methodological Issues in Human and Animal Research:* (Vol. 164) (pp. 175–210). Rockville, MD: NIDA.

Lewis, K. W., & Bosque, E. M. (1995). Deficient hypoxia awakening response in infants of smoking mothers: Possible relationship to sudden infant death syndrome. *Journal of Pediatrics, 127,* 691–699.

Linden, P. (1995). Drug addiction during pregnancy: A call for increased social responsibility. *American University Journal of Gender & the Law, 4.*

Mancall, P. C. (1995). *Deadly medicine: Indians and Alcohol in Early America.* Ithaca, NY: Cornell University Press.

Marks, J. (1973). Undertreatment of medical inpatients with narcotic analgesics. *Annals of Internal Medicine, 78,* 173–181.

Martens, W. (2001). Do alcoholic liver transplantation candidates merit lower medical priority than non-alcoholic candidates? *Transplant International, 14,* 170–175.

Mattson, S. N., Riley, E. P., Sowell, E. R., & Jernigan, T. L. (1996). A decrease in size of the basal ganglia in children with fetal alcohol syndrome. *Alcoholism: Clinical and Experimental Research, 20,* 1088–1093.

Minnesota Statutes Annotated § 253B. 02 (2007).

Murdock, C. G. (1998). *Domesticating Drink: Women, Men, and Alcohol in America, 1870–1940.* Baltimore, MD: Johns Hopkins University Press.

Neuberger, J., Adams, D., MacMaster, P., Maidment, A., & Speed, M. (1998). Assessing priorities for allocation of donor liver grafts. *British Medical Journal, 317,* 172–175.

Neuberger, J., & James, O. (1999). Guidelines for selection of patients for liver transplantation in the era of donor-organ shortage. *Lancet, 354,* 1636–1639.

O'Connor, P. G., & Kosten, T. R. (2000). Management of opioid intoxication and withdrawal. In A. W. Graham & T. K. Schulz (Eds.), *Principles of Addiction Medicine,* (pp. 457–464). Chevy Chase, MD: American Society of Addiction Medicine.

Office of Applied Statistics, Substance Abuse and Mental Health Services Administration. (2005). Substance use during pregnancy: 2002 and 2003 update. *The National Survey on Drug Use and Health (NSDUH) Report.* Last accessed January 2008. Available at <http://www.oas.samhsa.gov>

Olson, H. C., O'Connor, M. J., & Fitzgerald, H. E. (2001). Lessons learned from study of the developmental impact of parental alcohol abuse. *Infant Mental Health Journal, 22,* 271–290.

Paltrow, L. (1999). Pregnant drug users, fetal persons, and the threat to *Roe v. Wade. Albany Law Review, 62,* 1029–1055.

Paredes, A. (1976). The history of the concept of alcoholism. In R. E. Tarter & A. A. Sugerman (Eds.), *Alcoholism.* Reading, MA: Addison Wesley Publishing Company.

Rayburn, W. F. (2007). Maternal and fetal effects from substance use. *Clinical Perinatology, 34,* 559–571.

Richardson, K. K. (1999). Adolescent pregnancy and substance use. *Journal of Obstetrical, Gynecological and Neonatal Nursing, 28,* 623–627.

Riley, E. P., Matson, S. N., Sowell, E. R., & Jernigan, T. L. (1995). Abnormalities of the corpus callosum in children perinatally exposed to alcohol. *Alcoholism: Clinical and Experimental Research, 19,* 1198–1202.

Rosenblatt, A. B., & Mekhail, N. A. (2005). Management of pain in addicted/illicit and legal substance abusing patients. *Pain Practice, 5,* 2–10.

Savage, S. R. (2002). Assessment for addiction in pain-treatment settings. *Clinical Journal of Pain, 18*, S28–S38.

Savage, S. R., Joranson, D. E., Covington, E. C., Schnoll, S. H., Heit, H. A., & Gilson, A. M. (2003). Definitions related to the medical use of opioids: Evolution towards universal agreement. *Journal of Pain and Symptom Management, 26*, 655–667.

Schoendorf, K. C., & Kiely, J. L. (1992). Relationship of sudden infant death syndrome to maternal smoking during and after pregnancy. *Pediatrics, 90*, 905–908.

Schueller, J. (1999). The use of cocaine by pregnant women: Child abuse or choice? *Journal of Legislation, 25*, 163–165.

Sherwood, R. A., Keating, J., Kavvadia, V., Greenough, A., & Peters, T. J. (1998). Substance misuse in early pregnancy and relationship to fetal outcome. *European Journal of Pediatrics, 158*, 488–491.

South Dakota Codified Laws § 34– 20A–63(3) (2007).

Spillane, J. F. (2000). *Cocaine: From Medical Marvel to Modern Menace in the United States, 1884–1920*. Baltimore, MD: Johns Hopkins University Press.

Streatfield, D. (2001). *Cocaine [An Unauthorized Biography]*. New York, NY: St. Martin's Press.

Suzuki, K., Minei, L. J., & Johnson, E. E. (1980). Effect of nicotine upon uterine blood flow in the pregnant rhesus monkey. *American Journal of Obstetrics and Gynecology, 136*, 1009–1013.

Swayze, V. W., II, Johnson, V. P., Hanson, J. W., & Piven, J. (1997). Magnetic resonance imaging of brain anomalies in fetal alcohol syndrome. *Pediatrics, 99*, 232–240.

Trotter, J. F., Fitz, J. G., & Claiven, P. A. (1996). Liver transplantation, patient selection and organ allocation. *North Carolina Medical Journal, 57*, 249–252.

United Network of Organ Sharing. (1998). *Annual Report of the U.S. Scientific Registry for Organ Transplantation and the Organ Procurement and Transplantation Network – Transplant Data: 1988–1997*. Richmond, VA: United Network of Organ Sharing.

United States v. Oakland Cannabis Buyers' Cooperative, 532 U.S. 483 (2001)

Valliant, G. E. (1988). What does long-term follow-up teach us about relapse and prevention of relapse in addiction? *British Journal of Addiction, 83*, 1147–1157.

Weinrieb, R. M., & Lucey, M. R. (2007). Treatment of addictive behaviors in liver transplant patients. *Liver Transplantation, 13*, S79–S82.

Weinrieb, R. M., Van Horn, D. H. A., McLellan, A. T., & Lucey, M. R. (2000). Interpreting the significance of drinking by alcohol-dependent liver transplant patients: Fostering candor is the key to recovery. *Liver Transplantation, 6*, 769–776.

Wisconsin Statutes Annotated §§ 48.193(1)(d)(2), 48.205 (2006).

World Medical Association. (2006). *Declaration of Geneva*. Geneva, Switzerland: World Medical Association Last accessed 4 February 2008. Available at <http://www.wma.net/e/policy/c8.htm>.

World Medical Association. (2006). *International Code of Medical Ethics*. Geneva, Switzerland: World Medical Association. Last accessed 4 February 2008. Available at <http://www.wma.net/e/policy/c8.htm>.

Zuckerman, B., Frank, D. A., Hingson, R., Amaro, H., Levenson, S. M., Kayne, H., Parker, S., Vinci, R., Aboagye, K., Fried, L. E., et al. (1989). Effects of maternal marijuana and cocaine on fetal growth. *New England Journal of Medicine, 320*, 762–768.

Chapter 7

Domestic Public Health Law

Lesley Stone
Georgetown University School of Foreign Service, Washington, DC, USA

Susan C. Kim
O'Neill Institute for National and Global Health Law, Georgetown University,
Washington, DC, USA

INTRODUCTION

The medicinal drug approval process in the United States and the agency that carries it out (the Food and Drug Administration (FDA)) are world-renowned for their safety and efficacy. The exceptions, where dangerous drugs are approved for use by the general population, are infrequent. While the FDA has broad power to keep drugs off the market and regulate their use, other agencies, such as the Department of Justice (DOJ), work to stem the flow and impact of illegal drugs.

The United States has one of the world's highest incarceration rates (Liptak, 2008), due in no small part to our drug policies. The "war on drugs," declared in the 1970s, has channeled billions of dollars into keeping drugs out of the reach of citizens. Yet, it has been criticized for being ineffective, unfair and disproportionately impacting minorities. This chapter will explore how we regulate drugs in the United States, as well as federal law and policy surrounding the enforcement of the regulations.

Legal and moral issues surrounding the classification of drug users as "abusers" or "offenders" versus "addicts" is a balance the United States is struggling with today. The enforcement paradigm holds that drug users have full moral culpability for their behavior and should be punished in order to protect society from those willing to break with social mores, or to serve as a deterrent to others that may be tempted to head down the same path. The medical paradigm holds that addiction is a disease that limits a person's ability to make rational choices and should be treated rather than punished. These frameworks are not absolute, and the challenge is to promulgate law and allocate resources in a way that successfully reduces the cost of addiction to society.

The first part of this chapter will provide the legal framework for controlled substances, summarizing relevant legislation for both legal and illegal drugs. The second part will discuss the role of the major federal agencies in addiction and drug control policy.

CONTROLLED SUBSTANCES

Over the past 100 years, drugs and the laws that relate to them have both become more complicated. In part this is because there is no clear consensus on how to approach drug addiction. While the fundamental goal of public policy has been to protect the nation from dangerous substances, the policies have been shaped both by public outrage over crime and by the views of individual policymakers.

The United States policy regarding narcotics, opiates and marijuana began in earnest in 1914. New federal agencies were established to deter drug use, and drug policy was heavily influenced by Henry Anslinger, a proponent of the enforcement model of drug policy. Since that time, federal drug law has become increasingly stringent.

Harrison Narcotics Act of 1914

Prior to the creation of a federal drug control agency, Congress passed the Harrison Narcotics Act in 1914 (38 Stat. 785 (1914)). The act is important to domestic drug control policy for two reasons: (1) it marks the first time the federal government made an active attempt to regulate the recreational use of drugs; and (2) the subsequent implementation of the act laid the conceptual framework for policymakers to take the view that addiction was not an illness, and to prefer the enforcement paradigm to a medical model.

Although narcotics had been readily available to the public before 1914, mounting domestic and international political pressures led Congress to pass the act. The ongoing political and social unrest caused by the opium trade in China was troubling to U.S. policymakers (Musto, 1999). They were also concerned by the increase in non-medical (i.e., recreational) use of opiates in the United States. During this time, the United States imported approximately 400,000 pounds of opium annually for a population of 90 million (compared to 50,000 pounds in five European countries, with a population of 164 million) (Rowe, 2006). Between 1870 and 1909, the population of the United States increased by 133%, but opium use during the same period increased by 351%. Policymakers wanted to ensure that the federal government would be able to regulate the trade and interstate commerce issues of narcotics by levying a tax.

The title of the act: "An Act to provide for the registration of, with collectors of internal revenue, and to impose a special tax upon all persons who produce, import, manufacture, compound, deal in, dispense, sell, distribute, or give away opium or coco leaves, their salts, derivatives, or preparations, and for other purposes," suggests that Congress intended to regulate trade of and generate revenue from the sale of narcotics. However, the legislative history of the act indicates that Congress was also concerned with stemming the increase in the recreational use of narcotics and saw the imposition of a tax as an effective deterrent.

The legislative history also indicates that during the course of their deliberations, policymakers understood addiction as an illness that would require maintenance by physicians. The language of the act was not explicit, but the legislative history suggests that policymakers wanted to ensure that physicians would be able to pre-scribe opiates to addicted individuals (H.R. Rep. No. 23. 63d Cong., First Sess. (1913); H.R. Rep. No. 1196. 63d Cong., Second Sess. (1914)). However, as a tax measure, the Internal Revenue Service (IRS) in the Department of the Treasury ultimately administered the act. The agency was granted the authority to implement the act, and with little medical expertise or guidance the agency enforced the law without regard to the idea that addiction was an illness. Physicians who prescribed narcotics to addicts were considered to be in violation of the act.

The Harrison Narcotics Act was the first step of the federal government's drug control policy. Enforcement picked up considerably when the Federal Bureau of Narcotics was created, with Henry Anslinger as its head.

Federal Bureau of Narcotics and Henry Anslinger

Contemporary domestic drug control policy was formed, in large part, when Henry Anslinger, the first Commissioner of the Federal Bureau of Narcotics (FBN) in 1930. The Drug Enforcement Administration (DEA) had not yet been created, and drug control policy was in its initial stages. The IRS had been responsible for the enforcement of the Harrison Act and another sub-stance control agency, the Bureau of Prohibition, was also housed within the Department of the Treasury. The predecessor to FBN, the Narcotic Division, began as a branch within the Bureau of Prohibition. As prohibition came to an end, the Department of the Treasury refocused its energy onto narcotics with the creation of the FBN.

Between 1930 and 1962, Anslinger served as the commissioner of the United States Department of the Treasury's Federal Bureau of Narcotics (FBN). Anslinger was opposed to all forms of recreational drug use, and under his guidance the agency's drug policies became more and more restric-tive. Anslinger had no formal scientific training and regularly garnered public and political support for the FBN's proposed regulations with sensationalized stories of the dangers of drugs (Carroll, 2003).

Before he was appointed commissioner of the FBN, Anslinger was assistant commissioner in the Bureau of Prohibition. He was a charismatic speaker, per-ceived by his superiors as an incorruptible figure (Rowe, 2006). When the fed-eral government determined that the unregulated use of recreational drugs led to a loss of revenue, they decided to establish an agency within the Department of the Treasury and called upon Anslinger to head it.

Anslinger had a single-minded approach to drug regulation – he was une-quivocally opposed to all recreational drug use; the extent of danger posed by a particular drug was not part of his calculus. Some critics have argued that his policies were influenced more by social politics than science. In the example of marijuana regulation, some have speculated that the backlash against the drug was fueled by racism (Musto, 1999; Rowe, 2006).

Marihuana Tax Act of 1937

As with opiates and narcotics, marijuana use predated the FBN. However, policymakers were not overly concerned with marijuana prior to 1937. Marijuana
seemed to have few negative health consequences and was generally perceived
as a nuisance, as opposed to a problem, by law enforcement. Despite this, by
1937, Congress passed the Marihuana Tax Act (Pub. L. No. 75–238, 50 Stat.
551 (repealed 1970)).

The act would regulate the use of the drug by requiring a license and a transfer tax on all commerce associated with it. Fibers from hemp and sterilized seed
would be exempt from the tax (Marihuana Tax Act, Chapter II, Section 1(b)).
Although the stated purpose of the act was to raise tax revenue, like the Harrison
Act, the actual purpose was to restrict recreational use of the drug.

In his testimony before the Senate in support of the act, Anslinger suggested
that marijuana had an enormously damaging effect on the intellect of young people, which could lead to acts of extreme violence. Moreover, he testified that marijuana was not needed by the medical field. Anslinger relied predominantly on
anecdotal evidence that had no scientific basis. For example, Anslinger testified
that the intellect of young people who smoked marijuana was so damaged that
they committed robbery, rape and murder (Carroll, 2003; Rowe, 2006). He further stated that marijuana use "frequently leads to insanity" (House Committee
on Ways and Means, *Taxation of Marihuana*, 75th Congress, First Session,
May 4, 1937).

To some degree, racism played a role in how easily policymakers went
along with Anslinger's specious statements on marijuana. The drug was primarily associated with two racial groups, Mexican migrant workers in the southwest and African–American jazz culture in southern states, such as Louisiana
(Rowe, 2006). Neither minority was particularly popular with the government or
the general public. Mexican laborers were the subject of an especially negative
public perception and stereotyped as being lazy, shiftless, prone to criminal activity and likely to use marijuana (Rowe, 2006).

It is unsurprising, therefore, that there was little dissent in the Senate hearings. The lone voice of opposition came from William Woodward, general
counsel of the American Medical Association (AMA). The AMA opposed an
absolute ban on marijuana because there was the unexplored potential for viable medical use (Rowe, 2006). Over the AMA's tentative objections, the act
was quickly passed by Congress.

Boggs Act of 1951

During World War II, Anslinger was sensitive to the resource constraints of the
federal government and did not request budget increases for the FBN during
the 1940s (Carroll, 2003). He did, however, ensure that federal drug regulation
remained at the forefront of the political arena with his annual budget testimony
before Congress (Carroll, 2003). After the war, Anslinger found increasing

political and public support to bolster the FBN's enforcement powers as the media shifted its focus to the rising crime rate within the country (Carroll, 2003). In particular, the public was concerned with the reports of crime and young people under the influence of drugs (Carroll, 2003).

Anslinger used public sentiment to the agency's advantage. Throughout the 1950s, he argued consistently for stricter policies against illicit drug use, including: (1) longer prison sentences to deter drug dealers (Hearing Before the Subcommittee of the Committee on Appropriations, House of Representatives, *Treasury Department – Post Office Appropriations for 1952*, 82nd Congress, First Session, February 16, 1951); and (2) that the FBN needed additional narcotics agents in order to stop narcotics trafficking (Carroll, 2003).

The Boggs Act of 1951 was heavily influenced by Anslinger's arguments. The act established mandatory minimum penalties for the possession or sale of narcotic drugs. It also provided incremental increases for repeated offenses, an indication that policymakers were aligned with Anslinger's presumption that longer sentences for drug abusers and sellers would serve as an effective deterrent.

Narcotic Control Act of 1956 (NCA)

Anslinger's views remained influential for decades. In multiple Senate committee hearings, he continued to focus on anecdotal evidence regarding the harm of drug use. Anslinger's drug control policies heavily favored punitive responses rather than prevention and treatment strategies. It was Anslinger's drug policies that led to the disappearance of treatment clinics and instead criminalized the use of recreational drugs. Despite his lack of scientific or medical background, he was perceived as the nation's expert in the field of drug policy (Carroll, 2003).

In addition, in the 1950s, the nation was deeply concerned with rising crime rates and juvenile delinquency. It was in this climate that the Narcotic Control Act (NCA) was passed. The act was rushed through Congress with little question or dissent and was signed into law in July 1956. The NCA increased the civil and criminal penalties for drug offenses, both possession and distribution, and strengthened enforcement authority of narcotics agents, who were given the authority to carry guns, serve warrants and arrest individuals without a warrant (70 Stat. 571 (1956)).

Minimum and maximum penalties for all drug offenses were increased. The first possession conviction would carry a prison term of two to ten years with the possibility of parole or probation; the third would carry a sentence of 10 to 40 years with no possibility of parole (Carroll, 2003). Individuals found guilty of selling drugs faced even harsher penalties under the act. For example, the maximum penalty for a person selling heroin to a minor allowed the jury to recommend the death penalty (Carroll, 2003). While the climate toward recreational drug use became more and more restrictive, regulation of medicinal drug use was also strengthened.

Food and Drug Administration (FDA)

Originally called the Division of Chemistry, and then subsequently the Bureau of Chemistry, the Food and Drug Administration (FDA) served a scientific function, housed within the Department of Agriculture. The Bureau of Chemistry conducted studies on food and investigated the adulteration of agricultural commodities (United States Food and Drug Administration, (FDA)). The modern, regulatory era of the FDA began in 1906 with the passage of the Federal Food and Drugs Act. The act charged the agency with its enforcement to ensure the safety of food and drugs sold to the general public (FDA). In 1927, the Bureau of Chemistry's name was changed to the Food, Drug and Insecticide Administration, when the nonregulatory research functions of the bureau were transferred to the Bureau of Chemistry and Soils. The agency's name was again revised in 1930 to its present-day descriptor.

The FDA remained under the Department of Agriculture until 1940, when it was moved to the new Federal Security Agency. In 1953, the agency was transferred to the Department of Health, Education and Welfare (HEW). The FDA found its current home in the Department of Health and Human Services (HHS) when the HHS became a separate entity from the HEW in 1980.

Although the Division of Chemistry began investigating the adulteration of agricultural commodities as early as 1867, it was with the arrival of Harvey Washington Wiley as chief chemist in 1883 that the agency emerged as a protector of the public's health. As a scientist, Wiley was concerned with the government's poor oversight over adulteration and misbranding of food and drugs. He expanded the division's empirical research in this area, exemplified by the 10-part study, *Foods and Food Adulterants*, published in 1887 to 1902 (United States Department of Agriculture (USDA), 1887–1902). Wiley mobilized a number of interest groups, such as physicians, pharmacists and state chemists, to advocate for stronger federal oversight of food and drug regulation.

His efforts coincided with a larger social movement led by journalists, such as Samuel Hopkins Adams, and authors, such as Upton Sinclair, which exposed the dangerous externalities of a rapidly industrializing nation. Sinclair's novel, *The Jungle*, outlined in graphic detail the filthy conditions at meat-packing plants, which led to public outcry and government intervention. As a result of Wiley's efforts and growing public sentiment that the market was not an adequate protector of food and drug safety, Congress passed the Pure Food and Drugs Act in 1906 (Pub. L. No. 59–384, 34 Stat. 768 (1906) (repealed 1938)).

In general, the act prohibited interstate transport of unlawful food and drugs. The act attempted to regulate product labeling, rather than address premarket approval. Drugs, which were defined in accordance with the standards of strength, quality and purity in the *United States Pharmacopoeia* and the *National Formulary*, could not be sold in any other condition unless deviations from the norm were plainly stated on the label. Drug and food labels could not be false or misleading and eleven dangerous ingredients had to be explicitly named on the label (Pub. L. No. 59–384, 34 Stat. 768 (1906) (repealed 1938)). These included substances such as alcohol, heroin and cocaine.

Despite his commitment to reform, Wiley was more focused on food safety regulation than on drug safety. It was not until his resignation in 1912 that the agency shifted its focus to a greater emphasis on drug policy.

Food, Drug and Cosmetic Act of 1938

The passage of the Food, Drug and Cosmetic Act of 1938 (FDCA) (Pub. L. No. 75–717, 52 Stat. 1040 (1938)) paralleled that of the Food and Drugs Act of 1906. As with food safety and the Food and Drugs Act, public outcry over improper drug and product regulation served as a catalyst for the FDCA. The law was pushed through Congress after the Elixir Sulfanilamide scandal in 1937. Marketed as a therapeutic "wonder-drug," Elixir Sulfanilamide was an untested drug sold to pediatric patients. The drug caused over 100 deaths, affecting mostly children. The ensuing public demands for legislative reforms led to the FDCA. Subsequent investigation found that the underlying solvent in the "elixir" was a highly toxic chemical analog of antifreeze.

The FDCA granted the FDA broad regulatory powers over cosmetics and drugs. It required proper labeling of drugs, as well as the provision of adequate directions for safe use. The FDCA also mandated a pre-market approval process for all drugs. Drug manufacturers were now required to prove to the FDA that a drug was safe for human use before it could be sold.

The FDA requires a rigorous and lengthy drug approval process before a drug can be sold at market (FDA). Prior to the Prescription Drug User Fee Act of 1992 (described below), the median approval time was almost two years (FDA, 2002). The FDA has a stringent, twelve-step drug review process (see Table 7.1). Additionally, the FDCA gave the agency more stringent enforcement and inspection powers. The FDA was granted formal permission to inspect factories and issue injunctions against non-compliant food and drug manufacturers.

The FDCA also gave the FDA the power to regulate which drugs would require a prescription and which could be sold directly to the consumer. Over the counter (OTC) drugs are those that do not require a prescription. Currently, there are more than 80 OTC drug categories, including acne and weight loss medications (FDA). According to the FDA, OTC drugs generally have these characteristics: (1) their benefits outweigh their risks; (2) the potential for misuse and abuse is low; (3) consumers can use them for self-diagnosed conditions; (4) they can be adequately labeled; and (5) health practitioners are not needed for the safe and effective use of the product (FDA).

Prescription Drug User Fee Act of 1992 (PDUFA)

Given the lengthy approval process for new drugs, manufacturers and patient groups began to complain. Patients were not getting access to life-saving

---

TABLE 7.1 Drug Review Steps

1) Preclinical (animal) testing.

2) An investigational new drug application (IND) outlines what the sponsor of a new drug proposes for human testing in clinical trials.

3) Phase 1 studies (typically involve 20 to 80 people).

4) Phase 2 studies (typically involve a few dozen to about 300 people).

5) Phase 3 studies (typically involve several hundred to about 3,000 people).

6) The pre-NDA period, just before a new drug application (NDA) is submitted. A common time for the FDA and drug sponsors to meet.

7) Submission of an NDA is the formal step asking the FDA to consider a drug for marketing approval.

8) After an NDA is received, the FDA has 60 days to decide whether to file it so it can be reviewed.

9) If the FDA files the NDA, an FDA review team is assigned to evaluate the sponsor's research on the drug's safety and effectiveness.

10) The FDA reviews information that goes on a drug's professional labeling (information on how to use the drug).

11) The FDA inspects the facilities where the drug will be manufactured as part of the approval process.

12) FDA reviewers will decide on the application, finding it either "approvable" or "not approvable."

Source: U.S. Food and Drug Administration, The FDA's Drug Review Process: Ensuring Drugs are Safe and Effective. Available at http://www.fda.gov/fdac/features/2002/402_drug.html.

---

medication and each one-month delay in the review of a new medicine cost the manufacturer an estimated $10 million (Congressional Research Service (CRS), 2008). The FDA complained that it did not have the funding to staff the reviewers needed to speed the process.

The remedy came in the form of the Prescription Drug User Fee Act (Pub. L. No. 102–571, 106 Stat. 4491 (1992)), which amended the FDCA in 1992 to allow fees to be collected from manufacturers. The fees, initially about $100,000 per application, have grown to over $1 million, while the average time for a new drug application decreased from about 2.5 years in 1993 to 13 months in 2006 (CRS, 2008). The FDA can use the fees to keep the public safe throughout the life of a product, not just during its approval. Using fees collected through PDUFA, the FDA has doubled the number of employees monitoring reports of side-effects of drugs that have already reached the market (CRS, 2008).

In order to charge fees, Congress must appropriate a level equal to the pre-PDUFA budget. Congress has kept this part of the bargain, but the proportion of human drug applications paid for by fees from industry has grown to 48.4% of the program budget (CRS, 2008). While the arrangement has wide support, critics fear that the integrity of FDA scientists may be compromised through the fee arrangement and that ever-shortening targets for new drug application review will lead to less rigorous study of the drugs placed on the United States market.

FEDERAL AGENCY AND POLICY: SUPPLY AND DEMAND

The framework for regulating drugs is only part of the story; policy regarding prevention, enforcement and treatment is set through a web of federal agencies. Although policy at the state level regarding enforcement and treatment is important, states' reliance on federal funding means that federal policy is paramount. Since the increase in drug use in the 1960s and 1970s, federal policy has struggled to find a balance between the punitive approach of the enforcement paradigm and the medical paradigm, which argues for a public health approach. The allocation of funding to enforcement, treatment and prevention demonstrates the current balance.

The agency tasked with coordinating the federal government's response to illegal drug use is the Office of National Drug Control Policy (ONDCP) in the Executive Branch (Pub. L. No. 100–690, 102 Stat. 4181 (1988)). In addition to setting national priorities and reviewing the budgets of the multiple other federal agencies with drug control programs, the ONDCP conducts research and a national media campaign focused on reducing illegal drug use in the United States.

The ONDCP describes the National Drug Control Strategy as being based on three pillars: "(1) Stopping Use Before It Starts; (2) Healing America's Drug Users; and (3) Disrupting the Market for Illicit Drugs" (Office of National Drug Control Policy (ONDCP), 2008). While the order of goals may give the impression that prevention and treatment are paramount to United States strategy, the budgets indicate that far more is spent on domestic law enforcement and interdiction than treatment or prevention (see Figure 7.1).

The 10 major agencies responsible for carrying out United States domestic drug policy include seven that host programs aimed at supply reduction: the Departments of Defense; Homeland Security; Justice; State; Transportation; Interior; and Treasury. Four others work mainly on demand reduction: the Departments of Education; Health and Human Services; Small Business Administration; and Veterans Affairs.

Reducing the Supply of Illegal Drugs in the United States

The annual budget for supply-reducing activities in the United States includes about $3.8 billion in domestic law enforcement and $3.2 billion in interdiction (ONDCP, 2008). The largest share of the resources goes to the Department of Defense (DOD), at $1.18 billion in 2008 (ONDCP, 2008). The DOD's Office of

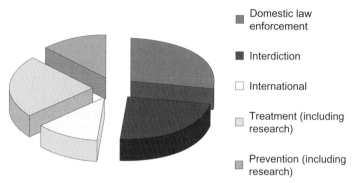

FIGURE 7.1 Budget Authority by Function: Financial Year 2008.

Counternarcotics, Counterproliferation and Global Threats is the focal point for DOD programs aimed at disrupting narcotics-related threats to national security. Coordinated through this office, the DOD monitors and supports interdiction of narcotics, collects intelligence on drug-related activities, and provides training for United States and foreign law enforcement branches with drug enforcement missions.

The DOD focuses on counternarcotics internationally in order to stem the flow of drugs into the United States, as well as the flow of funds to terrorist groups that benefit from the drug trade. In countries like Afghanistan and Colombia, the DOD supplies training, communications support, infrastructure and intelligence to curtail illicit drug rings. Domestically, the DOD aims its resources at intelligence gathering on smuggling rings, training and monitoring. The DOD has also developed programs for deterring drug use among its ranks, including random drug-testing, drug education and treatment.

The Department of Homeland Security also has drug control as part of its mission. It is comprised of multiple entities, three of which are tasked with drug control: Customs and Border Protection (CBP); Immigration and Customs Enforcement (ICE); and the Coast Guard. Essentially, these three act to control illicit drug movement at United States borders. CBP has almost 19,000 officers that work towards drug enforcement (including border patrol agents). Their authority extends to carriers, persons and commodities moving between the United States and other countries, while ICE focuses on investigative and intelligence activities. Meanwhile, the Coast Guard is the main maritime law enforcement agency, responsible for the interdiction of illicit drugs on United States waterways.

Together, these three entities seize millions of pounds of illegal drugs each year. In 2007, the Coast Guard broke its record for largest cocaine seizure when it seized 42,000 pounds of cocaine from a ship off the coast of Panama. The street value of this seizure alone was approximately $300 million (Chertoff, 2007).

Perhaps the most widely-known agency when it comes to illicit drug use is the Drug Enforcement Administration (DEA) of the Department of Justice (DOJ), one of the main enforcement agencies of the United States government. The DEA is the successor to a line of agencies that stemmed from the Federal Bureau of Narcotics, discussed above. The DEA's mission is to "enforce the controlled substances laws and regulations of the United States" (DEA). The DEA aims its resources at disrupting and dismantling the infrastructure of the illegal drug market. In the pursuit of its mission, it also advises and trains state and local law enforcement officials and participates in international enforcement initiatives. DEA agents seized $3.46 billion in assets and drugs in 2007 alone (ONDCP, 2008).

The DEA is not the only entity that focuses on drugs within the Department of Justice. In order to help integrate United States domestic enforcement efforts, the Organized Crime Drug Enforcement Task Force (OCDETF) Program was established in 1982 within the DOJ. The program involves several federal agencies, including the Bureau of Alcohol, Tobacco, Firearms and Explosives, the Federal Bureau of Investigation (FBI), the Internal Revenue Service (IRS), as well as United States attorneys who are expert in criminal and tax law. Combining the resources (including expertise and statutory authority) of several agencies allows the government to pursue related components of drug trafficking, such as money laundering and illegal gun sales.

In addition to these major government initiatives, a few executive agencies have ancillary drug control programs that work to support their mission. The Department of Transportation focuses its efforts domestically on our roadways, with the main goal of reducing the incidence of impaired driving. Its programs conduct research on impaired driving, train law enforcement in the topic, including in the Standardized Field Sobriety Test that police use to determine whether a driver is under the influence, and conduct outreach efforts to the public on the dangers of drunk and drug-impaired driving.

At the international level, the Department of State's Bureau of International Narcotics and Law Enforcement Affairs works overseas to eradicate drug crops, encourage alternative development, and stop the spread and sale of illegal drugs. With programs that support drug hot spots such as the Andean Region (Bolivia, Colombia, Peru, Ecuador, Brazil, and Panama) and Afghanistan, the Department of State also manages international relations and the United States presence in international organizations such as the International Narcotics Control Board. Through these agencies, the government commits substantial resources to interrupting the drug trade, both within the United States and abroad.

The Other Side of the Coin: Reducing Demand for Drugs in the United States

While the United States spends $9.2 billion on disrupting the market for illegal drugs, about half of that is spent by the federal government on prevention

($1.5 billion) and treatment ($3.4 billion) (ONDCP, 2008). The biggest player in prevention and treatment is the Department of Health and Human Services, with the Department of Education and several other small programs filling in services designed primarily for targeted populations.

The Department of Health and Human Services includes two large entities responsible for research into prevention and treatment for addiction: the Substance Abuse and Mental Health Services Administration (SAMHSA) and the National Institute on Drug Abuse (NIDA). SAMHSA was formed in 1992 from a predecessor – the Alcohol, Drug Abuse, and Mental Health Administration, whose roots go back to the Public Health Service in 1930 (SAMHSA, 2006). It is the primary federal agency responsible for improving the quality of prevention and treatment services for substance abuse (GAO, 2004).

A large proportion of its funding is dedicated to block grants to states allocated by formulas based on population and need, although most grants are discretionary (Stoil, 2006). SAMHSA's programs also include "Access to Recovery," which provides grants to states for vouchers to clients to purchase substance abuse services from an approved provider. SAMHSA's block grants provide an average of 42% of the expenses of state agencies responsible for substance abuse (CRS, 2008). Thus, even though health is predominantly the purview of states (Gostin, 2008), federal policy has a great influence over state programs.

Box 7.1 Needle Exchange Programs

Since 1998, federal funds have not been permitted to be used for needle exchange programs. Needle exchange programs (NEPs) allow intravenous drug users to exchange a used needle for a clean one as a method of reducing the spread of blood-borne infection, including HIV/AIDS. The overwhelming body of scientific evidence indicates that needle exchange programs help reduce the spread of blood-borne infection and do not increase drug use in the community (NIH, 1997; Waxman & Cumming, 2006). Yet, in spite of their usefulness, NEPs have been slow to grow throughout the United States. As of 2007, there were 185 programs in 36 states (MMWR, 2007). In a country that is approximately 3.5 million square miles, this means that the majority of injection drug users do not have access to a NEP. Because the federal government, including SAMHSA and NIDA, provides substantial leadership on effective drug treatment and prevention policy, the absence of federal funds for NEPs not only results in less money being available for these effective programs, but also results in confusion about their effectiveness at the state policymaking level.

In addition to block and discretionary grants aimed at prevention and supporting treatment, SAMHSA disseminates information on best practices for substance abuse prevention and treatment, and collects national data on behavioral health issues, including the annual National Survey on Drug Use and Health (NSDUH). The NSDUH tracks trends in drug use by conducting personal interviews with thousands of people over the age of 12 each year. State and federal policymakers can then use this information to measure the effectiveness of drug prevention and treatment programs and understand new trends in drug use (SAMHSA, 2007).

Funding for SAMHSA has not increased since 2000; adjusting SAMHSA funding for inflation since 2000, there has been a net decrease in funding. The programs supported serve about two million of the 23.28 million Americans that need treatment for an alcohol or drug use problem (SAMHSA, 2006).

While SAMHSA focuses on building capacity and effectiveness of treatment programs through grants, the National Institute on Drug Abuse (NIDA) focuses on scientific studies that help to understand the mechanisms of addiction. NIDA was established in 1974 by Congress to mount a scientific response to the increased drug abuse of the 1960s and 1970s. It became part of the National Institutes of Health at HHS in 1992. Its research portfolio includes basic, clinical and epidemiological research into the cause of drug abuse and addiction, course of the disease, and how to treat and prevent addiction.

At one time, NIDA supported over 85% of all biomedical and behavioral drug abuse research in the world (Mathias, 1999). NIDA research is responsible for developing a urine drug test and understanding nicotine's pivotal role in tobacco dependence, among other discoveries that have changed the way we think about drugs and addiction. NIDA's mission follows the drug trends of the time; in the 1980s, more research was directed at crack cocaine and HIV/AIDS, because of the role of injection drug use in transmitting the infection (Mathias, 1999). More recent initiatives include the Medications Development Division (dedicated to finding new medications to improve drug abuse treatment), work in epigenetics (studying the lasting impact **drug use has on the structure of DNA**), and addiction immunotherapy (ONDCP, 2008).

The work at NIDA and SAMHSA leads to new ways of thinking about addiction and its consequences, as well as new treatments. How quickly these prevention and treatment techniques are adopted will depend largely on how successful the agencies are at educating the stakeholders, as well as economic factors such as what treatments are covered by insurance. The Institute of Medicine has identified an incredible gap between the publication of research and its effect on the ground – changes in treatment delivery (IOM, 1998). Clearly, such a gap diminishes the usefulness of cutting-edge science to those currently dealing with drug or alcohol addiction.

Also under the HHS umbrella, the Centers for Medicare and Medicaid Services (CMS) play a pivotal role in determining how quickly treatment modalities are adopted. If CMS adopts a treatment as effective, private insurers are likely to follow suit. In 2008, alcohol and drug screening, as well as a 15-minute intervention for alcohol or drug abuse, were added to the panoply of services for which CMS will reimburse doctors (ONDCP, 2008).

Given the strength of information developed by NIDA and SAMHSA regarding the effectiveness of screening and brief intervention and the leadership of CMS, the practice is likely to become widespread.

In addition to the programs at the Department of Health and Human Services, a number of other federal programs support prevention and treatment in target populations. The Safe and Drug Free Schools and Communities Act authorizes the Department of Education to distribute grants to states to support local educational agencies and community programs that help prevent students from abusing drugs and alcohol. The program also funds student drug testing programs and a Student Drug Testing Institute that will help schools design drug testing programs as part of their prevention efforts (ONDCP, 2008).

The Bureau of Prisons (BOP) (a division of the Department of Justice) is legally mandated to provide drug treatment to eligible inmates. Given the historical tightening of criminal law surrounding illegal drug use, a predictably large proportion of incarcerated individuals has a history of drug abuse (Mumola & Karberg, 2006). Consequently, the BOP has drug screening programs, drug abuse education, and residential and nonresidential treatment programs for inmates. Some nonviolent offenders may earn a reduction in their sentence for successfully completing a program.

However, while extensive funding has been poured into drug control policy by the United States in the past few decades, the proportion of funding that supports the enforcement paradigm continues to dwarf the proportion spent on prevention and treatment. The tension between these two paradigms is one reason that prevention and harm reduction strategies that have been proven to be effective are difficult to implement.

CONCLUSION

The past century in American drug law and policy has focused on the tightening of access to drugs. Recreational drugs have been increasingly restricted and penalties for breaking the law more punitive. In some areas, such as the drug approval process, this increased vigilance has doubtless improved public safety. In other areas, it has led to high rates of incarceration. While federal spending on enforcement in the United States and abroad continues apace, agencies focusing on treatment and prevention remain under-funded.

The history of the enforcement paradigm's entrenchment in culture and law make increasing resources for the medical paradigm difficult. New discoveries in addiction and treatment may help future lawmakers direct federal policy and funds more effectively.

REFERENCES

38 Stat. 785 (1914).
70 Stat. 571 (1956).

Anti-Drug Abuse Act of 1988. (1988). Pub. L. No. 100–690, 102 Stat. 4181.

Carroll, R. (2003). Under the influence: Harry Anslinger's role in shaping America's drug policy. In J. Erlin & J. Spillane (Eds.), *Federal drug control: The evolution of policy and practice*, p. 66. New York, NY: Pharmaceutical Products Press.

Chertoff, M., Allen, T., & Tandy, K. (2007). *Coast Guard Record Maritime Cocaine Seizure.* Remarks by Homeland Security Secretary Michael Chertoff, U.S. Coast Guard commandant Admiral Thad Allen and Drug Enforcement Administration Administrator Karen Tandy, (March 21). Retrieved 8 August 2008 from <http://www.dhs.gov/xnews/releases/pr_1174566428378.shtm/>

Congressional Research Service. (2008). *Substance Abuse and Mental Health Services Administration (SAMHSA): Reauthorization Issues* (p. 2). Washington, DC: Sundararaman, R.

Congressional Research Service. (2008). *The Prescription Drug User Fee Act: History, Reauthorization in 2007, and Effect on FDA* Publication number RL33914, (p. 2). Washington, DC: Thaul, S.

DEA Mission Statement. Available at <http://www.usdoj.gov/dea/agency/mission.htm/>

GAO. (2004). *Substance Abuse and Mental Health Services Administration.* Washington, DC: GAO.

Gostin, L. (2008). *Public Health Law: Power, Duty, Restraint* (2nd ed). Berkeley, CA: University of California Press.

H.R. Rep. No. 23. 63d Cong., First Sess. (1913); H.R. Rep. No. 1196. 63d Cong., 2d Sess. (1914).

Hearing before the Subcommittee of the Committee on Appropriations, House of Representatives. (February 16, 1951). *Treasury Department – Post Office Appropriations for 1952*, 82nd Congress, First Session, p. 272.

House Committee on Ways and Means. (May 4, 1937). *Taxation of Marihuana*, 75th Congress, First Session, pp.117–118.

IOM. (1998). *Bridging the Gap between Practice and Research: Forging Partnerships with Community-Based Drug and Alcohol Treatment.* Washington, DC: National Academy Press.

Liptak, A. (2008). Inmate count in U.S. dwarfs other nations 23 April, p. A1. *New York Times.*

Marihuana Tax Act, Chapter II, Section 1(b).

Mathias, R. (1999). NIDA marks 25 years of progress in drug abuse research. *NIDA Notes*, 14.

Mumola, C. J., & Karberg, J. C. (2006). *Drug use and dependence, state and federal prisoners, 2004.* Bureau of Justice Statistics Special Report.

Musto, D. (1999). *The American disease, origins of narcotic control* (3rd ed). New York, NY: Oxford University Press (pp. 25–53).

National Institutes of Health. (1997). Interventions to prevent HIV risk behaviors. *National Institutes of Health, 15*(2), 1–41.

Office of National Drug Control Policy. (2008). *National drug control strategy: FY 2009 budget summary.* Washington, DC: Office of National Drug Control Policy.

Pub. L. No. 59–384, 34 Stat. 768, codified at 21 USC §§ 1–15 (1934), repealed by the Federal Food, Drug, and Cosmetic Act of 1938, § 902(a), Pub. L. No. 75–717, 52 Stat. 1040, 1059, codified at 21 USC § 301 (1994).

Pub. L. No. 102–571, 106 Stat. 4491 (1992).

Pub. L. No. 75–238, 50 Stat. 551 (repealed 1970).

Pub. L. No. 75–717, 52 Stat. 1040 (1938).

Rowe, T. (2006). *Federal Narcotics Laws and the War on Drugs: Money Down a Rat Hole.* New York, NY: Haworth Press (pp. 14–16).

SAMHSA. (2006). *SAMHSA Strategic Plan: FY 2006 – FY 2011* (p. 4). Washington, DC: SAMHSA.

SAMHSA. (2007). *Results from the 2006 National Survey on Drug Use and Health: National Findings.* Retrieved 8 August 2008 from <http://www.oas.samhsa.gov/nsduh/2k6nsduh/2k6Results.pdf/>.

Stoil, M. (2006). SAMHSA at the end of the Curie years. *Behavioral Healthcare, 26,* 10–14.

U.S. Department of Agriculture. (2005). Syringe Exchange Programs. *MMWR,* November 9, 2007/*56*(44), 1164–1167.

U.S. Department of Agriculture. (1887–1902). *Food and Food Adulterants, Part One–Part Ten* Government Printing Office. Washington, DC: Wiley, H.

U.S. Food and Drug Administration. *History of the FDA.* Available at <http://www.fda.gov/oc/history/historyoffda/default.htm/>

U.S. Food and Drug Administration. *Milestones in U.S. Food and Drug Law History.* Available at <http://www.fda.gov/opacom/backgrounders/miles.html/>

U.S. Food and Drug Administration. *The FDA's Drug Review Process: Ensuring Drugs are Safe and Effective.* Available at <http://www.fda.gov/fdac/features/2002/402_drug.html/>

U.S. Food and Drug Administration, Center for Drug Evaluation and Research. *Drug Approval Application Process.* Available at <http://www.fda.gov/cder/regulatory/applications/default.htm/>

U.S. Food and Drug Administration, Center for Drug Evaluation and Research. *FDA's Drug Review and Approval Times.* Available at <http://www.fda.gov/cder/reports/reviewtimes/default.htm/>

U.S. Food and Drug Administration, Office of Nonprescription Products. *Introduction.* Available at <http://www.fda.gov/cder/Offices/otc/default.htm/>

Waxman, H., & Cummings, E. (2006). Letter from Henry Waxman and Elijah Cummings to Condoleezza Rice, (March 15). Available at <http://reform.democrats.house.gov/documents/20060315121257-51998.pdf/>

Chapter 8

International Law, Public Health and Addiction

Peter J. Hammer, JD, PhD
Wayne State University Law School, Detroit, MI, USA

What is the relationship between international law, public health and addiction? This chapter addresses three straightforward questions: (1) what is international law; (2) how does international law relate to addiction; and (3) why is international law relevant to domestic practitioners struggling with the legal, medical and policy dimensions of addiction? The notion of practitioner is intentionally left vague. It includes research scientists studying addiction and physicians treating addiction. It includes lawyers and judges dealing with the legal aspects of addiction. It also includes social workers, community activists and policy-makers confronting the problems of addiction and thinking creatively about law reform. The focus on practitioners reflects a deeper interest in the ways that members of global civil society are playing an increasingly important role in shaping the contours of international law.

The interface between addiction and international law embraces a range of different substances: drugs, alcohol and tobacco. Drugs and alcohol have long been subjects of international law. The first International Opium Convention was adopted in 1912 (Fidler, 2001). The precursor to the World Health Organization (WHO), the health component of the short-lived League of Nations, began addressing alcoholism as a medical problem as early as 1928 (Fidler, 2001, p. 844). In contrast, despite its addictive characteristics and now obvious adverse health effects, tobacco was not an historic target of international control. Indeed, rather than restrictions, international law in the free trade regimes of the General Agreement on Tariffs and Trade (GATT) and the World Trade Organization (WTO) has been used to force open tobacco markets, especially in developing countries. However, times change, as well as do laws. The WHO Framework Convention on Tobacco Control (2003) commits countries to ambitious tobacco control regimes and illustrates a creative use of international law as a tool for policy reform and public health advocacy.

Without doubt, however, the dominant focus of international law and addiction has been, and continues to be, drugs and other controlled substances.

Not surprisingly, the tensions one finds at the international level roughly mirror the policy tensions and disputes found at the domestic level. On one side is the law enforcement perspective, with its focus on supply-side control, criminalization and the coercive power of the state. On the other side is the public health perspective, with its focus on demand-side control, treatment, education and the softer instruments of state power. At both the domestic and the international level, law enforcement and supply-side restrictions dominate, leaving public health and demand-side control playing subsidiary roles.

WHAT IS INTERNATIONAL LAW?

From a traditional perspective, international law is all about treaties and treaty-making. Here, international law is the exclusive domain of nation states. Nation states are the only relevant actors in international law and they are its primary objects. But this is not the only way to view international law. Particularly when international law confronts complex social issues, such as public health, nation states are joined with a growing array of international organizations, nongovernmental organizations (NGOs) and legions of other nonstate actors, comprising an increasingly vibrant international civil society. These dynamics stretch traditional concepts and call for more progressive understandings of international law that acknowledge the significance of nonstate actors and tools other than treaty-making.

It is standard in international law to differentiate between "hard law" and "soft law." Hard law consists primarily of formal treaties adopted by independent sovereign states. In theory, hard law creates binding legal obligations. Soft law, in contrast, consists of items such as resolutions passed by the United Nations' General Assembly or recommendations adopted by the WHO's World Health Assembly. Soft law creates no formal legal obligations. While this distinction is often helpful, it masks certain complications. Hard law is often not that hard and soft law is not always that soft as the traditional view suggests. Why is this so? The force behind international law is frequently more political than legal. International law exists in a realm where there are very limited enforcement mechanisms. As such, treaty obligations can be disregarded without obvious consequences, and many obligations routinely are ignored. Conversely, if the political environment is conducive to compliance with an international mandate, then the obligation (hard or soft) will likely be obeyed. The political environment and not the law is often the more important consideration. This suggests a more functional definition of international law that focuses not on law as an end in itself, but on law and other instrumentality as mechanisms designed to facilitate effective forms of international cooperation. Table 8.1 is helpful in understanding the multiple layers of the international legal landscape.

Traditional views of international law occupy boxes A and B. More progressive views of international law seek to fold boxes C, D, E and F into the analysis. Even in progressive views, however, boxes A and B remain critical.

TABLE 8.1 The Multiple Dimensions of International Law

	Hard Law	Soft Law
Nation states	A	B
International organizations	C	D
Civil society	E	F

Nation states will always remain essential building blocks for international law. Similarly, treaties will always remain important tools in regulating the conduct of nation states, and in defining the norms and expectations of the international community. But law is just one of many components capable of facilitating effective forms of cooperation. In progressive understandings, there is a clear movement from "nations" to "networks" as the primary units for addressing complex international problems. In these networks, the administrative infrastructures of international organizations are important, as are members of a global civil society, including practitioners in the field of addiction.

The discussion of international law and addiction in this chapter will highlight the continued relevance of traditional views, particularly as they relate to supply-side control and problems of law enforcement. The chapter will also examine, however, more progressive approaches, particularly as they relate to demand-side control and the influence of public health perspectives.

INTERNATIONAL LAW IN THE FIELD OF ADDICTION

The law and policy governing addiction provides a helpful framework for teaching the basics of international law. There is no shortage of hard law. Treaties play a particularly important role in the international law of drug control. The hard law realm of drug control is dominated by supply-side concerns and focuses on the exercise of the traditional police powers of the nation state. The international drug control regime seeks to limit access to narcotics and other drugs. Illicit uses are criminalized and the problems of addiction are filtered predominately through the lens of law enforcement. Public health, largely embodied in the policies and practices of the World Health Organization, provides a contrasting set of approaches to the problems of addiction. In this realm, one finds a greater concentration on demand-side concerns, a greater utilization of soft law tools and reliance on broad informal networks rather than on nation states. Here, addiction is viewed as a medical and social problem, and contrasting policies are formed from this premise.

Addiction: The Perspective of Drug Control

Hard law: Treaties for Drug Control

The archetypal form of a hard law is a formal treaty. For the last century, international law has focused primarily on efforts to restrict the availability of controlled substances, but this was not always the case. Laws are always reflections of social choices. Therefore, laws (treaties) will change as social choices change. Raustiala (1999) and McCoy (2000) both note the irony that over a three-hundred-year period, international policy for drugs like opium has moved from regimes of free trade to regimes of prohibition. Before banning trade in opium, the British fought wars to keep foreign markets open. This changed with changing social attitudes, solidifying in the early days of the twentieth century. At the primary urging of the United States, the Hague Opium Convention was adopted in 1912. A central problem facing policymakers, however, was that opium and cocaine (also subject to the convention) have legitimate as well as illegitimate uses. Adopting a regulatory model, the convention created a series of licensing and permitting requirements designed to limit trade and sale for legitimate medical purposes, and to prohibit all other uses. Countries adopting the international convention were obligated to adopt national legislation bringing their laws into compliance with the new standards. The United States enacted the Harrison Narcotics Act in 1914, requiring a doctor's prescription to purchase narcotics and forging an early link between American domestic and international drug policy (McCoy, 2000, p. 326).

All economists know that legal prohibitions create illegal markets. An international regime of supply-side law enforcement would, therefore, be needed to enforce the new international prohibitions. Under the auspices of the League of Nations, the 1936 convention was adopted to address supply-side narcotic control in response to a growing illegal trade. The convention recognized trafficking as a criminal offense, committed signing nations to establish new agencies to supervise drug suppression, and sought to enable greater international cooperation to control the illicit trade in drugs (Raustiala, 1999, pp. 106–107).

Modern drug control efforts are a post-World War II attempt to build on, consolidate and extend these initial approaches. There are three major international drug control treaties now in force:

- The Single Convention on Narcotic Drugs (1961) (amended by a 1972 Protocol);
- The Convention on Psychotropic Substances (1971);
- The UN Convention against Illicit Traffic in Narcotic Drugs and Psychotropic Substances (1988) (Raustiala, 1999; Wiener, 1999; Levitsky, 2003; Thomas, 2003; Aoyagi, 2005).

As suggested by its name, the Single Convention on Narcotic Drugs (1961) was an effort to codify the pre-existing *ad hoc* system of multilateral treaties into a single document. The convention also sought to create a simplified and streamlined infrastructure for the administration and implementation of the new drug control regime, creating the International Narcotics Control Board (INCB). Consistent with past practices, the convention sought to establish national mechanisms that made narcotic substances available for legitimate scientific and medical purposes, while preventing their illicit trade. As such, the treaty commits nations to establish elaborate regulatory processes to control the production, distribution, export and import of narcotics. Thomas (2003) argues that this was consistent with the "administrative" or "medical" model of past drug control efforts. The new international drug control regime, however, also incorporated and extended the prohibitionist elements of previous conventions. The 1961 convention required states to enact national legislation criminalizing the unlawful production and trade in narcotics. It also required states to establish conspiracy as a crime, making it easier to prosecute these offenses (Thomas, 2003, p. 561).

The Convention on Psychotropic Substances (1971) recognized that narcotics were not the only substances requiring international cooperation to control. The same regulatory machinery previously developed for narcotics would now be applied to hallucinogens, amphetamines and barbiturates. The convention extended the practice of using different schedules of substances triggering different levels of regulatory control, as well as an international process delegated to the World Health Organization (WHO) for prospectively adding, removing and transferring substances from these schedules.

While containing the seeds of a punitive criminal approach, the focus of the 1961 and 1971 conventions was still largely regulatory, seeking to restrict illicit access to drugs by controlling the channels of trade and production. Unfortunately, by any measure of assessment, these treaties were not effective in controlling the trafficking of illicit drugs. The United Nations Convention against Illicit Traffic in Narcotic Drugs and Psychotropic Substances (1988) recognized these failures and sought to add to the tools available for law enforcement. The convention commits signatories to fight money laundering, confiscate illegally produced drugs, and cooperate in the prosecution and extradition of criminal suspects. The 1988 convention also expands the focus of drug control efforts to include trade in precursor chemicals and equipment.

Economic theories of revealed preferences teach that actions reflect priorities and preferences. The priorities reflected in these hard law treaties reflect a concern over drugs, as opposed to alcohol or tobacco, as objects of regulation. Within the domain of drugs, these treaties reflect a nation-state preference for supply-side control rather than demand-side controls. Even on the supply-side, there is an increasing preference for criminalization and law enforcement as policy tools, as opposed to regulation. These trends are even more pronounced if one considers the Convention on Transnational Organized Crime (2000) as part of the drug control regime. Nevertheless, as will be detailed later, each of these treaties contains some concessions concerning the importance of treatment and rehabilitation.

Soft Law Declarations on Drug Control

Each of the above conventions is a treaty. Since international law is a consent-based system, no country is bound by a treaty unless it expressly adopts its provisions. Once enacted, each signatory is theoretically obligated by its terms. But treaties are not the only way that the international community seeks to influence the policy and conduct of nation states. Soft law tools reflect a range of devices nations and international organizations can use to pursue policy objectives. These declarations are not "law" in the sense that they create independent legal obligations on the part of nation states. Nevertheless, resolutions, declarations, guidelines and recommendations can help identify problems, motivate actors and encourage concerted corrective action. Soft law provides part of the international instrumentality that can facilitate effective forms of cooperation.

There are countless United Nations resolutions and declarations concerning drug control. Similarly, the WHO lists more than 25 World Health Assembly resolutions relating to substance abuse. Discussion here will be limited to three United Nations General Assembly Resolutions passed during a United Nations Special Session in June 1998 to address the world drug problem (Wiener, 1999). The conference marked the 10-year anniversary of the 1988 Convention against Illicit Traffic in Narcotic Drugs and Psychotropic Substances. At the end of the session three resolutions were adopted:

- Political Declaration on Global Drug Control (1998a);
- Declaration on the Guiding Principles of Drug Demand Reduction (1998b);
- Measures to Enhance International Cooperation to Counter the World Drug Problem (1998c).

The first resolution defines the problem. The second calls for greater demand-side reductions. The third envisions greater coordinated actions on the supply side. It acknowledges the need for action to address the growing problem of amphetaminetype stimulants and their precursor chemicals, as well as the need for strengthened international cooperation to facilitate judicial cooperation and to take more sustained action against money laundering.

A special session of the United Nations is a political event. It seeks to draw attention to an issue and motivate action. Like any political event, it will have its supporters, as well as its detractors. The United Nations event also provided a focal point for criticisms of the global war on drugs (Wiener, 1999, p. 783). Since global efforts closely mirror the United States war on drugs, so do the international policy arguments that surround it. The focus on demand reduction was welcomed by critics, but they questioned the depth of the international commitment to its implementation. Sharper criticism was directed to the continued focus on law enforcement and criminalization as the appropriate paradigm to address the problem. The positions and counter-positions on the so-called war on drugs are now well-established parts of the political landscape. The continuing tension underlying these debates is suggestive of the still unresolved policy questions in the international fight against addictive substances.

International Organizations and the Infrastructure of Drug Control

Drug control illustrates both the potential and limitations of international law. Hard and soft law provides nations with tools to pursue national and international objectives, but there is no guarantee that these efforts will be successful. There are many challenges to effective cooperation. What distinguishes international law from national law, with narrow exceptions, is the absence of coercive enforcement mechanisms. When people break domestic laws, they confront the coercive arm of the state – fines and imprisonment. This is not true for international law. What is the meaning of "law" in the absence of mechanisms for its enforcement? This is an endemic paradox in international law. But coercion is not the only instrument available to facilitate compliance. Coercion is neither necessary nor sufficient. Indeed, the failings of the American war of drugs, where criminalization and imprisonment are central components, suggest the limitations of coercion as a policy strategy in the drug control arena.

In the international realm, cooperation must typically be obtained in the absence of physical coercion. Consequently, the creation of frameworks capable of facilitating effective forms of cooperation between self-interested states lies at the heart of constructing effective international regimes. This can be done through positive incentives, threats of political retaliation and the selection of policy objectives that are perceived to yield benefits to all participants. Cooperation can also be facilitated through effective governance structures which, in turn, may necessitate elaborate administrative and bureaucratic infrastructures.

Cooperative frameworks can be of a formal or informal nature. International institutions themselves (the United Nations or the World Health Organization) can be viewed as formal institutional mechanisms to extend the scope of effective cooperation between nation states. Over the years, an elaborate array of bureaucratic structures has emerged to assist the implementation of the international drug enforcement regime.

The United Nations' Economic and Social Council is ultimately responsible for the United Nations' drug-related activities. Three entities under the Economic and Social Council are charged with the policy and operational details under the three drug control conventions:

- Commission on Narcotic Drugs (CND);
- International Narcotic Control Board (INCB);
- United Nations Office on Drugs and Crime (UNODC).

Established by the Economic and Social Council in 1946, the CND is the central policymaking body of the United Nations in drug-related matters (United Nations Office on Drugs and Crime, 2008a). The Commission is charged with analyzing the world drug situation and developing proposals to strengthen the international drug control system. The UN General Assembly expanded the CND's mandate in 1991 and 1998 to be the governing body for the newly created Fund of the United Nations International Drug Control Programme (UNDCP) and the United Nations Office on Drugs and Crime (UNODC). CND is also responsible, based on the substantive recommendations of the World Health Organization, for deciding to place, remove or transfer narcotics and psychotropic substances on the various schedules created by the 1961 and 1971 conventions. In 1999, CND was internally reorganized to better address its dual mission. The reorganization created a normative component focusing on CND's policy role and an operational component, focusing on CND's role as the governing body of UNDCP.

The International Narcotics Control Board (INCB) is an independent, quasijudicial monitoring body charged with implementing the drug control conventions (INCB, 2008). The INCB is responsible for ensuring operational compliance with the treaty regime. In this capacity, it works closely with individual nation states. The INCB seeks to identify weaknesses in national licensing and regulatory programs for controlled substances, and to assist states in making changes and improvements. Its quasi-judicial function is connected with this monitoring and consultation. If the INCB believes that a nation is out of compliance with convention obligations, it can ask for an explanation and if the explanation is not satisfactory, request remedial efforts. If these efforts are not successful, the INCB can bring the matter to the attention of the CND and the UN Economic and Social Council. In the end, however, the INCB acknowledges that its ultimate success rests in finding ways to work constructively with nation states, improving their commitment and ability to maintain compliance with their treaty commitments.

The drug control conventions have numerous reporting requirements for their signatories. The INCB receives, evaluates and processes this information for the UN Economic and Social Council in the form of an annual report (International Narcotic Control Board, 2007). The report assesses the state of drug enforcement and treaty compliance in various parts of the world. It also seeks to identify problems and trends, and recommend appropriate strategies and countermeasures.

One of the strongest incentives for countries to comply with their international obligations, however, lies outside of the UN system. Like the INCB, the United States also assesses national compliance with international drug control efforts. Unlike the INCB, when the United States deems a country to be out of compliance it triggers direct economic and political consequences (Raustiala, 1999, p. 110). This provides a powerful inducement for countries to work constructively with the INCB that is not found in many other areas of United Nations activities. A nation faces potentially far graver consequences if it is out of compliance with its drug control obligations than if it is out of compliance, for example, with its human rights obligations.

The United Nations Office for Drugs and Crimes (UNODC) was established in 1997 (United Nations Office on Drugs and Crime, 2008b). The UNODC seeks to integrate the international fights against drugs, crime and terrorism. The UNODC, in conjunction with the CND and the INCB, works to ensure implementation and compliance with the treaty-based drug control regime. Its work, however, goes substantially beyond the express mandates of the drug control conventions. The UNODC faces many difficult challenges. How does it implement its law enforcement objectives within often dysfunctional nation-state systems? In attempting to create an effective cooperative regime for drug control, UNODC increasingly employs soft law tools in service of its hard law mandate. Institutional economics teaches that political and bureaucratic institutions are critical to the effective implementation of law. Sound policy cannot be pursued without sound institutions. UNODC is paying greater attention to governance, corruption and rule of law concerns as part of its mandate. UNODC also acknowledges that demand-side efforts are relevant to its law enforcement mission. For example, UNODC has developed a Treatment and Rehabilitation Toolkit intended to identify and outline best practices in the area. It has also prepared a number of papers and reports, such as *Drug Abuse Treatment and Rehabilitation: A Practical Planning and Implementation Guide* (2003), examining these problems. While UNODC acknowledges a role for demand-side reduction, its primary focus remains on the supply-side and the tools of law enforcement.

Addiction: The Perspective of Public Health

World Health Organization: Hard Law Foundations and Actions

Established in 1948, the World Health Organization (WHO) is the leading international organization charged with addressing health-related issues. The WHO is a specialized agency of the United Nations, with its own constitution and budget. The WHO's mission is to advance international health, broadly defined as: "a state of complete physical, mental and social well-being and not merely the absence of disease or infirmity" (WHO, 2006a). It has historically struggled with a mandate that mixes the distinct functional attributes of scientific and technical expertise with a policymaking role that is unavoidably normative.

The WHO is directly involved with certain aspects of the international drug control regime. In its capacity as the international technical expert on science and medicine, the WHO's Expert Committee on Drug Dependence plays an important role in advising the Commission on Narcotic Drugs (CND) in placing, removing or transferring substances on the regulatory schedules of the 1961 and 1971 conventions. This is one of the organization's few express hard law obligations. "The evaluation of substances by this committee is one of the few tasks of the WHO, if not the only one, based on international treaties" (WHO, 2006b, p. 1).

The WHO's constitution gives the organization substantial lawmaking authority. Article 19 gives the WHO the power to sponsor health-related treaties that can then be put forward for individual national ratification (WHO, 2006a). Article 21 gives the WHO unique regulatory authority within a specified range of areas (WHO, 2006a). Unlike treaties that require individual state ratification before they become effective, a WHO regulation will be binding on member states, unless that state specifically opts out. This power was radical in 1948 when the WHO constitution was adopted, and marked an important move away from the traditional model of international law.

Ironically, the WHO has seldom exercised its hard law authority. Outside the domain of scientific nomenclature (the technical side of its mandate), the WHO has only used its regulatory authority on two occasions, with more than half a century separating each episode. Both regulations concerned the control of infectious diseases. In 1951, the WHO adopted the International Health Regulations (IHR) dealing with the historic scourges of small pox, plague, yellow fever, cholera and relapsing fever. Like the 1961 Single Convention on Narcotic Drugs, the original IHR was an effort to synthesize a century's worth of *ad hoc* international efforts at disease control. Having its basis firmly in the past, rather than the future, the IHR was a dead letter even on adoption. The IHR was completely unprepared to deal with the re-emergence of infectious diseases such as AIDS, SARS and the avian flu virus. As such, the IHR was completely revised and updated in 2005, constituting the second and last exercise of the WHO's regulatory authority (WHO, 2008a). The WHO's treaty-making power has been even more dormant. The WHO's only exercise of its treaty-making authority was the adoption of the Framework Convention on Tobacco Control (2003), targeting not drugs, but the addictive substance of tobacco. The convention commits signing countries to implement a comprehensive legislative agenda of tobacco control policies, ranging from excise taxes to education campaigns and restrictions on advertising. The implications of this convention will be discussed later.

The neglect of its hard lawmaking authority – treaties and regulations – is not a complete abdication by the WHO of its responsibilities, but rather a suggestion that the WHO has historically chosen to act through soft rather than hard law instrumentality. There are no shortages of WHO reports, studies, resolutions and recommendations. Among public health professionals, education, counseling and consensus building have a long tradition. While sanctions, penalties and coercion also play a role in public health, the WHO has historically been more comfortable in the soft law domain of international law.

World Health Organization: Soft Law Approach to the Problems of Substance Abuse

Some generalizations concerning drugs are easy. In the traditional hard law domain of nation state diplomacy, drug control efforts focus primarily on the supply-side with an emphasis on criminalization and stricter law enforcement.

This is the view of the police officer. Physicians and social workers view the problem of illicit drugs differently. Their focus is on the demand-side, with a more expressed recognition of the social and medical dimensions of the problem. Not surprisingly, the WHO adopts the later perspective. For the WHO, addiction is primarily a public health problem.

In the past, the WHO maintained separate departments of Substance Abuse and Mental Health. In 2000, these departments were merged to form the Department of Mental Health and Substance Abuse. The mission of the newly-merged department is to: "[r]educe the burden associated with mental, neurological and substance use disorders and to promote mental health worldwide" (WHO, 2008b). The WHO approaches the problem of substance abuse from the perspective of mental health and treatment, not law enforcement. The WHO describes the department's broad range of activities relating to substance abuse:

> The Management of Substance Abuse Team is concerned with the management of problems related to the use of all psychoactive substances. It emphasizes the development, testing and evaluation of costeffective interventions for substance use disorders as well as the generation, compilation and dissemination of scientific information on substance use and dependence, their health and social consequences. It supports countries in advocacy and capacity building for the prevention and management of substance use disorders in all vulnerable groups. It seeks an integrated approach to all substance use problems within the healthcare system, in particular primary care.
>
> (WHO, 2008c)

In the realm of soft law, the focus often shifts from nations to networks. The WHO Management of Substance Abuse Team can be seen as a hub in an international network of scientists, physicians, social workers, activists and policymakers interested in the problem of substance abuse. The relevant tools here are different from those of traditional hard law. Information and knowledge, not punishment and coercion, are the primary sources of power. The self-defined "strategic approach" of the department is revealing in this regard:

- A reliable *information base* on mental health, neurological and substance abuse problems and service systems;
- *Evidence-based technical guidance* on mental health and substance abuse;
- Strengthening *policies* and *systems* for mental, neurological and substance abuse care;
- Strengthening *capacity* on mental health and substance abuse policies and systems to deliver services that are effective, adequate and respect the human rights of affected individuals, and respond to emerging mental health problems such as emergencies and HIV/AIDS (WHO, 2008b).

Core functions of the Substance Abuse Team are listed as: (1) partnering with relevant stakeholders; (2) managing information; (3) technical guidance; and (4) policy support (WHO, 2008b). Effective action on these issues entails the formation of effective networks to enable international and domestic action (facilitating complex forms of cooperation).

While the law enforcement perspective as reflected in the UN Office on Drugs and Crime logically links "the problem" of drug control with the problems of organized crime and terrorism, the WHO's public health frame assumes a different logic. The WHO's interest in substance abuse extends beyond the substances regulated by the various drug control conventions. Drug abuse logically links with other addictive substances, such as alcohol and tobacco. One of the WHO's more important undertaking involves the Alcohol, Smoking and Substance Involvement Screening Test (ASSIST) (WHO, 2008d). ASSIST is an eight-item instrument designed to screen for health risks and problems associated with any psychoactive substance. The instrument is designed to be implemented in the clinical healthcare setting and is designed to better address problems of addiction in the context of primary care. The focus is on identification and treatment – not punishment. The frontline workers are doctors and nurses, not policemen.

As a part of a social network, the Department of Mental Health and Substance Abuse starts to cross paths and overlap with other internal WHO divisions, as well as external organizations. For example, the WHO also maintains an Expert Committee on the Problems Related to Alcohol Consumption. As the web extends outward, one finds the WHO TobaccoFree Initiative, WHO Global Alcohol Database, and the WHO Collaborative Project on Identification and Management of Alcohol-related Problems in Primary Health Care. Outside the WHO, one connects with other international organizations as part of the drug control regime previously discussed: the United Nations Office on Drugs and Crime (UNODC); the Commission on Narcotic Drugs (CND); and the International Narcotics Control Board (INCB). One also connects with other UN agencies that have social and economic missions, such as the International Labor Organization (ILO), which runs projects on workplace drug and alcohol abuse prevention, and the United Nations Children's Fund (UNICEF), which works with substance abuse problems as they pertain to children. Finally, one quickly moves beyond international and governmental organizations to a wide array of professional, civic and nongovernmental organizations, as the hard and soft law dimensions of addiction connect with components of civil society at both the domestic and international levels.

WHY IS INTERNATIONAL LAW RELEVANT TO ADDICTION PRACTITIONERS?

This section has at least two objectives. The first is to connect what may appear to be distant topics of international law to the readership of this volume. The second is to suggest ways that members of civil society can and do participate in the formation and implementation of international law – filling in boxes E and F of Table 8.1.

Physicians and Scientists

Nations, Networks and the Recognition of Multiple Communities

Traditional international law defines a frame exclusively consisting of nation states. In this world, concepts of national boundaries and citizenship have primary and profound meaning. While we are all citizens of some country, we simultaneously participate in numerous other overlapping communities. Scientists, in particular, have always identified with an epistemic community of fellow scientists that transcended simple notions of the nation state. The growing networks of nations, international organizations and civil society underscore this reality.

The National Institute on Drug Addiction (NIDA), as part of the National Institute of Health, serves as an illustration. NIDA is part of the United States federal government. Its mission, however, is largely scientific and research-based. In this regard, it shares much in common with the comparable international efforts of the WHO. The scientists who work in both domains serve as natural bridges. Some of these connections assume a formal, institutional nature. For example, NIDA maintains an international program, the mission of which is to foster international research and the exchange of scientific information by researchers around the globe (NIDA, 2008). NIDA sponsors international conferences, collaborative opportunities and research partnerships. Other connections are less formal, consisting of the scientists and physicians working on addiction-related issues and sharing ideas and understandings.

Resources and Information

International law, particularly in its soft law dimensions, provides a range of resources to practitioners working in the field of addiction. The growth of the Internet and the increasing sophistication of the websites of international organizations make these resources readily available. The WHO Substance Abuse Team serves as just one illustration. The WHO breaks down the work of the Substance Abuse Team into: (1) activities; (2) research tools; and (3) publications. Examining some of their activities suggests the breadth and intensity of the WHO's work, as well as the range of resources that are potentially available to domestic practitioners.

Activities

- Public health problems caused by harmful use of alcohol;
- Alcohol epidemiology and monitoring;
- ASSIST Project – Alcohol, Smoking and Substance Involvement Screening Test;
- Treatment of opioid dependence;
- WHO collaborative research project on drug dependence treatment and HIV/AIDS;

- Assessment of prevention and treatment systems for substance use disorders;
- Screening and brief intervention for alcohol problems in primary healthcare – Alcohol Use Disorders Identification Test (AUDIT);
- Gender, alcohol and culture: an international study (GENACIS);
- WHO Drug Injection Study Phase II;
- Alcohol and injuries;
- UNODC/WHO Global Initiative on Primary Prevention of Substance Abuse;
- Amphetamine-type stimulants;
- Indigenous peoples and substance use;
- Special project on street children;
- Volatile solvent use (WHO, 2008e).

A wide range of research tools and publications are available on topics ranging from psychoactive substances to alcohol, epidemiology and assessment, prevention, treatment and vulnerable populations.

Defining Benchmarks

What use are these international resources to local practitioners? The WHO's research is focused on establishing better scientific and epidemiological understandings of addiction, and in identifying best practices in intervention and treatment. To the extent that a growing international consensus emerges in an area where domestic law needs standards and criteria, or to the extent that an international standard might challenge or inform the scope of existing legal and policy benchmarks, international standards are a potential resource for advocating for the creation or redefinition of domestic legal norms.

There is a domestic analog to the "hard law" and "soft law" distinction at the international level. Hard law at the domestic level consists of statutes, administrative regulations and common law standards. Soft law consists of how the gaps in the hard law are filled, particularly as it relates to areas of technical expertise. The technical–scientific competence of lawyers, judges and legislatures is obviously constrained. In legal matters requiring technical expertise, the law often defers to the expertise of those professions with claims to greater knowledge. In these areas, the law is more soft and subject to influence by expert practitioners. To the extent that the expert community is influenced by international factors, there is a ready channel for these resources to be incorporated into domestic legal processes.

Lawyers and Judges

International Law as a Source of Domestic Law

Treaties are hard law, and create binding legal obligations on the part of nation states. When a country ratifies a treaty, it has the force of law. This is true for the purposes of external relations, as well as certain internal legal commitments. The drug control conventions, for example, impose obligations for countries to cooperate among themselves, combating money laundering and facilitating extradition. The conventions also require states to enact legislation in areas that might ordinarily be thought of as purely domestic concerns, such as criminalizing certain drug offenses and licensing the production and sale of controlled substances.

Ordinarily, the United States is hostile to the use of international law as a source of domestic legal obligation. Drug control presents an interesting exception. For more than a century, the United States has championed the cause of international efforts to combat narcotics and other drugs. As the United States domestic war on drugs assumed a stronger law enforcement and criminalization emphasis over time, so has the international drug control regime. Rather than international law being a source of domestic obligation for the United States, it is fair to ask whether the United States domestic policy is not, in fact, the primary source of international law. Given the United States commitment to the war on drugs, it is in its own perceived self-interest to fully comply with its supply-side international drug control obligations and to see that other countries also do so.

The role of international law on the demand-side of the equation is a different matter. There are a number of treaties and conventions that create obligations for their signatories to address demand-side aspects of addiction. The Appendix to the General Declaration on the Guiding Principles of Drug Demand Reduction (1998) lists many of the hard and soft law obligations states have assumed in this regard. Some of the more important provisions are as follows:

- Article 38 of the Single Convention on Narcotic Drugs of 1961, as amended by the 1972 Protocol;
- Article 20 of the Convention on Psychotropic Substances of 1971;
- Article 14 of the United Nations Convention against Illicit Traffic in Narcotic Drugs and Psychotropic Substances of 1988;
- Article 33 of the Convention on the Rights of the Child (United Nations, Declaration on the Guiding Principles of Drug Demand Reduction 1998).

This list suggests some of the difficulties in trying to use international law within the United States to create or enforce legal obligations for the treatment of substance abuse. Most American judges, lawyers and politicians see the American legal system as sufficient unto itself. As a reflection of this American exceptionalism, international law is often viewed as important for everyone else in the world, but not for the United States. For example, the UN declaration lists the International Convention on the Rights of the Child as a source of hard law obligation to protect children against the harm of drugs. But the convention only binds those countries that sign and ratify it. The United States and Somalia are the only two countries in the world that have not ratified the convention. Therefore, the Convention on the Rights of the Child creates no direct legal obligations on the part of the United States. This anti-international sentiment runs deep in the American legal system. Some Supreme Court justices openly disdain consideration of foreign and international legal opinion. Politically, there have been reactionary calls to impeach federal judges who have sought to acknowledge a greater role for international law in United States courts.

Significantly, however, the United States has signed all of the international drug control conventions. These conventions establish lengthy and detailed sets of obligations on the supply-side of the drug control equation. In contrast, demand-side obligations are far fewer in number and substantially less developed in scope (Wiener, 1999). The only provision in the 1961 convention addressing these concerns is Article 38, entitled *Treatment of Drug Addicts*. In its original form, it provided as follows:

1. The parties shall give special attention to the provision of facilities for the medical treatment, care and rehabilitation of drug addicts.
2. If a party has a serious problem of drug addiction and its economic resources permit, it is desirable that it establish adequate facilities for the effective treatment of drug addicts.

No standards or guidelines were adopted. Moreover, none of the key terms, such as "adequate facilities" or "effective treatment" were defined in the convention (Wiener, 1999, p. 767).

The 1971 convention addressed the issue in only slightly greater detail. Article 20, Measures against the Abuse of Psychotropic Substances, provides as follows:

1. The parties shall take all practicable measures for the prevention of abuse of psychotropic substances and for the early identification, treatment, education, aftercare, rehabilitation and social reintegration of the persons involved, and shall coordinate their efforts to these ends.
2. The parties shall as far as possible promote the training of personnel in the treatment, aftercare, rehabilitation and social reintegration of abusers of psychotropic substances.
3. The parties shall assist persons whose work so requires to gain an understanding of the problems of abuse of psychotropic substances and of its prevention, and shall also promote such understanding among the general public if there is a risk that abuse of psychotropic substances will become widespread.

The 1972 protocol amended Article 38 of the 1961 convention to bring it into conformity with the demand-side provision of the 1971 convention. Again, however, no effort was made to define concepts such as early identification, treatment, education, aftercare, rehabilitation and social reintegration. (Recognizing this vacuum, Article 14 of the 1988 convention directs states to consider adopting the policies and recommendations of "the United Nations, specialized agencies of the United Nations such as the World Health Organization and other competent international organizations.")

How might American lawyers use these provisions? There is a basis for action. The 1961 convention, amended by the 1972 protocol and the 1971 convention obligate nations to: "take all practicable measures for the prevention of abuse ... and for the early identification, treatment, education, aftercare, rehabilitation and social reintegration." The 1988 convention directs states to adopt: "appropriate measures aimed at eliminating or reducing illicit demand" for drugs. Still, it is difficult to see how lawyers or advocates could use these provisions either to demonstrate that existing demand-side initiatives in the United States are inadequate, or to force the implementation of new or different demand-side treatments. In contrast to the WHO Framework Convention on Tobacco Control (2003), which outlines a comprehensive domestic legislative agenda for tobacco control, the drug control conventions provide little substantive guidance as to demand-side issues. As a result, these conventions have had little impact on domestic legislation. Ironically, one of the most active domestic uses of international law in this field are efforts to parlay the United States international obligations under the various drug control conventions to oppose state initiatives that would decriminalize substances like marijuana or expand the range of their medical uses (Rasmussen & Benson, 2003). The mainstay of international and domestic efforts remains a strong emphasis on supply-side, not demand-side initiatives.

International Law as a Source for Normative Criteria

While international law is unlikely to be a substantial source of hard law obligations in the field of addiction treatment, it has greater potential as a source of normative criteria and guidance. Both the hard and soft law dimensions of international law provide resources to help frame legal and policy questions and to help shape normative criteria for legal action. In a legal system that is generally hostile to international influences as a source of law, and where the hard law guidance on demand-side issues is so anemic, it may be more strategic to employ international law in a supporting role. Particularly where Article 14 of the 1988 convention calls for states to consider the guidelines and recommendations of the international organizations like the WHO, the stage could be set for demonstrating the relevance of the wide array of WHO soft law initiatives detailed earlier. A similar function could be played by lawyers in shaping forensic testimony. Law is necessarily bounded by the geography of nation states in ways that science is not. There is substantially more flexibility in the legal system when it comes to discretionary aspects of legal questions, or in the law's necessary deference to other sources of professional expertise. A lawyer who is well-versed in the soft law world of the policies and recommendations of the WHO on issues of addiction is in a much better position to envision creative roles for forensic experts.

Social Workers, Community Activists, Policymakers and Sufferers of Addiction

Who speaks on behalf of the sufferers of addiction? How can affected communities better speak on their own behalf? This section moves beyond the staid realm of the courtroom and the formal roles of lawyer and judge and expert witnesses. Does international law have any role to play in advocacy, activism and policy reform in the area of addiction?

Addiction and Human Rights

In the traditional view, international law focuses on the interaction between independent sovereign states. Not surprisingly then, the state's treatment of and the state's obligations towards its own citizens were not traditional subjects of international law. The post-World War II human rights revolution substantially changed this understanding. Human rights are about the entitlements of individuals, not nation states. The express subject of human rights is the nature of the state's obligations towards its citizens. Conversely, in the traditional realm of state-to-state relations, there was little ability for individuals to interject themselves into discussions of international law or to make demands on the international community. Human rights law changed this orientation as well. Individuals matter in the new perspective. The individual has "rights," and, in appropriate circumstances, individuals can assert demands against the state.

Health as a human right, and more specifically mental heath as a human right, affords a useful frame for advocates of those afflicted by addiction. The frame and rhetoric inspired by human rights can be a powerful aid in the cause of policy reform. If substance abuse is fundamentally an issue of mental health and people have a right to mental healthcare, then the proper policy response is treatment, not incarceration. The human rights frame humanizes the sufferers of addiction, while the criminalization frame has a tendency to blame and demonize them. Further, recognizing the significance of the human rights frame might provide new models for action. There are many well-established tools and tactics employed by human rights activists. Those concerned about addiction can examine which of these tools might be helpful in their own campaigns.

One must also be realistic. There are problems and limitations with the human rights frame. As with all international law, the absence of meaningful enforcement mechanisms seriously constrains what can be accomplished in the name of human rights. Its political resonance is much greater than its direct legal resonance. Whether the human rights frame can prove effective depends on the underlying political context. Here, the instincts of the community activist and the politician will be much more instructive than those of the lawyer or physician.

International Advocacy and the Framework Convention on Tobacco Control

Human rights are not the only international tool for activism regarding addictive substances. Tobacco is an addictive substance and a great public health threat. Historically, however, the trade in tobacco has been licit and state-sanctioned, as trade in opium once was, rather than illicit and condemned. Indeed, a multi-billion dollar industry has grown up around tobacco (much as it has around illegal drugs). This industry lobbies mightily for its own interests. The political and economic clout that the tobacco industry can marshal has made it difficult to get tobacco control legislation through national legislatures, particularly in developing countries.

The WHO Framework Convention on Tobacco Control (2003) is an example of the innovative use of international law to address an important public health problem. A traditional international law narrative would focus on the convention as the willful enactment of the member states comprising the World Health Assembly. This narrative is at best only partially correct. The Framework Convention on Tobacco Control is better understood as the product of the concerted effort and advocacy of the public health community. The medical case against smoking is undeniable. The global public health threat of tobacco is real and growing, as the industry tries to expand markets in developing countries. Waging a nation-by-nation legislative campaign would be long, expensive and of questionable effectiveness, given the counter political influence of the tobacco industry. In response to this public health threat, the public health community strategically invoked, for the first time, the treaty-making authority of the WHO. The World Health Assembly draws its membership from national health ministries, not departments of state or treasury. Its membership is a reflection of the broader epistemic community of public health experts. Communities matter. The treaty that the WHO drafted and put forth was substantially stronger from a public health perspective than any treaty that would have been negotiated in a different political forum. The strategy was also significant. It is much harder for a country to reject a single public health treaty with the imprimatur of the World Health Organization than it would be to reject piecemeal antismoking legislation advocated by its own ministry of health. Further, the Framework Convention on Tobacco Control was designed to require adoption without reservations, meaning that the countries must accept it as a take-it-or-leave-it deal. The political equation was carefully crafted to maximize the chances of ratification.

The WHO Framework Convention on Tobacco Control (2003) is an interesting model of how the instrumentality of international law can be brought to bear as a vehicle for advocacy and activism to combat an addictive substance. The question is whether similar political forces could be brought to bear in support of a different public health problem. Problems of substance abuse do not have the same scientific and political consensus as tobacco. The politics of the war on drugs is also substantially different. Consequently, the tools and tactics of the public health community would have to be correspondingly different. Nevertheless, possibilities exist. Law remains a reflection of social choice. If society were to change its attitudes towards problems of addiction, it would necessarily entail different choices and different laws. Attitudes and laws have changed substantially with respect to tobacco. Attitudes may also change with respect to drugs. Opium went from a licit to an illicit commodity. The public health community and other members of civil society are in a position to influence the attitudes that will shape the future of international law in the field of addiction as well. The WHO Framework Convention on Tobacco Control is a case in point.

REFERENCES

Aoyagi, M. T. (2005). Beyond punitive prohibition: liberalizing the dialogue on international drug policy. *N.Y.U. J. Int'l L. & Pol.*, *37*(3), 555–610.

Convention on Psychotropic Substances. (1971). From http://www.unodc.org/pdf/convention_1971_en.pdf

Convention on Transnational Organized Crime. (2000). From http://www.unodc.org/pdf/crime/a_res_55/res5525e.pdf

Fidler, D. P. (2001). The globalization of public health: the first 100 years of international health diplomacy. *Bulletin of the World Health Organization*, *79*(9), 842–849.

International Narcotic Control Board. (2008). *Mandate and Functions*. From http://www.incb.org/incb/mandate.html

International Narcotic Control Board. (2007). *Report of the International Narcotics Control Board for 2007*. From http://www.incb.org/incb/en/annualreport2007.html

Levitsky, M. (2003). Transnational criminal networks and international security. *Syracuse J. Int'l L & Com.*, *30*(2), 227–240.

McCoy, A. W. (2000). From free trade to prohibition: a critical history of the modern Asian opium trade. *Fordham Urb. L. J*, *28*(1), 307–349.

National Institute on Drug Addiction. (2008). *Welcome to the National Institute on Drug Abuse (NIDA) International Program Home Page*. From http://international.drugabuse.gov/index.html

Rasmussen, D. W., & Benson, B. L. (2003). Rationalizing drug policy under federalism. *Fl. St. U. L. Rev*, *30*(4), 679–734.

Raustiala, K. (1999). Law, liberalization and international narcotics trafficking. *N.Y.U. J. Int'l L. & Pol.*, *32*(1), 89–145.

Single Convention on Narcotic Drugs. (1961). (Amended by 1972 protocol). From http://www.unodc.org/pdf/convention_1961_en.pdf

Thomas, C. (2003). Disciplining globalization: international law, illegal trade, and the case of narcotics. *Mich. J. Int'l L.*, *24*(2), 549–575.

UN Convention against Illicit Traffic in Narcotic Drugs and Psychotropic Substances. (1988). From http://www.unodc.org/pdf/convention_1988_en.pdf

United Nations. (1998a). *Political Declaration on Global Drug Control*. From http://www.un.org/ga/20special/poldecla.htm

United Nations. (1998b). *Declaration on the Guiding Principles of Drug Demand Reduction*. From http://www.un.org/ga/20special/demand.htm

United Nations. (1998c). Measures to Enhance International Cooperation to Counter the World Drug Problem. From http://www.un.org/ga/20special/coop.htm

United Nations Office on Drugs and Crime. (2003). *Drug Abuse Treatment and Rehabilitation: A Practical Planning and Implementation Guide*. From http://www.unodc. org/docs/treatment/Guide_E.pdf

United Nations Office on Drugs and Crime. (2008a). *The Commission on Narcotic Drugs: Its Mandate and Functions*. From http://www.unodc.org/unodc/commissions/CND/ 01itsmandateandfunctions.html

United Nations Office on Drugs and Crime. (2008b). *About UNODC*. From http://www.unodc.org/ unodc/en/aboutunodc/index.html

Wiener, T. M. (1999). Drug policy priorities in the wake of the June 1998 drug summit. *Brooklyn J. Int'l L.*, *25*(3), 759–789.

WHO. (2003). *WHO Framework Convention on Tobacco Control*. From http://www.who.int/ tobacco/framework/WHO_FCTC_english.pdf

WHO. (2006a). *Constitution*. From http://www.who.int/governance/eb/who_constitution_en.pdf

WHO. (2006b). *WHO Expert Committee on Drug Dependence*. Thirty-fourth Report. From http:// www.whqlibdoc.who.int/trs/WHO_TRS_942_eng.pdf

WHO. (2008a). *International Health Regulations (2005)*, (2nd ed.). From http://www.who. int/csr/ihr/IHR_2005_en.pdf

WHO. (2008b). *Department of Mental Health and Substance Abuse (MSD)*. From http://www.who. int/nmh/about/msd/en/index.html

WHO. (2008c). *Management of Substance Abuse*. From http://www.who.int/substance_abuse/en/

WHO. (2008d). The ASSIST project – Alcohol, Smoking and Substance Involvement Screening Test. From http://www.who.int/substance_abuse/activities/assist/en/

WHO. (2008e). *Our Activities*. From http://www.who.int/substance_abuse/activities/en/

Chapter 9

Medical Malpractice

Mark Cooney, JD

Thomas M. Cooley Law School, Lansing, MI, USA

OVERVIEW OF MEDICAL MALPRACTICE LAW

The Essential Elements

Medical malpractice refers to a medical professional's negligence in treating or diagnosing a patient (*Trimel v. Lawrence Community Hosp Rehab. Ctr.*, 2001). Patients suing for medical malpractice must therefore prove the elements of an ordinary negligence claim, as modified to reflect the medical context (*Ditch v. Waynesboro Hosp.*, 2007, appeal granted on other grounds; see also *Seeber v. Ebeling*, 2006). The patient must establish "(1) a duty owed by the physician to the patient; (2) a breach of duty from the physician to the patient; (3) that the breach of duty was the proximate cause of, or a substantial factor in, bringing about the harm suffered by the patient; and (4) damages suffered by the patient that were a direct result of that harm" (*Vicari v. Spiegel*, 2007; see also *Perez v. Bakel*, 2007).

The Standard of Care: Duty and Breach

A physician owes "a duty to use reasonable and ordinary care and diligence" in diagnosing and treating his or her patients (*Rios v. Bigler*, 1994, applying Kansas law). The physician must "use his or her best judgment" and "exercise that reasonable degree of learning, skill and experience which is ordinarily possessed by other physicians in the same or similar locations under like circumstances" (*Idem*). As this language reflects, the law only requires what is reasonable and ordinary; it does not require physicians to ensure favorable results or guarantee cures (*Charles F. Broughton, D.M.D., P.C. v. Riehle*, 1987). When the physician's care falls below this standard of reasonableness, the physician has breached his or her duty (*Mills v. Berrios*, 2006). Whether a physician breached his or her duty is ordinarily a question for the jury to decide (*Atkinson v. Scheer*, 1998).

Patients must establish the applicable standard of care and its breach with testimony by a qualified expert, except in those rare cases when the medical negligence and the injury's cause are obvious even to laypersons from their common knowledge and experience (see, e.g., *Bacon v. Mercy Hosp.*, 1988; *Housel v. James*, 2007 (applying Wash. Rev. Code Ann. § 7.70.040(1) (West, 2007)); *Vicari v. Spiegel*, 2007). In some jurisdictions, proposed experts must match very specific statutory qualifications to testify against a physician (see e.g., 18 Del. Code Ann. § 6854 (Matthew Bender, 1999); Mich. Comp. Laws Ann. § 600.2169 (West, 2000)). In jurisdictions without a statutory rule, courts apply their state law version of Federal Rule of Evidence 702, which allows testimony by experts who are qualified by knowledge, skill, experience, training, or education (Fed. R. Ev. *Idem* 702). Chapter 10, "Expert Witness in Civil and Criminal Testimony," addresses in far greater detail the role of experts in medical malpractice cases.

Causation of Damages

Patients suing for medical malpractice must prove that the physician's breach of duty "was the proximate cause of, or a substantial factor in, bringing about the harm suffered by the patient" (*Vicari v. Spiegel*, 2007). "The proximate cause of an event is that act or omission which, in natural and continuing sequence, unbroken by an efficient intervening cause, produces the event, and without which that event would not have occurred" (*Atkinson*, quoting *Beale v. Jones*, 1970). There may be more than one proximate cause of an event (*Idem*).

To satisfy the proximate cause element, patients must actually prove two separate elements: cause in fact and legal cause (*Bergman v. Kelsey*, 2007). The cause in fact element "generally requires showing that 'but for' the defendant's actions, the plaintiff's injury would not have occurred" (*Craig v. Oakwood Hosp.*, 2004). Legal cause, on the other hand, "presents a question of foreseeability," and it is established "if an injury was foreseeable as the type of harm that a reasonable person would expect to see as a likely result of his or her conduct" (*Bergman*).

As with the breach of duty element, in all but the most obvious cases, patients must present expert testimony showing that the physician's breach "was a substantial factor in causing the harm suffered" (*Winschel v. Jain*, 2007). The jury ordinarily decides whether the patient has established proximate cause (*Bergman*).

APPLICATION TO ADDICTION CASES

Standard of Care and Breach

Cases Finding Sufficient Evidence of Negligence

"[D]octors make professional judgments about the relative risks and benefits of a drug – and whether it is appropriate to prescribe it for their patients" (*In re Zyprexa Prod. Liab. Litigation*, 2008). Thus, a physician "has the duty to know the drug that he is prescribing and to properly monitor the patient" (*McKee v. American Home Products, Corp.*, 1989).

A doctor can breach the standard of care by unnecessarily prescribing narcotics. For example, in *Ballenger v. Crowell* (1978), the patient suffered from a chronic neurological disorder. For 14 years, the patient's physician prescribed addictive narcotics for pain relief, including Pantopon and morphine. The patient became addicted 2 years into his treatment, and, some 12 years later, left his physician's care and voluntarily entered a hospital for treatment of his addiction. The patient's expert testified that the physician's continued prescription of addictive narcotics was "not normal and was not recommended" (*Idem* at 291). Nevertheless, the trial court dismissed the case on motion, finding that there was no proof of negligence warranting a trial on the merits.

The North Carolina Court of Appeals reversed, holding that there was sufficient evidence of negligence to let the question go to the jury (*Idem*). The court reasoned that there was evidence tending "to show that standard medical practice no longer considered addiction necessary" to treat the patient's disease and that the physician "should have known more care was required than the mere writing of ever-increasing prescriptions" (*Idem*).

A similar federal decision found that a physician was negligent in continuously prescribing multiple pain medications to a known addict. In *Osborne v. United States* (2001), the physician treated the patient for 17 years, initially for back pain. The patient's chart from a previous hospitalization noted his addiction to a narcotic pain medication, Demerol (*Idem* at 481–482). The physician nevertheless prescribed various addictive pain medications, including Valium and Tylenol #4 (*Idem* at 482). This pattern continued for years, with the physician giving the patient routine prescriptions for Valium, Percocet and Percodan, despite noting the patient's drug and alcohol abuse (*Idem* at 482). Not even the patient's imprisonment for selling cocaine stopped this pattern. On the patient's release from prison, the physician resumed prescribing various addictive pain medications for years, often simultaneously (*Idem* at 483–484). While under the influence of two of these medications, Butalbital and codeine, the patient caused a fatal car accident. In addition to suing the patient, the accident victims sued the physician, alleging that his negligent prescription of multiple addictive medications was a cause of the accident (*Idem* at 480–481).

After hearing expert testimony indicating that the physician's "medication regimen would be inappropriate treatment for chronic pain over a protracted period" (*Idem* at 491), the court held that the physician's persistent prescription of "addictive medications over a period of several years to a known drug and alcohol abuser … fell below the appropriate standard of medical care and treatment" (*Idem* at 493). The court faulted the physician for prescribing these medications "in combination" despite *Physician's Desk Reference* (PDR) warnings that they were addictive and should not be given to drug- or alcohol-addicted patients (*Idem* at 498). The PDR also specifically warned that patients taking those medications should not drive (*Idem*).

A New York appellate court likewise found sufficient proof of negligence where a physician continued to prescribe OxyContin despite indications that the patient had become addicted and was suffering withdrawal symptoms (*Vito v. North Medical Family Physicians, P.C.*, 2005). The court concluded that there was "a rational process by which the jury could have found" that the physician was negligent (*Idem*). Therefore, the trial judge erred in taking the issue from the jury and granting the physician's motion for a directed verdict at the close of the patient's proofs (*Idem*).

These cases reveal that physicians may face liability for giving unending prescriptions of addictive medications to addicted patients or to patients with a known history of addiction. It is also noteworthy that the physicians in these cases, while treating known addicts, prescribed multiple addictive medications simultaneously, no doubt fueling the perception of carelessness.

Cases Finding Insufficient Evidence of Negligence

On the other hand, courts have rejected malpractice claims where patients could not articulate an accepted standard of care for prescribing addictive medications under the circumstances. The cases in this category also involved physicians who recognized actual or potential addiction and took affirmative steps to curtail the patients' use of addictive medications – steps that were often ignored by the patients.

For example, in *Schunk v. United States* (1992), a Vietnam War veteran with a 10-year history of drug and alcohol abuse sought pain treatment at various VA hospitals and clinics. Often the patient demanded pain medication on arrival and became angry when VA doctors refused to prescribe them (*Idem* at 75, 77). The patient also asked VA doctors to prescribe medications that his private physician had prescribed, such as Tylox and Valium, complaining that he couldn't otherwise afford to renew those prescriptions. VA doctors reacted by substituting mild anti-inflammatories and tranquilizers for benzodiazepines or analgesics, and a psychiatric department doctor discussed possible drug dependency with the patient and recommended hospitalization for detoxification (*Idem*). When VA doctors did prescribe Valium, it was a one-month prescription in the same amount that the patient's private doctor had prescribed in the past. VA doctors also gave the patient a 10-day Tylox refill, but only after warning him that the drug could be habit-forming (*Idem*). In the next two months, the VA clinic gave the patient 6-day and 13-day Tylox refills. But the clinic gave him no more drugs the next year, when the patient instead got medications exclusively from his private doctor (*Idem* at 77, 78).

The patient eventually returned to the VA hospital complaining of anxiety, and doctors gave him non-refillable one-month prescriptions for Valium (*Idem* at 78). They advised the patient to cut down his Valium use, and then stopped giving him Valium altogether when the VA adopted a national policy against dispensing Valium on an outpatient basis (*Idem*). VA doctors substituted one-month prescriptions of other benzodiazepines and, after admitting the patient for hallucinations, kept him on the same medication levels he'd been receiving from his private doctors. The VA hospital assigned the patient a psychiatric team and tried to wean him from his addictive medications (*Idem* at 78), but the patient refused inpatient detoxification and stopped treating with the VA hospital. The patient later sued, alleging that the VA hospitals and doctors negligently prescribed him addictive medications (*Idem* at 73, 79).

The court held that the VA doctors' "continued prescriptions, together with recommendations to detoxify, were appropriate" (*Idem* at 83). The court first noted that the patient's expert "failed to identify what the accepted standards of practice were at the time" (*Idem*). But the court found that the applicable standard "was amply demonstrated" by the patient's private physicians, who had for years given the patient one-month prescriptions to Valium and codeine, and had also prescribed other medications "for prolonged periods" (*Idem*). Given this evidence, the court found that the VA doctors' 30-day prescriptions were not "open-ended" or "irresponsible," as alleged (*Idem*).

VA doctors were again exonerated in *Rubin v. United States* (1999), where the court, like the *Schunk* court, emphasized the lack of established pain-management standards in the profession. In *Rubin*, the estate of a longtime VA hospital outpatient who died from a morphine overdose alleged that VA doctors fueled the patient's addiction by refilling his prescriptions too early and by injecting the patient with morphine whenever he requested it (*Idem* at 583). The estate also alleged that VA doctors negligently failed to monitor the patient properly or ensure proper counseling, despite knowing that he was abusing his medications (*Idem*).

After weighing the expert testimony, the court held that the patient's proofs did not establish negligence (*Idem*). The court reasoned that when the VA doctors treated the patient for his "intractable, non-malignant pain" during the early 1990s, there was "no consensus among physicians practicing the art of controlling such pain as to which of several differing sets of standards then being used to do so was the appropriate one" (*Idem* at 598). Even the American Pain Society's 1997 standards acknowledged that there was no "nationally-accepted consensus for the treatment of chronic pain not due to cancer" (*Idem* at 598–599). Moreover, the VA doctors' treatment "substantially complied" with the position statement issued by the West Virginia Board of Medicine three years after the patient's death (*Idem* at 599).

The Ohio Court of Appeals upheld a defense verdict in its *Johnson v. Doctors' Clinic* (1977) opinion, which underscored the patient's failure to cooperate with the physician's efforts to end the patient's addiction. The patient in *Johnson* suffered serious internal injuries in a car accident five years before becoming the physician's patient. In those five years, the patient was repeatedly hospitalized and became dependent on narcotics. While he was under the physician's care, the patient continued to receive "heavy dosages" of narcotic pain medications, including Percodan, on an outpatient basis (*Idem* at *1). The physician explained that the narcotics kept the patient "functional until such time as he could be admitted to recognized drug treatment centers" (*Idem*). The physician hospitalized the patient without narcotics on a number of occasions and later admitted the patient to two drug-treatment centers, only to have the patient withdraw from those centers and return home (*Idem*). The patient also failed to cooperate with the physician's methadone maintenance program and eventually overdosed on Phenabarbital, which the physician had not prescribed (*Idem* at *2).

The patient's estate argued that the verdict for the physician should be reversed because the overwhelming weight of the evidence showed that the physician negligently prescribed excessive amounts of narcotics, causing the patient's addiction and death. The Ohio Court of Appeals rejected this argument, holding that the patient's estate was not entitled to a new trial. The court reasoned that the jury's verdict could not be reversed if it was supported by some reliable and credible evidence, and the court found that there was sufficient evidence (*Idem*).

Effect of Physician's Violation of Statutes or Regulations

Some medical malpractice addiction cases have included allegations that the defendant physician violated codified laws governing the prescription of narcotic drugs. If a patient proves such a violation, the question becomes whether, in a civil malpractice suit, that violation establishes malpractice as a matter of law or is merely evidence of malpractice that the jury may accept or reject.

New Jersey case law intimates that violating administrative regulations governing prescription drugs can constitute negligence as a matter of law. In *Taglieri v. Moss* (2004), the patient began treating with the defendant physician after years of using narcotics for headaches and for postsurgery pain relief. For four years, the physician wrote postdated and undated prescriptions for various schedule II narcotics in heavy doses – including writing prescriptions "three or four days apart, each for quantities of 80 or 120 pills" (*Idem* at 283, 284). This, the patient alleged, violated regulations enacted under New Jersey's Controlled Dangerous Substances Act (*Taglieri*, at 283; N.J. Stat. Ann. § 24:21–1 (West, 1997; Supp. 2008) *et seq.*; see also N.J. Admin. Code § 8:65–7.5(a) and § 8:65–7.9)). The physician admitted knowing that New Jersey law prohibited prescribing refills for narcotic drugs (*Taglieri*, at 284). The patient's expert also testified that the physician's prescriptions far exceeded "the quantity that would be medically supportable," referring to both their amount and frequency (*Idem*).

The trial court found the evidence of malpractice so substantial that it granted the patient's motion for partial summary judgment on the negligence issue. The trial court concluded that the physician's "willful violations of the administrative regulations constituted negligence as a matter of law" (*Idem* at 283). The appellate court affirmed this decision, but stopped short of explicitly stating that proof of statutory or regulatory violations alone establishes a breach of the standard of care (*Idem* at 286). Instead, the appellate court skirted that finer legal question, noting simply that the evidence against the physician was so strong that the trial court's decision was correct: "Whether the violation of these regulations is admissible as evidence of a deviation from the applicable standard of care, or establishes a deviation as a matter of law, the evidence here is so one-sided that partial summary judgment … on the issue of [the physician's] deviation must be affirmed" (*Idem*).

In another opinion placing heavy emphasis on the physician's statutory duties, the Ohio Court of Appeals accepted that proof of statutory violations is evidence of malpractice, but did not state that those violations established negligence *per se*. The court in *Conrad-Hutsell v. Colturi* (2002) observed that under Ohio's statutes and administrative codes, physicians are required to exercise reasonable care in prescribing drugs, including taking into account the potential for abuse or addiction (*Idem* at *2 (citing Ohio Admin. Code § 4731–11–02)). Based on these provisions, the court concluded that the defendant physician "clearly had statutory duties" to the patient when prescribing controlled substances, which required him "to follow certain procedures when utilizing controlled substances" in her treatment (*Idem* at *2, *3). The court found that the evidence showing violations of these provisions, including the physician's failure to refer the patient for drug abuse counseling or rehabilitation, created a jury question (*Idem*). Thus, the trial court erred in granting a directed verdict in the physician's favor.

Relevance of the Physician's Desk Reference, Manufacturer Inserts and Medical Literature

The national cases give mixed signals on whether the *Physician's Desk Reference* (PDR) or medical literature should play a role in determining the standard of care for prescribing addictive medications. The PDR is "an encyclopedia of medications, written and compiled by drug manufacturers, that is published annually" (*Spensieri v. Lasky*, 1999, at 547). It is "a means for drug manufacturers to make physicians aware of possible side-effects of the drug in question," and the information in it "must comply with the FDA's guidelines for the proper labeling of prescription drugs" (*Idem*).

Given its wide use and perceived authoritativeness in the medical profession, some courts have found that a physician's deviation from clear and unambiguous PDR guidelines establishes a *prima facie* case of negligence (*Ohligschlager v. Proctor Comm. Hosp.*, 1973; *Mulder v. Parke Davis & Co.*, 1970, as modified by *Lhotka v. Larsen*, 1976). Likewise, where both physician and patient offer PDR excerpts as exhibits, the court may view this as "essentially a stipulation to use this information," which can establish the physician's duty to warn the patient about the potential side-effects outlined in the PDR (*Stebbins v. Concord Wrigley Drugs*, 1987).

However, the more common view is that PDR or manufacturer warnings, alone, do not establish the standard of care. Instead, the PDR guidelines must be combined with expert testimony to establish malpractice (*Craft v. Peebles*, 1989; *Ramon v. Farr*, 1995; *Morlino v. Medical Ctr.*, 1998). New York, for example, has "reject[ed] the contention that the PDR constitutes *prima facie* evidence of a standard of care" (*Spensieri v. Lasky*, 1999, at 548). Although acknowledging that the PDR "may have some significance in identifying a doctor's standard of care in the administration and use of prescription drugs," the New York Court of Appeals held that it is "not the sole determinant" (*Idem*). Instead, the PDR guidelines must be "analyzed in the context of the medical condition of the patient," and expert testimony "is necessary to interpret whether the drug in question presented an unacceptable risk for the patient" (*Idem*). The court explained that "[d]rug manufacturers compose the information found in the PDR to comport with FDA regulations, to serve advertising needs, to provide necessary information to a doctor and to limit their liability" (*Idem*). Thus, "[t]he purposes behind the PDR render its content ill-suited to serve as *prima facie* evidence of a standard of care" (*Idem*).

Similarly, in a disciplinary case involving a physician charged with improperly prescribing controlled substances, the Ohio Court of Appeals rejected a hearing examiner's heavy reliance on medical journal articles as proof of the standard of care (*Liss v. State Med. Bd. of Ohio*, 1992). The court explained that those articles "at most" reflected the "optimal standard of care," rather than the controlling "minimum standard of care" (*Idem*). The medical board could not "convert these guidelines into affirmative evidence of the minimum standard of care absent some expert testimony" (*Idem* at *5).

A number of cases show that PDR warnings, when coupled with expert testimony, can play a significant role in determining liability. In *Osborn v. United States* (2001), for example, a federal court applying West Virginia law relied on PDR warnings in finding that the defendant physician negligently prescribed addictive medications to a known addict. Describing the PDR as "a commonly accepted reference used by the medical profession and informed laity," the court found that the physician's failure to heed PDR warnings about the drugs' addictive effects and the hazards they posed for patients operating automobiles was proof of the physician's negligence (*Idem* at 498–499). The court also considered expert testimony in reaching its decision.

Effect of Poor Record-Keeping

A number of courts have found that a physician's failure to maintain accurate records of narcotic prescriptions can establish malpractice – or at least support a finding of malpractice when combined with other evidence. In *Vito v. North Medical Family Physicians, P.C.* (2005), New York's Appellate Division reversed a trial court's directed verdict in favor of a physician who allegedly mistreated the patient's lower back injury by, among other things, prescribing excessive amounts of OxyContin (*Idem* at 798). The patient claimed that the physician "failed to keep proper records," which, combined with the allegedly negligent prescription of narcotics, caused the patient's addiction (*Idem*).

The Appellate Division held that the case should have been submitted to the jury, concluding that there was "a rational process by which a jury could have found that [the physician] was negligent ... in failing to keep proper business records and in prescribing and continuing [the patient] on OxyContin" (*Idem*). Even the two dissenting judges did not substantially differ with the majority on this aspect of the case. Although they rejected the notion that poor record-keeping alone could amount to medical negligence, they agreed that evidence of poor record-keeping could, when combined with other evidence, be relevant in showing that the physician was careless in prescribing narcotics: "[T]he expert opinion testimony concerning record-keeping properly would have been considered by the jury in connection with the claim of [the patient] that [the physician] negligently caused him to become addicted to OxyContin" (*Idem* at 799 (Hurlbutt, J.P., and Smith, J., dissenting)).

The Ohio Court of Appeals has also recognized that evidence of faulty record-keeping can support a finding of negligence. Noting that Ohio doctors have a statutory obligation to "complete and maintain accurate medical records" reflecting the date, use and purpose of any controlled substances (Ohio Rev. Code § 3719.06(C) (Matthew Bender, 2005; Supp., 2008); Ohio Admin. Code § 4731–11–02(D)), the court in *Conrad-Hutsell v. Colturi* (2002) found that a physician's failure to date a prescription or to keep a record of another prescription "could have interfered with [the physician's] ability to effectively monitor" the patient's drug use in the manner required by law (at *2, *3). Thus, there was a triable question of fact concerning whether, among other things, the physician was negligent in "fail[ing] to maintain accurate records concerning the amount of and frequency" of the patient's prescriptions (*Idem* at *3).

Causation of Damages

Addiction cases are ripe for defense arguments attacking the plaintiff's proofs on the causation element. This is especially true in cases where the patient has been treated by multiple physicians or has secured drugs from other sources. Below is a discussion of cases finding sufficient proof of causation, as well as cases in which the chain of causation was too tenuous for liability to attach.

Cases Finding Sufficient Evidence of Causation

As mentioned previously, to prove causation a patient must show that his or her injuries were foreseeable to the treating physician (legal cause) and in fact resulted from the physician's negligence (cause in fact). These causation elements are satisfied in addiction cases where a patient proves that the physician's negligence in prescribing addictive medications caused the patient's addiction, and that the patient's addiction was foreseeable. This is illustrated by cases like *Vito v. North Medical Family Physicians, P.C.* (2005), where the court found sufficient evidence that the physician's negligence in continually prescribing OxyContin without keeping proper records caused the patient's addiction and later withdrawal (*Idem* at 798).

The foreseeable harm resulting from the negligent prescription of addictive medications is not necessarily limited to harm suffered by the patient. The causal nexus between negligence and injury may still exist when the harm is suffered by third persons outside the physician–patient relationship.

In *Osborne v. United States* (2001), for instance, the harm was suffered by innocent motorists who fell victim to an addicted patient's decision to drive while under the influence of drugs prescribed by his physician. In *Osborne*, the defendant physician prescribed multiple addictive pain medications, often simultaneously, for years despite knowing that the patient was addicted to them and that the patient mixed them with alcohol. While under the influence of two of these medications, Butalbital and codeine, the patient caused a fatal car accident, driving head-on into oncoming traffic. The physician had prescribed these medications "in combination," despite PDR warnings that they were addictive and should not be given to drug- or alcohol-addicted patients (*Idem* at 498). The PDR also specifically warned that patients using these medications should not drive (*Idem*). The accident victims sued the physician, alleging that his negligent prescription of multiple addictive medications was one of the accident's causes (*Idem* at 480–481).

The court agreed, concluding that the physician's "negligence was a proximate cause of the accident" (*Idem* at 499). It observed that the patient was "dangerous to himself and the public" while under the influence of the medications (*Idem*), and that the physician knew that the patient was taking the medications in amounts that would "severely impair his ability to function" (*Idem*). Given the patient's past disregard for medical warnings and instructions, it was foreseeable to the physician that the patient would operate a motor vehicle while under the influence of the medications, as was the case on the day of the fatal accident (*Idem*). Therefore, the physician's negligence was a proximate cause of the accident victims' injuries.

Cases Finding Insufficient Evidence of Causation

However, a significant body of case law reveals that addicted patients face formidable legal obstacles in satisfying the causation element. A notable example is *Posner v. Walker* (2006), where the Florida Court of Appeals overturned a multi-million-dollar verdict in the patient's favor because there was no proof that the defendant physician's alleged negligence, more likely than not, caused the patient's fatal overdose. In *Posner*, the patient suffered a series of injuries over a four-year span, resulting in a pinched nerve and severe pain in her lower back and leg. The physician, an orthopedic surgeon, treated the patient off-and-on for six years, including prescribing intravenous pain medications, prescription-strength Tylenol and Percocet. Eventually, the physician assembled a pain-management medical team that included an addictionologist.

The physician also instructed the patient to obtain medication only from him. Nevertheless, without her physician's knowledge, the patient began seeing another doctor, who prescribed various injectable drugs and gave the patient a syringe. A few days before the patient's death, the defendant physician gave the patient a prescription for MS Contin pills for her ongoing pain, unaware that three days earlier the patient's "secret" doctor had prescribed injectable morphine, Valium and Percocet (*Idem* at 663). The patient died in her sleep of a "combined overdose" (*Idem* at 664).

The court held that the jury's verdict in the patient's favor could not stand "due to the [patient's] failure to establish a causal link" between the physician's alleged negligence and the patient's death (*Idem* at 665). The court reasoned, for example, that there was no proof that a so-called "exit strategy" to wean the patient off the medications would have, more likely than not, prevented the patient's continued addiction and death (*Idem* at 666). Likewise, the estate could not show that the physician's continued prescription of addictive medications caused the patient's death, because the physician did not provide the medications that killed the patient; the fatal medications came from a different doctor (*Idem*). There was also no evidence showing what the patient or the patient's family would have done had the physician encouraged more family involvement in the patient's treatment. In fact, the evidence tended to show that the patient was a very private person, especially concerning her medical care (*Idem*).

Posner is one of a number of cases showing how precarious a plaintiff's causation argument is when there is evidence that the patient sought and received addictive medications from multiple physicians. *Schunk v. United States* (1992) is another example. In that case, a longtime drug abuser sought and received addictive pain medications from multiple VA hospitals, as well as private physicians. For instance, when the patient arrived at a VA hospital suffering from hallucinations after a lengthy treatment history with codeine-based medications, he was admitted and maintained on the same medication levels he'd been receiving from his private doctors (*Idem* at 78). When VA doctors created a formal treatment plan that included efforts to wean the patient from his addictive medications, the patient refused inpatient detoxification and ceased all treatment with the VA hospital. While continuing to take codeine-based medications obtained from other sources, the patient sued, alleging that the VA hospitals negligently prescribed him addictive medications (*Idem* at 73, 79).

The court held that the patient "failed to prove that the VA's treatment caused or perpetuated his dependency upon medication" (*Idem* at 83). The court emphasized that after leaving the VA's care, the patient took the same medications for years while under his private doctors' care, and the patient "never sought detoxification" (*Idem*). In fact, whenever the VA stopped the patient's Valium or Tylox supply, he "simply obtained the drugs from private physicians" (*Idem*). Thus, the court found "no reason to think" that the patient would have stopped using those medications if the VA had stopped prescribing them earlier (*Idem*). Moreover, the patient had a history of refusing his doctors' advice, and "no matter what the VA did or did not do, this [patient] would have sabotaged the [VA] doctors' efforts" (*Idem*). Given this evidence, the court concluded that the VA's alleged negligence "was not a substantial factor in causing or perpetuating" the patient's addictions (*Idem*).

Sometimes the inability to establish causation can be traced to more technical evidentiary shortcomings, such as the patient's failure to provide necessary expert testimony. For example, the court in *Rubin v. United States* (1999) held that the estate of a longtime VA outpatient could not establish that the patient's death from "probable morphine intoxication" was caused by the VA doctors' alleged negligence in providing morphine too liberally (*Idem* at 599). The court reasoned that although the estate's expert testified that the VA doctors were negligent, he offered no opinion on whether their negligence caused the patient's death (*Idem* at 586, 599). Instead of offering an opinion on causation, the expert, who was not a toxicologist, deferred to the state medical examiner's toxicology report. The court found the report insufficient to establish a causal connection, however, because the toxicologist who wrote it never stated that his findings were made "with reasonable medical or toxicological certainty or probability" (*Idem* at 599).

Similarly, in *Stebbins v. Concord Wrigley Drugs* (1987), evidence that the PDR warned of Tofranil's "potential" side-effects was insufficient to prove that the patient's use of the drug at bedtime caused a car accident the next morning (*Idem* at 385).

Experts

As many of the cases discussed above show, the rules concerning expert testimony almost invariably influence a court's analysis of the duty, breach and causation issues. This chapter acknowledges those rules only to the extent necessary to outline certain legal principles or to explain a court's decision and reasoning. For a full treatment of the relevant rules concerning experts refer to Chapter 10.

INFORMED CONSENT

The doctrine of informed consent "imposes on a physician, before he subjects his patient to medical treatment, the duty to explain the procedure to the patient and to warn him of any material risks or dangers inherent in or collateral to the therapy, so as to enable the patient to make an intelligent and informed choice about whether or not to undergo such treatment" (*Sard v. Hardy*, 1977). This duty requires physicians to reveal to patients "the nature of the ailment, the nature of the proposed treatment, the probability of success of the contemplated therapy and its alternatives, and the risk of unfortunate consequences associated with such treatment" (*Idem*). For a patient's consent to be effective, "it must have been an 'informed' consent, one that is given after the patient has received a fair and reasonable explanation of the contemplated treatment or procedure" (*Idem* at 1019).

The informed consent doctrine "follows logically from the universally-recognized rule that a physician, treating a mentally competent adult under non-emergency circumstances, cannot properly undertake to perform surgery or administer other therapy without the prior consent of his patient" (*Idem*, citing *Mohr v. Williams*, 1905). The doctrine reflects that patients have the "right to exercise control" over their own bodies (*Idem*).

Absent informed consent, "the treating physician is considered to have committed a technical battery" (*Kaskie v. Wright*, 1991). But the majority view is that a medical malpractice claim based on the lack of informed consent should be treated as a tort claim for negligence rather than a claim for assault or battery (see *Molé v. Jutton*, 2004, and cases cited there). Some states have even enacted statutes barring malpractice suits alleging assault and battery (Ariz. Rev. Stat. Ann. § 12–562 (West, 2003; Supp. 2008)).

Lack of informed consent is an accepted common-law theory for malpractice in many jurisdictions (see discussion in *Duncan v. Scottsdale Med. Imaging, Ltd.*, 2003). In some states, informed consent claims are governed by statute (see, e.g., N.C. Gen. Stat. Ann. § 90–21.13 (Matthew Bender, 2007); Tenn. Code Ann. § 29–26–118 (Lexis, 2000)). Georgia's statute, for example, recognizes that the lack of informed consent can give rise to a medical malpractice claim, but "shall not constitute a separate cause of action" (Ga. Code Ann. § 31–9–6.1(d) (Lexis, 2006)). Some states have statutes requiring physicians prescribing controlled substances to keep "evidence of informed consent" in the patient's chart (see, e.g., N.J. Admin. Code § 13.35–7.6(g)(4)).

The "learned intermediary" defense available to prescription drug manufacturers in product liability cases underscores the physician's obligation to inform patients of the adverse side-effects posed by prescription drugs. "The doctor, functioning as a learned intermediary between the prescription drug manufacturer and the patient, decides which available drug best fits the patient's needs and chooses which facts from the various warnings should be conveyed to the patient, and the extent of disclosure is a matter of medical judgment" (*Kirk v. Michael Reese Hosp. & Med. Ctr.*, 1987). Thus, as for tort liability, drug manufacturers are absolved of any duty to warn the patient of these side-effects, that duty resting squarely on the prescribing physician's shoulders (*Idem*).

A patient alleging that his or her physician failed to disclose a risk of treatment must prove that there was a material risk unknown to the patient, that the physician failed to disclose that risk, and that disclosure of the risk would have led a reasonable person in the patient's position to reject the treatment (*Tompkins v. Bryan*, 2008). Evidence that the physician failed to warn of possible addiction and that the patient became addicted creates a jury-submissible question on the informed consent issue (see *Mueller v. Mueller*, 1974).

Expert testimony is usually necessary to establish the scope of disclosure required of a reasonable physician under the circumstances (*Hill v. Squibb & Sons, E.R.*, 1979). Expert testimony on whether a physician obtained the patient's informed consent to treatment with narcotics is relevant and admissible in addiction cases, sometimes even if the expert witness does not share the same area of specialization as the defendant physician (see *Conrad-Hutsell v. Colturi*, 2002, at *6).

Although the lack of informed consent is most commonly seen as a patient's substantive theory of recovery, courts may also consider informed consent when deciding whether certain defenses are viable. For example, in *Aquino v. United States* (2005), the defendant psychiatrist argued that the patient assumed the risk of addiction to Vicodin and Valium by accepting the psychiatrist's prescriptions. The court rejected this argument, citing expert testimony that the psychiatrist prescribed those drugs without first obtaining the patient's informed consent (*Idem* at *5). The court specifically rejected the psychiatrist's argument that patients with a history of addiction are responsible for declining prescriptions to addictive medications (*Idem*). There was no evidence showing that the psychiatrist warned the patient that he could become addicted to these medications, or that the patient knew they were addictive (*Idem*). Moreover, the patient's expert testified that the onus is on doctors – not patients – to recognize which patients are prone to addiction (*Idem*).

There is another noteworthy twist on the informed consent issue as it relates to addiction. Courts have occasionally been called on to consider whether a physician's duty to disclose material risks includes a duty to disclose the *physician's* addiction to drugs or alcohol. The Georgia Supreme Court declined to impose such a duty in *Albany Urology Clinic, P.C., v. Cleveland* (2000). In that case, the patient sued for fraud and battery, alleging that he would not have consented to surgery had he known that his urologist used illegal drugs while off work and when not on call. Although the court found the urologist's behavior "reprehensible," it nevertheless held that "absent inquiry by a patient or client, there is neither a common law nor a statutory duty on the part of either physicians or other professionals to disclose to their patients or clients unspecified life factors which might be subjectively considered to adversely affect the professional's performance" (*Idem* at 778). The court added that its holding did not deprive the patient of a remedy given his ability to recover under a traditional medical malpractice theory (*Idem* at 780).

A Pennsylvania court reached the same conclusion in *Kaskie v. Wright* (1991), where a minor patient's parents sued a surgeon, in part, for failing to disclose before surgery that he was an alcoholic who had lost his license to practice medicine in that state (*Idem* at 214). The court rejected that claim as a matter of law, refusing to "expand the informed consent doctrine to include matters not specifically germane to surgical or operative treatment" (*Idem* at 217).

DEFENSES

Comparative Negligence

Overview

Historically, a plaintiff who was partially at fault for his or her own injuries was completely barred from recovering damages (65 C.J.S. *Negligence* §§ 292–93 (2000)). But most jurisdictions abandoned this "contributory negligence" rule, which many felt was unfairly harsh in cases where the plaintiff's culpability was small (*Idem*). Most jurisdictions replaced their longstanding contributory negligence rule with a "comparative negligence" rule.

Like contributory negligence, comparative negligence refers to a plaintiff's own fault, meaning the plaintiff's failure to exercise reasonable care to protect his or her own safety (*Idem* at § 291). Under the typical common-law comparative negligence model, a tort plaintiff who shares some fault may still recover damages, but that recovery is reduced by an amount corresponding to the plaintiff's own percentage of fault (*Idem*). Thus, the doctrine allows culpable defendants to reduce, but not eliminate, their payment obligation if they can prove that the plaintiff was partially at fault (*Idem*).

Many states have modified this comparative negligence rule in one way or another through legislation. For instance, in some states plaintiffs who are more than 50% at fault are barred from recovering noneconomic damages (such as damages for pain and suffering), but they may still recover a reduced percentage of economic damages (such as loss of wages) (see, e.g., Mich. Comp. Laws Ann. § 600.2959 (West, 2000)). Under some comparative fault statutes, a certain level of fault, or fault attributed to certain conduct (like intoxication) can be a complete bar to recovery (see e.g., Mich. Comp. Laws Ann. § 600.2955a (West, 2000); Neb. Rev. Stat. § 25–21,185.09 (1995)). These statutes mark a middle ground of sorts between the old contributory negligence rule, which acted as a complete bar, and a pure comparative negligence rule, which would allow recovery – albeit a small one – by a plaintiff who was 99% at fault.

Application to Malpractice Addiction Cases

In whatever form, the comparative negligence defense has long been a part of medical malpractice jurisprudence. Perhaps its most common incarnation in the medical malpractice context concerns patients' alleged negligence for failing to follow their doctors' instructions during or after treatment (see Kemper, 2000).

However, the doctrine poses some potential challenges for courts and attorneys in medical malpractice cases concerning addiction. This is because the very essence of addiction is the patient's psychological or physiological inability to avoid the hazardous conduct causing the harm: excessive drug use. A patient who has proven all the elements of a medical malpractice claim in the addiction context has, by definition, proven that the physician's negligent treatment caused or exacerbated the patient's inability to avoid the dangerous behavior at issue.

Courts considering the comparative negligence question in addiction cases are thus trying to reconcile settled legal principles requiring plaintiff accountability with the practical reality that drug addiction is inherently characterized by seemingly irrational and self-destructive behavior.

In a number of early addiction cases applying the old contributory negligence rule, courts were sensitive to the nature of addiction and refused to find fault with patients who followed their doctors' orders to take addictive drugs. For instance, in *Ballenger v. Crowell* (1978), the North Carolina Court of Appeals, citing cases from various jurisdictions, emphasized that "a patient is to be permitted to rely on his doctor without becoming a culpable partner of what turns out to be his doctor's negligence" (*Idem* at 291; see also *King v. Solomon*, 1948; *Los Alamos Med. Ctr., Inc. v. Coe*, 1954). "The fact that the patient becomes addicted, continues in the doctor's care and knowingly continues his addiction will not make him contributorily negligent unless he himself is doing something wrong or unless he knows his doctor is negligent" (*Ballenger*, at 291).

Applying these principles to the facts at hand, the *Ballenger* court declared that the patient could not be found guilty of contributory negligence for behaving like an addict after his trusted doctor prescribed addictive drugs and told the patient that addiction was necessary to the patient's treatment:

> In the case *sub judice*, [the patient] believed that he had to be addicted for the rest of his life because [his physician] had told him so. That once he became an addict he began to behave like one, and wheedled prescriptions, is not surprising, and does not make him contributorily negligent (*Idem*).

A New Mexico court presiding over a pharmacist malpractice case also questioned whether an addict's behavior could support a finding of contributory negligence. The court stated that if the patient was "deprived of her willpower and was so addicted to the use of the medication that she could not control her conduct, there would be a real question of whether her acts thereafter could be classed as contributory negligence" (*Johnson v. Primm*, 1964). The court added that when the jury considered the patient's conduct, her conduct was "not to be judged by the same standards as would apply to an ordinary or average adult" (*Idem* at 430).

It is possible that the strident protection offered to addicted patients in *Ballenger* and its contemporaries owes something to the fact that those were cases from the contributory negligence era, and therefore the patients' claims would have been barred completely had the courts held that the patients shared even a small percentage of fault. However, concerns over completely barring an addicted patient's recovery have also arisen in more recent cases. For instance, in the 2006 case *Messinger v. Forsman* (2006), the Nebraska Court of Appeals reversed a defense verdict, holding that the patient was prejudiced by the trial judge's failure to instruct the jury under Nebraska's comparative negligence statute, which would have allowed the jury to assess percentages of fault (*Messinger*, at *8). Although the Nebraska statute uses the throwback term "contributory" instead of "comparative," the statute's substantive rules are undoubtedly comparative, in that they do not automatically bar recovery because of a plaintiff's negligence, instead assessing damages on a percentage basis unless the plaintiff's fault exceeds that of the defendants (see *Idem* at *8) ("in short, what used to be contributory negligence has now become comparative negligence, even though § 25–21,185.09 still uses the term 'contributory negligence'"). The lack of this instruction, the court of appeals surmised, had given the jury the impression that proof of the patient's fault completely barred his recovery and compelled a verdict for the physician (*Idem*). Under Nebraska's statute, the patient's recovery would have been completely barred only if the jury decided that his fault exceeded that of his physician.

Notwithstanding *Messinger*'s seemingly patient-friendly tone, the case shows that in the courtroom, addicted patients can indeed be faulted for their conduct even if that conduct is typical of addiction. In *Messinger*, that fault included the patient's alcohol and marijuana abuse while taking the prescribed narcotics, as well as his manipulation of doctors to get prescriptions (*Idem* at *7). The court accepted that this behavior, although bearing the typical hallmarks of addiction, evidenced the patient's failure to follow medical instructions (*Idem*).

Messinger exemplifies the modern approach; despite the nature of addiction, courts will allow juries to consider whether addicted patients were negligent in failing to follow their physician's instructions. Another example is *Stephens v. Draffin* (1997), where the South Carolina Supreme Court affirmed a trial verdict finding the patient 50% at fault for his continued Percocette addiction. The case turned on a finer legal question concerning when the claim accrued, which determined whether the court should apply South Carolina's old contributory negligence rule or its new comparative negligence rule. Nevertheless, the opinion reveals that courts are willing to allow juries to consider whether addicted patients are partially at fault for their condition, especially when there is evidence that the physician warned the patient about continued use of the addictive drug (see *Idem* at 308–309).

The Louisiana Court of Appeals' decision in *Gauthreaux v. Frank* (1998) similarly illustrates that a physician whose malpractice involves the diagnosis or treatment of drug dependency will not necessarily shoulder 100% of the fault. The *Gauthreaux* court affirmed a jury verdict assessing 70% fault to the defendant psychiatrist and 30% fault to the patient. The patient had complained that the psychiatrist misdiagnosed her with Ativan and Xanax dependency. She also alleged that during an unnecessarily prolonged stay at the psychiatrist's clinic, the psychiatrist prescribed multiple medications, including Prozac, which adversely affected her.

The court held that the jury's assessment of 30% fault against the patient was supported by "ample medical testimony and other evidence that [the patient] did not comply with her treating physicians' orders regarding use of medication" (*Idem* at 1000).

The evidence showed, for example, that the patient did not use Xanax and Ativan properly before her admission to the clinic; rejected necessary medications and group therapy while in the clinic; and "resumed taking Xanax and Ativan several months after her discharge, even though it had not been prescribed" (*Idem* at 1000–1001). Because the jury had the benefit of hearing and reviewing a "plethora of medical evidence" and testimony, the court found that the verdict assessing 30% fault to the patient clearly demonstrated the jury's belief that she was "partly at fault for the unsatisfactory treatment she underwent" at the clinic (*Idem* at 1001). The court could not, after reviewing the evidence, "say the jury was clearly wrong" in reaching this decision (*Idem*).

These cases reflect the modern fault-allocation approach that requires juries to consider the conduct of both patient and physician, and to assess fault to one, both, or perhaps neither. Absent some statutory authority to the contrary, courts will likely reject creative arguments by physicians wishing to revisit the days when a patient's fault acted as an automatic and complete bar to the patient's recovery. For instance, a Tennessee court rejected a physician's argument that a patient's conduct while addicted – which included mixing pain medications with alcohol – warranted outright dismissal of the patient's case on "public policy" grounds (*Higgins v. Crecraft*, 1991, at *8). The court observed that although the patient's behavior "may or may not support a defense of contributory negligence," it was up to a jury to decide "the nature and extent of the [patient's] misconduct and its causal relation to the injuries" (*Idem*).

Assumption of Risk

Comparative negligence's close cousin is the "assumption of risk" doctrine. This defense completely bars recovery by a party who was fully aware of the risk posed by another's conduct, yet voluntarily confronted that risk despite this knowledge (see Restatement (Second) of Torts § 496A (1965)). Jurisdictions may differ on the rule's finer points, but often the doctrine is parsed into "primary" and "secondary" assumption of risk, as well as "express" and "implied" assumption of risk.

Primary assumption of risk recognizes nothing more than that under the circumstances, the defendant owed the plaintiff no duty or breached no duty to the plaintiff (57B Am. Jur. 2d *Negligence* § 763 (2004)). Secondary assumption of the risk, on the other hand, arises when the defendant owed a duty to protect the plaintiff from some danger, but the plaintiff intelligently chose to confront the danger, nonetheless (*Idem* at § 764).

Assumption of risk can be express or implied. It is express "when a plaintiff assumes the risk of injury by expressly releasing a defendant from liability for negligent acts," meaning that the plaintiff has consented to exposing himself or herself to the defendant's negligence (*Allen v. Dover Co-Recreational Softball League*, 2002). Implied assumption of risk exists when there is no express consent, but the evidence shows that the plaintiff "knowingly encounter[ed] a risk created by the defendant's negligence" (*Cunningham v. Helping Hands, Inc.*, 2003).

In states that have adopted comparative negligence schemes that allow jurors to assess the parties' percentages of fault, the assumption of risk defense has usually been superseded by or merged with those comparative negligence rules (57B Am. Jur. 2d *Negligence* § 764 (2004)).

An Ohio Court of Appeals decision captures these dynamics in the context of a medical malpractice addiction case. In *Conrad-Hutsel v. Colturi* (2002), a physician prescribed narcotics, including Percocet and Tylenol #3 with Codeine, to a patient with Crohn's disease. The patient began exceeding the instructed dosages and "exhibited classic drug addicted behavior when attempting to acquire additional narcotics" (*Idem* at *4). The trial judge directed a verdict in the physician's favor under the "primary" assumption of risk rule, finding that the patient assumed the risk of addiction by intentionally taking narcotics exceeding the prescribed dosages despite knowing the risk of addiction (*Idem*).

Noting that *primary* assumption of risk hinges on the lack of proof establishing a duty or a breach of duty, the Ohio Court of Appeals reversed. The court of appeals noted that Ohio codified law requires doctors to use reasonable care in prescribing drugs. Those code provisions list factors that doctors must consider before prescribing controlled substances, such as the potential for addiction. There was also evidence from which reasonable minds could conclude that the physician failed to fulfill those requirements and thus "created a risk of addiction." Therefore, the *primary* assumption of risk doctrine did not apply. In reaching this conclusion, the court of appeals forcefully rejected the notion that a patient's knowledge of potential addiction or a patient's addictive behavior could act as an absolute bar to suit:

> Clearly, [the patient] exceeded [her physician's] instructions regarding the amount of narcotics to use … and exhibited classic drug addicted behavior …. We, however, disagree that such behavior by a patient automatically relieves a physician from any duty to monitor the patient for signs of abuse and *ipso facto* relieves a physician from any liability for continuing to prescribe narcotics even though abuse or overuse is suspected. Such a finding is against public policy and renders meaningless a physician's statutory obligations to his patients (*Idem* at *4).

But the court of appeals did not reject *all* assumption of risk defenses. The jury, it concluded, could still find that the patient's claim was barred "on the basis of implied assumption of risk or contributory negligence" (*Idem* at *5). In other words, even though the existence of a duty and evidence of a possible breach made the *primary* assumption of risk doctrine inapplicable, an Ohio jury could still possibly reject the patient's claim based on her conduct, even if the jury found that the physician breached his duty.

In a case with a criminal law twist, a federal court refused to summarily dismiss a malpractice suit based on assumption of risk where there was evidence that the defendant psychiatrist abused his unique position of trust and coerced his addicted patient to participate in an illegal prescription drug distribution scheme (*Aquino v. United States*, 2005, at * 4). The court reasoned that the patient and doctor were not on "equal footing," and therefore the court could not find that the addicted patient's illegal "favors" for his psychiatrist were truly voluntary (*Idem*).

Statute of Limitations

A statute of limitations defense depends on the unique provisions found in each state's statute. States vary somewhat in their malpractice limitation provisions, but a survey of national cases reveals some common timeliness issues that arise in addiction cases. This section will focus on the most common timeliness questions in the addiction context, which often concern when the claim accrued or when the patient should have discovered the claim.

An understanding of the common statutory framework is helpful to this discussion. Most states offer two possible timeframes in which to sue: (1) the general limitations period that begins to run when the claim accrues; and (2) a second, "grace," period that begins to run when the patient discovered or should have discovered the claim. An example of this typical approach is found in Washington's medical malpractice statute of limitations, which allows patients to sue within three years of the physician's negligent act or omission, or within one year of when the patient discovered or reasonably should have discovered that an injury was caused by that act or omission (Wash. Rev. Code § 4.16.350 (West, 2005; Supp. 2008)). (The statute of limitations analysis in all jurisdictions may be further complicated by alternate timeframes in death cases, or by tolling based on a patient's minority or other legal disability. Malpractice suits may also be governed by a statute of repose.)

Many states also recognize a court-made "continued course of treatment" rule that treats an "entire course of continuing negligent treatment as one claim" (*Caughell v. Group Health Coop. of Puget Sound*, 1994). Under the continued course of treatment rule, a malpractice suit based on a continuous course of negligent treatment is timely if the patient can show that the last negligent act or omission occurred within the statutory limitations period – in Washington, for example, if the last negligent act or omission occurred within three years of when the patient filed suit (*Idem* at 905, 907).

The relative flexibility offered by these typical timeliness rules benefits patients who claim that their addiction stemmed from their doctors' unrestrained prescription of addictive medications for extended time periods. The Washington Supreme Court's decision in *Caughell v. Group Health Coop. of Puget Sound* (1994, *Idem* at 907) illustrates this. In *Caughell*, the patient alleged that her physician negligently prescribed Valium and Etrafon to her for over 20 years "without monitoring for physical and psychological side effects," causing her to become addicted (*Idem*). The court declared the patient's suit timely, reasoning that the Valium prescriptions continued until at least

March 1988, which was within three years of the patient's January 1991 complaint (*Idem*). Moreover, even though the physician discontinued Etrafon prescriptions more than three years before suit was filed, the patient convinced the court that the physician's failure to properly monitor her after withdrawing this medication constituted negligence and that this negligence extended to within three years of the patient's suit (*Idem*).

North Carolina courts have taken a very similar approach. In *Ballenger v. Crowell* (1978), the North Carolina Court of Appeals applied a continuing course of treatment rule – with a discovery component – to find that the trial court had improperly dismissed a 1976 suit arising from the prescription of narcotics from 1960 to 1974 (*Idem* at 292). Under this rule, the court explained, the patient's claim did not accrue in 1962, when the patient first became addicted to the drugs. Rather, the claim accrued when the patient–physician relationship ended in 1974, or when the patient "knew or should have known of his injury," whichever occurred earlier (*Idem* at 294). The court found that even though the patient knew of his addiction as early as 1962, he did not necessarily know that his doctor's prescription of narcotics was unnecessary, and thus negligent, until the physician–patient relationship ended (*Idem*). Because there was a factual question concerning when the patient knew or should have known that the narcotic prescription was unnecessary, the court concluded that a jury should have decided the timeliness issue, making summary dismissal inappropriate (*Idem* at 294–295).

The Tennessee Court of Appeals has also applied the continuing treatment rule in the addiction context, emphasizing how difficult it can be to assign a specific discovery date or duration to drug addiction. In *Higgins v. Crecraft* (1991, at *8), the patient sued within one year of his physician's last negligent prescription and within one year of the patient's hospitalization for addiction. The physician argued that the suit was nevertheless untimely because the patient knew he was addicted five or six months earlier. Under Tennessee's statute of limitations, the physician argued, the one-year limitations period began to run from that discovery date (see *Idem* at *3).

After a lengthy discussion of Tennessee's continuing treatment rule, the court held that "because of the peculiar nature of addiction, the question of when the [patient] acquired effective knowledge that he had been tortiously injured is a question of fact for the jury," thus precluding summary dismissal of the patient's case (*Idem* at *7). The court explained that the physician's argument might have been well-founded "[i]f addiction were a sudden, identifiable, one-time trauma, such as a broken leg, or the contraction of an infection" (*Idem* at *4). But, the court explained, "the word addiction is not so finely defined as to support a ruling of law as to its inception, nature or duration" (*Idem*).

Federal courts, however, may be less generous in applying the continuous treatment rule to medical malpractice claims brought under the Federal Tort Claims Act. In *Schunk v. United States* (1992), for example, the court acknowledged that the continuous treatment tolling rule applies to medical malpractice claims brought under the FTCA, but the court refused to apply it where the addicted patient had been treated by two different VA hospitals and multiple doctors within those hospitals (*Idem* at 82). The court believed that the continuous treatment rule only tolls the limitations period when the patient is continuously treated by "the same doctor or hospital" (*Idem* citing *Camire v. United States*, 1976). The court also believed that the defendant physician in *Schunk* would have been prejudiced by the passage of time, noting the unavailability of important medical records that might have supported his defenses (*Idem*).

ACKNOWLEDGMENT

The author wishes to acknowledge and thank Nicole Coroiu for her invaluable help with the research for this chapter.

REFERENCES

Albany Urology Clinic, P.C., v. Cleveland (528 S.E.2d 777 (Ga., 2000)).
Allen v. Dover Co-Recreational Softball League, 807 A.2d 1274, 1281 (N.H., 2002).
Aquino v. United States (2005 WL 1288002 (W.D. Wash. May 27, 2005)).
Atkinson v. Scheer, 508 S.E.2d 68, 71 (Va., 1998).
Bacon v. Mercy Hosp., 756 P.2d 416, 420 (Kan., 1988).
Ballenger v. Crowell (247 S.E.2d 287 (N.C. App., 1978)).
Beale v. Jones, 171 S.E.2d 851, 853 (Va., 1970).
Bergman v. Kelsey, 873 N.E.2d 486, 500 (Ill. App. 1st Dist., 2007).
Camire v. United States, 535 F.2d 749, 750 (2d Cir., 1976).
Caughell v. Group Health Coop. of Puget Sound, 876 P.2d 898, 905 (Wash., 1994).
Charles F. Broughton, D.M.D., P.C. v. Riehle, 512 N.E.2d 1133, 1137 (Ind. App. 1st Dist., 1987).
Conrad-Hutsel v. Colturi (2002 WL 1290844 (Ohio App. 6th Dist. May 24, 2002)).
Craft v. Peebles, 893 P.2d 138, 151 (Haw., 1989).
Craig v. Oakwood Hosp., 684 N.W.2d 296, 309 (Mich., 2004).
Cunningham v. Helping Hands, Inc., 575 S.E.2d 549, 552 (S.C., 2003).
Ditch v. Waynesboro Hosp., 917 A.2d 317, 322 (Pa. Super., 2007), appeal granted on other grounds, 934 A.2d 1150 (Pa., 2007).
Duncan v. Scottsdale Med. Imaging, Ltd., 70 P.3d 435, 438–39 (Ariz., 2003).
Gauthreaux v. Frank (718 So. 2d 985 (La. Ct. App. 4th Cir., 1998), app. denied, 729 So. 2d 567 (La. 1998)).
Higgins v. Crecraft (1991 WL 20387 (Tenn. App. Feb. 21, 1991)).
Hill v. Squibb & Sons, E.R., 592 P.2d 1383, 1389–90 (Mont., 1979).
Housel v. James, 172 P.2d 712, 717 (Wash. App. Div. 3, 2007).
In re Zyprexa Prod. Liab. Litigation, 253 F.R.D. 69, 106 (E.D. N.Y., 2008).
Johnson v. Doctors' Clinic, 1977 WL 199152 (Ohio App. 9th Dist. Dec. 21, 1977).
Johnson v. Primm, 396 P.2d 426, 429 (N.M., 1964).
Kaskie v. Wright, 589 A.2d 213, 216 (Pa. Super., 1991).
Kemper, K. A. (2000). Contributory *Negligence or Comparative Negligence Based on Failure of Patient to Follow Instructions as Defense in Action against Physician or Surgeon for Medical Malpractice*, 84 A.L.R.5th 619.

King v. Solomon, 81 N.E.2d 838 (Mass., 1948).

Kirk v. Michael Reese Hosp. Med. Ctr., 513 N.E.2d 387, 393 (Ill., 1987).

Lhotka v. Larsen, 238 N.W.2d 870, 873–74 (Minn., 1976).

Liss v. State Med. Bd. of Ohio, 1992 WL 238884 at *4 (Ohio App. 10th Dist. Sept. 24, 1992).

Los Alamos Med. Ctr., Inc. v. Coe, 275 P.2d 175 (N.M., 1954).

McKee v. American Home Products, Corp., 782 P.2d 1045, 1049 (Wash., 1989).

Messinger v. Forsman (2006 WL 1163955 (Neb. App. May 2, 2006)).

Mills v. Berrios, 851 N.E.2d 1066, 1070 (Ind. App., 2006).

Mohr v. Williams, 104 N.W. 12, 15 (Minn., 1905).

Molé v. Jutton, 846 A.2d 1035, 1042 (Md. App., 2004).

Morlino v. Medical Ctr., 706 A.2d 721, 728–29 (N.J., 1998).

Mueller v. Mueller, 221 N.W.2d 39, 41 (S.D., 1974).

Mulder v. Parke Davis & Co., 181 N.W.2d 882, 887 (Minn., 1970).

Ohligschlager v. Proctor Comm. Hosp., 303 N.E.2d 392, 398 (Ill., 1973).

Osborn v. United States (166 F. Supp. 2d 479 (S.D. W. Va., 2001).

Perez v. Bakel, 862 N.E.2d 289, 293 (Ind. App., 2007).

Posner v. Walker (930 So. 2d 659 (Fla. App. 3d Dist., 2006)).

Ramon v. Farr, 770 P.2d 131, 135 (Utah, 1995).

Rios v. Bigler, 847 F. Supp. 1538, 1542 (D. Kan., 1994).

Rubin v. United States (88 F. Supp. 2d 581 (S.D. W. Va., 1999)).

Sard v. Hardy, 379 A.2d 1014, 1020 (Md., 1977).

Schunk v. United States (783 F. Supp. 72 (E.D. N. Y., 1992)).

Seeber v. Ebeling, 141 P.3d 1180, 1185 (Kan. App., 2006).

Spensieri v. Lasky, 723 N.E.2d 544, (N.Y., 1999).

Stebbins v. Concord Wrigley Drugs, 416 N.W.2d 381, 385 (Mich. App., 1987).

Stephens v. Draffin (488 S.E.2d 307 (S.C., 1997)).

Taglieri v. Moss (842 A.2d 280 (N.J. App., 2004)).

Tompkins v. Bryan, 975 So. 2d 723, 725 (La. App. 2d Cir., 2008).

Trimel v. Lawrence Community Hosp Rehab. Ctr., 764 A.2d 203, 207 (Conn. App., 2001), appeal dismissed, 784 A.2d 889 (Conn., 2001).

Vicari v. Spiegel, 936 A.2d 503, 510 (Pa. Super., 2007).

Vito v. North Medical Family Physicians, P.C., 791 N.Y.S.2d 797, 798 (N.Y. App. Div., 2005).

Winschel v. Jain, 925 A.2d 782, 789 (Pa. Super., 2007).

Chapter 10

Expert Witness in Civil and Criminal Testimony

Norman S. Miller, MD, JD, PLLC
Department of Medicine, College of Human Medicine, Michigan State University, East Lansing, MI, USA

An expert witness is a witness who, by virtue of skill, education, experience, or training, is held to have knowledge in a particular subject above that of the average layperson. In civil trials, there has been some criticism of the use of expert witnesses as they are often employed by both sides to advocate conflicting opinions, ultimately leaving a jury of laymen to decide which expert to believe. Despite the controversy, the importance of expert witnesses has been well-established throughout American law. Expert testimony and evidence has become a critical component of many civil and criminal cases, particularly in cases involving drug and alcohol addiction.

EXPERT QUALIFICATIONS

Federal Rule of Evidence 702

An expert need not be an "outstanding practitioner in the field in which he professes expertise" (*United States v. Barker*, 1977). The federal rule governing expert qualifications is Federal Evidence Rule 702, which provides that a witness may qualify as an expert by reason of "knowledge, skill, experience, training, or education" (Fed. R. Evid. 702). In an advisory committee's note to this rule, it states: "[T]he expert is viewed, not in a narrow sense, but as a person qualified by 'knowledge, skill, experience, training, or education'. Thus, within the scope of the rule are not only experts in the strictest sense of the word, e.g., physicians, physicists and architects, but also the large groups sometimes called 'skilled' witnesses, such as bankers or landowners testifying to land values" (Fed. R. Evid. 104(a)). Determining such qualifications of an expert is a matter for the trial court (Fed. R. Evid. 104(a)).

159

Legal Precedent

In *Cruz-Vazquez v. Mennonite General Hospital, Inc.*, a 2009 case, defense counsel moved to exclude expert testimony the plaintiff had offered. The court, citing Federal Evidence Rule 702, stated that although the plaintiff's expert was in fact a medical doctor with some experience in the pertinent fields: "this experience is not adequate to qualify him as an expert witness in this case, because in recent years his work has drastically changed ... from a practicing physician to a professional witness focusing exclusively on testimony on behalf of plaintiffs" (*Cruz-Vazquez v. Mennonite Gen. Hosp., Inc.*, 2009, at 206). The court held that the plaintiff's expert testimony was to be excluded, and subsequently granted summary judgment in favor of the defendants (*Cruz-Vazquez v. Mennonite Gen. Hosp., Inc.*, at 211).

Federal Rule of Evidence 703

Another important federal rule governing expert testimony is Federal Evidence Rule 703, which stipulates that "[t]he facts or data in a particular case upon which an expert bases an opinion or inference may be those perceived by or made known to the expert at or before the hearing. If of a type reasonably relied upon by experts in the particular field in forming opinions and inferences upon the subject, the facts or data need not be admissible in evidence" (Fed. R. Evid. 703). Case law has shown that: "the District Court has wide discretion in its determination to admit and exclude evidence, and this is particularly true in the case of expert testimony" (*Hamling v. United States*, 1974). Not only must an expert have appropriate qualifications, but their proposed testimony must also meet certain criteria for reliability. Recently, the Supreme Court has revitalized the role of the trial judge in screening expert testimony that is likely to be misleading (see *Daubert v. Merrell Dow Pharmaceuticals*, 1993; *Kumho Tire v. Carmichael*, 1998).

Legal Precedent

This case law has advocated the "gatekeeper" model approach, in which a trial judge must consider the evidence to be presented and determine whether an expert's "testimony both rests on a reliable foundation and is relevant to the task at hand" (*Daubert v. Merrell Dow Pharmaceuticals, Inc.*, 1993). In *Daubert v. Merrell Dow Pharmaceuticals, Inc.* (1993), the court emphasized four questions about the testimony of prospective experts; whether a "theory or technique ... can be (and has been) tested;" whether the theory or technique "has been subjected to peer review and publication;" whether there is a high "known or potential rate of error" with the particular technique; and lastly, whether there are "standards controlling the technique's operation" (*Daubert v. Merrell Dow Pharmaceuticals, Inc.*, 1993). While the trial judge must decide whether the expert's knowledge of the subject matter is likely to assist the jury in arriving at the truth, if there is conflicting expert testimony at trial, it is for the jury to decide which of the experts to believe.

ROLE OF EXPERTS

There are many ways in which experts may be used for legal purposes. Initially, a party can hire an expert to help evaluate the case. The expert will provide an expert opinion and, much like work product protected by the attorney/client privilege, this opinion will not be subject to the rules of discovery. These experts (also referred to as non-testifying experts), do not have to satisfy the requirements of the Federal Rules of Evidence. Testifying experts, however, are not protected by such a privilege. The identity of the expert witness must be disclosed, and nearly all documents used in preparation for testimony are open to discovery. Additionally, testifying experts must satisfy the requirements of the Federal Rules of Evidence.

At trial, testifying experts are examined directly by the attorney who employed them, as well as being cross-examined by the opposing counsel. During the direct examination period of the trial, the attorney is to ask non-leading questions, and attempts to establish the expert's credibility based on credentials, training, experience, style and trustworthiness. The purpose of the cross-examination period, on the other hand, is to discredit adversary testimony and to attack collateral issues such as the expert's credentials and background.

DUTIES OF EXPERTS

As previously stated, an expert witness is a witness who, by virtue of skill, education, experience, or training, is held to have knowledge in a particular subject beyond that of a layperson. There are two basic categories in which expert testimony is admissible. The primary category is for matters in which the jury is forced to draw conclusions on the existence of facts that are specifically within the expert's scope or expertise and which are not considered common knowledge. In this category, the expert is able to testify with authority on the issues in question, enabling the jury to draw a conclusion. The second category is for matters in which the conclusions to be drawn from the facts stated depend on a professional or scientific knowledge above that of an average layperson. In this category, experts set forth the facts and state their conclusion based on those facts, and the jury is then free to accept or reject that conclusion. Expert witnesses may offer opinions, whereas fact witnesses may not. Additionally, expert witnesses are entitled to an expert witness fee, whereas fact witnesses receive ordinary witness fees which are generally much lower.

Typically, in cases involving drug and alcohol addiction, experts are relied upon for opinions on a person's mental capacity, a person's criminal intent, a healthcare provider's standard of care, a care provider's negligence and the like. Additionally, expert witnesses may provide expert evidence about facts from within their scope of expertise. Experts bear a heavy responsibility, especially in criminal and penal trials, and perjury by an expert is a punishable crime (see *Kline v. State*, 1984, psychologist convicted of perjury in the Ted Bundy trial for claiming he had a doctorate).

Principles of Addictions and the Law

MENS REA AND CAPACITY

In criminal cases, insanity is a complete, but affirmative defense. The first famous legal test for insanity was established in 1843 in the *M'Naughton Case*. This rule created a presumption of sanity, unless the defense proved "at the time of committing the act, the accused was laboring under such a defect of reason, from disease of the mind, as not to know the nature and quality of the act he was doing or, if he did know it, that he did not know what he was doing was wrong" (*M'Naughton Case*, 1849). Since an insanity defense is difficult to claim in cases involving drug or alcohol addiction, a diminished capacity defense is often used in conjunction with, or instead of, an insanity defense.

Diminished capacity is the impairment or absence of ability to form intent to commit a crime. A diminished capacity defense is a partial defense to charges that require that the defendant possess a particular *mens rea* during the commission of the crime. *Mens rea* is defined as "guilty mind," and encompasses both general and specific intent. In criminal cases, whether a crime arises from a willful misconduct or a disease, such as an addiction, affects the person's intent to commit a crime. Experts are needed to determine whether or not the accused was in fact of diminished capacity at the time of the offense.

In 1984, President Ronald Reagan signed the Comprehensive Crime Control Act, which established the Insanity Defense Reform Act, 18 U.S.C. § 17 (IDRA). This act requires that, for a federal insanity defense, the defendant prove, by "clear and convincing evidence," that "at the time of the commission of the acts constituting the offense, the defendant, as a result of a severe mental disease or defect, was unable to appreciate the nature and quality or the wrongfulness of his acts" (18 U.S.C. § 17). In *State v. Klein*, the definition of "mental disease" was expanded to include substance dependence, which is often explicitly excluded from legal definitions of mental disease (*State v. Klein*, 2005). This is the federal standard to be applied by the jury after hearing the medical testimony from prosecution and defense experts.

EXPERT ROLE IN CRIMINAL CASES

In criminal cases, forensic scientists and forensic psychologists are often used. For purposes of rebutting or establishing *mens rea*, a party will often use a psychologist as an expert. Additionally, it is important in criminal cases to establish whether the accused had diminished capacity or was insane at the time of the offense, trial and at the time of arraignment. Under the IDRA and the proceeding case law, trial courts are given vast discretion in limiting evidence, including expert testimony, used to establish a diminished capacity defense.

Legal Precedent

In *United States v. Twine*, the defendant was convicted of transmitting via telephone and mail threats to kidnap and injure. At trial, the defendant introduced evidence of mental defect, including expert psychiatric testimony. On appeal, the court stated that: "we agree with the courts in *Frisbee*, *Gold*, and *Pohlot* that the 1984 act does not abolish the diminished capacity defense" (*U.S. v. Twine*, 1988). "[A] careful reading of the 1984 act and its history persuades us that Congress intended to restrict a defendant's ability to excuse guilt with mental defect evidence, curtailing the insanity defense. But Congress did not intend to eliminate a defendant's ability to disprove guilt with mental defect evidence" (*U.S. v. Twine*, 1988). Thus, case law has interpreted the IDRA as giving broad discretion to the trial courts in determining, on a case-by-case basis, the admission of such evidence in establishing a diminished capacity defense.

MEDICAL MALPRACTICE

In medical malpractice cases, the plaintiff carries the burden of proving a medical professional committed negligence by a preponderance of the evidence. Negligence is defined as having a dereliction or breach of duty which is a direct cause of damage. There are four elements of a negligence claim, all of which the plaintiff must establish. First, the plaintiff must show that a legal duty was owed to them by the defendant. Second, the plaintiff must show that the duty was breached, in that the healthcare provider failed to conform to the relevant standard of care. The third element that a plaintiff must prove is that the breach caused the injury. Lastly, a plaintiff must show that the injury resulted in damages, which may be financial or emotional. Generally, medical malpractice occurs when a healthcare provider fails to prevent foreseeable injuries, intentionally engages in misconduct in caring for the patient, fails to provide correct test results, or fails to provide proper medical treatment. For the purpose of establishing or rebutting each of the elements of a negligence claim, experts are likely to be used.

EXPERT ROLE IN MEDICAL MALPRACTICE CASES

Medical Experts

There are generally two types of experts used in all cases of medical malpractice, medical experts and damage experts. A medical expert is an unbiased expert from within the medical field where the negligence is alleged to have occurred. This expert may provide medical and scientific opinions and testimony. The reputation and experience of an expert are vital to the value of their testimony at trial. Medical malpractice expert witnesses can be psychiatrists, pediatricians, neurosurgeons, or any other type of expert pertinent to the case at bar.

The duty of such an expert is to provide precise and detailed information and testimony about whether the healthcare provider failed to provide the requisite standard of care. The standard of care is generally thought of as the degree of care which a reasonably prudent physician would exercise in the same or similar circumstances. A medical expert will provide testimony as to the required standard of care, will point out any and all deviations and violations to the relevant standard of care, and will provide their expert opinion on how the injury was caused by that violation. A good medical expert is able to put these complex issues into understandable, clear, coherent and consistent terms, so that they are easily understood by both the judge and jury.

Before filing a legal action, some jurisdictions require expert testimony in medical malpractice cases in evaluating the merits of a malpractice claim. In these states, it is required by law that a competent and qualified medical professional, in the same area of expertise as the defendant, review the claim and be willing to testify that the standard of care was breached. In Michigan, for example, an expert witness in a medical malpractice case is required to be a licensed healthcare professional either teaching or practicing in the same specialty as the defendant he is to testify against, and the expert witness must also have the same board certifications as the defendant (Mich. Comp. Laws (MCL) Ann., § 600.2169 (West, 2000)).

Michigan Medical Malpractice: A Medical Expert's Role

Some states have enacted tort reform as a way to limit frivolous medical malpractice lawsuits. In Michigan, for example, a statute requires that, after careful medical review, the plaintiff counsel serve on each defendant a comprehensive document called a Notice of Intent. The plaintiff then has to wait 182 days (six months) before filing suit against the defendants to whom he served the notice of intent (MCL 600.2912b). In filing suit, Michigan law also requires the plaintiff counsel to locate and hire a qualified medical expert to prepare and provide sworn affidavits confirming that the defendant committed malpractice as support for the plaintiff's claim; this is called an Affidavit of Meritorious Defense (affidavit of merit) (MCL 600.2169; MCL 600.2912d).

For an expert to be qualified for an affidavit of merit, the expert must have the same qualifications, licensure and board certifications as the defendant at the time of the alleged malpractice (MCL 600.2169). Furthermore, for the year prior to the alleged malpractice, the expert must also have devoted a majority of his professional time either actively practicing in the same specialty, or to teaching in the same specialty as the defendant practices. Therefore, if there is more than one defendant with different qualifications, as is often the case in medical malpractice suits, the plaintiff must hire a different expert to submit an affidavit of merit against each of the defendants. For an affidavit of merit, the expert must first review the notice of intent. In the affidavit, an expert must state the applicable standard of care, how the applicable standard of care was breached, what the defendant should have done to comply with the standard or to avoid the breach, and that the breach was the proximate cause of the injury to the plaintiff.

Within 91 days of the plaintiff filing suit and an affidavit of merit, the defendant must file an affidavit of merit. In an affidavit of merit submitted on behalf of a defendant, the expert must state the applicable standard of care and how the defendant complied with the requisite standard of care (MCL 600.2912e). Often, filing an affidavit of merit is a much easier process for the defense counsel than for plaintiff counsel, because plaintiffs have very little documentation to work from in filing an affidavit of merit. So, while a defense team can readily obtain information from the defendants regarding the applicable certifications and qualifications to match to an expert, the plaintiff does not have such access and must make a reasonable assessment of the qualifications based on the limited source material at hand.

Given the complex and technical nature of medical malpractice law in Michigan, attorneys will often hire an expert, usually the expert who submitted the affidavit of merit, to consult during litigation. Per court rules, this expert must be disclosed to the opposing counsel, and may have to participate in a deposition and testify at trial. In the deposition and at trial, the expert will be questioned about the facts of the case, his qualifications, and his understanding and opinion about the applicable standard of care and alleged breach.

Admissibility of a Medical Expert

Generally, Federal Rules of Evidence 702 and 703, previously discussed in this chapter, serve as the guidelines for admissibility of a medical malpractice expert's testimony in court. There are, however, several states that deviate from this standard. Additionally, there are no uniform standards as to the credentialing requirements of medical experts. While the federal and state rules provide a guideline for a judge in determining admissibility of expert testimony, the trial judge must still decide whether the testimony is admissible by considering whether the expert's opinion has been reviewed by peers, whether there are errors in the evidence used in the expert's evaluation, whether the evidence used is sound, if the testimony is generally accepted within the medical profession, and whether the medical expert's conclusion is unbiased and based on a scientifically-sound and medically-valid method.

Legal Precedent

Legal precedent shows that not only are medical experts essential to a successful medical malpractice claim, but also that the discovery rules and requirements concerning an expert's qualifications need to be astringently adhered to. In *Law v. Camp*, the plaintiff lost his medical malpractice claim in part because he failed to follow the Connecticut discovery rule pertaining to the disclosure of medical expert witnesses. The court stated: "[b]ecause the success of malpractice claims in Connecticut depends on expert testimony, the defendants could not assess the strength of their case until [plaintiff's] experts were disclosed and deposed" (*Law v. Camp*, 2001).

Damage Experts

Damage experts are often used by both parties to a medical malpractice case. Generally, a damage expert will be an economist or an accountant. While many of the direct economic damages resulting from an alleged act of medical malpractice are fairly straightforward, damages from pain and suffering are much more uncertain. Damage experts aid in not only assessing the direct financial and economic losses, but they also assist in matching a dollar amount to the less certain damages that have resulted. Essentially, damage experts provide a backbone to the final element in a negligence claim, that the alleged malpractice resulted in damage to the plaintiff.

In some states, such as Michigan, there are caps for noneconomic damages in medical malpractice cases. Noneconomic damages are composed of pain and suffering, physical impairment, physical disfigurement and inconvenience. In Michigan, in 1993, the damage cap for all plaintiffs was set at $280,000, except for instances of impairment of cognitive capacity, instances of paralysis due to brain or spinal cord injury, or loss of reproductive ability, in which the damage cap for noneconomic damages was set at $500,000 (Mich. Comp. Laws Ann. § 600.1483 (West 1996)). These damage caps increase annually with the cost of living (Mich. Comp. Laws Ann. § 600.1483 (West 1996)). Additionally, any jury award in excess of the damage cap must be reduced by the trial court (Mich. Comp. Laws Ann. § 600.6304(5) (West 2000)). In such jurisdictions, damage experts are essential to a plaintiff's case, as they are able to construct seemingly noneconomic damages in an economic way so that the damage award can be maximized.

CONCLUSION

An expert witness, in either a criminal or medical malpractice case involving addiction, often plays a vital role in the outcome of the litigation. In criminal cases, an expert can testify as to the mental status and capacity of a defendant when the crime took place. Such testimony will affect not only what the defendant is charged with at trial, but also what the defendant is ultimately convicted of and sentenced to. Additionally, in medical malpractice cases, an expert participates in determining the merits of a claim before it is even filed with the court, and then continues to play a role throughout litigation.

REFERENCES

Cruz-Vazquez v. Mennonite Gen. Hosp., Inc., 613 F. Supp.2d 202, 206, 211 (D. Puerto Rico 2009).
Daubert v. Merrell Dow Pharmaceuticals, 509 U.S. 579 (1993).
Hamling v. United States, 418 U.S. 87, 108 (U.S.Cal. 1974).
Kline v. State, 444 So.2d 1102 (Fla. Ct. App. 1984).
Kumho Tire v. Carmichael, 526 U.S. 137 (1998).
Law v. Camp, 15 Fed Appx. 24, 26 2001 WL 868354, 3 (C.A.2 (Conn.)), 2001).
M'Naughton Case (10 Cl.2nd F. 200; 1849).
State v. Klein, 124 P.3d 644 (Wash. 2005).
U.S. v. Twine, 853 F.2d 676, 679 (C.A.9 (Wash.), 1988).
United States v. Barker, 553 F.2d 1013, 1024 (6th Cir. 1977).

Chapter 11

Forensic Considerations in Blood Alcohol Evaluation

Werner U. Spitz, MD

Wayne State University School of Medicine, University of Windsor, Ontario, Canada

INTRODUCTION

Alcoholic beverages are pleasant, entertaining and socially acceptable, but too often abused. Alcohol is a drug with predictable effects. When we think of alcohol or alcoholic beverages, we mean ethyl alcohol, also known as ethanol. Pure ethyl alcohol, i.e., 100%, also known as absolute alcohol, not to be confused with the brand Absolut, is odorless and colorless; in a clear bottle it looks like water. Many other alcohols, if ingested, are toxic, such as isopropanol (rubbing alcohol) which depresses the central nervous system (CNS). Wood alcohol (methanol), sold as sterno, often causes blindness due to formic acid formation which is toxic to the retina. Ethylene glycol, which is used in antifreeze, causes renal failure and cerebral manifestations due to formation of calcium oxalate crystals, which can be readily identified microscopically in urine with polarized light.

ALCOHOLISM

Alcoholics are resourceful when it comes to satisfying their addiction. In the past, alcoholics sometimes removed the odor and color from toxic compounds, which they believed were alcohol suitable for consumption, by straining the product through bread which they placed in the bottom of a sock. The offensive odor and often bright color were added by the manufacturer for the purpose of identification and to discourage drinking. The blue color of glass cleaner is one such example.

Vanilla extracts used for baking are sometimes consumed for their alcoholic content, and grocery stores have reported finding empty vanilla bottles on the floor. Pure vanilla extract is made by extraction of vanilla from vanilla beans in an alcohol solution. The United States Food and Drug Administration regulations require pure vanilla extract to contain a minimum of 35% alcohol and 13.35 ounces of vanilla bean per gallon (United States Food and Drug Administration, 2009). Double and triple strength extracts are available. Many cough syrups and mouthwashes also contain ethanol.

It is estimated that in the United States, 2/3 of all adults use alcohol occasionally and more than 12% can be considered to be heavy drinkers. Alcoholism is a disease. The life expectancy of alcoholics is 10–15 years shorter than that of non-alcoholics. Alcohol is toxic to the liver. Fatty infiltration of the liver occurs in heavy drinkers, especially binge drinkers, where alcohol is substituted for food for prolonged periods of time. The liver becomes saturated with fat, enlarged, intensely yellow, soft and greasy. A cut through such a liver shows no focal areas that differ in color or consistency. There is no evidence of fibrotic changes. Complete abstinence from alcohol consumption and a balanced diet return a fatty liver to normal, unless genetic predisposition and persistent binge drinking proceed to micronodular cirrhosis where the liver is shrunken, pale, hard, with nodules surrounded by fibrous tissue. A cirrhotic liver is not reversible. Many substances are toxic to the liver causing fatty infiltration and other damage; vitamin A in high doses, often used in eye treatments, is one example. The cause of a fatty liver is not always apparent.

High blood alcohol concentrations, in excess of 0.2% to 0.25%, suggest chronic consumption, a heavy drinker. A casual drinker would be unlikely to reach those levels. Excessive alcohol consumption irritates the gastric lining, causing vomiting in the casual drinker. Hangover is caused by acute gastritis after too much drinking the night before.

Alcohol in moderate amounts causes euphoria, dehydration and vasodilatation, i.e., dilated blood vessels, thus red, bloodshot eyes and flushed skin. At high concentrations, alcohol depresses the central nervous system. The mechanism of death from acute alcohol intoxication is from paralysis of the respiratory center in the brain, causing respiratory arrest. Death from alcohol intoxication is death by asphyxia.

In my experience, deaths from acute alcohol intoxication have been observed in cases with blood alcohol concentrations as low as 0.29%. In a person found outdoors in the wintertime, in a cold climate, the contributory effect of exposure must be considered. According to Perper (Perper et al., 1986), some alcoholics not only develop an increased tolerance, but often are functional at blood alcohol concentrations generally considered to be potentially fatal. It has been found that high blood alcohol concentrations do not necessarily result in evidence of visible intoxication in all cases.

Chronic consumption of alcoholic beverages increases tolerance. Significant individual differences in the degree of tolerance exist in what will cause physical dependence. Some people develop tolerance, others do not. According to Garriott (1993), 8–20% of chronic alcoholics eventually develop cirrhosis. Some alcoholics develop cirrhosis, while others do not. It would seem that a genetic link exists in these differences. An autopsy on a known skid row alcoholic in his 60s, with a blood alcohol concentration of 0.30%, who was struck by an automobile when crossing a street, showed a perfectly structured liver with no evidence of fatty change or cirrhosis. Both his parents had also been alcoholics.

Half of all suicides involve consumption of alcohol. The blood alcohol levels in suicides vary from low to highly intoxicating. Low blood alcohol levels in suicides are probably due to the fact that depression sets in during the declining phase of the blood alcohol concentration, after the euphoric effect has worn off.

Alcohol is not absorbed through intact skin. However, large open wounds, as in second degree burns, will allow absorption. A young child with second degree burns from scalding had a postmortem blood alcohol level of 0.05% after his mother used rubbing alcohol in an effort to reduce his fever. A worker in his 50s, unloading a truck carrying barrels of absolute alcohol, sued his employer for toxic manifestations alleging absorption of alcohol through the skin when he was doused with the contents of a ruptured barrel. On admission to the hospital, both his eyes were markedly red from irritation, but his blood alcohol concentration was zero. Swabbing of the skin using alcohol does not contaminate a blood sample withdrawn for blood alcohol determination. Nevertheless, it may be advantageous to use some other type of antiseptic to avoid such allegations.

Alcohol contributes to violence, injury and death. In the United States, at least 50% of motor vehicle crashes are related to alcohol consumption. According to the National Highway Traffic Safety Administration (NHTSA), in 2002 32% of fatally-injured drivers had a blood alcohol concentration of at least 0.08%. In 2005, there were 16,885 alcohol related fatalities, 39% of the total traffic fatalities for the year. In 2006, 17,602 people were killed in the U.S. in alcohol-related motor vehicle crashes, and an estimated 13,470 people were killed in traffic crashes that involved at least one driver or motorcycle operator with a blood alcohol concentration of 0.08% or higher (NHTSA, 2007).

According to the United States Department of Justice (DOJ), in 2002 approximately one million violent crimes occurred in the United States. Of these, 30% of the offenders had been drinking alcoholic beverages, according to the victims. Two-thirds of victims of violence by an intimate partner (spouse or former spouse, boyfriend or girlfriend) indicated alcohol consumption was a factor, whereas, 31% of stranger-involved violent crimes were reported to have implicated alcohol. The DOJ reports that one in five violent victimizations involved perceived alcohol use by the offender (United States Department of Justice, 2002).

The odor of alcoholic beverages is either from by-products of alcohol manufacture or artificially added congeners to achieve the desired flavor and odor, not from the alcohol itself. Pure alcohol is odorless. Congeners give the alcoholic beverage a smell which the consumer associates with quality. The smell of alcohol on someone's breath or emanating from their skin and clothes indicates that alcohol has been consumed, but by no means reflects an alcohol level. I have observed many times an intense odor of alcohol on a body with low levels of blood alcohol and sometimes with no blood alcohol at all. Congeners remain longer in the body than alcohol.

Alcohol, after being swallowed, enters the stomach, and then is absorbed into the blood. Only 20% of the total alcohol consumed is absorbed from the stomach, 80% is absorbed from the small intestine. On an empty stomach, it takes 15–20 minutes to feel the effect of an alcoholic beverage, a bottle of beer, a shot of liquor, or a glass of wine. Consumption of alcohol mixed with carbonated beverages causes more rapid and more complete absorption.

Food in the stomach will delay alcohol absorption to approximately an hour, especially if the food is greasy or oily. Food acts as a sponge which traps the alcohol, releasing it gradually. Thus, a few drinks with dinner may completely change the pattern of absorption to the extent that the ultimate blood alcohol level may be much lower than had the person eaten less, or nothing. The composition of the meal may also play a role. Common bar food, such as a hamburger and French fries will delay absorption. In a person who has had their stomach surgically removed, alcohol enters the blood much faster. Following gastrectomy, an individual would become intoxicated in half the time or less. A middle-aged man, with a history of gastrectomy, was observed exiting his vehicle parked against the wall of a pizza restaurant. He entered a liquor store nearby to purchase a six pack of beer. He then consumed one beer after the other in the parking lot. Within minutes, he started his car and proceeded through the wall into the pizza parlor, killing a patron.

Because it may take 15–20 minutes for an alcoholic beverage to be absorbed into the bloodstream from the stomach and the small intestine, the last drink consumed, such as "one for the road" does not affect the driver until after he leaves the bar. Consequently, someone who has been to a bar and had say, a shot and a beer before departing, who then gets into an accident shortly after leaving and has blood drawn an hour later, may have a higher blood alcohol level at the hospital than he would have had at the time of the crash. During the hour which elapsed, the alcohol which he drank on leaving would have entered the bloodstream and reached the brain. Alcohol in the stomach, prior to absorption, has no effect.

We use a customary burn-off rate, which is the rate at which alcohol is eliminated from the body, i.e., metabolized; this rate is approximately 20 mg per hour (0.02%). Some researchers consider 0.018% and still others consider 0.015%, the latter in novice drinkers. In borderline cases, these differences may play a significant role, insofar as the question needs to be answered whether a particular driver had above or below the legal limit allowable under the law. We have conducted blood alcohol analyses to determine burn-off rates on over 100 persons between the mid-20s to mid-40s. The participants consumed a six pack of beer on an empty stomach. We found that the majority eliminated 0.02% per hour, with some eliminating more. A rule of thumb indicates that in a person with average body weight (approximately 170 pounds) one drink generates 0.02% blood alcohol. Such a drink would be equivalent to one regular 12-ounce beer, 1–1.25 ounces of 80-proof liquor, or one four-ounce glass of average red wine.

Four drinks consumed in one hour by an average weight individual would cause a blood alcohol concentration of approximately 0.08% at the end of the hour. Four drinks consumed in three hours would cause a blood alcohol concentration of approximately 0.03%. Most adult individuals who are used to consumption of alcoholic beverages will eliminate an average of one drink, 0.02% per hour. This means one 12-ounce can of beer, or one shot of 80-proof liquor, or four ounces of red wine, is eliminated from the blood per hour.

An alcoholic may eliminate as much as double the amount of alcohol per hour compared to non-alcoholics, i.e., 0.04% per hour, except in the case of cirrhosis or other severe liver conditions, where alcohol may linger in the system due to reduced metabolic activity of a failing liver. Alcohol is mainly broken down in the liver by oxidation. It is eliminated from the body by the kidneys in the urine, but also in the sweat and breath. The concentration of alcohol in the urine cannot be utilized to determine an accurate and reliable blood level. The urine concentration is only indicative of alcohol consumption. Alcohol in the urine is essentially outside the body. One may legitimately say "now in the bladder, next in the toilet."

With regards to vitreous, which is eye fluid, obtained in an autopsy, poor blood supply causes alcohol to linger in the eye fluid, representing blood levels that occurred earlier. However, the vitreous is an important source for alcohol, drug and other chemical testing. As to alcohol, the vitreous concentration lags behind by about two hours. The eye being segregated in a bony structure, away from other organs, protects it from contamination and decomposition.

With regards to elimination of alcohol by way of the breath, the concentration in alveolar breath is less than that in the blood. In accordance with Henry's law, alcohol distributes between pulmonary blood and alveolar air in a ratio of 2,100 to 1, which means that 2,100 mL of alveolar air contains the same weight of alcohol as 1 mL of blood.

Prima facie evidence of drunk driving has changed over the years. When I first came to this country in 1959, it was 0.15%, now it is 0.08%, almost half. Many European countries consider drunk driving at 0.05% or less. The American Medical Association has urged the states to reduce the legal limit of blood alcohol concentration and continues to do so, in view of research that shows impairment in handling emergency situations in traffic at almost any level. There is no such thing as legal intoxication. The term *prima facie* evidence refers to drunkenness at the wheel, i.e., while driving only.

Two individuals in a motor vehicle, both with a blood alcohol concentration over 0.20%, stopped at a train crossing where a train, approximately 30 feet down track, blowing its whistle, was about to move forward; the driver of the car tried to cross the track but was struck by the train and both he and his friend were killed. Under the circumstances, I must assume that he misjudged the

TABLE 11.1 Effects of Blood Alcohol

Concentration	Effects
0.00–0.04%	No noticeable effect to mild euphoria. Concentrations below 0.05 – behavioral changes under laboratory conditions
0.05–0.09%	Reduced inhibitions, increased self-confidence, reduced attention span, decreased judgment, especially involving time and distance
0.10–0.14%	Nystagmus, euphoria, confusion and loss of judgment, reduced motor control, delayed reaction time, instability, loss of balance, inability to assess distance
0.15–0.29%	Loss of muscular control, uncoordinated, staggering, exaggerated emotions, dizziness, reduced pain response, confusion and slurring of speech
0.30–0.39%	Dazed, stupor, lack of muscular control, marked decrease in response to stimuli, possibly comatose
0.4% and above	Anesthesia, respiratory depression, deep coma, death

distance between himself and the locomotive. We judge the speed at which we are traveling by viewing houses, utility poles, trees and other stationary objects, but we are unable to perform this task correctly when intoxicated (see Table 11.1). Many motor vehicle accidents are due to excessive speed.

The argument is sometimes made that the blood specimen was contaminated by the use of non-sterile instruments. Non-sterile instruments may introduce bacteria into the blood, causing fermentation within the specimen and alcohol formation. This would be a legitimate argument if the specimen were shipped to a laboratory over several days. However, if the specimen analysis occurs in-house and is submitted to the laboratory and analyzed or refrigerated promptly, the requirement of sterility of the instruments is excessive and logic dictates that cleanliness by rinsing would suffice, since fermentation requires time.

Blood should never be obtained through an intact chest wall and preferably should be withdrawn from the femoral artery or vein, to avoid a possible later claim that the specimen was contaminated by gastric contents from the esophagus, thus introducing gastric contents into the specimen. The esophagus is located right behind the heart and the needle commonly used for blood withdrawal at autopsies is 3.5 to 4 inches in length, long enough to readily pass through the heart and enter the esophagus (Spitz, 2006).

Blood drawn from a decomposing body may yield a flawed alcohol concentration since decomposition involves fermentation and blood sugar will allow fermentation to occur. Up to as much as 0.10% alcohol may be found in blood from a decomposing body. We have frequently found lower alcohol concentrations in blood specimens obtained from bodies in a state of early decomposition and in cases where blood was shipped without a preservative, such as sodium fluoride or other antibacterial agent.

Vitreous can be obtained for alcohol analysis from a mild to moderately decomposed body. If the vitreous contains no alcohol, alcohol found in blood can be assumed to have formed postmortem. However, since the vitreous lags behind the blood in alcohol content, it could be that alcohol has not yet reached the vitreous. Therefore, caution must be used when interpreting the results. It may be necessary to expand the inquiry into circumstantial evidence and witness statements.

Advanced decomposition, especially in the summer, is often seen in bodies recovered from the water, such as oceans, lakes and rivers. There is often suspicion in such a body regarding the cause of death, since the body surface may be changed by deterioration. In such bodies, vitreous, if obtainable, is of special importance. Blood alcohol level, in fresh water drowning, may be reduced by dilution, since inhaled water enters the blood circulation. By the same token, transfusions and administration of intravenous fluids in hospitals also dilute blood alcohol concentrations. Therefore, it is advisable that in hospital cases, admission blood specimens drawn prior to fluid administration be obtained from the emergency room and analyzed. The specimen will reflect conditions at the time the specimen was drawn which is closest to the time the injury occurred, i.e., before IVs were hung and time passed allowing burn-off. In cases of death, after lengthy survival, with or without life support, having results of such analysis may be invaluable.

There is no alcohol production in the live body, it must be consumed. No drug can cause the body to eliminate alcohol faster, not even coffee. Drinking coffee makes for a wide-awake drunk. Under normal circumstances, in the dead body, blood alcohol concentration in the body does not change in the period from death until autopsy. Of course this assumes, in case of delay, that the body was refrigerated.

Embalming fluids may contain methanol and/or other alcohols; however, ethanol is not a standard component. Therefore, any ethanol present in an embalmed body was ingested prior to death. There is no blood available in an embalmed body, therefore urine or vitreous would be the only available source for examination since tissue testing would not yield reliable results and data obtained by tissue analysis would certainly not stand up in court.

When blood is centrifuged or when fresh blood is placed in a tube and allowed to sediment, the blood will separate into serum in the top half of the tube, while the cells will precipitate to the bottom. Hospital laboratories usually use serum, i.e., spun down blood, for all their blood analyses. Serum is water soluble and easier, faster and more economical to work with. In a hospital setting, blood alcohol concentration is usually quantitated using serum. Alcohol is water soluble. The concentration of alcohol in serum is 12 to 20% higher than that in whole blood. When the law indicates that 0.08% or 80 mg per 100 mL of blood is *prima facie* evidence of drunk driving, this level applies to whole blood analysis. PBTs used by police to determine drunk driving are calibrated to correspond to whole blood alcohol analysis.

Blood which is shed on the floor, the road, inside a vehicle or anywhere outside the body may be contaminated, and should not be used for alcohol testing. A hematoma inside the body may be used for analysis, if no other specimen is available. A subdural hematoma, or other recent intracranial blood clot, may help determine an approximate blood alcohol concentration which existed at the time the bleeding occurred. Subdural hemorrhage may be delayed.

A young woman crossing the road was struck by a motor vehicle and was admitted unconscious to the hospital. She had a blood alcohol concentration of 0.12% on admission. Efforts to reduce brain swelling due to head injuries improved her state of consciousness some 11 hours after admission. The young lady eventually died of pneumonia. A subdural hematoma removed at autopsy was negative for alcohol, due to the fact that the subdural bleed occurred at a time when alcohol in the peripheral blood had metabolized, some 21 hours after the accident, when brain swelling subsided, allowing previously compressed injured blood vessels to bleed (Cassin & Spitz, 1983).

The presence of another drug, most often depressants and sedatives, when taken with alcohol may have disastrous consequences. Narcotics, tranquilizers, antihistamines and other anti-allergic medications, cold and sleeping medications are common offenders, when taken with alcohol. Alcohol when mixed with any of these drugs has an additive effect. Whereas some individuals may commit suicide in this fashion, most often these are accidental deaths.

Alcoholics in withdrawal may develop delirium tremens (DTs), even if they have some alcohol in their system but not enough. DTs usually begin 48 to 72 hours after alcohol withdrawal, with anxiety, confusion, sleeplessness, sweating and profound depression. Hallucinations, restlessness and fear may also occur. Fast pulse and elevated temperature are frequently observed. People usually recover within one to three weeks, but recurrences are likely with resumption of alcohol consumption.

With regards to driving a motorcycle, there is a definite relationship between low-level blood alcohol concentrations and motorcycle operation. Maintaining balance on a two-wheel vehicle is almost dependant on sobriety, since even low levels of alcohol in the blood alter motor skills. According to Robinson (Robinson et al., 1990), decreased performance was documented at a level of 0.038%, and 58% of motorcycle fatalities involved alcohol consumption.

REFERENCES

Cassin, B. J., & Spitz, W. U. (1983). Concentration of alcohol in delayed subdural hematoma. *Journal of Forensic Sciences*, 28(4), 1013–1015.

Garriott, J. C. (1993). *Medicolegal Aspects of Alcohol Determination in Biological Specimens*. Tucson, AZ: Lawyers and Judges Publishing Co.

National Highway Traffic Safety Administration. (2007). Alcohol Related Traffic Fatalities, 2002–2006.

Perper, J. A., Twerski, A., & Wienand, J. W. (1986). Tolerance at high blood alcohol concentrations: A study of 110 cases and review of the literature. *Journal of Forensic Sciences, 31*(1), 212–221.

Robinson, A., Ketchum, C. H., Colburn, N., & Meyer, R. (1990). Effect of ethyl alcohol on reaction times as measured on a motorcycle simulator. *Issue Series Title: Clinical Chemistry (Abstract), 36*, 1170.

Spitz, W. U. (2006). *Spitz and Fisher's Medicolegal Investigation of Death.* Springfield, IL: Charles C. Thomas.

United States Department of Justice. (2002). *Alcohol and violent crimes.*

United States Food and Drug Administration. (2009). *Vanilla extract standards.*

Chapter 12

Pharmacological Drug Effects on Brain and Behavior

Richard A. Greer, MD
Division of Forensic Psychiatry, University of Florida, College of Medicine, Department of Psychiatry, Gainsville, FL, USA

Mark S. Gold, MD
Department of Psychiatry, University of Florida College of Medicine & McKnight Brain Institute, Depts of Psychiatry, Neuroscience, Anesthesiology, Community Health & Family Medicine, Gainesville, FL, USA

INTRODUCTION

Psychoactive substances including alcohol acutely, and often chronically, affect the way an individual feels and thinks. This chapter will focus on the properties of psychoactive substances which are abused, including alcohol, illicit drugs and prescribed medications. These substances not only affect the mood, but also have significant effects on cognition, behavior and physiology, therefore substantially altering our perceptions and social function. The biological mechanisms of neuropsychological reward, cravings and withdrawal will be discussed, as these processes have great relevance in understanding the disease model of addiction and how best to evaluate and treat individuals who suffer from these disorders.

Drug and alcohol abuse can be traced back for many centuries. The heavy use of hard liquor can be traced back to colonial America. The widespread use of narcotics can be seen in the nineteenth century. Cigarette smoking became widespread in the middle of the twentieth century. The ubiquitous use of marijuana among young people became socially acceptable in the 1960s. The cocaine epidemic in the United States became a prominent social issue in the 1980s. At the present time, society considers the use of coffee, the Internet, gambling, pornography, etc., as psychoactive in nature, and the ramifications of abuse have been repeatedly described in deleterious terms. The National Institute of Mental Health Epidemiologic Catchment Area Study, conducted in five major cities around the United States, determined lifetime prevalence rates of alcohol disorders to be approximately 13.5% in large metropolitan areas (Regier et al., 1990). The 2007 National Survey on Drug Use and Health findings show alcohol dependence or abuse prevalence for persons aged 12 or older to be 7.5% of the overall population, but 23% in large metropolitan areas (Substance Abuse and Mental Health Services Administration (SAMHSA), 2008). Drug disorders alone occur in approximately 9% of our population and 29% of individuals experience comorbid mental and addictive disorders. In addition, those who suffer from alcohol or drug abuse are seven times more likely to experience another addictive disorder, and 37% of those with alcohol abuse and 53% of those with drug abuse have comorbid mental disorders (Merlo & Gold, 2008). Conversely, those with bipolar disorder have had an almost 61% prevalence rate of comorbid substance abuse, while those with schizophrenia have a 47% comorbidity.

Characteristic pharmacological and pharmacokinetic features are important in understanding the acute and chronic effects of a substance on an individual. In addition, there are individual differences among users, considering the individual's own physiology and psychology. This chapter will therefore focus primarily on psychoactive substances of abuse, which can be broadly defined as central nervous system stimulants and depressants. Central nervous system stimulants include cocaine and amphetamines. Central nervous system depressants include alcohol, opioids, barbiturates and benzodiazepines. Marijuana, performance-enhancing drugs (steroids) and psychedelic drugs such as PCP and LSD, fall outside this division. However, physiological and psychological aspects of the most common types of these substances of abuse will be discussed (see Table 12.1).

Influence of Neurobiology and Neurotransmitters

The neurotransmitter dopamine, and its function in the neurological "reward" system, especially the nucleus accumbens and the ventral tegmental area, has been implicated extensively in drug and alcohol addiction. The release of dopamine and the nucleus accumbens has been associated repeatedly with craving for cocaine (Phillips et al., 2003; Merlo & Gold, 2008). In addition, morphine, marijuana, nicotine and alcohol administration have also resulted in increased dopamine release in the nucleus accumbens (Gonzalez et al., 2004; Dackis & O'Brien, 2005). These same drugs are associated with molecular adaption in dopamine transporters (Volkow & Li, 2005), as well as opioid receptors, nicotinic receptors and G-aminobutyric acid (GABA) (Bruijnzeel et al., 2004). Furthermore, several of these drugs of abuse are known to activate the brain's endogenous opioid and cannabinoid systems, within the pathway connecting the ventral tegmental area and the nucleus accumbens (Anderson et al., 2008; Merlo & Gold, 2008).

Addiction may represent a single disease. If this is so, one would expect a fairly common neurobiology. As such, treatments that work for one addictive disease might also treat multiple addictive behaviors. For example, Naltrexone has been utilized in the treatment of opioid abuse prevention, alcohol dependence, gambling, eating disorders, etc. (Merlo & Gold, 2008). This may also be supported by the mechanism and action of opioid blockers such as naltrexone (Burattini et al., 2008), partial opioid agonists such as buprenorphine (Bruijnzeel et al., 2007) and agonists such as methadone (Leri et al., 2009).

Radiographic neuroimaging studies, including the use of MRI, PET (positron emission tomography) and SPECT (single photon emission CT), as well as functional MRI, have helped confirm the addiction pathways and changes in brain structure and function associated with these substances (Volkow et al., 2004). A review of the literature indicates that structural abnormalities take place in the frontal cortex, prefrontal cortex, basal ganglia and amygdala (Fowler et al., 2007). For example, a review of functional imaging studies indicates the caudate nucleus, singulate and prefrontal cortex become activated during a drug "high" and the nucleus accumbens becomes activated during periods of craving. PET scans and SPECT scans have revealed the role of the striatal dopamine pathway in drug-related reward and craving (Volkow et al., 2004). Finally, the dopamine enhancement that causes the pleasurable "high" associated with these drugs of abuse is believed to diminish the drug user's ability to experience pleasure with regard to other activities (Hortin et al., 2006). More recent findings suggest that drug effects on brain structure and function, on a molecular and cellular basis, may be longstanding (Fowler et al., 2007).

Molecular Mechanisms and Neurobiological Consequences of Drug and Alcohol Use

Using animal models, there have been significant advances in the understanding of neural circuitry and cellular mechanisms involved in drug and alcohol addiction (Kalivas & O'Brien, 2008). Nestler has described changes associated with drug addiction on a molecular level, which has been considered a form of neural plasticity, resulting from long-term drug use (Nestler, 2001). Other studies have reviewed existing animal and human protein research on the cellular effects of opioids, amphetamines and alcohol, in the prefrontal cortex, striatum and hippocampus (Kobeissy et al., 2008). They have reported that morphine administration is associated with dysregulation of proteins involved in several cellular functions (e.g., metabolism, synaptic transmission, etc.). Methamphetamine administration appears to negatively alter cellular function in other ways, such as mitochondrial dysfunction and synaptic transmission (Sekine et al., 2008). The impact of chronic alcohol use also reveals similar dysfunction in signaling and cytoskeleton organization. Data suggest drug abuse may result in permanent damage on a cellular structure and function level. Wang and colleagues have described studies which assess inflammatory response and damage caused by drugs, such as amphetamines, and evaluating the time before brain function recovers following drug use (Wang et al., 2004).

TABLE 12.1 Physical and Behavioral Effects of Addictive Substances

Legal status L/P/I*	Substance	Behavioral abuse symptoms (when high)	Physical brain changes (MRI, PET, SPECT)**	Physical withdrawal symptoms	Behavioral withdrawal symptoms	FDA-approved pharmacological treatments
L	Alcohol	Emotional restraint gone, feeling of warmth, impaired judgment, confusion, slurred speech, gait staggering	Increased dopamine, damage to cellular structure level and function, dysfunction in neural signaling	Diaphoresis, tachycardia, nausea, vomiting, fever, convulsions, craving, delirium tremens	Anxiety, depression, aggression	Disulfiram, acamprosate, oral naltrexone, extended-release injectable naltrexone
P	Amphetamines (used by prescription to treat narcolepsy, ADHD, obesity)	Increased energy, improved focus, loss of interest in food or sex, general feeling of wellness	Significant deficit in brain reward function, increased level of dopamine and glutamate	Headache, dry mouth, irregular heart rate, increased blood pressure, fever and sweating	Anhedonia, anxious, moody, insomnia, appetite changes, bizarre mannerisms, hostility, aggression	**None** as of April, 2009. Those being investigated include: baclofen, topiramate, nifedipine, disulfiram
I	Methamphetamine (if smoked, Ice)	Extreme confidence, excessive talking, uninterested in sex, food, or friends, false sense of power, aggression	Microglial activation, decreased dopamine transporters, frontal cortex degeneration, neurotoxicity	Intense craving, excessive sleep, increased heart rate, convulsions, twitching or jerking, coma	Poor decision-making, severe depression, violent behavior, paranoia, hallucinations	**None** as of April, 2009. Prometa protocol (using flumazenil, gabapentin, hydroxyzine and vitamins) modafinil, lobeline

I	Cannabis (marijuana, pot)	Bloodshot eyes, dilated pupils, time sense slowed, crave food, especially sweets	Extra-cellular CRF levels, activation of brain reward stress system	Craving, headaches, dry mouth, nausea, restlessness, sweating, stomach pain	Anxiety, irritability, depression, physical tension, decreases in appetite and mood	**None** as of April, 2009. Those being investigated include: dronabinol, rimonabant
I	Cocaine (if smoked, Crack)	Dilated pupils, increased heart rate and blood pressure, lack of fatigue, fast speech, runny nose	Brain CRF systems activated, brain reward function decreased, cystine–glutamate exchange deficit	Nausea, blurred vision, chest pain, fever, muscle spasms, severe drug craving	Anxiety, depression, agitation, paranoia, auditory hallucinations	**None** as of April, 2009. Those being investigated include: selegiline, naltrexone, disulfiram, rasagiline, nifedipine
P	Opioids (Heroin)	Constricted pupils, euphoric mood, slowed breathing, sedation	Increased dopamine, damage to cellular structure and function, neural signaling deficit	Dysphoria, diarrhea, hyperalgesia, seizures, intense cravings, sweating, vomiting, dilated pupils	Irritability, agitation, anxiety, depression, insomnia, aggression	Naltrexone, buprenorphine, methadone, naloxone are approved; others under investigation

*L/P/I = Legal, Prescription, Illegal;

**MRI, PET, SPECT = magnetic resonance imaging, positron emission tomography, single photon emission CT.

Finally, drugs of abuse also induce adaptation in neuronal substrates than those involved in the acute reinforcing affects of drug abuse. Cessation of drug use leads to the recruitment of brain systems associated with behavioral and physiological responses to stressors (Liu et al., 2008). Corticotropin-releasing factor (CRF) is a neuropeptid which induces both behavioral and physiological responses resembling those observed during exposure to stress. Withdrawal from drugs of abuse induces the activation of brain CRF systems, and the antagonism of brain CRF receptors alleviates the negative systems associated with drug withdrawal (Romualdi et al., 2007). It has been repeatedly hypothesized that the negative affective state associated with the cessation of drug use provides the motivation for continued drug self-administration (Bruijnzeel & Gold, 2005).

Cocaine

Cocaine withdrawal leads to depression, anxiety, agitation, paranoia and drug craving. This may last for several days (Semlitz & Gold, 1986). Animal model research indicates that withdrawal of cocaine induces a negative emotional response that exceeds those associated with withdrawal from other drugs, including nicotine or morphine (Koob, 2003). Animal models have been developed to investigate the motivational effects of cocaine withdrawal to better understand the neuronal mechanisms that underlie cocaine dependence (Baker et al., 2003). For example, rat intracranial self-stimulation is used widely to study loss of interest or pleasure in activities, which is one of the core symptoms of depression, associated with withdrawal from drugs of abuse. Withdrawal from drugs of abuse appears to elevate brain reward thresholds, which may be interpreted as a decrease in brain reward function (Bruijnzeel et al., 2006). Research has indicated that 15 minutes after intravenous self-administration of cocaine, brain reward thresholds are decreased. However, 24 hours after the self-administration of cocaine, brain reward thresholds are increased (Kenny et al., 2003). The increase in brain reward thresholds has been shown to correlate with the amount of cocaine consumed during the binge. The severity of cocaine withdrawal symptoms, as measured by the cocaine selective severity assessment, is a powerful predictor of treatment outcome (Kampman et al., 2001).

Cocaine withdrawal is also characterized by anxiety symptoms (Chhatwal & Ressler, 2007). It has been hypothesized that these anxiety symptoms provide another motivational factor for continuation of cocaine use. Anxiety symptoms associated with cocaine withdrawal have been extensively investigated. More recent research has focused on the role of the neuropeptid CRF in anxiety effects associated with cocaine withdrawal (Romualdi et al., 2007). CRF plays a central role in mediating the effects of stress on the hypothalamic–pituitary–adrenocortical (HPA) axis. CRF in the hypothalamus is released in the pituitary portal system on exposure to stress, and induces adrenocorticotrophic hormone (ACTH) from the pituitary by the means of a CRF receptor. Withdrawal from cocaine induces a very strong activation of brain CRF systems

(Kalivas, 2007). Richter and Weiss allowed rats to self-administer cocaine for 12 hours. They measured extra cellular CRF levels in the central amygdala until 12 hours after the session. Four hours after the self-administration session, extra-cellular CRF levels started to rise to approximately 400% of baseline levels (Richter & Weiss, 1999). Increased activity of brain CRF systems appears to induce heightened anxiety, as experienced by cocaine users going through withdrawal (Moussawi et al., 2009).

Amphetamines

Withdrawal symptoms from amphetamines include dysphoria, fatigue, insomnia, appetite disturbance, agitation and other somatic symptoms. In rats, assessed with self-stimulation paradigm, withdrawal from amphetamines leads to significant anhedonia. In addition, it appears the deficit in brain reward function associated with amphetamine withdrawal is proportional to the duration of amphetamine use (Lin et al., 1999). Antidepressants that decrease the reuptake of serotonin and/or noradrenalin appear to attenuate this withdrawal phenomenon (Cryan et al., 2002). Taken as a whole, studies indicate that withdrawal from amphetamines induces a significant deficit in brain reward function (Koob, 2009). Furthermore, the similarity between symptoms of amphetamines in rodents and major depression in people indicates amphetamine withdrawal is a reasonable model to study for major depression. Amphetamine withdrawal anhedonia appears to be attenuated at least partly by serotonin enhancement (Koob, 2009). Finally, it appears the amphetamine withdrawal model of depression has some ability to discern between fast and slow onset of action with pharmacological agents.

Alcohol

Withdrawal from alcohol has been associated with significant anxiety and depression (Bolton et al., 2008). Unlike stimulants, alcohol withdrawal may include severe physical symptoms such as diaphoresis, tachycardia, nausea and vomiting, fever and convulsions. Multiple animal models have been developed to investigate the physical symptoms of alcohol withdrawal. However, models which focus on anxiety-like symptoms induced by alcohol withdrawal appear most relevant (Neznanova et al., 2009). Research with rats, using benzodiazepines as treatment of alcohol withdrawal-induced anxiety has shown promising results. However, due to the cross tolerance of benzodiazepines and alcohol, the former may simply be a substitute for alcohol. Currently there are four pharmacotherapeutic agents approved by the United States Food and Drug Administration for human treatment of alcohol abuse and dependence; these are disulfiram, acamprosate, oral naltrexone and extended-release injectable naltrexone (Garbutt, 2009).

Recent research has provided evidence that the hyperactive brain CRF system may also be associated with increased anxiety associated with alcohol withdrawal (Bruijnzeel & Gold, 2005; Barr et al., 2008). Alcohol withdrawal also appears to increase extra-cellular CRF levels in the nucleus of the striatal terminalas, a brain area implicated in anxiety behavior (Walker et al., 2003). Additionally, CRF levels appear to return to baseline with subsequent alcohol intake (Olive et al., 2002). Therefore, findings indicate that alcohol withdrawal induces an activation of the brain CRF system, and antagonism of CRF receptors decreases the anxiety behavior associated with alcohol withdrawal. Finally, alcohol withdrawal is also characterized by depressive symptoms (Fergusson et al., 2009). The withdrawal from alcohol, similar to stimulants, appears to induce a deficit in brain reward function in rats that persists for approximately 48 hours after the cessation of alcohol use (Adams et al., 2008).

Cannabis

There has been significant controversy regarding whether chronic cannabis use gives rise to dependency. However, research indicates the cessation of cannabis in individuals does give rise to affective and physical withdrawal symptoms (Nordstrom & Levin, 2007). The abstinence from cannabis increases anxiety, irritability and depression, and may cause increased insomnia and stomach pain. Furthermore, those individuals withdrawing from cannabis demonstrated more aggressive behavior (Nordstrom & Levin, 2007). The fact that cannabis withdrawal symptoms may be relatively mild, compared to other drugs of abuse, may be attributable to the pharmacokinetics of cannabis. Cannabis is lipid-soluble and accumulates in the fatty tissue. Because of the slow release of cannabinoids from fatty tissue, withdrawal symptoms may be less. This theory is supported by the observation that cannabinoid withdrawal symptoms are more obvious after the administration of a cannabinoid antagonist (Haller et al., 2004).

Once again, withdrawal from cannabinoids appears to be associated with activation of the brain stress system (Yucel et al., 2008). Research indicates that antagonists of cannabinoid receptors cause elevated extra cellular CRF levels in rats and were associated with increased somatic withdrawal signs (Bruijnzeel & Gold, 2005). These studies indicate that precipitated cannabinoid withdrawal leads to increased anxious behavior, somatic symptoms, and an activation of the brain reward stress system, leading to increased activity of the CRF system, and that endogenous cannabinoids exert an inhibitory control over anxiety-like states (Chhatwal & Ressler, 2007).

Performance-Enhancing Drugs

Anabolic androgenic steroids are naturally-occurring male hormones involved in a variety of physiological functions. Testosterone is the most commonly known steroid. Anabolic means "building" and androgenic relates to male characteristics. Steroids may be categorized as endogenous or naturally-occurring, such as testosterone, or exogenous otherwise known as synthetics, such as Danazol. Synthetic testosterone was first developed by the Nazis, producing dramatic improvements in strength and power. Subsequently exogenous synthetic testosterone was used in pain patients and those who were physically disabled (Martin et al., 2007).

Serious medical side-effects of steroids include liver function abnormalities, liver and kidney tumors, endocrine and reproductive problems, testicular atrophy, cardiac effects and psychiatric symptoms (Rylkova et al., 2007). These deleterious consequences are also exaggerated by the common practice of "stacking" steroids, using 10 times or more than the recommended medical dose, or the repeated use of multiple drugs.

Human growth hormone is again a naturally-occurring polypeptide hormone produced in the pituitary gland, and one of the major hormones influencing growth and development. The major function of HGA is protein synthesis, speeding muscle tissue repair and building muscle and muscle tone (Martin et al., 2007). It is also involved in the control of growth (height) from birth to adulthood. It was discovered by Dr Harvey Cushing in 1912. It has been used to treat dwarfism in children. Synthetic or human growth hormone is now available in a variety of forms. Most human growth hormone is used in medicine, and unfortunately at times diverted to sports doping. Most athletes tend to abuse human growth hormone because of unsubstantiated reports that it is as effective as anabolic steroids, with fewer side-effects. Human growth hormone is also used as a steroid substitute, to prevent muscle loss after the discontinuation of steroids. According to controlled studies, human growth hormone does not increase muscle strength, however, reports on human growth hormone performance enhancement in sport are limited. Nevertheless, the abuse of human growth hormone abuse in sports appears to be escalating (Conrad & Potter, 2004). Finally, side-effects associated with human growth hormone may lead to life-threatening health conditions, especially since estimates are that athletes use up to 10 times the therapeutic dose of this drug. Side-effects include abnormal bone growth, hypertension, cardiovascular disease, cardiomyopathy, glucose intolerance, colon polyps, cancer and decreased lifespan (Perls et al., 2005).

Opioids

Opioids have been used medicinally for many centuries and are one of the most effective drugs for providing moderate to severe pain relief. Hippocrates (460–357 BC), however, recommended physicians prescribe opium sparingly because of its deleterious affects due to excessive or prolonged use. Opioid abuse and addiction has become an increasingly significant problem in our society. According to "the trans and drug-related emergency department" visits in the United States, the lifetime prevalence for prescription opioid abuse in adults was estimated to be 6.8% in 1992, but 22.1% in 2002. It has become apparent that opioid effects differ significantly between individuals and between acute and chronic or repeated administration. It has also become apparent that individuals differ widely with regard to their susceptibility to addiction following prolonged use of opioids.

Generally, the acute effects of opioid administration are robust. Acute opioid injection is often associated with pain relief, reliably produced respiratory depression; it is also anti-tussive and decreases gastrointestinal motility. However, psychological affects vary from euphoria to uncomfortably mind-altering. Over time, tolerance and dependence develops. The former may occur with regard to the euphoric or mood effect, as well as the antinocicepitive or analgesic affect (Morgan et al., 2006).

Chronic opioid use appears to not only change the responsiveness to a particular opioid dose, but may also produce physiological and behavioral changes, which become apparent when opioid use is stopped (Miller & Gold, 2006). Withdrawal effects may include the opposite of acute opioid administration, and dysphoria, diarrhea, enhanced sensitivity to painful stimuli (hyperalgesia) have all been described. Thus, the avoidance of a withdrawal syndrome is often thought to be a powerful motivator in continued opioid use. Furthermore, the chronic use of opioids is hypothesized to induce changes in the neural function that are physiologically adaptive in nature, but are likely to attribute to tolerance and dependence and may give rise to drug addictive behavior.

Currently, three endogenous morphine-binding sites in brain membranes have been identified and are associated with endogenously-produced opioid function. These three receptor types are the MOP (mu) DOP (delta) and KOP (kappa) receptors that are structurally similar, but encoded by different genes (Kieffer, 1999). A variety of protein ligands bind opioid receptors and are similar to the structure of morphine, including codeine, methadone, buprenorphine and fentanyl. Behavioral consequences of activating different opioid receptors can be opposing in some individuals and similar in others. For example, both mu and kappa agonists are analgesic. However, mu agonists are rewarding and kappa are aversive when tested in behavioral assays. In addition to differing potent and pharmacogenetics, opioids also differ in their activity at opioid receptors (Shoblock & Maidment, 2006). For example, methadone is a relatively effective agonist at the mu opioid receptor, whereas buprenorphine is a weak partial agonist. Furthermore, in addition to modulating the effects of opioid drugs, the endogenous opioid system is highly relevant in the reward activity of other drugs of abuse. Contet and colleagues have demonstrated that animals lacking mu opioid receptors display behaviors indicating diminished reward for alcohol, marijuana and nicotine (Contet et al., 2004).

Conversely, opioid receptor antagonist, such as naloxone, when administered to drug naïve rodents, is highly aversive, suggesting endogenous opioid signals are an aspect of natural homeostasis. Naloxone aversion is not observed in mice lacking the mu opioid receptor, leading to the hypothesis that naloxone produces aversion by antagonizing proekephalan-derived activation of the mu receptor

TABLE 12.2 Frequently Abused Substances

NAME	PRESCRIPTION TREATMENT FOR:
Codeine	Cough, mild pain
Methadone	Opiate abuse, primarily heroin addiction
Morphine	Pain, moderate to severe
Percocet	Pain, moderate to severe
Percodan	Pain, moderate to severe
Vicoden	Pain, moderate to severe
Oxycodone	Pain, severe
Hydrocodone	Pain, severe
Ativan	Anxiety
Valium	Anxiety
Librium	Anxiety
Xanax	Anxiety
Haldol	Psychosis
Thorazine	Psychosis
Nembutal	Sleep disorders
Seconal	Sleep disorders
Amytal	Sleep disorders
Soma	Muscle relaxant
Ritalin	Attention deficit disorders
Cylert	Attention deficit disorders
Adderall	Attention deficit disorders
NAME	**OTC TREATMENT FOR:**
Drixoral Cough Liquid Caps	Cold, cough, congestion
Robitussin AC	Cold, cough, congestion
Decotuss – HD	Cold, cough, congestion

which occurs under normal conditions *in vivo* (Shoblock & Maidment, 2006). Taken as a whole, this research suggests the opioid system is critical in many addictive behaviors, and modulates the reward effects of various natural events.

Further analysis of the opioid system indicates adaptations take place on a cellular level. Nirenberg and colleagues described an opioid-responsive cultured cell line in which morphine's ability to cyclic amp responses became dramatically attenuated following chronic exposure, and in which removal of morphine produced an opposing affect on cellular cyclic amp levels (Sharma et al., 1977). This has led to a more general understanding of opioid addiction in terms of a homeostatic or regulatory process at the level of individual opioid responsive neurons. This may further be understood as a reduced signaling response, beginning at the receptor level but taking place with a down-regulation of the total receptor complement and additional intracellular biochemical mechanisms which control opioid receptors and contribute to a functional change in the endogenous opioid system, thereby distinguishing acute, chronic and regulatory effects of various opioid drugs (Whistler et al., 1999).

CONCLUSION

In summary, substance abuse and addiction disorders are the most costly of all neuropsychiatric disorders in this country (Uhl & Grow, 2004). Animal models have made a profound impact on the study of each drug of abuse with the new, more realistic, studies making addiction the easiest of the neuropsychiatric diseases to study (see Table 12.2). New neuroimaging techniques have greatly advanced our understanding of the neural systems involved in addictive drugs, as well as in their withdrawal. Neurobiology and psychology together bring change associated with abuse and addiction, thus leading the way for development of new treatments (Robinson, 2004). Biological research is relevant to reducing this public health problem by developing evidence-based approaches to the evaluation and treatment of drug addiction. Certainly, a more comprehensive view of the biological aspects of drug abuse, including the signaling pathways, reward system, withdrawal/stress response, etc., relates to the compulsive and uncontrollable abuse of psychoactive drugs. By considering their mechanisms of action on a genetic, molecular and cellular level, which give rise to craving, withdrawal and relapse phenomena, individuals who experience this disease may be more appropriately managed. The understanding of various methodological approaches involved in the research of drug abuse is likely to improve our understanding of this most costly of neuropsychiatric disorders.

REFERENCES

Adams, C. L., Cowen, M. S., Short, J. L., & Lawrence, A. J. (2008). Combined antagonism of glutamate mGlu5 and adenosine A_{2A} receptors interact to regulate alcohol-seeking in rats. *International Journal of Neuropsychopharmacology, 11*, 229–241.

Anderson, S. M., Famous, K. R., Sadri-Vakili, G., Kumaresan, V., Schmidt, H. D., Bass, C. E., Terwilliger, E. F., Cha, J. H., & Pierce, R. C. (2008). CaMKII: a biochemical bridge linking accumbens dopamine and glutamate systems in cocaine seeking. *Nature Neuroscience, 11*(3), 344–353.

Baker, D. A., McFarland, K., Lake, R. W., Shen, H., Tang, X. C., Toda, S., & Kalivas, P. W. (2003). Neuroadaptions in cystine-glutamate exchange underlie cocaine relapse. *Nature Neuroscience, 6*(7), 743–749.

Barr, C. S., Dvoskin, R. L., Yuan, Q., Lipsky, R. H., Gupte, M., Hu, X., Zhou, Z., Schwandt, M. L., Lindell, S. G., McKee, M., Becker, M. L., Kling, M. A., Gold, P. W., Higley, D., Heilig, M., Suomi, S. J., & Goldman, D. (2008). CRH haplotype as a factor influencing cerebrospinal fluid levels of corticotropin-releasing hormone, hypothalamic-pituitary-adrenal axis activity, temperament, and alcohol consumption in Rhesus Macaques. *Archives of General Psychiatry, 65*(8), 934–944.

Bolton, J. M., Robinson, J., & Sareen, J. (2008). Self-medication of mood disorders with alcohol and drugs in the National Epidemiologic Survey on Alcohol and Related Conditions. *Journal Affective Disorders, 115*(3), 367–375.

Bruijnzeel, A. W., & Gold, M. S. (2005). The role of corticotropin-releasing factor-like peptides in cannabis, nicotine, and alcohol dependence. *Brain Research Reviews, 49*, 505–528.

Bruijnzeel, A. W., Repetto, M., & Gold, M. S. (2004). Neurobiological mechanisms in addictive and psychiatric disorders. *Psychiatric Clinics of North America, 27*, 661–674.

Bruijnzeel, A. W., Lewis, B., Bajpai, L. K., Morey, T. E., Dennis, D. M., & Gold, M. (2006). Severe deficit in brain reward function associated with fentanyl withdrawal in rats. *Biological Psychiatry, 59*, 477–480.

Bruijnzeel, A. W., Marcinkiewcz, C., Issac, S., Booth, M. M., Dennis, D. M., & Gold, M. S. (2007). The effects of buprenorphine on fentanyl withdrawal in rats. *Psychopharmacology, 191*, 931–941.

Burattini, C., Burbassi, S., Aicardi, G., & Cervo, L. (2008). Effects of naltrexone on cocaine- and sucrose-seeking behaviour in response to associated stimuli in rats. *International Journal of Neuropsychopharmacology, 11*, 103–109.

Chhatwal, J. P., & Ressler, K. J. (2007). Modulation of fear and anxiety by the endogenous cannabinoid system. *CNS Spectrums, 12*, 211–220.

Conrad, P., & Potter, D. (2004). Human growth hormone and the temptations of biomedical enhancement. *Sociology of Health & Illness, 26*(2), 184–215.

Contet, C., Kieffer, B. L., & Befort, K. (2004). Mu opioid receptor: a gateway to drug addiction. *Current Opinions in NeuroBiology, 14*(3), 370–378.

Cryan, J. F., Markou, A., & Lucki, I. (2002). Assessing antidepressant activity in rodents: recent developments and future needs. *Trends Pharmacological Science, 23*(5), 238–245.

Dackis, C., & O'Brien, C. (2005). Neurobiology of addiction: treatment and public policy ramifications. *Nature Neuroscience, 8*(11), 1431–1436.

Fergusson, D. M., Boden, J. M., & Horwood, J. (2009). Tests of causal links between alcohol abuse or dependence and major depression. *Archives of General Psychiatry, 66*(3), 260–266.

Fowler, J. S., Volkow, N. D., Kassed, C. A., & Chang, L. (2007). Imaging the addicted human brain. *Science Practical Perspective, 3*(2), 4–16.

Garbutt, J. C. (2009). Promoting recovery in alcohol-dependent patients. *Journal of Substance Abuse Treatment, 36*(Suppl. 1), S3–S4.

Gonzalez, R. A., Job, M. O., & Doyon, W. M. (2004). The role of mesolimbic dopamine in the development and maintenance of ethanol reinforcement. *Pharmacological Therapy, 103*(2), 121–146.

Haller, J., Varga, B., Ledent, C., & Freund, T. F. (2004). CB1 cannabinoid receptors mediate anxiolytic effects: Convergent genetic and pharmacological evidence with CB1-specific agents. *Behavioural Pharmacology, 15*(4), 299–304.

Hortin, G. L., Jortani, S. A., Ritchie, J. C., Jr, Valdes, R., Jr, & Chan, D. W. (2006). Proteomics: a new diagnostic frontier. *Clinical Chemistry, 52*(7), 1218–1222.

Kalivas, P. W. (2007). Neurobiology of cocaine addiction: Implications for new pharmacotherapy. *The American Journal on Addictions, 16*, 71–78.

Kalivas, P. W., & O'Brien, C. (2008). Drug addiction as a pathology of staged neuroplasticity. *Neuropsychopharmacology, 33*, 166–180.

Kampman, K. M., Alterman, A. I., Volpicelli, J. R., Maany, I., Mullere, E. S., Luce, D., Mulholland, E. M., Jawad, A. F., Parikh, G. A., Mulvaney, F. D., Weinrieb, R. M., & O'Brien, C. P. (2001). Cocaine withdrawal symptoms and initial urine toxicology results predict treatment attrition in outpatient cocaine dependence treatment. *Psychological Addictive Behavior, 15*(1), 52–59.

Kenny, P. J., Polis, I., Koob, G. F., & Markou, A. (2003). Low dose cocaine self-administration transiently increases but high dose cocaine persistently decreases brain reward function in rats. *European Journal Neuroscience, 17*(1), 191–195.

Kieffer, B. L. (1999). Opioids: First lessons from knockout mice. *Trends in Pharmacological Science, 20*(1), 19–26.

Kobeissy, F. H., Sadasivan, S., Liu, J., Gold, M. S., & Wang, K. K. (2008). Psychiatric research: Psychoproteomics, degradomics and systems biology. *Experimental Reviews Proteomics, 5*(2), 293–314.

Koob, G. F. (2003). Neuroadaptive mechanisms of addiction: studies on the extended amygdala. *European Neuropsychopharmacology, 13*(6), 442–452.

Koob, G. F. (2009). Neurobiological substrates for the dark side of compulsivity in addiction. *Neuropharmacology, 56*, 18–31.

Leri, F., Zhou, Y., Goddard, B., Levy, A. M., Jacklin, D., & Kreek, M. J. (2009). Steady-state methadone blocks cocaine seeking and cocaine-induced gene expression alterations in the rat brain. *European Neuropsychopharmacology, 19*, 238–249.

Lin, D., Koob, G. F., & Markou, A. (1999). Differential effects of withdrawal from chronic amphetamine or fluoxetine administration on brain stimulation reward in the rat – interactions between the two drugs. *Psychopharmacology (Berl), 145*(3), 283–294.

Liu, J., Pan, H., Gold, M. S., Derendorf, H., & Bruijnzeel, A. W. (2008). Effects of fentanyl dose and exposure duration on the affective and somatic signs of fentanyl withdrawal in rats. *Neuropharmacology, 55*(5), 812–818.

Martin, D. M., Baron, D. A., & Gold, M. S. (2007). A review of performance-enhancing drugs in professional sports and their spread to amateur athletics, adolescents, and other at-risk populations. *Journal of Addictive Diseases, 25*(Suppl. 1), 5–15.

Merlo, L. J., & Gold, M. S. (2008). Special report – Frontiers in psychiatric research: Addiction research: The state of the art in 2008. *Psychiatric Times, 25*(7), 52–57.

Miller, N. S., & Gold, M. S. (2006). Opiate prescription medication dependence and pain perceptions. *Journal of Addictive Diseases, 26*(Suppl. 1), 65–72.

Morgan, D., Frost-Pineda, K., & Gold, M. S. (2006). Medical and nonmedical use of prescription opioids: Epidemiology and prevalence. *Psychiatric Annals, 36*(6), 404–409.

Moussawi, K., Pacchioni, A., Moran, M., Olive, M. F., Gass, J. T., Lavin, A., & Kalivas, P. W. (2009). N-Acetylcysteine reverses cocaine-induced metaplasticity. *Nature Neuroscience, 12*(2), 182–189.

Nestler, E. J. (2001). Molecular basis of long-term plasticity underlying addiction. *National Review of Neuroscience, 2*(2), 119–128.

Neznanova, O., Björk, K., Rimondini, R., Hansson, A. C., Hyytiä, P., Helig, M., & Sommer, W. H. (2009). Acute ethanol challenge inhibits glycogen synthase Kinase-3ß in the rat perfrontal cortex. *International Journal of Neuropsychopharmacology, 12*, 275–280.

Olive, M. F., Koenig, H. N., Nannini, M. A., & Hodge, C. W. (2002). Elevated extracellular CRF levels in the bed nucleus of the stria terminalis during ethanol withdrawal and reduction by subsequent ethanol intake. *Pharmacology Biochemical Behavior, 72*(1–2), 213–220.

Perls, T. T., Reisman, N. R., & Olshansky, S. J. (2005). Provision or distribution of growth hormone for "antiaging:" clinical and legal issues. *Journal of the American Medical Association, 294*(16), 2086–2090.

Phillips, P. E., Stuber, G. D., Heien, M. L., Wightman, R. M., & Carelli, R. M. (2003). Subsecond dopamine release promotes cocaine seeking. *Nature, 422*(6932), 614–618.

Regier, D. A., Farmer, M. E., Rae, D. S., Locke, B. Z., Keith, S. J., Judd, L. L., & Goodwin, F. K. (1990). Comorbidity of mental disorders with alcohol and other drug abuse. Results from the Epidemiologic Catchment Areas (ECA) Study. *Journal of the American Medical Association, 264*(19), 2511–2518.

Richter, R. M., & Weiss, F. (1999). *In vivo* CRF release in rat amygdala is increased during cocaine withdrawal in self-administrating rats. *Synapse, 32*(4), 254–261.

Robinson, T. E. (2004). Addicted rats. *Science, 305*, 951–953.

Romualdi, P., Di Benedetto, M., D'Addario, C., Collins, S. L., Wade, D., Candeletti, S., & Izenwasser, S. (2007). Chronic cocaine produces dereases in N/OFQ peptide levels in select rat brain regions. *Journal of Molecular Neuroscience, 31*, 159–164.

Rylkova, D., Bruijnzeel, A. W., & Gold, M. S. (2007). Anabolic steroid abuse: Neurobiological substrates and psychiatric comorbidity. *Journal of Addictive Diseases, 25*(Suppl. 1), 33–45.

Sekine, Y., Ouchi, Y., Sugihara, G., Takei, N., Yoshikawa, E., Nakamura, K., Iwata, Y., Tsuchiya, K. J., Suda, S., Suzuki, K., Kawai, M., Takebayashi, K., Yamamoto, S., Matsuzaki, H., Ueki, T., Mori, N., Gold, M. S., & Cadet, J. L. (2008). Methamphetamine causes microglial activation in the brains of human abusers. *The Journal of Neuroscience, 28*(22), 5756–5761.

Semlitz, L., & Gold, M. S. (1986). Adolescent drug abuse. Diagnosis, treatment and prevention. *Psychiatric Clinics of North America, 9*(3), 455–473.

Sharma, S. K., Klee, W. A., & Nirenberg, M. (1977). Opiate-dependent modulation of adenylate cyclase. *Proc National Academy Science USA, 74*(8), 3365–3369.

Shoblock, J. R., & Maidment, N. T. (2006). Constitutively active Mu opioid receptors mediate the enhanced conditioned adversive effect of naloxone in morphine-dependent mice. *Neuropsychopharmacology, 31*, 171–177.

Substance Abuse and Mental Health Services Administration (SAMHSA). (2008). *Results from the 2007 National Survey on Drug Use and Health: National Findings* Office of Applied Studies, NSDUH Series H–34, DHHS Publication No. SMA 08–4343. Rockville, MD: SAMHSA.

Uhl, G. R., & Grow, R. W. (2004). The burden of complex genetics in brain disorders. *Archives of General Psychiatry, 61*(3), 223–229.

Volkow, N. D., Fowler, J. S., Wang, G. J., & Swanson, J. M. (2004). Dopamine in drug abuse addiction: results from imaging studies and treatment implications. *Molecular Psychiatry, 9*(6), 557–569.

Volkow, N. D., & Li, T. K. (2005). The neuroscience of addiction. *Nature Neuroscience, 8*(11), 1429–1430.

Walker, D. L., Toufexis, D. J., & Davis, M. (2003). Role of the bed nucleus of the stria terminalis versus the amygdala in fear, stress and anxiety. *European Journal of Pharmacology, 463*(1–3), 199–216.

Wang, G. J., Volkow, N. D., Chang, L., Miller, E., Sedler, M., Hitzemann, R., Zhu, W., Logan, J., Ma, Y., & Fowler, J. S. (2004). Partial recovery of brain metabolism in methamphetamine abusers after protracted abstinence. *American Journal of Psychiatry, 161*(2), 242–248.

Whistler, J. L., Chuang, H. H., Chu, P., Jan, L. Y., & von Zastrow, M. (1999). Functional disassociation of mu opioid receptor signaling and endocytosis: implications of the biology of opiate tolerance and addiction. *Neuron, 23*(4), 737–746.

Yucel, M., Solowij, N., Respondek, C., Whittle, S., Fornito, A., Pantelis, C., & Lubman, I. (2008). Regional brain abnormalities associated with long-term heavy cannabis use. *Archives of General Psychiatry, 65*(6), 694–701.

Chapter 13

Forensic Toxicology

Michele L. Merves, PhD and Bruce A. Goldberger, PhD
Department of Pathology, Immunology and Laboratory Medicine, University of Florida College of Medicine, Gainesville, FL, USA

INTRODUCTION

"What is there that is not poison? All things are poison and nothing without poison. Solely the dose determines that a thing is not a poison."

Paracelsus (from Paracelsus' Third Defense)

According to the American Board of Forensic Toxicology (ABFT), forensic toxicology is "the study and practice of the application of toxicology to the purposes of the law." (Toxicology is the study of poisons. The term "poison" has a very broad meaning and refers to any substance that causes injury or death of an organism through a chemical process.) Forensic toxicology demands the pursuit of scientific discovery within the rigors of the legal system in order to emphasize truth (accuracy), justice (impartiality) and the public good. It began in the United States in the early 1900s, shortly after the development of the coroner and medical examiner systems. With many technological and procedural advances, the field has matured into three distinct disciplines: postmortem forensic toxicology; human performance forensic toxicology; and forensic urine drug testing. These disciplines overlap significantly; however, each one was developed to aid the judicial system in different ways. Table 13.1 is a list of websites related to the practice of forensic toxicology.

According to the Society of Forensic Toxicologists (SOFT), postmortem forensic toxicology determines the "absence or presence of drugs and their metabolites, chemicals such as ethanol and other volatile substances, carbon monoxide and other gases, metals and other toxic chemicals in human fluids and tissues, and evaluates their role as a determinant or contributory factor in the cause and manner of death." Human performance forensic toxicology, also known as behavioral toxicology: "determines the absence or presence of ethanol and other drugs and chemicals in blood, breath or other appropriate specimen(s) and evaluates their role in modifying human performance or behavior." Forensic urine drug testing: "determines the absence or presence of drugs and their metabolites in urine to demonstrate prior use or abuse."

TABLE 13.1 Forensic Toxicology-Related Websites

American Academy of Forensic Sciences	www.aafs.org
American Board of Forensic Toxicology	www.abft.org
College of American Pathologists	www.cap.org
Drug and Alcohol Testing Industry Association	www.datia.org
International Association for Chemical Testing	www.iactonline.org
International Council on Alcohol, Drugs and Traffic Safety	www.icadts.org
National Institute on Drug Abuse	www.nida.nih.gov
Society of Forensic Toxicologists	www.soft-tox.org
Substance Abuse & Mental Health Services Administration	www.drugfreeworkplace.gov
The International Association of Forensic Toxicologists	www.tiaft.org

As noted in these definitions pharmaceutical and illicit drugs are the most common analytes, but other chemicals such as volatiles, metals, corrosive agents and organic compounds may also be targeted in forensic toxicology. These definitions not only discuss the analytes, but also the key biological matrices. Blood is often collected, but alternative specimens such as urine, oral fluid and hair may be useful.

In forensic toxicology, each specimen is tracked by detailed documentation, from the time of its collection to the time of its disposal. Furthermore, each positive result is confirmed by a second analytical test before being reported. These two aspects of forensic toxicology, the chain of custody and the multiple analytical testing procedures (dual-testing philosophy) required for each case, are some of the most important distinctions between this field and its clinical counterparts. Detailed instructions for the chain of custody and analytical testing procedures, as well as every other aspect of the laboratory, are maintained in the standard operating procedural manual (SOP), another important aspect of forensic toxicology.

POSTMORTEM FORENSIC TOXICOLOGY

Postmortem forensic toxicology plays a key ancillary role in medicolegal death investigation. In the United States, these death investigations are conducted through the medical examiner or coroner system, and the medical examiner or coroner is responsible for the certification of the cause and manner of death. Depending on the jurisdiction, an appointed forensic pathologist (medical examiner) or elected official (coroner) will conduct an autopsy, request ancillary testing (e.g., toxicology), review medical records and other related documents in order to determine the cause and manner of death of an individual. Death certificates for individuals that died from natural causes are often signed by the treating physician. Most jurisdictions, if not all, require that all "unnatural" deaths are investigated by the medical examiner or coroner system.

The medical examiner or coroner authorizes the collection of specimens, which are often sent to a forensic toxicology laboratory for analysis with the chain of custody documentation. Depending on the nature of the case, a variety of specimens are collected to help assess the role of drugs in the death of the decedent. Typical specimens include blood, urine, bile, vitreous humor (ocular fluid) and stomach contents. However, tissue specimens such as liver, kidney, lung, spleen, brain, blood clots (hematomas), hair and nails may be useful. Any medication and drug paraphernalia found at the death scene are valuable.

The type of specimen collection container is very important to the preservation of the specimen, especially blood. The most common collection tubes employed are vacuum-sealed glass tubes (e.g., Vacutainer©). These collection tubes contain various preservatives, indicated by the color of the cap. For example, the two most commonly used tubes in forensic toxicology are the red-top (no additives) and gray-top (sodium fluoride and potassium oxalate) tubes. Sodium fluoride and potassium oxalate are important to prevent bacterial growth, as well as to preserve the integrity of the specimen and drug analytes present in the fluid.

HUMAN PERFORMANCE FORENSIC TOXICOLOGY

Human performance forensic toxicology, which is also known as behavioral toxicology, is primarily designed to establish relationships between changes in behavior with the concentrations of drug(s) that elicit those changes. The most common applications include the recognition of the effects of ethanol and other drugs on driving performance and/or work-related tasks. Ideally, the effects on behavior are documented through observations, such as those from safety violations, accidents and/or standardized field sobriety tests. These observations are corroborated by positive toxicology results. Blood and breath are the primary specimens utilized to document impairment in individuals, although other specimens such as oral fluid (saliva) may be used in some jurisdictions.

FORENSIC URINE DRUG TESTING

Forensic urine drug testing is often referred to as workplace drug testing, even though various public and private agencies and organizations mandate this type of drug testing. Some examples include the criminal justice system, amateur and professional athletics, and many public and private corporations. The United States military was the first to introduce the concept of a drug-free workplace, but many quickly followed with requirements for testing individuals seeking employment and, in some circumstances, current employees.

As indicated in the name, urine is the usual specimen collected; however, hair is an alternative specimen to urine used by some employers to increase the window of detection. The most common drug and drug classes tested are amphetamines, cannabinoids, cocaine, opioids and phencyclidine (also known as the NIDA or SAMHSA Five). The goal of forensic urine drug testing is to document the use of banned substances, not to necessarily correlate behavior to drug use. Urine is popular because it is very compatible with cost-effective and automated screening instrumentation. Due to the potential for adulteration, forensic urine drug testing laboratories are often adapting their testing methodology to readily identify adulterated specimens.

Standard Operating Procedural Manual

Guidelines for each laboratory are provided in the laboratory's standard operating procedure (SOP) manual. The SOP should include recommendations and requirements for chain of custody, collection, transport and receipt of a specimen, drug and drug metabolite analysis, generation and certification of the final report, quality assurance and quality control procedures, personnel education and training, and all other aspects of the laboratory practice. At minimum, this SOP is reviewed annually by appropriate personnel, and all changes are documented.

Chain of Custody

The chain of custody is the administrative process that monitors and tracks the specimen from collection to disposal. It includes paperwork containing the names of individuals that handled the specimen for any reason including collection, transport and receipt. Even after destroying the specimen, the written record is kept for many years, often indefinitely. This documentation is critical for reporting the results and maintaining confidence in the collection, testing and reporting processes. As mentioned previously, the SOP for each laboratory must maintain the instructions for appropriate chain of custody procedures and forms.

Dual-Testing Philosophy

"As a general matter of scientific and forensic principle, the detection or initial identification of drugs and other toxins should be confirmed whenever possible by a second technique based on a different chemical principle."

(American Academy of Forensic Sciences Toxicology Section and Society of Forensic Toxicologists (1985))

Forensic toxicology is an applied science that often has financial and time constraints. Therefore, a dual-testing philosophy was developed in order to provide a cost-effective service that yields legally-defensible results. The first step is often referred to as the screen and the second step as confirmation. The screening test is designed to differentiate specimens containing the analyte(s) of interest from those without any analyte(s) of interest. Ideally, the technique is relatively quick, inexpensive, semi-quantitative, and does not permit false negative test results. To achieve these goals, cross-reactivity is often a key component. In this context, cross-reactivity refers to the ability of an analytical test to indicate a positive result for multiple analytes with similar chemical structures (e.g., an opiate assay may be able to detect morphine, hydromorphone, hydrocodone, oxycodone, codeine and other similar analytes). Since this screening test does not distinguish which analyte produced the positive test result, the positive screen test results are considered *presumptive* and the specimen must be subjected to confirmation testing. The confirmation test should employ, whenever possible, a different analytical technique from the screening test. It is imperative that the confirmation test does not produce false positive test results.

Many analytical procedures have been developed, optimized and validated for the screening and confirmation testing process. Some of the most common techniques include immunoassay, gas chromatography, gas chromatography–mass spectrometry and liquid chromatography–mass spectrometry.

Sample Preparation

Sample preparation is a key component in the drug analysis process. Depending on the complexity of the biological matrix and the detection method, varying degrees of sample preparation may be necessary. Some methods (e.g., colorimetric) may not require any sample preparation, whereas others may require hydrolysis of the conjugated metabolites or protein precipitation. Furthermore, many assays require the isolation of the analyte(s) from the biological matrix. Two such types of isolation techniques are liquid–liquid extraction (LLE) and solid–phase extraction (SPE). It is important to note that many of these sample preparation techniques are compatible with liquid specimens, but solid specimens may also be used. These "solids" (e.g., liver, brain, other biological tissues, or pills) can be measured according to weight, diluted with a liquid (e.g., buffer) and homogenized prior to the extraction.

Liquid–Liquid Extraction

Liquid–liquid extraction (LLE) methods are often cost effective, simple and very robust. They utilize the physicochemical properties (e.g., pKa and polarity) of the analyte(s) in order to isolate the analyte(s) from the aqueous matrices into an organic solvent. Variations of LLE can be helpful such as "back extraction," which isolates the analyte back into an aqueous phase from the organic phase in order to remove additional interferents. LLE methods are commonly employed in forensic toxicology laboratories because often they have minimal steps and provide adequate sensitivity. However, the technique may become tedious with the separation of the two phases and can generate large volumes of liquid waste.

Solid–Phase Extraction

Solid–phase extraction (SPE) has become an important isolation technique in forensic toxicology laboratories. Since its inception less than 50 years ago, this technology has advanced significantly and can be used to separate many types of analytes from complex matrices. SPE cartridges contain solid polymers with nonpolar, polar, or bipolar functional groups. Selectivity is optimized based on the properties of these polymers. For example, nonpolar analytes will have affinity for nonpolar polymers, polar analytes for polar polymers, and bipolar polymers for many types of drugs containing nonpolar and polar functional groups. Often, analytes are loaded onto the conditioned polymers and interferents washed away by manipulating the chemical environment in accordance with the physicochemical properties of the analytes. The target analytes are then removed from the polymers using appropriate solvents with higher affinities for the analytes than the polymer has for the analytes. Conversely, some SPE techniques utilize resins that have affinities for the interferents instead of the analytes, allowing the target analytes to pass through into a collection chamber.

Detection Techniques

A diverse repertoire of analytical techniques exists for the detection of drugs and other analytes. Many of them are specific and selective enough to quantitate these compounds, allowing their use for either screening and/or confirmation. Depending on the resources of the laboratory, various combinations of detection techniques can be used. Some of the most common techniques used in the screening process are immunoassay, gas chromatography, gas chromatography–mass spectrometry and liquid chromatography–mass spectrometry. Gas chromatography–mass spectrometry and liquid chromatography–mass spectrometry are common confirmation techniques, but others may be used.

Immunoassay

Commercial screening techniques such as enzyme immunoassay (EIA), enzyme-linked immunosorbent assay (ELISA) and fluorescence polarization immunoassay (FPIA) are designed to detect a drug or class of drugs by utilizing an immunologic-based reaction coupled with a variety of detection techniques (e.g., enzymatic, colorimetric). Major advantages of these screening techniques include minimal sample preparation, automation and cross-reactivity. For example, immunoassays designed to detect morphine may also cross-react to some degree with metabolites of morphine (e.g., morphine-3-glucuronide) and other opioids such as codeine, hydromorphone, hydrocodone and oxycodone.

Gas Chromatography

Gas chromatography (GC) is a robust separation technique that uses a gaseous mobile phase and a liquid or solid stationary phase to isolate compounds. Often, liquid samples are introduced into the heated injection port of the gas chromatograph, where they are quickly volatilized and introduced into the gaseous mobile phase. By flowing through a column that is either packed or coated with the stationary phase, the compounds are separated, based on their physicochemical properties and interaction with the stationary phase. Therefore, the retention time of these compounds is important for identification. Many detectors are amenable to gas chromatography, such as the flame ionization detector, nitrogen phosphorous detector, electron capture detector, or mass spectrometer. Gas chromatography–mass spectrometry (GC–MS) has excellent sensitivity and specificity and is commonly used for confirmation testing in forensic toxicology.

Headspace gas chromatography, which is a GC coupled with a headspace sampling technique, is commonly used in forensic toxicology for the detection and quantitation of volatile compounds (e.g., ethanol and others such as methanol, acetone and isopropanol). Simply stated, the headspace gas above a liquid sample in a sealed vial can be injected into the GC instead of the liquid sample. This gas mixes with the gaseous mobile phase and behaves similar to a volatized liquid sample. This reproducible and quantitative technique is very advantageous, because it requires minimal sample preparation.

Liquid Chromatography

Similar to GC, liquid chromatography (LC) is a reproducible separation technique; however, the mobile phase is a liquid, not a gas, and the solid stationary phase tends to be a packed column with a fraction of the length of its GC counterpart. Various detection techniques are amenable with LC such as UV–VIS detection and mass spectrometry. LC coupled with tandem mass spectrometry (discussed in the next section) is gaining popularity due to increased sensitivity and specificity with reduced background contamination.

Mass Spectrometry

As mentioned previously, mass spectrometry (MS) is a common detection technique, typically coupled with GC or LC. Its ability to uniquely and reproducibly identify, as well as quantitate target analytes makes MS extremely important in forensic toxicology. MS is complex with many components, most of which are under vacuum to minimize background contamination.

After the analytes exit the GC or LC, they enter the ionization chamber. The most common ionization in GC–MS is electron impact ionization. However, LC–MS requires an ionization technique that can handle larger volumes and higher pressures, such as electrospray ionization (ESI) or atmospheric pressure chemical ionization (APCI). Once ionized, the analyte will fragment in a repro-ducible manner creating a drug "fingerprint" based on its chemical structure. Fragments are selected by optimizing the electrical and magnetic fields of the mass analyzer component (e.g., quadrupole or ion trap) of the MS. The final key component of most mass spectrometers is the electron multiplier, which amplifies the signal.

Tandem mass spectrometry (MS/MS) can be coupled with GC (GC–MS/MS) or LC (LC–MS/MS). It refers to multiple mass analyzers in series with an additional ionization chamber in between (e.g., triple quadrupole), or the capability of the existing mass analyzer to further fragment the targeted ions (e.g., ion trap). Tandem mass spectrometry can often increase sensitivity by reducing background contamination.

Method Validation

Due to strict medicolegal scrutiny, any procedure utilized in a forensic toxi-cology laboratory must be validated and continually monitored with quality control (QC) and quality assurance (QA) procedures. (The terms quality con-trol and quality assurance are often used interchangeably. However, quality control refers to checks and balances placed on each batch to ensure consist-ency and reliability. Quality assurance refers to the overall program that over-sees all aspects of the laboratory. Quality control is a key component of quality assurance.)

Due to constraints that are often placed on the development of new ana-lytical methods (e.g., pre-established administrative reporting limits or exist-ing QA/QC requirements), proper goals for a new methodology should be set before beginning the development process. Furthermore, these analytical meth-ods should be developed and optimized under the "Good Laboratory Practice" (GLP) standards issued by governing agencies. Analytical method develop-ment may include factors such as the selection of a reference standard, internal standard, derivatizing reagent, ions for selected ion monitoring in mass spec-trometry and instrumentation. Further validation of the method should include parameters that evaluate all relevant aspects of the procedure, such as intra- and inter-day accuracy and precision, recovery, limits of detection (sensitivity) and quantitation, range of linearity, specificity, stability, carryover potential and robustness. This validation process is often done using controls verified from previous procedures or national/international standards (e.g., NIST). Ideally, the method is further validated using authentic specimens. Once an analytical method is validated and implemented in the laboratory, it must be continually monitored by quality control and quality assurance processes. This is typically done by including control specimens, both negative and positive, in each batch. These control values should be monitored within each batch and between each batch, to identify potential errors with the assay.

Quality assurance programs should be in place for all aspects of the laboratory, not just analytical methodology. Such programs include proficiency testing from external organizations, continuing education for employees and accreditation of laboratories.

REFERENCES

Baselt, R. C. (2001). *Drug effects on psychomotor performance.* Foster City, CA: Biomedical Publications.

Baselt, R. C. (2008). *Disposition of toxic drugs and chemicals in man* (8th ed.). Foster City, CA: Biomedical Publications.

Brunton, L. L., Lazo, J. S., & Parker, K. L. (Eds.), (2006). *Goodman & Gilman's the pharmacological basis of therapeutics* (11th ed.). New York, NY: McGraw-Hill.

Cravey, R. H., & Baselt, R. C. (Eds.), (1981). *Introduction to forensic toxicology.* Foster City, CA: Biomedical Publications.

Flomenbaum, N. E., Goldfrank, L. R., Hoffman, R. S., Howland, M. A., Lewin, N. A., & Nelson, L. S. (Eds.), (2006). *Goldfrank's toxicologic emergencies* (8th ed.). New York, NY: McGraw-Hill.

Goldberger, B. A., Huestis, M. A., & Wilkins, D. G. (1997). Commonly practiced quality control and quality assurance procedures for gas chromatography/mass spectrometry analysis in forensic urine drug-testing laboratories. *Forensic Sciences Review, 9,* 60–80.

Jickells, S., & Negrusz, A. (Eds.), (2008). *Clarke's analytical forensic toxicology.* London, UK: The Pharmaceutical Press.

Karch, S. B. (2007). Drug abuse handbook (2nd ed.). Boca Raton, FL: CRC Press.

Klaassen, C. D. (Ed.). (2000). *Casarett & doull's toxicology: The basic science of poisons* (7th ed.). New York, NY: McGraw-Hill.

Levine, B. (Ed.). (2009). *Principles of forensic toxicology* (3th ed.). Washington, DC: AACC Press.

Merves, M. L., & Goldberger, B. A. (2007). Quality assurance, quality control, and method validation in chromatographic applications. In R. L. Bertholf & R. E. Winecker (Eds.), *Chromatographic methods in clinical chemistry & toxicology* (pp. 1–14). Chichester, UK: John Wiley & Sons, Ltd.

Moffat, A. C., Osselton, M. D., & Widdop, B. (Eds.), (2003). *Clarke's analysis of drugs and poisons* (3rd ed.). London, UK: The Pharmaceutical Press.

Ropero-Miller, J. D., & Goldberger, B. A. (Eds.), (2009). *Handbook of workplace drug testing.* Washington, DC: AACC Press.

Chapter 14

Forensic Psychiatry, Substance Use and Mental Illness

Joel M. Silberberg, MD
Division of Psychiatry and Law, Feinberg School of Medicine, Northwestern University, Chicago, IL, USA

Adair Crosley
Northwestern University School of Law, Chicago, IL, USA

INTRODUCTION

Approximately 20% of Americans will have a problem with substance abuse during their lifetime. Substance use or abuse plays an important role in criminal issues and in civil issues, such as competence to practice a profession or parental fitness. It is therefore important that judges, attorneys, forensic psychiatrists, forensic psychologists and other actors at all levels in the criminal and civil process understand the basic issues of substance abuse and addiction (dependence) and their interaction with the legal system.

This chapter will tackle five goals and objectives for those individuals who work at the intersection of substance abuse and addiction and the legal system. The focus will primarily be on the relationship between substance abuse and addiction, and competence to stand trial and affirmative defenses. We will also address some civil and treatment issues that are written about in more detail in other chapters of this book. As a first goal, we try to provide the reader with basic current epidemiological data. Second, we aim to educate the reader on the basic legal concepts such as competence and affirmative defenses, and on key statutes relevant for the addicted. Third, we will describe the inherent tension between free will, public safety and the disease concept of substance addiction. Fourth, we will briefly describe criminal and civil competence for the addicted. Finally, we will briefly cover treatment issues for this population in different clinical settings.

EPIDEMIOLOGY

Psychoactive substances (substances) are chemicals that affect the way an individual feels, thinks, behaves and functions on an interpersonal and social level.

Alcohol, illicit drugs and certain prescribed drugs can produce acute intoxication or withdrawal, and lead to substance abuse or addiction (dependence).
Addiction and dependence are often used interchangeably in the literature. The
five-city National Institute of Mental Health Epidemiologic Catchment Area
study found lifetime prevalence rates of 13.5% for alcohol disorders alone,
6.1% for drug disorders alone, 22.5% for mental disorder alone and 29% for
comorbid mental and addictive disorders (Robins & Regier, 1991). The study
reported 37% of those with alcohol disorders and 53% of those with drug disorders had a comorbid mental disorder. The comorbity rate for bipolar disorder
was 60%, for schizophrenia 47% and for mood disorders 32%.

Experts note that the overwhelming majority of incarcerated inmates are or
have been involved in serious use of drugs or alcohol (Lamb & Weinberger,
1998; Belenko, 2000). Alcohol use has strong associations to serious crimes
such as assault, robbery, rape and murder (Bradford et al., 1992; Beckson et al.,
2003; Haggard-Grann et al., 2006). A study showed 68% of those with comorbid substance abuse and bipolar disorder had criminal histories (Friedman
et al., 2005). Bipolar disorder with co-occurring substance abuse has a high
likelihood of increasing a woman's tendency toward criminal behavior. There
is an over-representation of women with bipolar disorder in the corrections system (Friedman et al., 2005).

In a different study, 39% of individuals diagnosed with antisocial personality (ASPD) had alcoholism and 43% of individuals diagnosed with borderline
personality had alcoholism (Cloninger et al., 1997). ASPD is found in 45% to
54% of heroin addicts and 40% to 50% of alcoholics (Kermani & Casteneda,
1996; Goldstein et al., 1998; Sakai et al., 2004).

The United States has never recovered from the movement of the chronic and
severely mentally ill from large state psychiatric hospitals into the community in
the 1960s, due to a lack of planning and funding ahead of time for suitable community resources. The United States prison system and the state forensic hospitals nearly tripled in size during the 1980s and 1990s to address, in part, this lack
of community treatment facilities (Harrison & Karberg, 2004). Today, the correctional system in the United States is the largest provider of mental health services. It is important to note that the rates of crime among those in the "healthy"
general population and those with a mental illness are nearly identical (Taylor
& Monahan, 1996; Monahan et al., 2001; Steadman et al., 1998; Juninger et al.,
2006). However, the connection between violence and crime strengthens when
the seriously mentally ill abuse substances (Hodgins et al., 1996). Regarding substance abuse in the criminal justice system, 72.9% of those in federal prison, 83%
in state prisons and 82.4% in state jails admitted to abusing at least one substance
(Drug Treatment in the Criminal Justice System, 2001).

Friedman et al. (2005) found that 50% to 65% of all inmates are drug-
dependent at the time of their arrest. In addition, 23% of female inmates were using
cocaine at the time of their arrest (Drug Treatment in the Criminal Justice System,
2001). Among adults of 18 years or older, 60.1% of those who were arrested in

the past year for a serious violent act or property offense were found to have used an illicit drug within the past year and 46.5% of adults who had been arrested for a serious offense, had used marijuana in the past year (Substance Abuse Mental Health Services Administration, 2002). Lightfoot and Hodgins report an alarming finding that over 50% of those convicted of murder are found to have actively abused a substance at the time they committed the crime – half of these involve alcohol intoxication (Lightfoot & Hodgins, 1988).

The prevalence of substance abuse and the need for effective treatment, particularly in the correctional/forensic setting, is on the rise. Seventy to eighty-five percent of state correctional inmates need some level of substance abuse treatment (Drug Treatment in the Criminal Justice System, 2001). The treatment of offenders with substance abuse and other co-occurring psychiatric illnesses within jails is especially important as they enter, and due to recidivism, re-enter general society as convicted criminals. Treatment offered to those in this group, as well as treatment offered to "pure" substance abusers, is limited. The prison system continues to struggle to provide rehabilitative services to inmates who suffer from substance use issues (Lamb & Weinberger, 2005; Narevic et al., 2006; Taxman et al., 2007). Onsite substance abuse treatment is only provided in 33% of jails (Substance Abuse and Mental Health Services Administration, 2002). Many of these inmates, regardless of whether they received treatment and of the overall quality of the treatment they received, are eventually, most of the time, released back into the community. A striking example of this release back into the community of this population is the recent mass release of prisoners authorized in California by Governor Arnold Schwarzenegger.

BASIC LEGAL CONCEPTS AND STATUTES

It is essential to discuss basic legal terms and forensic psychiatry concepts to understand the relationship between substance abuse or addiction, mental health, and crime and the law. British common law describes that *actus rea*, the forbidden act, and *mens rea*, the guilty mind, are both required to commit a punishable crime. The Model Penal Code (Model Penal Code, 1962) describes the four components of *mens rea* as: "purposefully, knowingly, recklessly and negligently." "Purposefully" is when the defendant's "conscious object [was] to engage in conduct of that nature or to cause such a result;" "knowingly" is when the defendant "is aware that it is practically certain that this conduct will cause such a result;" "recklessly" is when the defendant "consciously disregards a substantial and unjustifiable risk" and the disregard of the risk "involves a gross deviation from the standard of conduct that a law-abiding person would observe in the actor's situation;" and "negligently" is when a defendant "should be aware of a substantial and unjustifiable risk," but inadvertently fails to act as a "reasonable person" in that situation.

At common law, only conduct that is committed purposefully, knowingly, or recklessly can be considered criminal. Crimes that require *specific intent* are those which must be committed purposefully or knowingly. Crimes that require *general intent* are those which must be committed purposely, knowingly, or recklessly. Although negligence is frequently alleged in civil cases, "negligent" conduct is not considered criminal unless designated so by statute. For example, negligent vehicular homicide is criminal in some states. The purposes of criminal punishment include general deterrence, retribution, rehabilitation and the protection of society. The United States has moved away from a rehabilitative model over the last two decades, but there is hope that this trend is reversing.

For ease of reading this chapter, it is important to note that a person convicted of a *misdemeanor* has a sentence limited to a maximum of 6 to 12 months and is usually confined to a jail. A jail also holds detainees who are currently awaiting trial. A *felony* is usually a specific-intent crime such as robbery, burglary, or, for example, the selling of crack cocaine. A person convicted of a *felony* usually has a sentence ranging from 12 months to life and is confined to a prison. In this chapter we will use the term "inmate" to describe both detainees and prisoners.

The law is formed over time by a combination of common law, statutes and case precedents. The principle of *stare decisis*, "let the decision stand," requires that courts stand by their own precedents and that an inferior court must follow the precedent of superior courts. How does one read a case precedent? The reader needs to pay attention to the *year* of the opinion and the *case syllabus*. The court that the decision is being appealed to *identifies the issue* in a two part question with regard to the *particular facts* of the case and the *applicable rules* of law. The *majority opinion* contains the *summary* of the *facts*, the *procedural history*, the *reasoning* and the *holding* which is the court's opinion on the legal questions. The *dissenting opinion* and *dicta* may indicate future thinking of the court about the issue. Many cases are decided on constitutional issues. Mental health and substance use or addiction cases often involve the Fifth Amendment right not to incriminate oneself, the Sixth Amendment right to assistance of counsel, the Eighth Amendment proscription of cruel and unusual punishment, and the Fourteenth Amendment (state court) and Fifth Amendment (federal court) right to due process and equal protection. Equal protection requires, for example, that people of all races be treated similarly under the law. Due process includes *substantive* due process, which is fundamental fairness, and *procedural* due process to carefully assess competing private and government interests (*Matthews v. Eldridge*, 1976). Federal law sets constitutional minimums throughout the country, but state and local legal statutes may provide more protections on a particular issue.

- You now have a sufficient basic understanding of the relationship between substance abuse or addiction and the law to discuss three precedent cases that specifically address important issues related to substance abuse, public safety and crime.

Robinson v. California (1962): Mr Robinson was discovered to have needle marks on his arms when he was stopped by Los Angeles police. At this time, the California Health and Safety Code made it a misdemeanor to be addicted to the use of narcotics, even in the absence of actual criminal behavior related to the addiction. Robinson was convicted according to this code and appealed to the California Supreme Court, which upheld the conviction. When the case reached the Supreme Court, in the majority opinion, Justice Stewart wrote that the California statute violated the cruel and unusual punishment proscription of the Eighth Amendment. The Supreme Court noted that mental illness, leprosy and venereal diseases, which had in the past been viewed as problems with morality and hence criminal, could not be constitutionally upheld as criminal. The court indicated that it was necessary to separate a defendant's acts from his status (addiction). This decision helped to remove other status crimes, such as homelessness and vagrancy, from statutes.

Powell v. Texas (1968): six years after *Robinson v. California* this case addressed the issue of whether it was cruel and unusual punishment to convict an alcoholic for public drunkenness. Mr Powell had been convicted in Texas for being intoxicated in public. His counsel raised the defense that alcoholism was a disease and that he was a chronic alcoholic. The Supreme Court was asked to apply the Robinson decision to prevent the state from punishing a chronic alcoholic for public drunkenness. Powell's conviction for public drunkenness was upheld, because the Supreme Court did not want to open the door to a constitutional basis for an insanity defense for substance abuse or addiction. If Powell's claim that he did not appear in public of his own volition when he was drunk was accepted, then no one could be held accountable under a compulsion that was a "very strong influence." For the court to have ruled otherwise would have possibly created a constitutional basis for an insanity defense for voluntarily intoxicated persons committing a crime such as rape. The defense of drunkenness does not result in exculpation of the offender.

Montana v. Egelhoff (1996): Mr Egelhoff was accused of shooting and killing two acquaintances after a night of heavy drinking. When arrested, his blood alcohol was 0.36 mg percent. He had amnesia for his two homicides. He was charged with deliberate homicide, which in Montana is a specific-intent crime involving purposefully or knowingly causing another's death. He was convicted at trial after offering the defense that his extreme intoxication had rendered him mentally incapable of committing murder. Montana's criminal code, however, required that the jury be instructed that voluntary intoxication could not be considered in determining the existence of his *mens rea* or mental state at the time of the crime. He appealed to the Montana Supreme Court that his Fourteenth Amendment rights to present all relevant evidence were violated. The Montana Supreme Court overturned his conviction. The United States Supreme Court agreed to review the case, and held that the Montana law was constitutional and did not violate a "fundamental principle of justice" because one fifth of the states had not adopted the ruling that intoxication could be considered in the determination of specific-intent formation. The court also reasoned that historically, alcohol was viewed more as an aggravating than mitigating factor for crime.

- You now have a basic understanding of the relationship between substance abuse or addiction and the law to address affirmative defenses as related to substance abuse and crime.

An *affirmative defense* is a plea to justify that an act was at least legally permissible, such as self-defense, or an excuse that admits the act was wrong but argues that the defendant should not be blamed for it in such situations as *duress, insanity, automatism, entrapment* or *necessity*. The *burden of production*, and in many states the *burden of persuasion*, is on the defendant in such cases. It is important to note that successful insanity defenses are raised in less than 1% of felony trials and are successful less than 25% of the time. The large majority of successful insanity defenses are for serious mental illness, such as schizophrenia.

In general, the law across the United States to date has prohibited the use of insanity defenses by addict defendants facing serious criminal charges. This stance is at odds with the prevailing view of the medical and mental health community in the United States, which has largely recognized that addiction is, in fact, a mental illness – the first requirement of any legally-recognized insanity defense. The text revision of the fourth edition of the *Diagnostic and Statistical Manual* (*DSM-IV-TR*) *of the American Psychiatric Association* describes substance dependence as a mental disorder which is a: "cluster of cognitive, behavioral and physiological symptoms indicating that the individual continues use of the substance despite significant substance-related problems ... there is a pattern of repeated self-administration that usually results in tolerance, withdrawal and compulsive drug-taking behavior." The diagnosis is made when there is a "maladaptive pattern of substance use, leading to clinically significant impairment or distress." *DSM-IV-TR* also describes criteria for a diagnosis of substance abuse in which there is a maladaptive pattern of use manifested by recurrent adverse consequences, such as risk of physical injury or legal, social, or interpersonal problems. Individuals may be diagnosed with substance abuse when they fulfill the appropriate criteria and have never met the criteria for substance dependence. *DSM-IV-TR* also describes diagnoses of intoxication and withdrawal for each individual substance. For any professional doing a forensic evaluation or relying on a forensic evaluation in court it is important that *DSM-IV-TR* warns: "there are significant risks that diagnostic information will be misused or understood" ... due to "the imperfect fit between the questions of ultimate concern to the law and the information contained in a clinical diagnosis." Usually a *DSM-IV-TR* mental disorder is not sufficient to establish the existence for legal purposes of a "mental disorder," "mental disability," "mental disease," or "mental defect." Additional information is usually required beyond that contained in the *DSM-IV-TR* diagnosis in determining whether an individual meets a specified legal standard (e.g., for competence, criminal responsibility, or disability). This additional information might include information about the individual's functional impairments and how the impairments affect the particular abilities in question.

Given that substance dependence is a recognized mental disorder, the question is under what circumstances the symptoms of substance dependence (addiction) would meet the second requirement of any legally recognized insanity defenses, namely, a link between the mental disorder and the criminal act. Federal and state courts are not unified with respect to the propriety of insanity defenses or the requirements for meeting the defense when allowed, but most courts that recognize an insanity defense recognize one of three standards, in some form or another.

Under the *M'Naghten* rule and its progeny, the requirement is that the criminal actor must not understand the nature or quality of his or her acts, or must not understand that what he or she does is wrong (*M'Naghten Case*, 1843). While suffering from serious perceptual or intellectual defects while intoxicated or from addiction psychosis, no such defects are otherwise implicated in substance addiction. Therefore, under this standard, if the addict defendant's level of intoxication at the time of the offense, as a result of his or her inability to control their drug use, was shown to undermine his or her ability to understand the quality, nature, or wrongfulness of his or her acts, he or she could be found less culpable. However, to the extent that the law requires a recognized mental disorder before considering the defendant's ability to appreciate his acts, the casual user or substance abuser who is not addicted would not be able to rely on this defense.

Under the *Durham* test, a defendant must show that his unlawful act was the "product" of mental disease or defect (*Durham v. United States*, 1954). Here, as long as the criminal act could be sufficiently tied to the substance dependence, the addict defendant could argue that he was not criminally responsible. This would be true whether the criminal act was the result of intoxication, addiction psychosis, or the pursuit of obtaining the drug in response to overwhelming fears of withdrawal. The first-time user or casual user who did not meet the diagnostic criterion for substance dependence or abuse would not qualify for this defense.

In 1962, the *American Law Institute* drafted an insanity standard which has subsequently been adopted by a number of state and federal courts, in one form or another. Under this standard: "[a] person is not responsible for criminal conduct if at the time of such conduct as a result of mental disease or defect he lacks substantial capacity either to appreciate the criminality [wrongfulness] of his conduct or to conform his conduct to the requirements of the law." Here, the addict defendant could rely on an insanity defense to exculpate himself to the extent that, as a result of intoxication or addiction psychosis, he did not appreciate the wrongfulness of his conduct or, as a result of the strong impulse to use and the fear of withdrawal, he was unable to conform his conduct to the requirements of the law. It should be noted that the Model Penal Code goes on to explicitly except mental disorders that are manifested only by repeated criminal or otherwise antisocial conduct. While this provision appears to be directly aimed at individuals with psychopathic or antisocial personality disorders, it seems that individuals suffering from substance addiction may fall under this exception, to the extent that repeated use of drugs for non-medical purposes (both illegal drugs and legal drugs illegally obtained), a feature of substance dependence, could be understood as "repeated" criminal conduct.

Hence, in American and English common law, voluntary intoxication does not fully excuse an offender who has committed a crime, and is not a defense under a not guilty by reason of insanity plea in a general-intent crime, although it may result in a diminished verdict or sentence (Slovenko, 2002). *Temporary insanity* or short-lived mental changes secondary to voluntary intoxication are not considered a mental disease or defect for the insanity defense, but may result in a diminished verdict or sentence, or in a finding of "guilty but mentally ill." In regard to the *duress defense*, neither the addict, despite great fear of physical or psychological withdrawal symptoms or dysphoria, nor the pedophile, despite strong desires for sexual contact with children that produce distress or dysfunction, can demonstrate fear of death or grievous bodily injury that would be required for a duress defense (Morse, 1999).

Alcohol and/or drug abuse or addiction may be considered as a *diminished responsibility* defense in circumstances such as acute pathological alcoholic intoxication, where very small amounts of alcohol may precipitate impulsive aggressive behavior. Slovenko describes that the intoxication may so impair the individual's judgment that he is unable to plan his behavior rationally, or to appreciate its consequences. He adds that this is a rare disorder that usually occurs in first-time users (Slovenko, 2002). Unwitting ingestion of a substance such as phencyclidine (PCP) may be considered as a *diminished responsibility* defense of *involuntary intoxication* when a person is given a drug without his knowledge, leading to prolonged psychosis. Involuntary intoxication can be totally exculpatory. This requires that the individual has consumed the substance due to duress or trickery, or behaved violently due to a previously unknown susceptibility to a recognized atypical reaction to a substance, or the intoxication resulted from previously unknown side-effects of a drug prescribed as a treatment (Pandina, 1996; Burglass, 1997). Under the concept of diminished capacity, a *mens rea* partial defense, *voluntary intoxication* could negate the capacity of an offender to form the specific-intent required by the definition of the criminal charge in a specific-intent crime (Weinstock et al., 1996). If the requisite specific-intent were nullified, guilt could be found only for a lesser included crime (e.g., manslaughter instead of second-degree murder) that does not require specific-intent (Weinstock et al., 1996). The mere fact of intoxication does not automatically mean that the defendant lacked the requisite specific intent. *Diminished capacity* and *diminished responsibility* have also been used in sentencing, where intoxication and addiction issues may be raised as mitigating factors. Due to recent tighter sentencing guidelines, such evidence is often brought out in pretrial plea-bargaining (Slovenko, 2002).

There is a complex relationship between alcoholic blackouts and criminal behavior. Alcoholic blackouts may be used as a *diminished capacity defense* if an *automatism* can be linked to the amnesia. An alcoholic blackout causes a form of amnesia about events that happened during a heavy period of drinking (Goodwin, 1995). Heavy drinking may induce an alcoholic blackout during which the person is awake and conscious, may be engaged in any type of activity or conversation, and may appear to the observer to be perfectly oriented (Kalant, 1996). Sometimes the event is later recalled. The frequency and type of blackout were surveyed in two healthy samples in a Dutch study. Van Oorsouw et al. (2000) reviewed the literature, and found that in the United States and the Netherlands, on average, 20% to 30% of offenders claim a form of amnesia after committing a crime and in a substantial number of these cases defendants invoke excessive alcohol consumption as an explanation for the amnesia. The results of their study suggest that *bona fide* blackouts during criminally-relevant behavior do occur, but that the reliability of those who raised blackout claims with blood alcohol levels below 250 mg percent should be questioned (van Oorsouw et al., 2000).

If chronic substance abuse has caused permanent and irreversible brain damage resulting in mental illness or cognitive dysfunction, an insanity defense may be possible in some jurisdictions under the concept of "settled insanity" (Kermani & Castaneda, 1996).

Settled insanity is defined as a "settled" or permanent condition caused by long-term substance abuse. In the absence of cognitive impairment of the processes involved in obtaining, retaining and utilizing knowledge (a possible result of chronic alcoholism, for example), the addict is assumed to have the capacity to behave rationally (Halleck, 1992). Chronic alcoholism may result in settled insanity and thus provide an insanity defense where prolonged intoxication may produce a brain syndrome characterized by a degree of confusion sufficient to lead to drastic misinterpretation of reality (Slovenko, 2002). For example, a patient with alcohol-induced dementia murders his spouse at the time she has been devoting more attention than usual to a previous lover. Is this jealous rage and premeditated murder, or is this an act driven by delusional jealousy and the poor impulse control of settled insanity? Most jurisdictions differentiate between settled insanity and temporary intoxication.

Affirmative Defense Statutes

States have varying statutes in regard to the insanity defense. For example, the Illinois Criminal Code recognizes an insanity defense to crime (Illinois Statutes, 2008). Case law suggests that addiction alone is an insufficient basis for an insanity defense in this state, but Illinois does not statutorily except addicts from using this defense (Illinois Statutes, 2008). Many other states that recognize insanity defenses similarly do not statutorily except addiction as a basis for the defense, even though relevant case law suggests that it would be insufficient. However, this is not the case everywhere in the United States: at least thirteen states statutory except persons acting under the influence of drugs or that are addicted to drugs from relying on an insanity defense. These states include Arizona, Arkansas, California, Colorado, Connecticut, Delaware, Maine, Missouri, Nevada, North Dakota, Utah and Wyoming. In the Arizona Revised Statutes (2008), the term "mental disease or defect" which forms the basis of an insanity defense "does not include disorders that result from acute voluntary intoxication or withdrawal from alcohol or drugs ...." Similarly, Colorado Revised Statutes (2008) state that: "'mental disease or defect' includes only those severely abnormal mental conditions that ... are not attributable to the voluntary ingestion of alcohol or any other psychoactive substance ...." Other states, including Connecticut, Delaware, Nevada and Wyoming, also exclude voluntary intoxication from the definition of "mental disease or defect." In these states, the statutes do not make clear whether voluntary intoxication at any time cannot be the basis of an insanity defense, or if only voluntary intoxication at the time of the offense specifically cannot be the basis for an insanity defense, as is the case in North Dakota and Utah. While this distinction may seem unimportant, in the case of an addict experiencing, and compelled by, the symptoms of withdrawal, and not actually intoxicated at the time of the offense, the difference could be quite meaningful.

These statutes, representing a number of states, both large and small and from all regions of the country, along with case law in other states, like Washington and Illinois, suggest a shared view that, under the law, for the purposes of an insanity defense, the medical model of addiction has not been fully embraced. A Washington case determined: "chronic addiction to alcohol does not, by itself, constitute insanity" (*State v. Wicks*, 1983). In these states, it is not just that addicts and drug users cannot meet the additional cognitive or volitional requirements of recognized insanity defenses, it is that drug use and addiction is itself not a recognized mental illness.

While addict defendants may be unable successfully to pursue insanity defenses, they may be found *guilty but mentally ill* in states that recognize such a statute. The guilty but mentally ill statutes are distinct from statutes authorizing a finding of guilty but insane or guilty except for insanity. In *People v. Ramsey* (1985), the court commented that the major purpose in creating the guilty but mentally ill verdict was to limit the number of persons who, in the eyes of the legislature, were improperly being relieved of all criminal responsibility by way of the insanity verdict. The court said that there was nothing impermissible about such a purpose, since it is within the power of the legislature to attempt to cure what it sees to be a misuse of the law. The court affirmed the conviction of a defendant found guilty of second-degree murder but mentally ill, and of a second defendant, found guilty but mentally ill on charges of armed robbery and assault with intent to commit robbery while armed.

The guilty but mentally ill verdict is intended to provide an "in-between" classification whereby a defendant bears the legal responsibility for criminal conduct, but is accorded the right to treatment, if found appropriate, for his or her mental illness. Under the particular circumstances of the following cases, the courts held that a defendant who had pleaded guilty but mentally ill to a criminal charge was not entitled to a hearing before the sentencing court on the issue of whether he was being provided sufficient psychiatric treatment by the department of corrections (*People v. Sorna*, 1979; *People v. McLeod*, 1980; *People v. Tenbrink*, 1979; *People v. Toner*, 1983). What occurs, in reality, is that many seriously mentally ill offenders, with or without comorbid substance abuse or addiction, that are found guilty but mentally ill linger in prisons untreated except for acute emergency situations such as suicide crisis.

INHERENT CONFLICT BETWEEN FREE WILL, PUBLIC SAFETY AND THE DISEASE CONCEPT AND SUBSTANCE ADDICTION

Free Will

A central tenet underlying American criminal law is the notion that the individual is an agent subject to free will (Morse, 2000). Any defense based on the proposition that an actor should be, for some reason, held not responsible for his criminal conduct must contend with and overcome this fundamental precept. Legal scholars and philosophers that have attempted to grapple with the question of whether addicts are less culpable for their criminal conduct than non-addicts have attempted to do so by asking whether addiction and its symptoms are powerful enough to overcome the assumption of free will embedded in American criminal law.

There are several circumstances in which an actor's blameworthiness for his or her conduct is either diminished or completely absent, many of which have been highlighted in the section of this chapter on basic legal concepts and statutes. Both legally and morally, an individual whose actions are the result of forces completely outside of his control is not responsible for those actions. For example, an epileptic experiencing a seizure is not responsible for any damage he or she causes. Individuals suffering from mental diseases or defects which render them incapable of making rational choices are generally excused from their behavior if the behavior is sufficiently tied to the mental deficiency. Actors whose conduct is the product of powerful, transitory influences that prevent them from making rational and moral choices are generally deemed less culpable than others making similarly irrational choices in the absence of such powerful influences. For this reason, crimes of passion are viewed differently from crimes committed in "cold blood." Similarly, actors whose conduct is the result of duress are generally viewed as not morally or legally culpable. For example, a person faced with the choice of killing three other innocent people or being killed herself is not considered blameworthy if she chooses to kill the three other people. While this is not considered the morally right choice, the law understands that most people, faced with such a decision, would be unable to do the right thing.

Recognizing that there are situations in which the assumption of free will can be defeated, the question becomes whether addiction is sufficiently like any of the situations described above to excuse actions that are the product of addiction. Before discussing how the legal scholars have answered this question, a discussion of the disease model of addiction is necessary.

Disease Concept

The defining feature of both substance dependence and substance abuse relates to the persistence of use in the face of serious and dramatic negative consequences. In the case of substance dependence, or addiction, the repeated use occurs in response to growing tolerance of the drug (i.e., the need to use more to feel the same effects) and an overwhelming fear of withdrawal (i.e., the belief that feeling "normal" is dependent on continued use of the drug).

Although addiction has important psychological and social consequences, it is fundamentally the result of biological processes (Nestler & Aghajanian, 1997). The prevailing view within the medical community today is that addiction is a brain disease involving brain structure and function (Leshner, 1997). Evidence suggests that the brains of addicts are meaningfully different from the brains of non-addicts although it is unclear to what extent such change is a cause or a product of drug addiction. This is in contrast to other models, such as cultural constructivist, political economy and utilitarian that view factors other than neurological processes as driving the addiction. Pervasive and critical changes in the brain at the molecular, cellular and structural levels, and its functioning, take place after prolonged use of drugs and these changes persist long after an individual has stopped taking drugs. When ingested by anyone, addicted or not, addictive substances affect the cerebral cortex, midbrain and cerebellum. However, the interactions between drugs and the brains of those who are addicted are different from the interactions that take place in the brains of those who are not addicted. Scientists have demonstrated that the addicted brain is meaningfully different from the non-addicted brain, as manifested by changes in brain metabolic activity, receptor availability, gene expression and responsiveness to environmental cues (National Institute on Drug Abuse, 2008).

The Conflict between Free Will, Public Safety and the Disease Model

Is addictive behavior involuntary or driven by free will? In addressing behavior in the context of substance intoxication and addiction, controversy exists regarding whether such conduct is volitional and willfully intended or whether it is automatic and beyond control. Compulsive use and "loss of control," despite knowledge of possible adverse consequences, is the hallmark of the disease model.

The prevailing view among the medical community represents a move away from the notion that an addict is a moral agent whose actions are the result of free will, the prevailing view under the law, and towards a view in which the conduct of the addict is the product of causal factors that determine choice. This is because of the powerful biological and chemical processes taking place in the brain of the addict, as well as the role of both genetic makeup and childhood environment – over which the addict certainly has no control – that are also important in the formation of addictive disorders. In other words, once addiction takes hold, neurobiological mechanisms make it increasingly hard for the addict to stop using the drug. As such, the continued use of drugs by an addicted individual cannot be seen as voluntary in the same way that the use of drugs is for non-addicted individuals. Watterson describes that the compulsion to get drunk is so disabling that an individual is deprived of the ability to avoid risk-creating intoxication; that "denial" prevents recognition of the lack of control; that alcoholism destroys the capacity to foresee the consequences of drinking; and that the compulsion overwhelms behavioral control, creating an equivalent of coercion (Watterson, 1991). Therefore, while initial drug use may be seen as the product of free will, continued use of a drug by an addict may be less the product of free will and more the result of the deterministic forces resulting from the neurochemical changes associated with prolonged use of drugs.

The fact that fundamental changes in the brain chemistry, structure and functioning of addicts result in cognitive impairments would mean that addict defendants may be found not culpable for acts performed as a result of their addiction – at least in places such as Illinois, where an insanity defense requires a "lack of appreciation" of the criminality of one's act. In other words, individuals who embrace the prevailing views of addiction within the medical community would be less inclined to view the addict acting in response to his addiction as fully culpable for certain acts.

Even among scholars who are more inclined to embrace the current medical views of addiction, there is still some reluctance to fully accept the implications of a purely medical or biological model of addiction. There is great difficulty in distinguishing between an allegedly "irresistible" desire and one simply not resisted (Morse, 1999). Morse argues that, despite recent advances in our understanding of addiction at the biological level, the essence of this brain disease is primarily behavioral. Accepting the view of addiction as a disease does not preclude one from acknowledging that a great deal of human agency is involved in addiction and the behaviors associated with addiction. The biological forces underlying the behavior of addicts do not negate the human agency involved in seeking and using drugs; possessing and using the substance in question are intentional acts the addict engages in to achieve the pleasure of intoxication or avoid the pain of inner withdrawal and inner tension, or both (Morse, 1999). Similarly, the compulsion excuse is problematic; the addict's choices are not so difficult that the "wrong" choice should be excused by society (Morse, 1986, 1999). For this reason, Morse ultimately concludes that most addicts are responsible for most criminal behavior that they engage in, even when such behavior is the product of substance dependence.

By-and-large, the medical model of addiction has not been widely accepted by the American public. Today, American society is largely unsympathetic toward the addict. The most charitable view is that addicts are products of their poor social situations. At worst, addicts are weak or bad people. In 1996, a representative sample of American adults were presented with a series of written vignettes describing individuals suffering from a set of symptoms associated with various mental illness, including alcohol dependence, major depressive disorder, schizophrenia and cocaine dependence. Less than half of adults in the survey indicated a belief that those suffering from alcohol and cocaine dependence were suffering from a mental illness (Link, 1999). Further, more than half of the respondents indicated that the symptoms described in the substance-dependant vignettes were very likely or somewhat likely the result of the sufferer's own bad character.

The addict fares somewhat better in the eyes of the law, as evidenced through statute, case law and the work of legal scholars. The case law suggests that while early on many defendants (and their lawyers) attempted to use the medical understanding of addiction to help further claims of impairment and reduced (if not absent) culpability, these arguments did not bring about a sea-change in the way courts were willing to treat addict defendants. The idea that there are biological mechanisms at play in addiction has gained some traction. However, the idea that these biological mechanisms somehow lessen criminal responsibility in addicts has not been fully embraced. Concerns with regard to public safety prevail over the disease concept. To date, neither American society nor the legal community seem poised to begin to view those that suffer from substance dependence in the same way that they have come to view those suffering from other serious mental illness.

CRIMINAL AND CIVIL COMPETENCE FOR THE ADDICTED

Competency (or *competence*) is the quality or condition of being legally qualified to perform an act and/or make decisions. Competence is that degree of mental soundness necessary to carry out certain legal acts. Clinicians opine on capacities relevant to competence. The general test is whether the person understands the nature of the specific act (volitional or decisional) and is aware of the duties and obligations it entails. Substance intoxication, withdrawal or addiction can interfere with any specific competence. An individual is presumed competent until incompetence is proven.

Competence to Stand Trial

Forensic psychiatry evaluations in the criminal competency sphere include competency to waive Miranda rights, competency to confess, competency to stand trial, competency to be sentenced and competency to be executed. Substance abuse or addiction often plays a role in the outcome or recommendations in these evaluations. Competency to stand trial (also known as fitness to proceed or adjudicative competence), is probably the most common evaluation done by psychiatrists for the court system (Gutheil & Appelbaum, 2000).

The Supreme Court defines competency to stand trial as the ability of a defendant to have a rational and factual understanding of the proceedings against him, and to assist and consult with an attorney with a reasonable degree of rational understanding (*Dusky v. United States*, 1960). Most states adopt a similar test of competency to stand trial. The mental illness should specifically inhibit functioning at the trial to render someone incompetent (Warren et al., 2006). Symptoms of mental illness *per se* do not render a person incompetent to stand trial. Defendants who are found incompetent to stand trial most likely have serious mental disorders or mental retardation, with psychosis being the most common (Warren et al., 2006). Thirty-two states rely primarily on outpatient competency assessments and only 10 primarily on inpatient evaluation (Grisso et al., 1996). The methods to restore competence include treatment of the defendant's mental illness and education about the trial process (Noffsinger, 2001). Access to substances need to be closely monitored in outpatient settings and even in the setting of a secure forensic hospital. These competence restoration programs involve written information and tests, and videotaped vignettes and role-playing, including mock trials to monitor improvement in competence-related capacities. Restoration in a person with acute mental illness with or without substance abuse or addiction usually takes six to eight months. In rare cases, substance abuse or addiction may cause significant cognitive deficits that prolong the process of restoration, and a small percentage of these individuals may never be restored to competence.

Mental illness is not always required to render an individual incompetent to stand trial or unrestorable to competence to stand trial (*Jackson v. Indiana*, 1972). Mr Jackson was a mentally-retarded deaf mute who was charged with two robberies. He was found incompetent to stand trial, based on his non-existent communication skills, mental retardation and lack of hearing. He was committed to the Indiana Department of Mental Health until his competency was restored. Jackson did not have a mental illness and his other deficiencies were not treatable. Jackson's lawyer filed an appeal saying that he would never be restored to competency, citing the deprivation of due process and equal protection under the Fourteenth Amendment and the proscription against cruel and unusual punishment under the Eighth Amendment. The Supreme Court ruled in favor of Mr Jackson, stating that due process requires that the nature and duration of confinement bear some reasonable relation to the purpose for which the individual is committed. Alcohol or drugs may lead to organic syndromes that may make it unlikely that competence be restored. In these situations, if it is unlikely that competence will be restored, the defendant must be released or civilly committed, as in the case of *Jackson v. Indiana*. Fortunately, 90% of defendants are restored to competency.

Substance abuse is often a confounding factor with regard to maintenance of competence to stand trial status. All too often, detainees or offenders are restored to competency in a state forensic hospital only to relapse when accessing drugs in jail while awaiting trial. Individuals restored on an outpatient basis who are awaiting trial need ongoing support to adhere to treatment and abstain from substances in order to get a speedy trial. Unfortunately, crowded court dockets, continuances and delayed trials often contribute to addiction relapse, rendering the competent defendant incompetent to stand trial.

Civil Competencies

Substance abuse or addiction affects a wide array of civil competencies. This chapter will briefly discuss examples in this regard. First, substance abuse may be a contributing factor with regard to adverse findings in custody evaluations, adoption proceedings and revocation of parental rights. In these cases, the court will be interested in the presence of a substance use disorder, impairment of an individual's capacity to perform parental duties, potential for behavior that would jeopardize the child, cooperation and participation in drug rehabilitation, potential for recovery from addiction and time course of recovery (Kermani & Castaneda, 1996).

Second, substance abuse or addiction may interfere with the competence to practice a profession or the performance of jobs involving the public safety, national security and driving (sobriety checkpoints). These are circumstances in which alcohol and drug testing is common (Kermani & Castaneda, 1996). The Supreme Court has held in several cases that widespread random testing of employees is allowed in jobs that affect public safety (West & Ackerman, 1993). Pursuant to these cases, workplace testing is performed for job applicant pre-employment screening, random testing and testing for cause. Drug tests in the workplace are usually reviewed by certified medical review officers to verify an intact forensic chain of custody, the legitimacy of psychoactive medications in the test sample, and to rule out false positives and negatives (Swotinsky & Smith, 1999). Many jobs also involve the competence to drive a vehicle. In this regard, police may test an individual for signs of intoxication, such as slurred speech (*Michigan v. Sitz*, 1990; *Pennsylvania v. Muniz*, 1990).

The court may request a forensic expert opinion about the validity of the results of alcohol or drug testing and the likely effects on job performance capacity with particular focus on public safety issues. With regard to substance abuse or addiction interfering with the competence to practice medicine, it is unethical for a physician to practice medicine while under the influence of a substance which impairs the ability to practice. Ten to fifteen percent of physicians are dependent on alcohol or drugs (Keeve, 1984). This is a conservative estimate, because physicians are generally reluctant to report impaired colleagues. Physicians have an ethical obligation to report impaired colleagues. States vary in the reporting requirement, ranging from no requirement of a physician to report another physician suspected of alcohol or drug abuse (California) to granting immunity to anyone who makes a good faith report (Texas).

Should substance abuse or addiction lead to disability the Americans with Disabilities Act (ADA) of 1990 protects individuals from discrimination. All individuals suffering from alcoholism must be given the choice of accepting treatment, before progressive discipline towards job-termination begins. The ADA limits employment protection to drug users who are not currently using illegal drugs or are in supervised treatment programs. The ADA excludes direct threat of harm to others that cannot be reasonably reduced through accommodation and misconduct due to alcohol abuse.

TREATMENT ISSUES FOR THIS POPULATION IN DIFFERENT CLINICAL SETTINGS

Clinical Assessment in Forensic Settings

General principles of assessment of alcoholic and substance abusers are the same in all settings, private or forensic. It is not uncommon, in a medical or mental health setting, to fail to diagnose a substance abuse problem because of the classical denial regarding substance abuse problems, which may be perceived as poor moral character, weakness of will, or criminality. Family members may further this denial by "enabling."

In forensic settings, all available records and collateral sources of information must be requested, as substance abusers are frequently unreliable historians. Arrest records and legal history may reveal arrests or convictions for driving under the influence or possession of a controlled substance. In the evaluation of a defendant in a forensic setting, malingering has always to be considered, because intoxication or addiction may be used as an excuse for an illegal act, or falsely denied to avoid legal problems.

Treatment in Forensic Settings

General principles of treatment of alcoholic and substance abusers are the same in all settings. Alcoholics Anonymous requires that once aware of the problem with substances and the consequences of abuse, the addict must accept responsibility for taking the steps necessary to achieve and maintain sobriety.

Relapse rates are high in substance abusers (25 to 97% after one year), but it is important to note that treatment results are similar to those found in the chronic medical disorders (McLellan et al., 2000). Treatment mandated (coerced) by the court has been found to be as effective as treatment obtained voluntarily by a highly-motivated individual (Miller & Flaherty, 2000). Substance abuse treatment is associated with reduction in crime (Wald et al., 1999).

Participation in Alcoholics Anonymous, Narcotics Anonymous, or similar self-help fellowships, individual psychotherapy and medication therapy are the best combination of remedies. Residential treatment provides individual and group treatment in a drug-free environment that conducts ongoing random alcohol and drug testing. On completion of a residential program, day hospital treatment or intensive evening programs permit living at home, job training and employment. Medications may be used to treat associated psychiatric comorbidity, or to support abstinence such as methadone for opiate dependence, or antabuse or naltrexone for alcohol dependence. Long-acting naltrexone is showing much promise in relapse prevention for alcohol dependence. A minimum of one year of treatment in one form or another is prudent, given the high rates of relapse within the first year of recovery.

Civil Commitment

Civil commitment for individuals with comorbid serious mental illness and substance addiction only allows for brief hospitalization and stabilization. The situation for substance-addicted individuals, without comorbid serious mental illness, varies in that the federal government and some states have commitment statutes regarding alcohol and drug abusers. None of these statutes commit for treatment unless the individual is demonstrated to be dangerous to self or others, or gravely disabled (Kermani & Castaneda, 1996). Some states, such as Texas, have separate commitment laws for substance abuse (versus other mental illness), and may require a bed in an approved alcohol and drug facility and rehabilitation program, which is often not easy to find.

Civil commitment may serve to protect an intended victim from a specific threat of violence. What happens when the individual is ready for discharge from substance abuse treatment? Federal regulations prohibit the disclosure of records or information concerning any patient in a federally-assisted alcohol or drug treatment program (42 CFR Part 2). Federal law supersedes any state or local law that is less restrictive in this regard. In some states, mental health professionals have a duty to take reasonable steps to protect an intended victim from a patient that has made a threat (*Tarasoff v. Regents of the University of California*, 1976). The presence of substance abuse or addiction most likely increases the risk of violence. In these situations, notification of a potential victim or law enforcement agency should not identify that the report is being made by a substance abuse program or that the individual making the threat is in substance abuse treatment.

Correctional Settings, Diversion and Coerced Treatment, Community Re-entry and Reintegration

Individuals with alcohol and mental illness in general are more likely than those with mental disorder alone to show violent or suicidal behavior (Swanson et al., 1999), be homeless (Drake & Wallach, 1989), be admitted to hospital and make greater use of emergency services (Bartels et al., 1993). Without post-release treatment referral and planning, relapse of substance abuse often leads to psychotropic medication non-adherence or *vice versa*. Drug and alcohol treatment successfully reduces rearrest, conviction and incarceration, particularly when therapeutic community modalities of treatment are utilized (Wald et al., 1999).

In jails, screening for active substance-induced disorders (intoxication, withdrawal or other psychiatric syndromes secondary to substance use) and substance use disorders (abuse and addiction) is an important mental health task. Factors predicting successful completion of an intensive jail-based substance user program include being age 26 or older, not having used methadone and having already received a sentence (Krebs et al., 2003). A longitudinal study of Monroe County, New York's jail treatment drug and alcohol program showed that jail substance-based treatment programs have demonstrated efficacy in decreasing criminal recidivism on release into the community in a one year follow-up period when compared with an inmate control group (Turley et al., 2004).

Prison-based substance abuse treatment services demonstrate significant treatment efficacy (Scott & Gerbasi, 2005). Screening for substance use disorders should occur again in the prison setting, because the transfer of medical and mental health information between jails and prisons is far from optimal. The "therapeutic community model," first pioneered by the British physician Maxwell Jones at the end of World War II, has been successfully modified for use in correctional settings, and in many states is housed separately from the general prison population. This program focuses on the inmate's substance abuse and related problems and lasts between six to twelve months (Deleon, 1997).

The forensic setting that has been portrayed in contemporary movies and books tends to give the impression that not guilty by reason of insanity acquitees "get away with murder." These individuals may in fact spend more time institutionalized for their crime than if they were sentenced to prison. There are well-validated instruments created for the formal assessment of violence potential (Appelbaum et al., 2000; Elbogen & Tomkins, 2000; Monahan et al., 2000, 2006). These instruments address the well-established fact that substance use increases rates of violence. While mental illness alone does not increase rates of violence when compared to the general population, the concurrent use of substances by the seriously mentally ill detainee or offender does increase rates of violence, and needs to be considered in prerelease evaluations and assessments. Many state forensic hospitals now enroll these individuals in a minimum six month stay on a Mental Illness and Substance Abuse (MISA) Unit in order to persuade the judge with regard to the safety of release of the individual from the forensic setting, and to prevent relapse of substance abuse and associated violence. MISA units play a particularly important role in the safe release into the community of insanity acquitees.

Diversion is a process whereby individuals arrested for drug-related offenses, typically of a nonviolent nature, may engage in a treatment program in order to avoid or reduce criminal charges. The rationale is that treatment of underlying addictive problems in the least restrictive setting will reduce future arrests or convictions. Compliance with requirements regarding treatment and sobriety, such as treatment participation and random toxicology reports, may affect sentencing, probation and parole. Diversion programs reduce the burden on local courts and the expansion of prison populations.

Coerced treatment for substance abuse or addiction can have just as good an outcome as voluntary treatment (Miller & Flaherty, 2000). Coerced postrelease treatment often involves random drug and alcohol testing, required Alcoholics and/or Narcotics Anonymous meeting attendance, and partial hospitalization programs specifically for substance addiction. Drug courts are a specific type of coerced treatment that integrates alcohol and other drug treatment services with justice system processing. Admission to drug courts can occur under probationary terms or diversion where records are expunged after successful treatment. Participants sign an agreement to participate with an understanding of the requirements of the program. Drug courts have been found to have a positive treatment outcome among substance abusers (Drug Courts Program Office, 1997). Post drug court follow-up is, of course, extremely important for continued success. Further studies about post drug court follow-up are needed.

Re-entry and reintegration is the process of returning to the community after incarceration/institutionalization. Prisons and jails, in particular, are part of the community in which they reside. Failure to treat and link forensic patients with substance addiction alone, or those with co-occurring substance addiction and mental illness, to effective community treatment programs leads to relapse of substance abuse and criminal recidivism.

The period immediately following release places the inmate at high risk for death. Binswanger et al. reviewed prison records of 30,237 inmates released from Washington state prisons during a four-year span. The leading causes of death within two weeks of release were drug overdose, cardiovascular disease, homicide and suicide (Binswanger et al., 2007). Inmates who have undergone alcohol detoxification should be counseled that repeated alcohol withdrawal is associated with increased risk for delirium tremens and death, and about medication-assisted treatment of alcoholism with naltrexone, acamprosate and disulfiram (Mayo-Smith et al., 2004). Inmates who have undergone opioid detoxification should be counseled regarding the increased risk of lethal overdose following release due to loss of tolerance. Correctional physician leaders should be encouraged to obtain licenses for the use of methadone and buprenorphine to provide optimal detoxification regimens, as well as to offer selected inmates the opportunity to begin medication-assisted therapy. These programs have been found to reduce rates of illicit drugs in correctional facilities and to reduce recidivism (Stallwitz & Stover, 2007).

CONCLUSION

We have attempted to review substance abuse and addiction and its consequences in the context of current laws, statutes and case precedents. The connection between substance abuse and specific civil competencies is nuanced, and has both criminal and civil consequences. Substance abuse and addiction and crime share a reciprocating, multifactorial and to some extent causal relationship. The law, driven by case precedent, has helped us to understand how we are to legally handle crimes committed in the presence of substance use in regard to accountability, punishment, protection and defense for the accused. Currently the legal system gives more sway to free will than to the disease model in issues such as the insanity defense. In time, it is possible that advancing scientific knowledge about substance use will move this pendulum towards greater influence by the disease model.

We hope that this chapter has also provided you with knowledge in the assessment of specific civil competencies impaired by substance abuse and addiction, and of the importance of prevention and early intervention. Finally, we hope that this chapter has empowered you in handling specific treatment situations in relation to the complex interaction between substance abuse and addiction and the morals, ethics and laws of the society in which we live.

REFERENCES

American Law Institute. (1962). *Model Penal Code* (Official Draft). Philadelphia, PA: American Law Institute.

American Medical Association. (2001a). H–95.983: Drug dependencies as diseases. <http://www.ama-assn.org/>.

American Psychiatric Association. (2000). *Diagnostic and Statistical Manual of Mental Disorders*, (4th ed.), Text Revision *(DSM–IV–TR)* . Washington, DC: American Psychiatric Association.

Appelbaum, P. S., Robbins, P. C., & Monahan, J. (2000). Violence and delusions: Data from the MacArthur Violence Risk Assessment Study. *American Journal of Psychiatry, 157*(4), 566–572.

Arizona Revised Statutes. (2008). Section 13–502.

Bartels, S. J., Teague, G. B., Drake, R. E., Clark, R. E., Bush, P. W., & Noordsy, D. L. (1993). Substance abuse in schizophrenia: Service utilization and costs. *Journal of Nervous and Mental Disease, 181*(4), 227–232.

Beckson, M., Bartzokis, G., & Weinstock, R. (2003). Substance abuse and addiction. In R. Rosner (Ed.), *Principles and Practice of Forensic Psychiatry* (pp. 672–684). New York, NY: Oxford University Press.

Belenko, S. R. (2000). *Drugs and drug policy in America: A Documentary History*. Westport, CT: Greenwood Press.

Binswanger, I. A., Stern, M. F., Deyo, R. A., Heagerty, P. J., Cheadle, A., Elmore, J. G., & Koepsell, T. D. (2007). Release from prison – a high risk of death for former inmates. *New England Journal of Medicine, 356*(2), 157–165.

Bradford, J. M. W., Greenberg, D. M., & Motayne, G. G. (1992). Substance abuse and criminal behavior. *Psychiatric Clinics of North America, 15*, 605–622.

Burglass, M. E. (1997). Forensics. In J. H. Lowinson, P. Ruiz, R. B. Millman, & J. G. Langrod (Eds.), *Substance abuse: A Comprehensive Textbook* (3rd ed.). Baltimore, MD: Williams & Wilkins.

Cloninger, C. R., Bayon, C., & Przybeck, T. R. (1997). Epidemiology and Axis I comorbidity of antisocial personality. In D. M. Stoff, J. Breiling, & J. D. Maser (Eds.), *Handbook of Antisocial Behavior*. New York, NY: John Wiley & Sons, Inc.

Code of Federal Regulations, Title 42, Part II: Confidentiality of Alcohol and Drug Abuse Patient Records.

Colorado Revised Statutes. (2008). Section 16–8–101.5.

Criminal Resource Manual. (1984). Insanity Reform Act, Federal Rule of Evidence

Deleon, G. (1997). Modified therapeutic communities. Emerging issues. In G. Deleon (Ed.), *Community as Method: Therapeutic Communities for Special Populations and Special Settings* (pp. 261–270). Westport, CT: Greenwood Publishing.

Drake, R. E., & Wallach, M. A. (1989). Substance abuse among chronically medically ill. *Hospital and Community Psychiatry, 40*, 1041–1046.

Drug Courts Program Office. (1997). *Defining Drug Courts: The Key Components*. Washington, DC: United States Department of Justice.

Durham v. United States. 214 F.2d 862, 875 (D.C. Cir. 1954).

Dusky v. United States. 362 U.S. 402 (1960).

Elbogen, E. B., & Tomkins, A. J. (2000). From the psychiatric hospital to the community: Integrating conditional release and contingency management. *Behavioral Sciences & the Law, 18*(4), 427–444.

Friedman, S., Shelton, M., Elhaj, O., Youngstrom, E. A., Rapport, D. J., Packer, K. A., Bilali, S. R., Jackson, K. S., Sakai, H. E., Resnick, P. J., Findling, R. L., & Calabrese, J. R. (2005). Gender differences in criminality: Bipolar disorder with co-occurring substance abuse. *Journal of American Academy of Psychiatry and the Law, 33*, 188–195.

Goldstein, R. B., Powers, S. I., McCusker, J., Lewis, B. F., Bigelow, C., & Mundt, K. A. (1998). Antisocial behavioral syndromes among residential drug abuse treatment clients. *Drug and Alcohol Dependence, 49*, 201–216.

Goodwin, D. W. (1995). Alcohol amnesia. *Addiction, 90*, 315–317.

Grisso, T., Cocozza, J. J., Steadman, H. J., Greer, A., & Fisher, W. H. (1996). A national survey of hospital-based and community-based approaches to pretrial mental health evaluations. *Psychiatric Services, 47*, 642–644.

Gutheil, T. G., & Appelbaum, P. S. (2000). Forensic evaluations. In T. G. Gutheil & P. S. Appelbaum (Eds.), *Clinical Handbook of Psychiatry and Law* (pp. 261–316). Philadelphia, PA: Lippincott Williams and Wilkins.

Haggard-Grann, U., Hallqvist, J., Langstrom, N., & Moller, J. (2006). The role of alcohol and drugs in triggering criminal violence: A case-crossover study. *Addiction, 101*, 100–108.

Halleck, S. L. (1992). Clinical assessment of the voluntariness of behavior. *Bulletin of the American Academy of Psychiatry and the Law, 20*, 221–236.

Harrison, P. M., & Karberg, J. C. (2004). *Prison and Jail Inmates at Midyear: 2000 Bulletin, Office of Justice Programs, Bureau of Justice Statistics*. Washington, DC: US Department of Justice.

Hodgins, S., Mednick, S. A., Brennan, P. A., Schulsinger, F., & Engberg, M. (1996). Mental disorder and crime. Evidence from a Danish birth cohort. *Archives of General Psychiatry*, *53*, 489–622.

Illinois Statutes. (2008). 720 Ill. 5/9–1.

Jackson v. Indiana, 406 U.S. 715 (1972).

Juninger, J., Claypoole, K., Laygo, R., & Crisanti, A. (2006). Effects of serious mental illness and substance abuse on criminal offenses. *Psychiatric Services*, *57*, 879–882.

Kalant, H. (1996). Intoxicated automatism: Legal concept v. scientific evidence. *Contemporary Drug Problems*, *23*, 631–648.

Keeve, P. (1984). Physicians at risk: Some epidemiologic considerations of alcoholism, drug abuse, and suicide. *Journal of Occupational Medicine*, *26*, 503–508.

Kermani, D. J., & Castaneda, R. C. (1996). Psychoactive substance use in forensic psychiatry. *American Journal of Drug and Alcohol Abuse*, *22*, 1–27.

Krebs, C. P., Brady, T., & Laird, G. (2003). Jail-based substance user treatment: An analysis of retention. *Substance Use and Misuse*, *38*, 1227–1258.

Lamb, H. R., & Weinberger, L. E. (1998). Persons with severe mental illness in jails and prisons: A review. *Psychiatry Services*, *49*(4), 483–490.

Lamb, H. R., & Weinberger, L. E. (2005). The shift of psychiatric inpatient care from hospitals to jails and prisons. *Journal of the American Academy of Psychiatry and the Law*, *33*, 529–534.

Lehman, W. (1990). Alcoholism, freedom, and moral responsibility. *International Journal of Law and Psychiatry*, *13*, 103–121.

Leshner, A. (1997). Addiction is a brain disease, and it matters. *Science*, *278*, 45–46.

Lightfoot, L. O., & Hodgins, D. (1988). A survey of alcohol and drug problems in incarcerated offenders. *International Journal of Addiction*, *23*, 688–706.

Link, G. (1999). Public conceptions of mental illness: Labels, causes, dangerousness, and social distance. *American Journal of Public Health*, *8*, 1328–1330.

M'Naghten Case, 8 Eng. Rep. 718, 722 (1843).

Matthews v. Eldridge, 424 U.S. 319, 335 (1976).

Mayo-Smith, M. F., Beecher, L. H., Fischer, T. L., Gorelick, D. A., Guillaume, J. L., Hill, A., Jara, G., & Kasser, C. (2004). Management of alcohol withdrawal delirium. An evidence based practice guideline. *Archives of Internal Medicine*, *164*, 1405–1412.

McLellan, A. T., Lewis, D. C., O'Brien, C. P., & Kleber, H. D. (2000). Drug dependence, a chronic medical illness: Implications for treatment, insurance, and outcomes evaluation. *Journal of the American Medical Association*, *284*, 1689–1695.

Michigan v. Sitz, 493 U.S. 806 (1990).

Miller, N. S., & Flaherty, J. A. (2000). Effectiveness of coerced addiction treatment (alternative consequences): A review of the clinical research. *Journal of Substance Abuse*, *18*, 9–16.

Monahan, J., Steadman, H. J., Silver, E., & Appelbaum, P. (2001). *Rethinking risk assessment: The MacArthur study of mental disorder and violence*. New York, NY: Oxford University Press.

Monahan, J., Steadman, H. J., Appelbaum, P. S., Robbins, P. C., Mulvey, E. P., Silver, E., Roth, L. H., & Grisso, T. (2000). Developing a clinically useful actuarial tool for assessing violence risk. *British Journal of Psychiatry*, *176*, 312–319.

Monahan, J., Steadman, H. J., Appelbaum, P. S., Grisso, T., Mulvey, E. P., Roth, L. H., Robbins, P. C., Banks, S., & Silver, E. (2006). The classification of violence risk. *Behavioral Sciences and the Law*, *24*(6), 721–730.

Montana v. Egelhoff, 116 S. Ct. 2013 (1996).

Morse, S. J. (1986). Psychology, determinism, and legal responsibility. In: *Nebraska symposium on motivation 1985*. Lincoln, NE: University of Nebraska Press.

Morse, S. J. (1999). Craziness and criminal responsibility. *Behavioral Science and the Law*, *17*, 147–164.

Morse, S. J. (2000). Hooked on hype: Addiction and responsibility. *Law and Philosophy*, *19*, 3–6.

Narevic, E., Garrity, T. F., Schoenberg, N. E., Hiller, M. L., Webster, J. M., Leukefeld, C. G., & Staton Tindall, M. (2006). Factors predicting unmet health services needs among incarcerated substance users. *Substance Use & Misuse*, *41*(8), 1077–1094.

National Institute on Drug Abuse. (2008). *Understanding Drug Abuse and Addiction*. U.S. Dept of Health and Human Services.

National Institute on Drug Use and Health. (2005). *Illicit Drug Use among Persons Arrested for Serious Crimes*, (December 16), Report. Office of Applied Studies, Substance Abuse Mental Health Services Administration.

Nestler, E., & Aghajanian, K. (1997). Molecular and cellular basis of addiction. *Science*, *278*, 58.

Noffsinger, S. G. (2001). Restoration to competency practice guidelines. *International Journal of Offender Therapy and Comparative Criminology*, *45*(2), 356–362.

Office of Applied Studies. (2002). *National Survey on Drug Use and Health*. Substance Abuse and Mental Health Services Administration.

Office of National Drug Control Policy. (2001). *Drug Treatment in the Criminal Justice System* (March), Fact sheet. Drug Policy Information Clearing House.

Pandina, R. J. (1996). Idiosyncratic alcohol intoxication: A construct that has lost its validity? In L. B. Schlesinger (Ed.), *Explorations in Clinical Psychopathology: Clinical Syndromes with Forensic Implications*, (pp. 142–148). Springfield, IL: Charles C. Thomas.

Parry, J. (1997). *Mental Disabilities and the Americans with Disabilities Act* (2nd ed.). Washington, DC: American Bar Association.

Pennsylvania v. Muniz, 110 S. Ct. 2638 (1990).

People v. McLeod, 407 Mich 632, 288 NW2d 909 (1980).

People v. Ramsey, 422 Mich 500, 375 NW2d 297, 71 ALR4th 661 (1985).

People v. Sorna, 88 Mich App 351, 276 NW2d 892 (1979).

People v. Tenbrink, 93 Mich App 326, 287 NW2d 223 (1979).

People v. Toner, 125 Mich App 439, 336 NW2d 22 (1983).

Powell v. Texas, 392 U.S. 514 (1968).

Robins, L. N., & Regier, D. A. (1991). Psychiatric Disorders in American: The Epidemiologic Catchment Area Study. New York, NY: Free Press.

Robinson v. California, 370 U.S. 660 (1962).

Roesenhan, L., & Seligman, M. (1995). *Abnormal Psychology* (3rd ed.). New York, NY: W. W. Norton (p. 512).

Sakai, J. T., Stallings, M. C., Mikulich-Gilberston, S. K., Corley, R. P., Young, S. E., Hopfer, C. J., & Crowley, T. J. (2004). Mate similarity for substance dependence and antisocial personality disorder symptoms among parents of patients and controls. *Drug and Alcohol Dependence*, *75*, 165–175.

Scott, C. L., & Gerbasi, J. B. (2005). Assessment of mental disorders in correctional settings. In: *Handbook of Correctional Mental Health* (1st ed.). Washington, DC: American Psychiatric Publishing, Inc (pp. 43–68) (1st ed.).

Slovenko, R. (2002). *Psychiatry in Law, Law in Psychiatry*. New York–London: Brunner Routledge (pp. 305–322).

Stallwitz, A., & Stover, H. (2007). The impact of substitution treatment in prisons – a literature review. *International Journal of Drug Policy*, *18*, 464–474.

State v. Wicks, 657 P.2d 781, 782 (Wash. 1983).

Steadman, H. J., Mulvey, E. P., Monahan, J., Robbins, P. C., Appelbaum, P., Grisso, T., Roth, L. H., & Silver, E. (1998). Violence by people discharged from acute psychiatric inpatient facilities and by others in the same neighborhoods. *Archives of General Psychiatry, 55*, 393–401.

Substance Abuse and Mental Health Services Administration. (2002). *Substance Abuse Services and Staffing in Adult Correctional Facilities.* The Drug and Alcohol Services Information System Report, Office of Applied Studies Report, Substance Abuse and Mental Health Services Administration, October 4.

Swanson, J., Holzer, C., & Ganju, V. (1999). Violence and psychotic disorder in the community: Evidence from the epidemiological catchment area study. *Hospital and Community Psychiatry, 41*, 761–770.

Swotinsky, R. B., & Smith, D. R. (1999). *The Medical Review Officer's Manual: MROCC's Guide to Drug Testing.* Beverly Farms, MA: OEM Press.

Symposium on Motivation 1985. Lincoln, NE: University of Nebraska Press.

Tarasoff v. Regents of the University of California, 17 Cal 3d 425 (1976).

Taxman, F. S., Perdoni, M. L., & Harrison, L. D. (2007). Drug treatment services for adult offenders: The state of the state. *Journal of Substance Abuse Treatment, 32*, 238–254.

Taylor, P. J., & Monahan, J. (1996). Commentary: Dangerous patients or dangerous diseases?. *British Medical Journal, 312*, 967–969.

Turley, A., Thornton, T., Johnson, C., & Azzolino, S. (2004). Jail drug and alcohol treatment program reduces recidivism in nonviolent offenders: A longitudinal study of Monroe County, New York's jail treatment drug and alcohol program. *International Journal of Offender Therapy and Comparative Criminology, 48*(6), 721–728.

United States Department of Health and Human Services. (1988). *The Mandatory Guidelines for Federal Workplace Drug Testing Programs: Final guidelines.* Washington, DC: U.S. Department of Health and Human Services.

van Oorsouw, K., Merckelbach, H., Ravelli, D., Nijman, H., & Mekking-Pompen, I. (2000). Alcoholic blackout for criminally relevant behavior. *The Journal of the American Academy of Psychiatry and the Law, 32*, 364–370.

Wald, H. P., Flaherty, M. T., & Pringle, J. L. (1999). Prevention in prisons. In R. T. Ammerman, P. J. Ott, & R. E. Tarter (Eds.), *Prevention and societal Impact of Drug and Alcohol Abuse* (pp. 369–381). Mahwah, NJ: Lawrence Erlbaum associates.

Warren, J. I., Murrie, D. C., Stejskal, W., Colwell, L. H., Morris, J., Chauhan, P., & Dietz, P. (2006). Opinion formation in evaluating the adjudicative competence and restorability of criminal defendants: A review of 8,000 evaluations. *Behavioral Sciences and the Law, 24*(2), 113–132.

Watterson, R. T. (1991). Just say no to the charges against you: Alcohol intoxication, mental capacity, and criminal responsibility. *Bulletin of the American Academy of Psychiatry and the Law, 19*, 277–290.

Weinstock, R. W., Leong, G. B., & Silva, J. A. (1996). California's diminished capacity defense: Evolution and transformation. *Bulletin of the American Academy of Psychiatry and Law, 24*, 347–366.

West, L. J., & Ackerman, D. L. (1993). The drug-testing controversy. *Journal of Drug Issues, 23*, 579–595.

Wilkinson, A. P., & Roberts, A. C. (2008). Annotation, insanity defenses. *American Jurisprudence, 2*, 615.

Chapter 15

Legal Rights of Fetuses and Young Children

Frank E. Vandervort, JD
University of Michigan, Ann Arbor, MI, USA

INTRODUCTION

The abuse of illicit drugs, prescription drugs and alcohol are substantial social problems in the United States (Simoni-Wastila & Strickler, 2004; SAMHSA, 2007). According to the *National Survey of Drug Use and Health*, in 2006 more than 20 million Americans aged 12 and older used an illicit drug within one month of being surveyed, a rate of 8.3%. According to the Institute of Health Policy at Brandeis University, some 18 million Americans have a problem with alcohol abuse, while five to six million Americans have a drug abuse problem (Institute for Health Policy, 2001). Simoni-Wastila and Strickler (2004) note that approximately 10 million Americans (7% of the population) used prescription drugs in 1999 for a non-medical purpose. They estimate that 1.3 million Americans over the age of 12 are problem users of prescription medication (Simoni-Wastila & Strickler, 2004). Approximately half of Americans surveyed in 2006 reported alcohol use within one month of being surveyed and 23% reported binge drinking in that same timeframe (SAMHSA, 2007). Moreover, researchers estimate that between eight and nine million children live in a household with a substance abusing parent (Substance Abuse and Mental Health Services Administration, 1999; Brown University Center for Alcohol and Addiction Studies, 2000).

Some of those using drugs are pregnant women. In 1990, it was estimated that between 100,000 and 375,000 women were using drugs during pregnancy (Ondersma et al., 2000). Although there is evidence that these numbers may have dropped somewhat (SAMHSA, 2007), the use of drugs and alcohol during pregnancy remains at concerning levels. Indeed, the 2006 National Survey on Drug Use and Health found that 4.0% of pregnant women had used illicit drugs within the past month while 11.8% reported use of alcohol within this same period (SAMHSA, 2007). Binge drinking by pregnant women in the 2006 survey was reported at 2.9% and heavy use of alcohol was reported by 0.7% of pregnant

Principles of Addictions and the Law: Applications in Forensic, Mental Health, and Medical Practice

women surveyed (SAMHSA, 2007). The use of these substances by pregnant women is thought by many to be a substantial social problem of concern to public health, legal and child welfare professionals (Drescher-Burke & Price, 2005; SAMHSA, 2007).

Policymakers and scholars debate what the proper response to the use of drugs and alcohol by pregnant women should be. Some argue that women who use drugs and alcohol during pregnancy should be criminally prosecuted and treated harshly by societal authorities (Drago, 2001). This approach has led to women being prosecuted for crimes ranging from child abuse (e.g., *Commonwealth v. Welch*, 1993; *Whitner v. State*, 1997; *State v. McKnight*, 2003) and delivery of drugs (*State v. Luster*, 1992) to homicide (*State v. McKnight*, 2003). Others have argued for a public health approach to prenatal exposure (Conn. Gen. Stat. § 17a–710, 2007; Del. Code § 1769A, 2008; S.D. Codified Laws § 34–23B–1, 2008). These advocates argue that the impact of substance abuse by pregnant women upon children is exaggerated, and that pregnant women who use drugs and alcohol should be treated with compassion (Armstrong & Abel, 2000; Eckenwiler, 2004; Armstrong, 2005). A number of states have declared that prenatal substance exposure should be treated as a public health problem, rather than a matter for the criminal law. Colorado has enacted a statute to provide nurse home visitors to visit with new mothers and their children, one rationale for which is the reduction in the use of drugs and alcohol that would negatively impact the baby (Colorado Revised Statutes 25–31–102, 2007).

This chapter addresses the following questions: what impact does prenatal exposure to alcohol and illicit drugs have upon a developing fetus; how does our legal system respond to pregnant women who use drugs and alcohol; do pregnant women commit a crime when they use these substances while pregnant and give birth to drug or alcohol exposed children? If they do, what crime, and how have courts responded to these charges? What rights, if any, do fetuses that have been exposed to drugs and alcohol *in utero* have? What rights do children who have been born exposed to alcohol and drugs have?

IMPACT OF PRENATAL DRUG EXPOSURE ON THE DEVELOPING FETUS

The precise impact of prenatal exposure to alcohol and illicit drugs on the developing fetus is unclear and may depend on a multiplicity of factors, such as the substance used, the timing of that use during the pregnancy, prenatal medical care and other environmental factors such as maternal poverty, whether the mother has a social support network and the presence of domestic violence in the home (Ondersma et al., 2000; Frank et al., 2001). It seems clear that there are some negative impacts (Roberts, 1997; Singer et al., 2004; Drescher-Burke & Price, 2005; Shankaran et al., 2007). Some substances, such as alcohol, appear to have clear negative effects on the development of the fetus, including impairment of cognitive functioning, poor academic performance and behavioral problems, and may be a contributing factor to juvenile delinquency (Fast et al., 1999; Drescher-Burke & Price, 2005). Similarly, *in utero* exposure to cocaine has been associated with decreased blood flow in the child's brain in adolescence, as measured by functional MRI scans (Rao et al., 2007). Other impacts are not as clear. In a systemic review of the literature, Frank and her colleagues (2001) concluded that prenatal exposure to cocaine itself – that is, when other complicating factors are controlled—has less negative impact on children than researchers previously believed.

IMPACT OF SUBSTANCE ABUSE ON CHILDREN

Prenatal exposure to drugs or alcohol may have lasting negative impacts on children (Dixon et al., 2007; Henry et al., 2007), including some which last well into adolescence (Crea et al., 2008). The actual impact of prenatal exposure on particular children may depend on the interaction with the impact of the exposure, together with the postnatal environment (Putnam, 2006; Henry et al., 2007; Dixon et al., 2008). Henry and his colleagues compared the results of various neurodevelopmental tests administered to children who had experienced postnatal trauma with those who experienced both prenatal alcohol exposure and postnatal trauma. They discovered that children who were exposed to alcohol *in utero* and then suffered postnatal trauma did less well than children who had experienced only postnatal trauma (Henry et al., 2007). They also found that children who experienced both prenatal exposure to alcohol and postnatal trauma had lower IQ scores than children who had experienced only postnatal trauma (Henry et al., 2007). Similarly, Singer and her colleagues (2002) studied 415 women and their neonates, 218 of which tested negative for cocaine exposure while 197 tested positive for cocaine at birth. These researchers controlled for confounding variables, such as use of tobacco, alcohol and marijuana, and among their findings were that cocaine-exposed children were twice as likely to experience developmental delay in the first two years of life.

NEED FOR AND ACCESS TO TREATMENT

In a 1998 study of 501 women who gave birth at two hospitals in Louisiana, researchers found that approximately 33% of the women surveyed needed treatment, while only 7% of the women wanted treatment (Louisiana Department of Health and Hospitals, Office of Alcohol and Drug Abuse, 1998). Even when a pregnant woman recognizes the need for treatment, she may find it difficult to access the appropriate level of care (Howell et al., 1999). Resources to pay for treatment present another barrier to adequate access to care. The need for pregnant women to obtain treatment, their willingness to enter treatment and their ability to obtain the necessary services may place the interest of the pregnant substance abuser into conflict with the rights of her fetus and the child the fetus will become.

Rights of Fetuses Generally

More than three decades ago, the United States Supreme Court found that: "the word 'person' as used in the Fourteenth Amendment [to the United States Constitution], does not include the unborn" (*Roe v. Wade*, 1973, p. 158). Nevertheless, because a viable fetus: "has the capability of meaningful life outside the mother's womb," the state has a compelling interest in the fetus's well-being on its reaching this stage of development (*Roe v. Wade*, p. 163). To protect the state's interest in the viable fetus, the court held, state regulation of the mother's behavior by imposing a restriction on abortion in the latter stages of pregnancy was both logically and biologically justified (subsequent developments in abortion law are beyond the scope of this chapter). In light of the Supreme Court's abortion jurisprudence, a number of state legislatures have defined the status and rights of fetuses in their statutory law (e.g., 720 ILCS 510.1, 2008; Wis. Stats. § 48.01, 2008). Illinois, for instance, defines an "unborn" child as a "human being," but expressly states that it is not the legislation's intent to interfere with a woman's right to abortion as determined in *Roe v. Wade* (720 ILCS 510.1). Somewhat similarly, the Wisconsin legislature has included unborn children in the state's Children's Code, which is designed to protect children from abuse and neglect (Wis. Stats. § 48.01, 2008).

A number of courts have addressed the rights of fetuses outside the abortion context, and when there is concern that the rights of the mother and the rights of the fetus are in conflict. For example, a number of courts have addressed a fetus's right to medical care when the mother does not wish to receive recommended treatment. One example of this is *In re Fetus Brown* (1998). In that case, Darlene Brown, a 26-year-old Jehovah's Witness who was approximately 34 weeks pregnant, refused a blood transfusion that doctors had recommended because of substantial blood loss during a cystoscopy and removal of a urethral mass. Before the procedure, doctors anticipated that she could lose 100 cubic centimeters of blood. In fact, she lost approximately 700 ccs of blood, so the physician performing the procedure ordered three units of blood for a transfusion. Ms Brown, who was conscious during the procedure, explained that her religious beliefs prohibited her from authorizing the transfusion and she refused consent. The doctor did not transfuse her, but used other procedures in an effort to stem the bleeding. After the procedure, Brown experienced a precipitous drop in her hemoglobin. The physician explained that the drop in hemoglobin was life-threatening to both Ms Brown and her fetus. After consulting with his patient and her husband, the doctor attempted other measures, consistent with Ms Brown's religious beliefs, to raise her hemoglobin. These alternate measures proved unsuccessful and her hemoglobin level continued to drop, eventually reaching the point where the doctor opined that Ms Brown's and the fetus's chances of survival were only approximately 5%.

Faced with these facts, the state petitioned the Cook County, Illinois Circuit Court for an order taking custody of the fetus for the purpose of ordering the provision of the recommended medical treatment. In order to protect the interests of the fetus in the legal proceedings, the court appointed the public guardian to represent the fetus's legal interests. At the hearing on the state's petition, the attending physician testified as to Ms Brown's condition. A hospital administrator testified that the hospital would agree to take temporary custody of the fetus for the purpose of authorizing the blood transfusion. Ms Brown, through her attorney and her husband, entered stipulations with the state regarding her condition and the care of Ms Brown's older children.

The court, at the conclusion of the hearing, appointed the hospital administrator temporary legal custodian of the fetus for the purpose of consenting to blood transfusions for Darlene Brown. In doing so, the court considered four interests at stake in the case. First, the court found that the transfusion was necessary to save Ms Brown's and the fetus's lives. Next, the court considered whether suicide was an issue, but determined that it was not because Ms. Brown willingly accepted all medical care except the transfusion. Third, the court determined that the state had a strong interest in protecting third parties, Ms Brown's other children, three- and eight-years-old, would be orphaned if she did not receive the transfusion. Finally, the court determined that the transfusion would be minimally invasive.

Ms Brown was subsequently transfused with six units of blood after being sedated, because she resisted the medical professionals' efforts to administer the transfusion. She gave birth to a healthy baby and the court dismissed the state's petition for temporary custody and closed the case.

Arguing that as a competent adult she had an absolute right to refuse the recommended medical treatment, Ms Brown appealed. The public guardian also appealed, asserting that the trial court committed legal error by appointing it to represent the interests of a fetus as separate and apart from the mother. The state, for its part, argued that its interest in the welfare of Ms Brown's viable fetus outweighed the minimal intrusion presented by the transfusion. The appellate court held that the: "state may not override a pregnant woman's competent treatment decision, including refusal of recommended invasive medical procedures, to potentially save the life of the viable fetus" (*In re Fetus Brown*, p. 405). The court also ruled that the circuit court judge had erred in appointing a guardian *ad litem* to represent the fetus, despite its viability.

Courts are split on the question of whether a child may bring a civil action against his or her mother for negligently inflicted prenatal injuries. Several courts have found that such a claim is viable (*Grodin v. Grodin*, 1980; *Stallman v. Youngquist*, 1988; *Bonte v. Bonte*, 1992; *National Cas. Co. v. Northern Trust Bank*, 2002); however, others have found that such claims are prohibited (*Stallman v. Youngquist*, 1988; *Chenault v. Huie*, 1999; *Remy v. MacDonald*, 2004). Courts have been more willing to recognize the rights of a person to bring a civil action for damages against a third person for injury suffered by a fetus (*Smith v. Brennan*, 1971; *Womack v. Buchhorn*, 1971). So, generally, while fetuses lack personhood under our constitution, they are not entirely deprived of all legal remedies for their mistreatment.

RIGHTS OF FETUSES: CIVIL CHILD PROTECTIVE PROCEEDINGS

The purpose of child protective proceedings is to protect children from abuse or neglect inflicted by their parents or legal guardians, rather than punishment of the parent (*In re Neil*, 1987; *In re Constance G.*, 1995; *In the Interests of J.P.H.*, 2006). Parental substance abuse is a major contributor to the abuse and neglect of children, although relatively few children living with a substance abusing parent are involved in the formal, state run child welfare system (Department of Health and Human Services, 1999). Between 90 and 100% of public child welfare agencies have received a referral for child maltreatment based on prenatal exposure to drugs or alcohol (Ondersma et al., 2000).

Substance abuse is thought to be a contributing factor in 70% of all child protection cases (Reid & Macchetto, 1999), while at least half of the child protection cases substantiated by state child welfare authorities involve parental substance abuse (Department of Health and Human Services, 1999). Prenatal substance abuse does not take place in a vacuum, but rather occurs in a social context. It seems clear that the postnatal environment is a crucial contributing factor in determining whether state child welfare authorities label prenatal exposure as child maltreatment (Roberts, 1997; Ondersma et al., 2000; Drescher-Burke, 2005; Henry et al., 2007). This comorbidity has been recognized in some states' laws. In California, for instance, if a child is born with a positive toxicology screen, the hospital personnel must make an assessment of the child's and mother's needs, as well as an assessment of risk to the child and, if necessary to protect the child's health, must make a referral to children's protective services (Cal Pen Code § 11165.13, 2007; Cal Health and Saf Code § 123605). Other states define prenatal exposure to illicit drugs or alcohol as child neglect *per se*. For example, Minnesota law provides that prenatal exposure to "a controlled substance … used by the mother for non-medical purposes" as neglect (Minn. Stats. § 626.556(2)(f)(6)). Other states define a separate category for infants prenatally exposed. Under Maine's law, the state's child welfare agency: "shall act to protect infants born identified as being affected by illegal substance abuse or suffering from withdrawal symptoms resulting from prenatal drug exposure, whether or not the prenatal exposure was to legal or illegal drugs, regardless of whether or not the infant is abused or neglected" (22 Maine Revised Statutes § 4004–B, 2007).

Much of state child welfare practice is molded by federal statutes such as the Child Abuse Prevention and Treatment Act (CAPTA)(42 U.S.C. § 5101, *et seq.*) and Titles IV–B (42 U.S.C. § 620, *et seq.*) and IV–E (42 U.S.C. § 670) of the Social Security Act. These statutes provide funding to the states to support their child welfare services programming so long as the states' programs comply with certain minimum federal requirements (Rollin et al., 2005). Before the enactment of the Keeping Children and Families Safe Act in 2003, the federal law did not require state child welfare systems to provide for the reporting of drug- and alcohol-exposed infants to child welfare authorities as a contingency to receipt of federal funding for child welfare services. This new act, however, amended CAPTA's provisions to require, as a contingency to receiving federal child welfare funds, that states adopt policies mandating the reporting of prenatal substance abuse (42 U.S.C. 5106a(b)(2)(A)(ii)).

Although federal law only recently incentivized states to mandate reporting of prenatal exposure, some states have long required mandated reporters to report the birth of an infant when it is believed that the infant was prenatally exposed to alcohol or drugs. For instance, since 1975 Michigan law has required medical professionals to report to children's protective services when he or she: "knows, or from the child's symptoms has reasonable cause to suspect, that a newborn infant has any amount of alcohol, a controlled substance, or the metabolite of a controlled substance in his or her body" unless its presence is as a result of medical treatment provided to the newborn or the mother (Michigan Compiled Law 722.623a). To be in compliance with the federal law, those states which did not require such reports before the adoption of the federal law in 2003 now contain such a provision.

Response to Report

While the states uniformly require that at-risk newborns exposed to alcohol or drugs *in utero* be reported, once reports are made it appears that the response by children's protective services is anything but uniform. Ondersma and his colleagues (2001) surveyed 200 child welfare professionals, from both urban and rural jurisdictions, to examine patterns of child protective services agencies' response to reports of drug-exposed neonates. They found that responses varied widely; some jurisdictions make no official response while others always immediately seek court approval to take the child into the state's protective custody.

While infants have likely been born exposed to drugs and alcohol for decades, the exposure of fetuses to alcohol and illicit substances really entered the nation's psyche in the mid-1980s with the advent of the crack cocaine "epidemic" (Roberts, 1997). More recently, child welfare authorities have expressed grave concern about the impact of methamphetamine use and production on children (Connell-Carrick, 2007). Researchers have identified numerous negative impacts on children from prenatal exposure to methamphetamine, including developmental delay, learning disability, low birth weight, premature birth, visual motor problems and difficulties with attention and verbal memory (Connell-Carrick, 2007, p. 134). These concerns have caused some jurisdictions to enact child protection laws unique to the exposure of children to methamphetamine and its production. In New York, for instance, the Social Services Law mandates that children's protective services workers receive information aimed at helping them to identify methamphetamine laboratories (NY Soc. Serv. Law § 413, 2007). Michigan's Child Protection Law requires that if the state's child protection authorities determine that a child has been exposed to or had contact with methamphetamine production they must file a petition within 24 hours, requesting that the family court take jurisdiction of the child (Mich. Comp. Laws Ann. 722.637, 2008).

Courts' Responses to Child Protection Actions on Behalf of Fetuses

Numerous state courts have addressed efforts by state child welfare authorities to protect the fetuses of substance-abusing women by taking temporary custody of the fetus under state laws allowing courts to take temporary custody of children who they find are abused or neglected (e.g., *In re Dittrick Infant*, 1977; *In re Baby X*, 1980; *In re Ruiz*, 1986; *In re Pima County*, 1995; *In the Interest of H*, 2003). Most courts that have addressed this issue have held that state child protection statutes do not permit courts to assert their authority over fetuses. The outcome of these cases has typically turned on the courts' interpretation of individual state statutes, specifically the intent of the legislature vis-à-vis substance-exposed fetuses at the time the statute was enacted. Some state statutes, currently or previously, have explicitly provided for the protection of fetuses. Thus, the central focus of these court opinions is whether at the time of the statute's enactment the legislature intended the law to protect a fetus (e.g., *In re Pima County*, 1995). This was the issue in *In the Interest of H*, a 2003 Colorado Court of Appeals case in which county officials brought a dependency and neglect proceeding seeking court jurisdiction over an unborn baby based on the mother's methamphetamine use. The trial court held that it lacked subject matter jurisdiction over the case, because the Colorado Children's Code did not intend for a court to assert authority over an unborn child. The Court of Appeals affirmed the lower court's ruling, noting that: "where, as here, the controlling statute does not specifically include the unborn child within its protection and the proceeding was commenced prior to the child's birth, most state courts have found jurisdiction lacking" (*In the Interest of H*, p. 496). In doing so, the court noted that prior to 1967 the state's Children's Code had specifically provided for the court to have child protective jurisdiction over fetuses "*from the time of their conception and during the months before birth*" (p. 496, emphasis in original), but that this provision of the law was changed. Similarly, in *In re Dittrick Infant* (1977), the Michigan Court of Appeals ruled that the state's juvenile courts cannot assert child protective jurisdiction over a fetus, because a fetus is not a "child" within the meaning of the applicable statutes.

Wisconsin's Children's Code explicitly provides the court the authority over fetuses to the same extent that it provides for jurisdiction over children once born. Among other things, the code permits the court to order an "expectant mother," whether an adult or a minor, to participate in outpatient substance abuse treatment services or to place an "expectant mother" in a residential substance abuse treatment program. Before doing so, the court must find that the "expectant mother" has been offered the relevant alcohol or drug treatment services and has refused them, and has not made a good faith effort to participate in an outpatient services program (Wis. Stat. § 48.345, Wis. Stat. 48.347 2008).

Courts' Responses to Substance Exposed Neonates

While courts have typically rejected efforts by state child protection authorities to take custody of fetuses, they generally recognize prenatal ingestion of alcohol or illicit drugs as a form of child maltreatment warranting the immediate assertion of temporary court authority over neonates, and authorize children's protective services personnel to remove these children from parental custody (e.g., *In re Baby X.*, 1980; *In re Troy D.*, 1989; *In the Matter of Stefanel Tyesha C.*, 1990; *In re Dustin T.*, 1992).

Some courts have squarely held that under their child protection statutes prenatal exposure to drugs or alcohol is in and of itself sufficient to make a case that a child is maltreated (e.g., *In re Troy D.* 1989). *In Troy D.*, an infant was born prematurely on 10 February 1988. At the time of his birth, both he and his mother tested positive for amphetamines and opiates. Six days after his birth, child protection authorities filed a petition with the court asking the court to assert its jurisdiction. The trial court took jurisdiction of the infant and the mother appealed. The Court of Appeal of California affirmed holding that: "the fact that Troy was diagnosed as being born under the influence of a dangerous drug is legally sufficient for the juvenile court to exercise jurisdiction" (p. 897). The Michigan Court of Appeals has recognized that: "a child has a legal right to begin life with a sound mind and body" (*In re Baby X*, p. 739). The court reasoned that: "it is within his best interests to examine all prenatal conduct bearing on that right" (p. 739). Thus, the court held that prenatal drug use is sufficient in itself for the court to assume jurisdiction over the child.

Other courts have held that a combination of prenatal exposure and environmental factors, such as the parent's continued use of substances, failure to enroll in substance abuse treatment or associating with drug dealers, is sufficient to support juvenile court action to protect the child (e.g., *In re Dustin T.*, 1992; *ex rel Dante M. v. Denise J.*, 1995). For instance, the Court of Special Appeals of Maryland held in *In re Dustin T.* that where state child protection authorities alleged in their petition that the mother's drug use affected the child's birth and continued to affect her living conditions after her son was born, there was sufficient evidence of parental neglect to warrant the court's assertion of jurisdiction over the child. In doing so, the court was careful to stress that the mother's drug use: "must be seen as being relevant to (although not necessarily determinative of) her ability to provide adequate care to Dustin" (p. 733). Similarly, New York's highest court has held that, while a positive toxicology screen at birth is not itself sufficient to support a finding of parental abuse or neglect, such a test together with the mother's history of drug use and her inability to properly care for other children was sufficient evidence of neglect to trigger the family court's jurisdiction of both the child born exposed and an older child in the mother's care (*Nassau County Dep't. Social Services ex rel Dante M. v. Denise J.*, 1995).

Courts, of course, must apply the law as established by the jurisdiction's legislature. South Carolina's legislature has enacted a statute which explicitly provides that a child born exposed to alcohol or drugs is presumed to be abused or neglected (S.C. Code Ann 20–7–736, 2007). The statute provides that if either the mother or the newborn tests positive for any controlled substance that was not the result of medical treatment, this is sufficient evidence of child maltreatment. The statute also establishes a presumption that in such circumstances the child: "cannot be protected from further harm without being removed from the custody of the mother" (S.C. Code Ann. 20–7–736(G)).

It is less clear whether a court may terminate parental rights based solely on the prenatal use of alcohol or drugs. The Michigan Court of Appeals specifically declined to address this question in In re Baby X, saying: "prenatal conduct will be considered along with postnatal conduct" (p. 739) in determining whether termination of parental rights is appropriate. A more definitive answer was provided by the Court of Appeals of Arizona in In the Matter of Pima County (1995). In that case, the mother had given birth to two children, A. and T. While the court did not set out the facts of the case in detail, it did state that: "it is undisputed that A. and T. were harmed by the mother's ingestion of alcohol during pregnancy" (pp. 556–557) and, after the children had been in foster care for an extended period of time, the state sought to terminate the mother's rights based on her prenatal use of alcohol and the father's rights based on his failure to protect the children from the mother's prenatal alcohol use. Relying on a then recently-decided criminal case in which it was held that a woman could not be charged under the state's criminal child abuse statute for prenatal conduct that caused harm to the child after birth, the court held that the prenatal ingestion of alcohol was not a sufficient rationale "in and of itself" to terminate the parent's rights (p. 558). Similarly, in In re Valerie D. (1992), the Connecticut Supreme Court found that the state's termination of parental rights statute was ambiguous regarding whether a parent's rights to a child could be terminated based on prenatal drug use. The court assumed that the mother's use of cocaine while pregnant, and the complications the child suffered after birth, placed the child in serious jeopardy. But the court stressed that the fundamental nature of the parent–child relationship, which is constitutionally protected, requires the child protection laws be strictly construed. The terms "child" and "parent" as used in the statute suggest a child who has been born rather than a fetus. The court carefully reviewed the legislature's intent in enacting the child protection laws, and concluded that the legislature did not intend for the termination of parental rights statute to apply to prenatal drug use. In so deciding, the court expressed concern that if the state could seek termination of parental rights based on prenatal substance use, it would invite similar petitions regarding behavior that, while unhealthy, is not illegal.

OTHER CIVIL REMEDIES

While courts have generally held that the law does not permit the assertion of child protection authority over fetuses, but does generally permit temporary jurisdiction over newborns based on prenatal drug use, in some situations state agencies or legislatures have sought to require pregnant women who use alcohol or drugs to take action to protect the fetus. The question inevitably arises whether such actions are permissible.

In *Cox v. Court of Common Pleas of Franklin County* (1988), an Ohio trial court issued an order directing Ms Cox, who was seven months pregnant, to refrain from using drugs and to submit to a medical evaluation. The mother had four other children that had been removed from her custody and placed with relatives, and at the time she was pregnant with this child there was an action pending to terminate their rights to those children. She was using drugs daily, producing 23 positive drug screens, and was enrolled in a methadone program. She had refused to seek any prenatal care. On appeal, the question was whether the state child protection statute provides the juvenile court the necessary statutory authority to issue orders regarding a pregnant woman. The appellate court held that it did not. Thus, the court was powerless to enter orders mandating that Ms Cox refrain from drug use or see a physician.

PUBLIC HEALTH APPROACHES

In an attempt to address problems of prenatal alcohol and drug use, a number of states have enacted statutes that take a public health, as opposed to a child protective or criminal punishment, orientation. For instance, one provision of the Delaware Code (Del. Code § 1769A, 2008) states:

> "A person certified to practice medicine who treats, advises, or counsels pregnant women for matters relating to pregnancy shall post warnings and give written and verbal warnings to all pregnant women regarding possible problems, complications, and injuries to themselves and/or to the fetus from the consumption or use of alcohol or cocaine, marijuana, heroin and other narcotics during pregnancy."

Similarly, South Dakota law requires both physicians and "any counselor" to counsel their patients regarding the potential impacts of substance abuse during pregnancy (S.D. Codified Laws § 34–23B–1, 2008), and also mandates that the state department of education provide to local school districts educational information on the impact of prenatal alcohol and drug use for all students in the first through twelfth grades (S.D. Codified Laws § 34–23B–3, 2008). That statute also requires that the relevant state agencies provide educational materials and direction to physicians to implement this requirement. Finally, Missouri law provides, but does not mandate, that various professionals including physicians, nurses, social workers and the like may refer a pregnant woman to a substance abuse treatment program (§ 191.725, *et seq.*, R.S.Mo.).

A number of states have enacted statutes mandating that public health officials establish treatment programs aimed at pregnant women (e.g., *Commonwealth of Kentucky v. Welch*, 1993; Conn. Gen. Stat. § 17a–710, 2007; Revised Statutes of Missouri §§ 191.725–191.745, 2008). Connecticut's law provides that the state's Department of Mental Health and Addiction Services must, to the extent that funding is available, establish comprehensive programs to address the needs of pregnant women who are abusing substances. These programs should include, in addition to direct substance abuse treatment, housing assistance, parenting skills classes and vocational training. Missouri's statutory law requires any physician who provides obstetrical or gynecological care to women to inform their patient about the risks of smoking cigarettes, as well as the risks of drug and alcohol use during pregnancy, and requires the patient to sign a written statement that this information has been received; this document must be retained in the patient's file (191.725 R.S.Mo., 2008). Further, state law provides that pregnant women are to be given "first priority" in obtaining substance abuse treatment, and no substance abuse treatment facility may deny a woman treatment services because she is pregnant (191.731 R.S.Mo., 2008). The state's Department of Health and Senior Services is statutorily required to develop protocols for assessing, based on risk assessment criteria, whether a particular woman is having a high-risk pregnancy because of possible substance abuse. Once a woman is assessed as being at high risk for substance abuse, the agency must then provide service coordination regarding social services, healthcare and mental health services (191.741 R.S.Mo., 2008).

Criminal Charges

Medical associations have consistently opposed efforts by prosecutorial authorities to charge women criminally for the use of illicit drugs or alcohol while pregnant (e.g., American Medical Association Board of Trustees, 1990). For example, the American Public Health Association filed a friend of the court brief with the Michigan Court of Appeals in *People v. Hardy* (1991), opposing the application of Michigan's law outlawing the delivery of cocaine to a woman who used the drug while she was pregnant. In that case, the woman was charged with "delivery" of cocaine for ingesting the drug while she was pregnant and thereby "delivering" it to her fetus. These associations often argue that charging pregnant women who use drugs will likely discourage them from seeking treatment. Some courts have adopted this argument as one rationale for prohibiting the criminal prosecution of women who use alcohol or illicit drugs during pregnancy (e.g., *State v. Gethers*, 1991).

Although medical professionals have recommended against the use of the criminal law as a coercive response to the problem of alcohol and drug use by pregnant women, prosecutors around the country have attempted to use criminal sanctions to respond to drug use by pregnant women. As with courts' child protection jurisdiction, the question of whether criminal charges may be sustained against a woman for prenatal use of alcohol or drugs is, in essence, one of statutory interpretation (e.g., *People v. Hardy*, 1991; *State of Ohio v. Gray*, 1992; *State v. Luster*, 1992; *Johnson v. State of Florida*, 1992; *Commonwealth v. Welch*, 1993). The overriding question is whether when it enacted the specific state criminal statute the legislature intended for a pregnant woman to be charged with a crime under the circumstances of the case.

While most courts have declined to uphold criminal charges against pregnant women who use alcohol or drugs (e.g., *People v. Hardy*, 1991; *State v. Luster*, 1992), one state, South Carolina, has consistently held that pregnant women who use drugs may be charged under various state statutes prohibiting criminal conduct. Thus, its courts have upheld criminal convictions of pregnant women who use drugs during pregnancy (*Whitner v. State*, 1997; *State v. McKnight*, 2003). South Carolina also produced a case, which was decided by the United States Supreme Court in 2001, which addressed the application of the Fourth Amendment's prohibition against unreasonable searches and seizures in the context of unauthorized drug screening of pregnant women (*Ferguson v. City of Charleston*, 2001). The outcomes of these cases turn on the specific crime charged and a careful reading of the language of the statute under which the charges were filed. We will look at courts' responses to individual criminal charges.

Search and Seizure and Consent

In 2001 the United States Supreme Court decided *Ferguson v. City of Charleston*, which addressed a Fourth Amendment challenge to a drug testing program of pregnant women who had not given consent for the drug screens, and in which the hospital's policy for drug testing pregnant women was developed in close collaboration with law enforcement personnel. In essence, if a pregnant woman tested positive for cocaine, the results were turned over to law enforcement and the woman was offered an opportunity to participate in substance abuse treatment (this last provision was added after the program of prosecution had been in place for about a year, so not every woman who tested positive was offered the opportunity to obtain treatment before the police were notified). In *Ferguson*, ten women who received obstetrical care at the Medical University of South Carolina tested positive for cocaine use and were arrested as a result. Of the ten women, six were offered treatment as an alternative to prosecution, while four were not. Each of the women either failed to complete treatment or continued using cocaine. Thus, each was charged with delivery of cocaine as a result of her drug usage during pregnancy. The women challenged the hospital's program of nonconsensual drug testing for the purpose of turning positive results over to law enforcement for prosecution, arguing that the hospital's action violated their Fourth Amendment right against unreasonable search and seizure. A federal district court jury found that the women had consented to the drug screens and ruled in favor of the defendant city. The women appealed to the United States Court of Appeals for the Fourth Circuit, which did not address the question of consent but ruled that the searches in the form of the drug screens a reasonable search given the "special needs" at play in the circumstances. The women then appealed to the United States Supreme Court which reversed the Fourth Circuit's holding that the searches were reasonable.

Writing for the Supreme Court, Justice John Paul Stevens framed the question to be answered by the court as: "whether the interest in using the threat of criminal sanctions to deter pregnant women from using cocaine can justify a departure from the general rule that an official nonconsensual search is unconstitutional if not authorized by a valid warrant" (p. 69). After careful analysis of the program and the law, the court's majority concluded that the primary purpose of the drug screening at the MUSC was for law enforcement purposes, and not for medical treatment of the women or their fetuses. Thus, the court found that the program violated the women's Fourth Amendment right against unreasonable searches and seizures.

Charges that Can be Sustained

State appellate courts around the country have addressed numerous cases in which the authorities have brought various charges against women for illicit drug use while pregnant.

Homicide

In *State v. McKnight* (2003) the South Carolina Supreme Court confronted the question of whether the state's homicide statute would support the conviction of a woman for drug use during pregnancy which resulted in the death of the fetus. Regina McKnight gave birth to a stillborn baby girl weighing five pounds. The baby was estimated to be 34–37 weeks gestation at the time of delivery. After the birth, an autopsy was conducted and the pathologist found evidence of a cocaine metabolite in the baby's system. The pathologist ruled the child's death a homicide, and Ms McKnight was criminally charged with homicide by child abuse. At her trial, the jury could not agree on a verdict, and the court declared a mistrial. She was retried and the jury found her guilty. The judge then sentenced Ms McKnight to 20 years in prison, the final eight to be suspended on her serving 12 years. She appealed, raising several legal issues. Among these were that at the time the legislature enacted the homicide by child abuse statute it did not intend for the term "child" to include a fetus. The South Carolina Supreme Court rejected this argument. The South Carolina courts had previously interpreted the term "child" in the child abuse statutes to include an unborn child, so the court reasoned the legislature was on notice regarding the courts' understanding of that term. In 2000 the legislature amended the homicide by child abuse statute without altering the definition of the term "child," so the legislature's intent was that the law be so interpreted. Additionally, the mother asserted that her constitutional right to be free from unreasonable searches and seizures was violated by the taking of the urine sample. However, she had signed a consent form which specifically noted that the results of the test may be turned over to law enforcement and could be used for legal purposes. The South Carolina Supreme Court found that the practice of taking "medical-legal (forensic)" drug screens did not violate her right to be free from unreasonable searches and seizures, because she had provided informed consent for the search. Thus, the court upheld her conviction and sentence for homicide.

Possession

At least two state appellate courts have addressed the application of state laws prohibiting the possession of illicit drugs in the context of prenatal use (*People v. Hardy*, 1991; *Commonwealth v. Pellegrini*, 1993). In *Pellegrini* the Supreme Judicial Court of Massachusetts (the state's highest court) was called upon to determine whether a criminal charge of possession of cocaine against a mother was viable where the charge was brought as a result of her newborn testing positive for metabolites of cocaine. The child was born on 2 July 1989. On 15 August of that year the child was taken to the hospital, because of injuries on his toes which were later determined to be the result of cigarette burns or a similar object. The mother was apparently transported to the hospital by the police and admitted that she had used drugs during her pregnancy. The prosecutor then brought the case before the grand jury, which issued an indictment for unlawful distribution of cocaine. The court subsequently dismissed the delivery charge. The prosecutor did not appeal the court's decision to dismiss the delivery charge, but did choose to pursue a charge of possession of cocaine. The trial court dismissed the possession charge after finding that the statute under which the state obtained evidence of her alleged drug use was intended to prosecute child abuse and not possession of drugs. The mother also asserted that she had a privacy interest in her infant's medical records which was violated when those records were turned over to state authorities for the purposes of prosecution. The Supreme Judicial Court rejected both of the mother's claims. It reasoned that the prosecutor, an officer of the executive branch of government, and not the court is properly charged with determining what criminal charges to bring. Regarding the mother's assertion of privacy in her son's medical records, the court observed that this argument assumed that the mother: "has the same privacy right in her child's medical record as she has in her own" (p. 721). The court rejected this proposition. "To permit parents to exclude medical or hospital records of their child on a privacy claim," the court reasoned, "could be adverse to the child's best interests" (p. 721). As a result, the prosecutor was permitted to introduce the medical records or testimony of medical witnesses regarding the content of those records for the purpose of supporting the alleged possession. The court was careful to stress that while the positive drug test at birth was sufficient to support the charge, it was not deciding whether a positive test without additional evidence would be sufficient to actually convict the mother of possession.

Child Neglect

It appears that South Carolina is the only state in which an appellate court has upheld a criminal conviction for child neglect as a result of prenatal drug use by a pregnant woman (*Whitner v. State*, 1997). In *Whitner*, a woman was charged with criminal child neglect after she gave birth to a child born with cocaine metabolites in his or her system. Based on the advice of her attorney, Ms Whitner entered a guilty plea and was sentenced to eight years in prison. She did not appeal, but later filed a motion for post-conviction relief.

She argued that the court lacked subject matter jurisdiction over her because the statute at issue did not apply to the use of drugs by pregnant women, and that her lawyer had ineffectively represented her because the lawyer did not explain to her that the child neglect statute may not apply to pregnant women who use illicit drugs. The trial court granted the mother the relief she sought. The prosecution appealed. On appeal the state supreme court held that a viable fetus is a "child" within the meaning of the state's criminal child neglect statute. For this reason, the court explained, the trial court in fact had subject matter jurisdiction over the case. Similarly, because the statute applied to protect a viable fetus, the mother's attorney was not ineffective when he advised her to plead guilty. The state Supreme Court reversed and reinstated the mother's guilty plea and sentence.

Use of Controlled Substances

Every state prohibits the use of controlled substances that are not prescribed by or administered under the supervision of one licensed by the state to prescribe such use (e.g., Mich. Comp. Laws 333.7404, 2007; § 195.017 R.S.Mo., 2008). The Michigan Court of Appeals, in *People v. Hardy* (1991), implied without holding that a pregnant woman who uses illicit drugs could properly be charged under the state's statute prohibiting the use of controlled substances which are not prescribed by a physician.

Charges that Cannot be Sustained

Most courts that have addressed the application of the criminal law to punish pregnant drug users have held that the specific statutes under which the charges were brought do not permit such a use. Most often, again, because the courts have held that the term "child" or "person" as used in the various statutes cannot be interpreted to include fetuses.

Delivery

A number of state appellate courts have addressed whether their state statutes prohibiting the delivery of drugs may be applied to punish a woman for "delivering" drugs to her fetus (e.g., *People v. Hardy*, 1991; *State v. Luster*, 1992; *Commonwealth v. Kemp*, 1992; *Johnson v. Florida*, 1992). The prosecution's theory of these cases is typically that some amount of the drug in question was delivered to the child after birth but before the umbilical cord is severed. In *State v. Luster*, the Court of Appeals of Georgia was called on to decide whether that state's laws prohibiting the unauthorized possession and delivery of drugs were meant to apply to a fetus. The mother, Darla Michelle Luster, was charged with two crimes, one count of possession and one count of delivery of cocaine to her daughter, Tiffany. The mother, through her attorney, asked the trial court to dismiss the delivery charge. The trial court granted her motion and dismissed the delivery charge. The prosecutor appealed, arguing that the statute in question contemplated that the use of cocaine by a pregnant woman would trigger the delivery provision. The Court of Appeals disagreed with the prosecution and affirmed the trial court's order dismissing the delivery charge. The statute in question prohibited one person from delivering a controlled substance, including cocaine, to another "person." The court reasoned that, pursuant to "Georgia law, the word 'person' in a criminal statute may not be construed to include a fetus unless the legislature has expressly included it" (p. 34).

Similarly, in *People v. Hardy* (1991), Ms Hardy gave birth to a child prenatally exposed to cocaine. She was charged with delivery of less than 50 grams of cocaine and second-degree child abuse. The trial court dismissed the child abuse charge, but refused to dismiss the delivery charge. The mother appealed the decision to permit the delivery charge to stand, the prosecution did not appeal regarding the child abuse charge. The Michigan Court of Appeals held that: "to prosecute the defendant for *delivery* of cocaine is so tenuous that we cannot reasonably infer that the legislature intended this application, absent unmistakable evidence of legislative intent." The court went on to note that: "we are not persuaded that a pregnant woman's use of cocaine, which might result in the postpartum transfer of cocaine metabolites through the umbilical cord to her infant, is the type of conduct that the legislature intended to be prosecuted under the *delivery* of cocaine statute" (emphasis in original).

Child Abuse or Endangerment

Prosecutors in numerous jurisdictions have sought to charge women under state child abuse or child endangerment statutes (*Commonwealth v. Kemp*, 1992; *Ohio v. Gray*, 1992; *Commonwealth v. Welch*, 1993; *Sheriff, Washoe County v. Encoe*, 1994; *State v. Wade*, 2007). Representative of this group of cases is *Sheriff, Washoe County v. Encoe* (1994), in which a woman was charged under Nevada's child endangerment statute for passing methamphetamine through the umbilical cord to her infant between the time the child left her womb and the time the umbilical cord was severed by her attending physician. The Nevada Supreme Court held that the legislature had not intended for a mother to be criminally prosecuted in such a circumstance.

Access to Substance Abuse Treatment Records

Disclosure of substance abuse treatment records is closely regulated by federal law (42 U.S.C § 290dd–2; 42 § C.F.R. 2.1). (This statute and the relevant federal regulations specifically provide that they are not violated when the holder of the record reports suspected child abuse or neglect to state child protection authorities. However, once such a report is made, the statute and federal regulations implementing the law apply to further disclosures of information relating to any civil or criminal proceeding brought pursuant to such a report (42 C.F.R. § 2.12(c)(6).) The federal law provides for records of such treatment to: "be confidential and be disclosed only for purposes and under the circumstances expressly authorized" in the statute (42 U.S.C. § 290dd–2(a)). The law provides that the patient may authorize the release of these treatment records, but in the absence of such a release, the records may be released only to other medical providers if there is a *bona fide* medical emergency that makes the release necessary to researchers conducting research so long as the recipient's identity is kept confidential, and by court order after a showing of good cause is made. In determining whether "good cause" exists to authorize the disclosure, courts must balance the need for disclosure on the one hand against the injury to the patient, the possible impact on the physician–patient relationship and the impact on the treatment services.

The statute explicitly protects the disclosure of substance abuse treatment records from use in investigating or prosecuting a criminal charge, except under narrowly-proscribed conditions (42 U.S.C. § 290dd–2(b)(2)(C)). While it does not specifically address the authority of state agencies to obtain such records when pursuing child protection cases, the statute does provide a general rule for permitting disclosure pursuant to a court order. The Department of Health and Human Services has issued comprehensive regulations pursuant to the statute (42 C.F.R. 2.1 *et seq.*). Those regulations address the authority of courts to order release of the records. First, the party seeking the disclosure must request an order from the court releasing the records (42 C.F.R. § 64(a)). Next, the court must give the individual to whom the records pertain and the treatment program which holds the records adequate opportunity to respond to the request for a court order, and generally should hold an *in camera* hearing (42 C.F.R. § 2.64(a), (c); *In re B.S.*, 1995). Before ordering the release, the court must find that the information contained in the record cannot be obtained in another way and that the balancing test discussed above must weigh in favor of disclosure (42 C.F.R. § 2.64(d)). Any disclosure of the records which the court may order must be limited: "to those parts of the patient's record which are essential to fulfill the objective of the order," must limit the disclosure only to those persons who are party to the legal proceeding, and must take any other necessary steps to protect the patient's privacy (42 C.F.R. 2.64(e)).

On occasion, state appellate courts have been called on to determine whether and under what circumstances courts adjudicating civil child protective proceedings should disclose substance abuse treatment records (*In re B.S.*, 1995; *In re Baby X*, 1980). These cases have addressed both the substance of whether the interests of the state in pursuing child protection proceedings outweigh the interests of the recipient of substance abuse treatment services (*In re Baby X*, 1980) and the procedure utilized by juvenile or family courts in ordering the release of such records (*In re B.S.*, 1995).

Substantively, courts which have addressed the issue have more often than not found that the need for disclosure of a parent's substance abuse treatment records outweighs the parent's interest in maintaining confidentiality and in any harm to the physician–patient privilege (e.g., *In the Matter of Dwayne G*,

1978; *In the Matter of the Doe Children*, 1978; *In re Baby X*, 1980; *Jane Doe v. Daviess County Division of Children and Family Services*, 1996). The Michigan Court of Appeals, in deciding *In re Baby X* (1980), held that: "in neglect proceedings confidentiality must give way to the best interest of the child. Where treatment records are found to be 'necessary and material' ... to the state's proof of neglect, a court of competent jurisdiction may authorize disclosure. Alleged drug or alcohol dependence (here, the alleged heroin addiction of Mother X) which causes a baby's withdrawal and failure to thrive is sufficient 'good cause' as required by the Federal statute ... to order production of records" (p. 741).

While the substantive decision is important, the means by which courts review requests for access to substance abuse records is also critical. The Vermont Supreme Court addressed numerous procedural issues regarding accessing substance abuse treatment records in *In re B.S.* (1995), a case in which a child had been in foster care and outside his mother's care for some period of time. First, the court ruled that where the information contained in the treatment record itself was otherwise available through the testimony of witnesses other than a substance abuse treatment provider or the record the family court erred in ordering a parent's substance abuse treatment records disclosed (*In re B.S.*, 1995). In that case, the state foster care worker had frequent conversations with the substance abuse counselor and could have testified to the content of those conversations. The Supreme Court held that the trial court erred when it failed to make specific findings as to the impact of the ordered disclosure on the physician–patient relationship, and when it failed to conduct an *in camera* review of the relevant records before ordering that they be released. The purpose of *in camera* review is to: "determine whether they reveal ... any unique and relevant information" (p. 1141). Lastly, the court indicated that the trial court's order was not drawn carefully enough to ensure that unnecessary disclosures of information did not take place. The federal regulations permit disclosure when: "necessary to protect against an existing threat to life or of serious bodily injury, including circumstances which constitute suspected child abuse and neglect and verbal threats against third parties" (42 C.F.R. § 2.63(a)). The trial court ruled that this provision permitted the disclosure. However, the Supreme Court disagreed, because the law provides for disclosure only when there is a threat to life or serious injury, which did not then exist because the child was placed outside the parent-recipient's home for some time by the time the records were requested.

Access to Records and HIPAA

In 1996 Congress enacted the Health Insurance Portability and Accountability Act (HIPAA) to protect the confidentiality of individuals' medical records (P.L. 104–191, 1996) (HIPAA addresses additional issues and provides additional protections that are not relevant to this discussion). Like protection of substance abuse treatment records, HIPAA permits a patient to consent to release of information. In the absence of consent a court may, under certain circumstances, order the release of a patient's medical records.

While HIPAA's protections are strong, generally providing a great deal of privacy protection for an individual's medical records, they are not without exception. So, the first question that must be addressed is whether HIPAA's provisions apply in the context of child protection proceedings. The statute provides that its provisions shall not: "be construed to invalidate or limit the authority, power, or procedures established under any law providing for the reporting of … child abuse … public health surveillance, or public health investigation or intervention" (42 U.S.C. § 1320d–7). As Howard Davidson, the Director of the American Bar Association's Center on Children and the Law, has argued: "this broadly-worded exception to HIPAA's privacy protections not only permits 'reporting' but also appears to permit disclosure of public health-related case information on child maltreatment and child fatalities to those conducting activities related to 'investigation' and 'intervention' in such cases" (Davidson, 2003, p. 12). The investigation of child maltreatment is clearly, in Davidson's view, a: "*public health matter* …" (p. 12, emphasis in original). Two state appellate court decisions support this interpretation of the law.

In *Haney v. Adams County Office of Family and Children* (2005), the Court of Appeals of Indiana addressed the admissibility of a psychological report that was not prepared in response to a court order for the purposes of the court proceeding (when a psychological or medical evaluation is conducted pursuant to a court's order, the person being examined or evaluated has only a limited right to confidentiality and the evaluation may be used in court). In that case, the children's father had undergone a psychological evaluation for purposes of obtaining disability benefits. At a subsequent termination of parental rights proceeding, the court admitted the psychological report at the request of the state child welfare agency. The father appealed, arguing that in doing so the court violated HIPAA's provisions because he did not consent to the admission. Analogizing to the previously-discussed provisions of federal law protecting substance abuse treatment records, the court found no violation of the HIPAA in admitting the psychological evaluation. Similarly, in *In the Matter of C.B.* (2007) the Court of Appeals of Indiana held that HIPAA has exceptions, which include proceedings to protect children from child maltreatment, and that the child's interest in receiving such protection outweighs the parent's right to the privacy of his or her medical records.

CONCLUSION

Prenatal substance abuse by pregnant women has been the subject of considerable public policy discussion and litigation. It seems clear that the use of substances while pregnant, when coupled with a difficult postnatal environment, poses a threat to children's well-being. Both legislatures and law enforcement officials have struggled to find proper responses to this important social issue.

Most courts have dramatically limited the criminal responses available to prosecutors to respond, while they have given much broader authority to take action in civil cases to protect the welfare of children born exposed to drugs and alcohol.

REFERENCES

American Medical Association Board of Trustees. (1990). Report: Legal interventions during pregnancy: Court-ordered medical treatment and legal penalties for potentially harmful behavior by pregnant women. *Journal of the American Medical Association, 264*(20), 2270–2663.

Armstrong, E. M. (2005). Drug and alcohol use during pregnancy: We need to protect, not punish, women. *Women's Health Issues, 15*, 45–47.

Armstrong, E. M., & Abel, E. L. (2000). Fetal alcohol syndrome: The origins of a moral panic. *Alcohol and Alcoholism, 35*, 276–282.

Bonte v. Bonte, 616 A.2d 464 (N.H. 1992).

Brown University Center for Alcohol and Addiction Studies. (2000). Position Paper on Drug Policy, Physician's Leadership on National Drug Policy.

Chenault v. Huie, 989 S.W.2d 474 (Tex. Ct. App. 1999).

Child Abuse Prevention and Treatment Act, 42 U.S.C. 5101 (2008).

Colorado Revised Statutes § 25–31–102.

Commonwealth v. Kemp, 18 Pa. D. & C. 4th 53 (Ct. Common Pleas Penn. 1992).

Commonwealth v. Pellegrini, 608 N.E. 2d 717 (Sup. Judicial Ct. Mass. 1993).

Commonwealth v. Welch, 864 S.W. 2d 280 (S. Ct. Ky. 1993).

Connecticut General Statutes § 17a–710 (2007).

Connell-Carrick, K. (2007). Methamphetamine and the changing face of child welfare: Practice principles for child welfare workers. *Child Welfare, 88*(3), 125–143.

Crea, T. M., Barth, R. P., Guo, S., & Brooks, D. (2008). Behavioral outcomes for substance-exposed adopted children: Fourteen years postadoption. *American Journal of Orthopsychiatry, 78*(1), 11–19.

Davidson, H. (2003). The impact of HIPAA on child abuse and neglect cases. *Child Law Practice, 22*(1), 11–13.

Delaware Code § 1769A (2008).

Department of Health and Human Services. (1999). *Blending perspectives and building common ground: A report to congress on substance abuse and child protection.* Washington, DC: Department of Health and Human Services.

Dixon, D. R., Kurtz, P. F., & Chin, M. D. (2008). A systemic review of challenging behaviors in children exposed prenatally to substances of abuse. *Research in Developmental Disabilities, 29*(6), 483–502.

Drago, J. (2001). Note: One for my baby, one more for the road: Legislation and counseling to prevent prenatal exposure to alcohol. *Cardozo Women's Saw Journal, 7*, 163–186.

Drescher-Burke, K., & Price, A. (2005). *Identifying, reporting, and responding to substance exposed newborns: An exploratory study of policies and practices.* Berkley, CA: The National Abandoned Infants Assistance Resource Center.

Eckenwiler, L. (2004). Why not retribution? The particularized imagination and justice for pregnant women. *Journal of Law, Medicine & Ethics, 32*, 89–99.

Fast, D. K., Conry, J., & Loock, C. A. (1999). Identifying fetal alcohol syndrome among youth in the criminal justice system. *Developmental and Behavioral Pediatrics, 20*, 370–372.

Ferguson v. City of Charleston, 532 U.S. 67 (2001).

Frank, D. A., Augustyn, M., Knight, W. G., Pell, T., & Zuckerman, B. (2001). Growth, development, and behavior in early childhood following prenatal cocaine exposure. *Journal of the American Medical Association, 285*, 613–625.

Grodin v. Grodin, 301 N.W.2d 869 (Mich. App. 1980).

Henry, J., Sloane, M., & Black-Pond, C. (2007). Neurobiology and neurodevelopmental impact of childhood traumatic stress and prenatal alcohol exposure. *Language, Speech, and Hearing Services in Schools, 38*, 99–108.

In re Baby X, 293 N.W. 2d 736 (Mich. Ct. App. 1980).

In re B.S., 659 A. 2d 1137 (Vt. Sup. Ct. 1995).

In re Constance G., 529 N.W. 2d 534 (Neb. 1995).

In re Dettrick Infant, 263 N.W. 2d 37 (Mich. Ct. App. 1977).

In re Dustin T., 614 A. 2d 999 (1992).

In re Fetus Brown, 689 N.E. 2d 397 (Ill. 1998).

In re Neil C., 521 A.2d 329 (Ct. App. Md. 1987).

In re Pima County Juvenile Severence Action NO. S–120171, 905 P. 2d 555 (Ariz. App. 1995).

In re Ruiz, 500 N.E. 2d 935 (Ohio Ct. Comm. Pleas 1986).

In re Troy D., 215 Cal. App. 3d 889; 263 Cal. Rptr. 869 (1989).

In re Valerie D., 613 A. 2d 748 (Conn. Sup. Ct. 1992).

In the Interest of H., 74 P.3d 494 (Colo. App. 2003).

In the Interest of J.P.H., 196 S.W. 3d 289 (Ct. App. Tex. 2006).

In the Matter of C.B., 865 N.E. 2d 1068 (2007).

In the Matter of Dwayne G., 411 NYS 2d 180 (Fam. Ct. 1978).

In the Matter of the Doe Children, 402 NYS 2d 958 (Fam. Ct. 1978).

In the Matter of Stefanel Tyesha C., 157 A.D. 2d 322; 556 N.Y.S. 2d 280 (1990).

Institute for Health Policy. (2001). *Substance abuse: The nation's number one health problem.* Waltham, MA: Brandeis University Press.

Jane Doe v. Daviess County Division of Children and Family Services, 669 N.E. 2d 192 (Ind. Ct. App. 1996).

Johnson v. Florida, 602 So. 2d 1288 (Sup. Ct. Fla. 1992).

Louisiana Office of Health and Hospitals. (1998). *Substance abuse treatment needs of pregnant women in Louisiana: Findings from a study of women giving birth in two hospitals.* Office of Alcohol and Drug Abuse.

Michigan Compiled Laws 722.623a (2008).

Nassau County Dep't. Social Services *ex rel Dante M. v. Denise J.*, 661 N.E. 2d 138 (Ct. App. N.Y. 1995).

National Cas. Co. v. Northern Trust Bank, 807 So. 2d 86 (Fla. Dist. Ct. App. 2002).

Ondersma, S. J., Malcoe, L. H., & Simpson, S. M. (2001). Child protective services' response to prenatal drug exposure: Results from a nationwide survey. *Child Abuse & Neglect, 25*, 657–668.

Ondersma, S. J., Simpson, S. M., Brestan, E. V., & Ward, M. (2000). Prenatal drug exposure and social policy: The search for an appropriate response. *Child Maltreatment, 5*, 93–108.

People v. Hardy, 469 N.W. 2d 50 (Mich. Ct. App. 1991).

Putnam, F. W. (2006). The impact of trauma on child development. *Juvenile and Family Court Journal, 57*(1), 1–11.

Rao, H., Wang, J., Giannetta, J., Korczykowski, M., Shera, D., Avants, B. B., Gee, J., Detre, J. A., & Hurt, H. (2007). Altered resting cerebral blood flow in adolescents with *in utero* cocaine exposure revealed by perfusion functional MRI. Retrieved 4 January 2008 from http://pediatrics. aappublications.org/cgi/content/full/120/5/e1245. *Pediatrics, 120*, e1245–e1254.

Reid, J., & Macchetto, P. (1999). *No safe haven: Children of substance-abusing parents.* New York, NY: National Center on Addiction and Substance Abuse, Columbia University.

Remy v. MacDonald, 801 N.E. 2d 260 (Mass. 2004).

Revised Statutes of Missouri. (2008). 191.725.

Revised Statutes of Missouri. (2008). 191.741.

Roberts, D. (1997). *Killing the black body: Race, reproduction and the meaning of liberty.* New York, NY: Pantheon Books.

Rollin, M., Vandervort, F., & Haralambie, A. M. (2005). Federal child welfare law and policy: Understanding the federal law and funding process. In M. Ventrell & D. N. Duquette (Eds.), *Child welfare law and practice: Representing children, parents, and state agencies in abuse, neglect and dependency cases.* Denver, CO: Bradford Publishing Company.

S.D. Codified Laws § 34–23B–1.

S.D. Codified Laws § 34–23B–3.

S.D. Codified Laws § 34–23B–8.

Shankaran, S., Lester, B. M., Das, A., Bauer, C. R., Bada, H. S., Lagasse, L., & Higgins, R. (2007). Impact of maternal substance abuse use during pregnancy on childhood outcome. *Seminars in Fetal & Neonatal Medicine, 12,* 143–150.

Sheriff, Washoe County v. Encoe, 885 P. 2d 596 (Nev. Sup. Ct. 1994).

Simoni-Wastila, L., & Strickler, G. (2004). Risk factors associated with problem use of prescription drugs. *American Journal of Public Health, 94,* 266–268.

Singer, L. T., Arendt, R., Minnes, S., Farkas, K., Salvator, A., Kirchner, H. L., & Kliegman, R. (2002). Cognitive and motor outcomes of cocaine-exposed infants. *Journal of the American Medical Association, 287,* 1952–1960.

Smith v. Brennan, 157 A.2d 497 (N.J. 1960).

Stallman v. Youngquist, 531 N.E. 2d 355 (Ill. 1988).

State v. Gethers, 585 So. 2d 1140 (Ct. App. Fla. 1991).

State v. Luster, 419 S.E. 2d 32 (Ga. App. 1992).

State v. McKnight. (2003). 576 S.E. 2d 168.

State v. Wade, 232 S.W. 3d 663 (Ct. App. Mo. 2007).

State of Ohio v. Gray, 584 N.E. 2d 710 (Sup. Ct. Ohio 1992).

Substance Abuse and Mental Health Services Administration (SAMHSA). (2007). *Results from the 2006 National Survey on Drug Use and Health: National Findings.* Retrieved 4 January 2008, from www.osa.samhsa.gov/nsduh/2k6nsduh/2k6Results.pdf

Substance Abuse and Mental Health Services Administration. (1999). *Blending perspectives and building common ground: A report to congress on substance abuse and child protection.*

Whitner v. State, 492 S.E. 2d 777 (S.C. Sup. Ct. 1997).

Wisconsin Statutes § 48.01 (2008).

Womack v. Buchhorn, 187 N.W. 2d 218 (Mich. 1971).

Chapter 16

Criminal Populations and Substance Abuse

Roger H. Peters
Department of Mental Health Law and Policy, Louis de la Parte, Florida Mental Health Institute, University of South Florida, FL, USA

John M. Ray
Department of Psychology, University of South Florida, FL, USA

Janine Kremling
Department of Criminal Justice, California State University at San Bernardino, CA, USA

INTRODUCTION

The link between substance abuse and criminal behavior is now well-recognized and has become better understood during the past 20 years as the courts, jails, prisons and community corrections have been inundated with growing numbers of drug-involved offenders (Field, 2002; National Institute on Drug Abuse, 2006). Over 70% of jail inmates test positive for illicit drugs at the time of arrest (Bureau of Justice Statistics, 2000). Substance abusers indicate significantly greater levels of criminal activity than non-users and have a history of more frequent arrest and incarceration (Collins et al., 1985; Ball, 1986), while those with more extensive criminal records are more likely to report prior substance abuse (Belenko & Peugh, 1998). In many cases, criminal behavior (e.g., property crime, prostitution, drug sales) results directly from attempts to support a drug habit.

The correctional system in the United States has experienced steady growth since the late 1980s, much of it directly related to law enforcement and judicial responses to substance abuse, and to the absence of sufficient community resources to prevent, treat and supervise persons with substance abuse problems (Peters & Wexler, 2005). During this period, jail populations have increased 78% and prison populations have increased 101%, resulting in 2.3 million persons incarcerated in United States prisons and jails, and representing the highest incarceration rate in the world (Sheldon, 2004; Walmsley, 2007; Warren, 2008). The expansion of the United States correctional system has been enormously costly and is now one of the largest budget items at the state level, competing with expenditures for education, healthcare and other social services. For example, spending on state prisons rose 400% from 1987 to 2007, and is expected to continue rising in the years ahead (Warren, 2008). The vast majority of United States correctional costs are linked to substance abuse, and represent approximately 10 times the amount spent by the states on substance abuse treatment, prevention and research (National Center on Addiction and Substance Abuse, 2001; Office of National Drug Control Policy, 2001).

Drug offenders account for approximately half of the growth in jails and prisons (Harrison & Beck, 2006). Not surprisingly, prevalence rates for substance use disorders among correctional populations are quite high, ranging from 68–74% for prisoners (National Institute of Justice, 2000; Karberg & James, 2005). Research indicates a growing gap between the need for substance abuse treatment in prisons and jails and services actually provided. For example, fewer than 20% of offenders with diagnosable substance use disorders receive treatment during incarceration (Karberg & James, 2005; Chandler et al., 2009) and only 10% receive treatment at any given time (Taxman et al., 2007). There is a significant need for expansion of all modalities of correctional drug treatment services, including residential, outpatient and short-term interventions (Belenko & Peugh, 2005).

INTERVENTIONS FOR SUBSTANCE ABUSE IN CORRECTIONAL FACILITIES

There are multiple challenges in developing substance abuse treatment services within the criminal justice system. Many prisons and jails are not architecturally or environmentally conducive to effective treatment, neither are they staffed at appropriate levels (Substance Abuse and Mental Health Services Administration, 2002; Peters, Matthews & Dvoskin, 2005). Illicit drugs are available in many correctional facilities (Simpler & Langhinrichsen-Rohling, 2005) despite existing security measures and periodic drug testing. National surveys indicate that despite the presence of some specialized prison-based treatment services, many correctional treatment programs are inadequate in scope and quality (Cropsey et al., 2007; Taxman et al., 2007), and they may not include evidence-based practices.

Correctional Treatment Programs

More advanced systems of drug treatment in the justice system include multi-tiered services that include outpatient, intensive outpatient, short- and long-term residential and re-entry/transition programs (Peters et al., 2005). For example, treatment services in the Federal Bureau of Prisons and several state prison systems are matched in duration and intensity to the level of addiction severity and other psychosocial needs of inmates (Weinman & Dignam, 2002; Peters et al., 2005). Cognitive–behavioral approaches are used most frequently in correctional substance abuse treatment programs, featuring development of drug coping skills, skills to identify and restructure "criminal thinking," motivational enhancement, relapse prevention and contingency management. Residential drug treatment programs, such as therapeutic communities, tend to embrace social learning models that provide regular feedback and reinforcement for behaviors occurring within the treatment units (De Leon, 2000).

Approximately 10% of offenders have co-occurring substance use and mental disorders (National GAINS Center, 2004) and there is a growing recognition that this population requires specialized services within the justice system. Offenders with co-occurring disorders have more pronounced problems related to employment, educational achievement, social skills, problem-solving skills, social supports and cognitive functioning (Mueser et al., 2003), and without comprehensive treatment and supervision services tend to cycle rapidly through the criminal justice system and community acute care systems (e.g., emergency rooms). A number of specialized correctional programs have recently been developed for offenders who have co-occurring disorders (Peters & Bekman, 2007), and these can significantly reduce recidivism and substance abuse (Sacks et al., 2004).

Accumulating research evidence over the past two decades indicates that treatment provided within the criminal justice system reduces substance abuse and recidivism. For example, treatment provided during prison can lead to significant reductions in arrests, recommitment and substance abuse during extended follow-up periods (Pearson & Lipton, 1999; Martin et al., 1999; Wexler et al., 1999; Prendergast et al., 2004). Positive benefits are augmented for programs that provide treatment while in custody and following release to the community (Martin et al., 1999; McCollister et al., 2003; Inciardi et al., 2004; Prendergast et al., 2004).

Drug-involved offenders who are released from jail or prison are faced with a number of challenges (e.g., employment, housing, reunification with family, stigma, supervision requirements) and have high rates of recidivism and reincarceration. Within a year of release from custody, 85% of these offenders return to drug use (Inciardi et al., 1997), and approximately two-thirds are rearrested within three years of release (Langan & Levin, 2002). One of the most significant obstacles to successful community reintegration is the absence of coordinated aftercare and transition services in the community (Peters & Bekman, 2007; Chandler et al., 2009). Few jails or prisons provide transition services, although research indicates that the most successful offender treatment programs are those that combine treatment in the institution with treatment for at least three months following release to the community (Knight et al., 1999; Martin et al., 1999; Wexler et al., 1999).

Legal Standards for Substance Abuse Treatment in Correctional Facilities

Prison and jail inmates have the right to medical care although the required care is generally limited to services needed to address serious medical needs, and does not include the majority of substance abuse treatment interventions. Threshold levels of care were set by the United States Supreme court in *Estelle v. Gamble* (1976), in which inmates were determined to have a right to receive medical care in correctional facilities to meet their serious medical needs. Although the courts have rejected a general right to substance abuse treatment in correctional facilities, substance abuse services have been required by the courts in situations involving "deliberate indifference" to serious medical needs, such as detoxification and identification of suicide risk. Such cases have typically resulted in requirements for screening and treatment of acute substance-related and life-threatening medical problems, but not for traditional substance abuse services such as outpatient or residential treatment. These cases have also resulted in requirements for implementation of training protocols for personnel charged with medical/substance abuse screening, which can entail distinguishing intoxication from other serious medical illnesses. Although the courts haven't determined whether treatment for drug and alcohol withdrawal is a constitutionally required service, recent appellate rulings support the contention that neglect or denial of such services may be tantamount to cruel and unusual punishment, in the case of inmates, or punishment without due process, pertaining to pre-trial detainees (Fiscella, Pless, Meldrum & Fiscella, 2004).

Although legal standards of care provide somewhat limited guidance in developing substance abuse treatment services in correctional settings, several professional organizations have developed their own sets of comprehensive standards. The National Commission on Correctional Health Care (NCCHC) describes standards for essential substance abuse treatment services in criminal justice settings. Included are recommended guidelines for medical management of intoxication and withdrawal, and comprehensive physical and mental health assessments provided soon after admission to jails and prisons (NCCHC, 2008a,b). The American Correctional Association (ACA) provides additional recommendations regarding substance abuse assessment, referral and placement procedures. These include: use of mandatory substance abuse screening during the initial health examination; use of standardized screening and referral approaches; reassessment over time; triage to drug treatment programs according to intensity and type of inmate needs; and use of drug testing and monitoring (American Correctional Association, 2004, 2006). In addition, the ACA provides much more specific detail in recommending the type of substance abuse treatment services that should be provided in jails and prisons, including development of individualized treatment plans, aftercare discharge plans, motivational incentives, inclusion of self-help groups and relapse prevention approaches.

JUDICIAL AND STATUTORY APPROACHES TO SUBSTANCE ABUSE

Civil Commitment for Substance Use Disorders

Following the Supreme Court's 1962 ruling in *Robinson v. California* (1962) that determined it was unconstitutional to prosecute a person for drug addiction, judicial approaches to addiction shifted from a largely punitive approach to a broader perspective that considered treatment alternatives to incarceration. The Supreme Court's decision did, however, explicitly allow for compulsory treatment by the states, which laid the legal groundwork for civil commitment of substance-dependent persons (Beane & Beck, 1991).

Thirty-one states have enacted involuntary civil commitment legislation (Kitzmann, 1997) related to drug and alcohol addiction, while other states have implemented "hybrid" laws that authorize this type of commitment under mental illness commitment laws. State commitment laws related to addiction typically predicate involuntary placement in detoxification and treatment facilities on findings that an individual presents an imminent danger to self or others as a result of drug or alcohol problems (Nace et al., 2007), is in need of substance abuse treatment, and is unable to meet the basic needs of sustenance, shelter and self-protection.

Procedures for civil commitment of addicted individuals may be initiated by any adult and, in the case of emergency, by any law enforcement officer or authorized treatment or care provider (Beane & Beck, 1991). Persons who are deemed dangerous to themselves or others may be held for evaluation and/or emergency services for a period ranging from 72 hours to two weeks, pending judicial review. Most statutes do not explicitly define the location of treatment and allow placement in a variety of secure settings (Garcia & Keilitz, 1991). Some states specifically allow for civil commitment to outpatient settings, although provisions are typically included that mandate residential treatment for persons who fail to comply with outpatient services. Procedural protections are provided to those who are civilly committed for substance use disorders, including notice, right to counsel, judicial review, and a clearly delineated period of commitment that ranges across the states from 30 days to three years. Opponents of civil commitment for substance use disorders cite the potential for abuse of coercive powers and civil rights infringement (Krongard, 2002). Several studies examining civil commitment for addictive disorders have demonstrated positive treatment outcomes for individuals mandated to treatment (Anglin et al., 1989; Farabee et al., 1998). For example, persons who are involuntarily committed to substance abuse treatment have equivalent or better outcomes than those who participate voluntarily (Nace et al., 2007).

Drug Courts

The judicial and correctional systems in the United States have been strained by a growing number of substance-involved offenders who are arrested for drug-related offenses and who often cycle rapidly through courts, jails, prisons and acute care services in the community. Largely in response to the ineffective judicial responses available to slow this "revolving door," drug court programs began to emerge in the early 1990s. Between 1989 and 2008, 2,140 drug courts were established in the United States and another 284 were in the planning stages. Drug courts have been implemented in all 50 states, the District of

Columbia, in several United States territories and in a number of United States Indian reservations (ONDCP, 2008).

Drug courts provide a coordinated response by the courts, community treatment providers, law enforcement, supervision officers and other service providers to divert nonviolent substance-involved offenders to ongoing involvement in drug treatment and judicial supervision. Participants enter drug court on a voluntary basis and are offered reduction or dismissal of charges contingent upon completion of drug court requirements, which typically include a year's involvement in substance use treatment, drug testing, supervision in the community and attendance at regular judicial hearings. Judges with specialized expertise in the drug court model oversee the programs and preside over regularly scheduled judicial (status) hearings. Drug court judges work closely with an integrated team of prosecutors, defense attorneys, treatment providers, case managers and supervision officers to implement a system of sanctions and rewards to be administered commensurate with progress in substance abuse treatment. In some circumstances, drug courts provide ancillary services, such as employment training, family counseling and other specialized training.

In light of the rapid expansion of drug courts and attempts to define minimum standards for drug court operations, the National Association of Drug Court Professionals (NADCP) has established a set of 10 "key components" of drug courts on which new problem-solving courts could model their structure (NADCP, 1997). These include the following:

1. Drug courts integrate alcohol and other drug treatment services with justice system case processing;
2. They use a non-adversarial approach, prosecution and defense counsel promote public safety while protecting participants' due process rights;
3. Eligible participants are identified early and promptly placed in the drug court program;
4. Drug courts provide access to a continuum of alcohol, drug and other related treatment and rehabilitation services;
5. Abstinence is monitored by frequent alcohol and other drug testing;
6. A coordinated strategy governs drug court responses to participants' compliance;
7. Ongoing judicial interaction with each drug court participant is essential;
8. Monitoring and evaluation measure the achievement of program goals and gauge effectiveness;
9. Continuing interdisciplinary education promotes effective drug court planning, implementation and operation;
10. Forging partnerships among drug courts, public agencies and community-based organizations generates local support and enhances drug court program effectiveness.

Research indicates that drug courts "outperform virtually all other strategies that have been attempted for drug involved offenders" (Marlowe, DeMatteo, &

Festinger, 2003). Research examining the efficacy of drug court programs tends to support this claim. A meta-analysis of 55 drug court outcome studies (Wilson et al., 2006) found that drug court participants are significantly less likely to reoffend than comparable groups of individuals who do not receive drug court program services. Involvement in drug courts was associated with an average 26% reduction in arrests during follow-up across the 55 studies examined. The two drug court studies examined that utilized a randomized design yielded slightly lower (14%) reductions in recidivism, but these still represented a significant improvement in comparison to groups that did not receive drug court services. Other large-scale studies of drug courts also support the effectiveness of these programs in reducing criminal behavior (Roman et al., 2003). Drug courts are also associated with lower rates of reconviction during extended follow-up periods (Rempel et al., 2003).

Participation in drug courts also leads to other positive outcomes, including reduced substance abuse and greater retention in treatment (Belenko, 1999; Cissner & Rempel, 2005). Whereas in general, drug abusers drop out of treatment at a rate of up to 80% within ninety days and 90% within a year, more than two-thirds of drug court participants complete treatment after a year or more (Huddleston et al., 2008). Review of drug court outcome studies indicates that the most effective programs use clearly defined sanction and reward contingencies and utilize single treatment providers (Wilson et al., 2006). Drug courts save more than $2,000 per year per participant when compared to incarceration and court costs of similar offenders who do not participate in drug court programs (Carey & Finigan, 2004).

The success of the drug court programs has led to the development of similar problem-solving courts for other offender populations. Variants on the drug court model for substance abusing offenders include juvenile drug courts, family/dependence courts (for cases in which abuse or neglect of a minor is present and parental substance use is viewed as a primary contributing factor), DUI/DWI courts, tribal courts, veterans courts, campus drug courts and re-entry courts. Each of these problem-solving courts provides an integrated approach between the judiciary, treatment providers, supervision staff and community service providers and requires sustained involvement in treatment. Other variants on the drug court model include domestic violence courts, mental health courts and probation/parole violation courts. In 2000, the Conference of Chief Justices and the Conference of State Court Administrators called for the integration of the most effective components of drug courts into all courts, with the express goal of replicating the drug court model's success in other populations (Huddleston et al., 2008).

State and Federal Drug Laws

Substance abusers are more likely than non-users to be arrested, incarcerated and to reoffend after release from incarceration (Wilson, 2000). Due to the need for more comprehensive services related to poor physical health, addiction history and mental health needs, substance abusers incur greater costs than other offenders while incarcerated (Leukefeld et al., 1998) and while in the community. The social and economic toll of substance abusers on society makes illicit drug use and its consequences a top priority for legislators, policymakers and law enforcement (Uniform Crime Reports/Federal Bureau of Investigations (UCR/FBI), 2003).

The most common approach to reducing the negative effects of illicit drug use has been deterrence via sentencing laws that impose strict penalties for the use, possession, and sale of drugs. Drug laws in the United States are regulated in accordance with the Comprehensive Drug Abuse Prevention Act of 1970. Title II of this legislation, known as the Controlled Substances Act (CSA), created the legal framework by which the United States Department of Health and Human Services and the United States Department of Justice regulate and enforce drug laws related to the manufacture, possession, transportation and sale of narcotics, stimulants, depressants, hallucinogens, anabolic steroids and chemicals used in the illegal production of controlled substances.

The CSA established a hierarchy of five "schedules" pertaining to the classification of illicit drugs. Generally, Schedule I is reserved for drugs with the greatest health risk and no recognized medicinal benefit, whereas Schedule V is assigned to the least dangerous drugs that have also demonstrated medical utility. Other factors used in determining a drug's placement within the CSA classification schedule include: the potential for abuse; state of the scientific knowledge of the drug's pharmacological effect; its historical and current pattern of abuse; the scope, duration and significance of abuse; its psychological or physiological dependence liability; and whether the substance is an immediate precursor of a substance already controlled (21 U.S.C. § 811(h)).

The CSA was designed to leave considerable discretion to individual states in the scheduling of drugs, enforcement of drug laws and associated penalties/sentencing (Courtwright, 2004). In 2002, a collaborative research study funded by the Robert Wood Johnson Foundation released a comprehensive assessment of drug laws in the United States (Chriqui et al., 2002). The report found that states generally follow the drug scheduling guidelines prescribed by the CSA, but exercise considerable discretion in implementing these guidelines. For example, although marijuana is a Schedule I drug, many states assign it to a lower schedule due to its potential medical use, and in several states marijuana is not scheduled. By 2000, 24 states and the District of Columbia had passed legislation authorizing the use of marijuana for medical purposes. However, the states vary considerably in allowing use of drugs for "medical necessity" and for federally-authorized medical research in allowing prescription by physicians, and in provisions for rescheduling of drugs (e.g., to a lower schedule).

States also vary in the quantity of drugs used to determine penalties under the law, or thresholds referred to as "quantity triggers." For example, some states designate just one quantity trigger level, while others provide complex hierarchical structures in which penalties increase with the quantity of drug involved. Quantity triggers also vary by substance type and offense category. For example, most states use two quantity triggers for sale of marijuana, but one to five triggers for possession of marijuana.

Penalties for violations of controlled substance statutes vary widely by state, but usually specify minimum and maximum fines and/or incarceration, which are determined by the specific drug and nature of the offense (i.e., sale versus possession of a controlled substance). Most states impose a maximum of one year in jail for conviction of possession of marijuana. Maximum prison sentences for other drug possession offenses range from 1–25 years. Convictions for drug sales can be much more severe, ranging from one year in jail to life imprisonment. Monetary fines for possession range from a maximum of $5,000 for a first time marijuana possession offense to $1,000,000 for the sale of methamphetamine. Some states don't specify maximum monetary penalties for the sale or possession of controlled substances. Offenders who have a history of prior drug offenses face stiffer penalties in most, but not all, states with sentencing guidelines varying by the type of substance.

Laws Regulating Drinking and Driving

States have been very active in enacting legislation to reduce driving under the influence of alcohol, which contributes to a significant number of annual traffic fatalities and other serious injuries in the United States. In 2007, state legislatures considered 173 bills that addressed driving under the influence (DUI) and driving while intoxicated (DWI), including initiatives focused on repeat offenders and use of ignition interlock devices (Savage et al., 2007). Under pressure from citizen groups, such as Mother's Against Drunk Driving, and faced with loss of highway funds for noncompliance with federal guidelines, all 50 states, the District of Columbia and Puerto Rico have enacted legislation that established the level of legal impairment for DUI/DWI offenses at 0.08% blood alcohol content (BAC) (Freeman, 2007; National Highway Safety Administration (NHTSA), 2008a). The states typically classify first offenses for drunk driving as misdemeanors of varying degree. Some states provide harsher penalties for first offenses, dependent on the BAC level or injury to victims.

Specific penalties for drunk driving convictions vary widely from state to state (Insurance Institute on Highway Safety (IIHS), 2008). Forty-one states impose suspension of a driver's license on conviction for drunk driving, with the length and terms of suspensions varying between states. Many states also provide license suspension for refusal to submit to sobriety testing by law enforcement officers. According to the IIHS (2008), these preconviction, noncriminal sanctions are more effective than traditional postconviction sanctions. If convicted, offenders in most states can drive only if their vehicles have been equipped with ignition interlock devices, which measure BAC and prevent operation of the vehicle on detection of alcohol use. Thirty-two states allow for impounding/forfeiture of the offender's vehicle.

Some states classify all repeat DUI/DWI offenses as felonies, but others do not charge for felonies until the third or fourth offense (NCSL, 2008). The duration of time between arrests is considered for repeat offenses in some states. For example, in Florida, first and second DUI/DWI offenses are misdemeanors, while third or subsequent offenses within 10 years are felonies. New York distinguishes between driving while impaired, which is a traffic violation, and driving while intoxicated, which is a misdemeanor for the first offense and a felony for subsequent offenses within 10 years.

Over half of fatal car accidents involve drivers with BAC levels in excess of 0.15 (NHTSA, 2008a). Forty-one states have enacted laws to deal with drivers whose BAC is considered to be excessive (IIHS, 2008), with the threshold usually defined as a BAC level of between 0.15 and 0.20. Penalties include increased license penalties, vehicle plate seizure, impound or immobility of the vehicle, mandatory alcoholism assessment and/or treatment, court-ordered supervision, implementation of ignition interlock, fines and fees, imprisonment and house arrest with electronic monitoring. Most states have enacted laws pertaining to cases of injury or death caused by drunk driving, with penalties including imprisonment and large fines. According to NHTSA (2008b), drivers under the age of 21 are twice as likely as adults to be involved in car accidents that involve use of alcohol. As a result, all 50 states have passed "zero-tolerance" laws that prohibit minors from driving with any measurable BAC alcohol (some states allow BAC's up to 0.02 to account for measurement error) (Carpenter, 2004; NHTSA, 2008b).

The effectiveness of penalties for DUI/DWI offenses has proven difficult to measure, due to the wide variability of legislation and enforcement practices in the United States. Research indicates evidence of only slight deterrent effects as a result of mandatory fines and jail sentences (Wagenaar et al., 2007), including an 8% decrease in fatal crashes associated with fines and a 5% decrease associated with mandatory jail time. Freeman (2007) found no evidence of reduction in alcohol-related car accident fatalities after BAC thresholds were lowered from 0.10 to 0.08, although fatalities were reduced in states that supplemented BAC laws with imposition of administrative license revocation. Enhanced sanctions for driving with excessive BAC (e.g., >0.20) appear to be effective. For example, in Minnesota, convicted drunk drivers with high BAC's who received enhanced sanctions (e.g., impounded vehicle plate) were less likely to reoffend within a two-year follow-up period (McCartt & Northrup, 2004). Similarly, there is strong evidence that "zero-tolerance" laws for minors reduce alcohol-related traffic fatalities (Carpenter, 2004).

INFORMATION SHARING BETWEEN THE JUSTICE AND TREATMENT SYSTEMS

A high level of coordination and information sharing is needed between the justice and treatment systems to identify persons who have substance use disorders, provide effective triage to treatment services, supervise participation in treatment and monitor progress following completion of treatment. Of key importance in this process is the ability to share critical information about offenders' need for substance abuse treatment and participation in treatment. However, there is frequently uncertainty among justice and treatment professionals regarding the nature of requirements for confidentiality of health-related information in these situations. Among the most important concerns are those related to the ability to share information related to offenders' involvement and progress in substance abuse treatment with correctional and detention facilities, the courts and law enforcement.

The Health Information Portability and Accountability Act (HIPAA, 1996) was enacted by the United States Congress in 1996. The Department of Health and Human Services issued two key regulations to guide implementation of the law. The Privacy Rule was established in 2003, and addresses the circumstances under which "protected health information" (PHI) may be shared. The Security Rule was established in 2005, and describes requirements for the security of electronic health records. The HIPAA Privacy Rule protects disclosure of PHI by "covered entities" that transmit this information electronically. Covered entities include health plans, healthcare clearinghouses and healthcare providers. Prisons, jails, the courts and law enforcement agencies are not covered entities under HIPAA, although some correctional facilities may fall under the HIPAA Privacy Rule requirements. For example, a "hybrid entity" is one in which a smaller component of a larger entity conducts procedures falling under the purview of the Privacy Rule. Correctional facilities (e.g., prisons) that provide onsite hospital, clinic, or substance abuse treatment services would be considered hybrid entities and subject to HIPAA Privacy Rule requirements. In addition, a company that provides contracted health services to a jail or prison would be considered a covered entity. Regardless of how services are provided, HIPAA provides for broad disclosure to corrections, courts, or law enforcement personnel without consent of the individual. Specifically, HIPAA permits unconsented disclosure to the courts, correctional facilities, or law enforcement in circumstances in which these entities maintain custody of the person in order to maintain necessary care, health, or safety of the offender, criminal justice/correctional staff, or third parties, and for the safety, security and good order of correctional facilities.

Whereas HIPAA covers all personal health information that identifies or can be used to identify an individual, the United States Code of Federal Regulations, Title 42, Volume 1, Part 2 (42 CFR Part 2) specifically regulates disclosure of information that can be used to identify a person as an alcohol or drug abuser, or a recipient of substance abuse treatment services. Information is considered identifiable, and thus subject to 42 CFR Part 2, unless all identifying information pertaining to the client and their associations is removed. Disclosure of PHI by substance abuse treatment providers to criminal justice entities is permitted under Part 2, as long as the individual has been referred as a condition of criminal sanction and the information is necessary to protect: (1) the individual's healthcare; (2) the safety of the individual or those with whom he/she has contact; (3) criminal justice (or other) professionals within the facility in which the individual is housed; or (4) the administration of health and safety parameters in the facility.

Several limitations to sharing PHI are stipulated by federal CFR regulations. Disclosure may be made only to personnel with a demonstrable need for the information in monitoring the offender's progress, such as prosecuting attorneys, court personnel and probation or parole officers. Additionally, the offender must provide written consent. The consent document must reflect the duration of consent, which must be reasonable in consideration of the duration of treatment ordered, the type of criminal proceeding, including the type of information needed for final disposition and when that disposition is scheduled, and other factors deemed important by parties involved. The federal CFR guidelines require that consent be revocable at any time. However, in the case of court-ordered treatment, revocation may be contingent upon a predetermined amount of time or treatment-related criterion (e.g., completion of a particular treatment program), which may not extend in time beyond the anticipated date of final disposition. Finally, allowance for redisclosure of information is limited to situations in which it is necessary to perform official duties commensurate with the terms set forth in the patient's written consent. In 42 CFR Part 2 disclosure of PHI is allowed in response to a court-ordered subpoena if the offender provides written consent specific to the information requested. Disclosure is permitted without consent only if the patient is reasonably notified and the court observes the requirements outlined in Subpart E of 42 CFR Part 2.

There is often uncertainty among criminal justice professionals and treatment providers regarding the relationship between state laws on confidentiality and the federal regulations. To reconcile differences between state and federal guidelines, it is important to determine if a state law is more protective of privacy, and if so, the state law must be followed. In many instances, state laws are more restrictive than HIPAA, and in those cases state law applies. There are also occasions in which state law is more restrictive than Part 2, and in those cases state law also applies. For programs providing services for offenders with co-occurring mental health disorders, Part 2 will govern rather than HIPAA because Part 2 is considerably more restrictive than HIPAA.

In summary, correctional facilities, courts and law enforcement are not covered entities under HIPAA. Some facilities are designated as "hybrid" entities, in which aspects of the institution (e.g., prison, jail) that meet the definition of a covered entity must comply with the HIPAA Privacy Rule. However, as noted previously, HIPAA permits broad disclosure to correctional and court personnel. Entities that meet the definition of "programs" as defined in 42 CFR Part 2 must comply with those regulations.

INTERNATIONAL APPROACHES TO CRIMINAL POPULATIONS AND SUBSTANCE ABUSE

Within the international community there are a wide variety of civil and criminal approaches to providing substance abuse treatment services for those with drug and alcohol problems. A number of countries, especially in Europe and Scandinavia, employ civil commitment to substance abuse treatment and court-ordered treatment as a result of a criminal offense. Civil commitment is not used as commonly as court-ordered treatment within the international community.

Among the European nations, Sweden makes the most extensive use of civil commitment to substance abuse treatment (Kildal & Kuhnle, 2005). In 2000, over 1,000 individuals were civilly committed to residential treatment for therapeutic addiction services in Sweden. Civil commitment to substance abuse treatment has a long tradition in Sweden and is based on the Swedish Act on Care of Addicts in Certain Cases, which allows the state to intervene extensively in the private life of its citizens to address mental health and substance abuse problems. Social service staff review individual cases and make referrals to a board of social welfare (Palm & Stenius, 2002) that is staffed by laypersons. This board determines the type of treatment needed, based on an assessment by a social worker and a physician. Civil commitment treatment in Sweden includes detoxification and drug education (Palm & Stenius, 2002). Persons who are civilly committed are not involved in decisions regarding treatment admission or the type of treatment program provided.

Civil commitment to substance abuse treatment is also provided in Switzerland, although it is used less frequently than in Sweden and is used primarily for situations related to guardianship (Stevens et al., 2003, 2005). In 1991, Switzerland initiated a civil commitment program to provide drug detoxification and treatment services, but participants experienced high relapse rates following release from treatment and the program was discontinued. In general, civil commitment to substance abuse treatment is used infrequently in Switzerland and in most of Europe (Grichting et al., 2002).

On the contrary, court-ordered treatment following arrest for criminal offenses is commonly used in Europe. For example, Switzerland refers persons to court-ordered treatment for drug-related offenses, and allows the offender to choose between prison or supervised residential or outpatient substance abuse treatment. The prison sentence is suspended until treatment has been successfully completed, but the entire sentence can be reinstated if treatment is not completed, regardless of the length of stay in treatment (Palm & Stenius, 2002). In Austria and Germany, offenders with substance abuse problems can also be diverted from incarceration and placed in supervised drug treatment if the sentence does not exceed two years in prison (Werdenich et al., 2004).

Legal Foundations for Treatment Provided in Justice Settings

In most European countries, statutes provide a number of options to address the needs of substance-involved persons in the civil and criminal justice systems. For example, in Germany legal mechanisms to address substance use disorders include: (1) civil commitment to a psychiatric facility for residential drug treatment;

(2) probation or parole, coupled with supervised residential or outpatient treatment in the community; (3) treatment in jail or prison, including methadone maintenance; and (4) deferment or reduction of criminal sentences, contingent on successful completion of substance abuse treatment (Boellinger, 2002).

In Canada, the Controlled Drug and Substances Act (1997) provides the legal framework for sentencing, sanctions and drug treatment services for substance-involved offenders. The most common option exercised by the Canadian courts is a deferred prison sentence that is served in the community and contingent on completion of supervision and substance abuse treatment requirements. As mentioned previously, Canada has also established a number of drug courts that provide diversion to long-term outpatient drug treatment, drug testing and community supervision. In England and Wales, Community Rehabilitation Orders (CROs) provide the basis for probation and community drug treatment for offenders aged 16 years and older. In the Netherlands, the Prison Act authorizes offenders to be placed in residential drug treatment "clinics" (Werdenich et al., 2004).

Whereas in most of Europe the legal authority for mandated treatment of offenders lies primarily with the judiciary, in some countries the authority to suspend criminal justice proceedings lies with the prosecutor. In Austria, the Law of Illicit Drugs allows the prosecutor to suspend proceedings if the offender enters a supervised drug treatment program. After completion of treatment, the prosecutor reviews the case and decides whether the offender has successfully fulfilled the treatment obligations, and determines whether criminal charges will be suspended or reinstated (Werdenich et al., 2004).

As noted previously, only a few countries outside the United States provide civil commitment for substance use disorders. In Switzerland, the legal basis for civil commitment is provided by the Swiss Civil Law, which authorizes a specialized Guardianship Court (Vormundschaftsgericht) to order involuntary treatment in a secure psychiatric facility (Grichting et al., 2002). The Swedish Act of Care enables use of civil commitment to substance abuse treatment for persons who are experiencing acute alcohol or drug psychosis, or for persons who are at risk of harming themselves or others due to substance abuse (Palm & Stenius, 2002).

Points of Intervention for Offender Drug Treatment

Within the international community there are four major points of criminal justice intervention for offenders in need of substance abuse treatment. Offenders can be referred into treatment at the time of arrest, during trial and sentencing, during incarceration and after release from prison (McSweeney et al., 2008). Referral at the point of arrest is commonly used in Australia, Denmark, England, the Netherlands and Sweden to refer drug users to treatment programs on a voluntary basis (Bull, 2005). For example, the State of Victoria in Australia recently implemented the Court Referral and Evaluation for Drug Intervention and Treatment program (CREDIT) (Victorian State Government, 2008). The program is designed to divert arrestees with substance abuse problems to treatment as part of bail proceedings. If a law enforcement officer suspects that the arrestee has a substance abuse problem, the officer can make a referral to a clinician for specialized evaluation. The clinician is based in the magistrate court and, with the court's approval, can divert the arrestee into a treatment program as part of the conditions of bail (Victorian State Government, 2008). No legal sanctions are provided if the court's recommendations for completion of treatment are followed. Enrollment in drug treatment is voluntary, and research indicates that the number of offenders who participate and complete treatment are quite low (McSweeney et al., 2004).

In European nations that employ diversion programs for drug-involved arrestees, treatment counselors are often on call or on site to assess the need for substance abuse treatment at the time of booking to jail or other detention facilities. If the offender appears to have an addiction problem, the drug counselor provides the individual with information regarding available drug treatment centers and other related services. However, no legal sanctions are provided if the offender decides not to contact the treatment agency following release from custody (Bull, 2005).

Within the international community, another major point of criminal justice intervention for drug-involved offenders is at the time of pretrial hearings, trial, or sentencing. The main goal of these interventions is to provide opportunities for involvement in treatment as an alternative to incarceration, to prevent subsequent criminal activity and to promote rehabilitation from substance use disorders (Koerner, 2002). As indicated previously, research indicates that drug courts and other offender diversion programs can be effective in reducing crime and illicit drug use (Wilson et al., 2006), and in enhancing health and social functioning (Freeman, 2002). One of the key ingredients to successful offender diversion/treatment programs appears to be duration of time spent in treatment. Offenders remaining in treatment for at least several months are more likely to be abstinent and are less likely to be rearrested (Greenfield et al., 2004; Simpson & Joe, 2004; McSweeney et al., 2006; National Institute on Drug Abuse, 2006). Another important predictor of treatment outcomes in diversion settings is whether offenders graduate from the diversion program. A major challenge faced by some diversion programs is the high attrition rate among court-based referrals for substance abuse treatment (Freeman, 2002; Meier, 2005).

Several options for diversion to treatment are exercised by the criminal courts in international settings. Offenders are often diverted to residential or outpatient drug treatment with the understanding that criminal charges will be dismissed pending completion of the program, or are mandated to treatment as part of their sentence. These strategies are used regularly by drug courts within the international community (Bean, 2002). Canada has implemented a number of drug courts that operate in similar fashion to those in the United States, but that employ "harm reduction" approaches, such as drug substitution treatment (e.g., methadone maintenance) (Walker, 2001). For example, the Toronto Drug Treatment Court provides a preplea program for nonviolent offenders. More serious offenders are also offered treatment, but only after having pleaded guilty (Fischer et al., 2002). Drug courts were established in Australia in 1999 that target serious offenders including those addicted to heroin (Walker, 2001).

In 1981, Germany established the statutory and administrative framework for drug treatment as an alternative to prison and detention (Koerner, 2002). Under this legislation, the government is required to provide appropriate treatment to offenders who have substance use disorders. If the offender enters a long-term residential treatment program or an outpatient treatment program, prosecution and/or sentencing can be deferred. The German correctional system also employs methadone maintenance and other substitution therapy approaches for drug-involved offenders, and research indicates that this has resulted in improved health and psychological functioning (Michels et al., 2007). In the Netherlands, offenders can be placed in residential treatment "clinics" that provide detoxification, psychological counseling, psychotherapy and motivational classes. Treatment progress is monitored by probation services and includes mandatory drug testing.

Another key point of intervention for drug-involved offenders is in custody settings. Over the last two decades, correctional substance abuse treatment programs in Europe have expanded significantly. The European Union encourages its member states to provide substance abuse treatment in prison (Kinnunen & Nilson, 1999), and most but not all provide these services (Stoever, 2001, 2002). For example, England and Wales have implemented the Counseling, Assessment, Referral, Advice and Throughcare (CARAT) program, offering assessment, detoxification and postrelease services for offenders with substance abuse problems (Kothary et al., 2002).

As noted previously, substitution treatment has emerged as a common modality of substance abuse treatment in European correctional systems. Among European nations, only Sweden and Greece do not provide substitution treatment in prison (Stoever, 2001). Research demonstrates that prison-based treatment and methadone programs can be effective, given appropriate duration of treatment (Hiller et al., 1999; Inciardi et al., 2004). However, most European prisoners receive rather short terms of incarceration, thus limiting the available time and opportunities for successful participation in substance abuse treatment (European Monitoring Centre for Drugs and Drug Addiction, 2003).

The most widespread substitution drug used in European correctional systems is methadone, which is employed either as a maintenance program (e.g., in Austria, Denmark, Luxemburg, Portugal and Spain) or for detoxification purposes (e.g., in Belgium, Germany, Italy and the Netherlands) (Kinnunen & Nilson, 1999; Gerlach, 2002; Stoever, 2002). For example, offenders in Austria who are convicted and sentenced to prison terms of up to three years can enter a substitution and/or other drug treatment program. On successful completion of the program the prison sentence is converted to probation supervision (Kinnunen & Nilson, 1999). Germany also employs nonmethadone substitutes, including buprenorphine, LAAM, dihydrocodeine and codeine (Gerlach, 2002). According to statutory provisions, substitution treatment in Germany is viewed as "routine treatment" and prisoners have the right to receive such treatment (Stoever, 2002).

The fourth point of criminal justice intervention for substance-involved offenders is at release from custody. The major goal of postrelease treatment programs is to prevent drug-involved offenders from relapsing and returning to criminal behavior. As in the United States, postrelease treatment programs are uncommon in Europe and in other areas outside the United States. As a result, drug-involved offenders frequently relapse when they return to their home communities and are faced with familiar cues and temptations related to drug use and crime (Hobbs et al., 2006). Australia has developed a postrelease community supervision program that assists offenders to remain abstinent through the use of electronic monitoring and supervised participation in treatment. However, few such coordinated release programs exist outside the United States (Hobbs et al., 2006).

CONCLUSION

The criminal justice system has been significantly altered as a result of widespread substance abuse problems and drug-related crime over the past two decades. Courts, jails, prisons and community corrections have all grown dramatically during this time, and are facing enormous challenges to reduce the revolving door of substance-involved offenders cycling through the justice system. In response to this trend, a number of substance abuse treatment programs have been implemented in correctional facilities, including residential and "outpatient" programs that employ cognitive–behavioral and motivational enhancement approaches and that focus on restructuring "criminal thinking." Specialized correctional treatment programs have also begun to address the needs of offenders with co-occurring mental and substance use disorders, who present additional risk for recidivism on release from custody. A growing number of correctional substance abuse programs have emerged in other countries, and these more prominently feature "harm reduction" approaches such as methadone maintenance.

Correctional facilities are also implementing re-entry initiatives so that offenders receiving drug treatment in jails and prisons can continue to receive these services in the community, following incarceration. In-custody substance abuse treatment and re-entry programs have been found to be quite effective in reducing criminal behavior and drug use during extended follow-up periods. The United States courts have not upheld the constitutional right to substance abuse treatment in correctional settings, other than for services that address serious medical needs. However, a number of professional associations (ACA, NCCHC) have developed sets of professional standards to guide development and implementation of substance abuse services in jails and prisons. Information-sharing between criminal justice and treatment professionals presents an ongoing set of challenges in coordinating effective offender treatment programs. Broad disclosure is provided under HIPAA between treatment providers and the courts, jails, prisons and law enforcement, although other state and federal confidentiality regulations also apply.

State and federal drug laws classify illicit drugs according to "schedules" that identify varying levels of health risk and benefits. There is considerable variability among the states in sentencing guidelines for drug offenses and enforcement of drug laws. Some states provide complex sentencing algorithms based on the quantity and type of illicit substances involved, and the penalties for drug offenses vary widely. Through the guidance of federal legislation, most states have enacted laws establishing legal impairment for driving while under the influence of alcohol and other drugs. Sentencing guidelines for DWI/DUI offenses vary significantly by state, and these offenses are not classified as felonies in some states until the second or third DWI/DUI arrest.

Civil commitment is available in the majority of states and in some European nations to provide emergency evaluation, treatment and monitoring of substance-involved persons who are in danger of harming themselves or others. These procedures allow for involuntary placement in both residential and outpatient treatment for specified periods of time. Court-ordered diversion and treatment programs provide another legal remedy for managing substance-abusing offenders, as an alternative to incarceration. Drug courts are perhaps the most visible example of drug diversion programs, and have been established in over 2,000 jurisdictions in the United States and in many foreign countries. Courts also frequently require involvement in drug treatment as a condition of sentencing, and court-ordered treatment is used extensively in the United States and in international settings. Research indicates that court-ordered substance abuse treatment is at least as effective as voluntary treatment, and that drug court programs result in significant cost savings and reductions in criminal recidivism.

REFERENCES

American Correctional Association. (2004). *Performance-based standards for adult local detention facilities* (4th ed.). Lanham, MD: American Correctional Association.

American Correctional Association. (2006). *Standards for adult correctional institutions* (4th ed.). Lanham, MD: American Correctional Association.

Anglin, M. D., Brecht, M., & Maddahian, E. (1989). Pretreatment characteristics and treatment performance of legally coerced versus voluntary methadone maintenance admissions. *Criminology, 27*(3), 537–557.

Ball, J. C. (1986). The hyper-criminal opiate addict. In B. D. Johnson & E. Wish (Eds.), *Crime rates among drug abusing offenders*. Final Report to the National Institute of Justice, (pp. 81–104). New York, NY: Narcotic and Drug Research, Inc.

Bean, P. (2002). Drug treatment courts, British style: The drug treatment court movement in Britain. *Substance Use and Misuse, 37*, 1595–1614.

Beane, E. A., & Beck, J. C. (1991). Court based civil commitment of alcoholics and substance abusers. *Bulletin of the American Academy of Psychiatry and the Law, 19*(4), 359–366.

Belenko, S. (1999). Research on drug courts: A critical review 1999 update. *National Drug Court Institute Review, 2*(2), 1–58.

Belenko, S., & Peugh, J. (1998). Fighting crime by treating substance abuse. *Issues in Science and Technology, Fall,* 53–60.

Belenko, S., & Peugh, J. (2005). Estimating drug treatment needs among state prison inmates. *Drug and Alcohol Dependence, 77,* 269–281.

Boellinger, L. (2002). Recent developments regarding drug law and policy in Germany and the European Community: The evolution of drug control in Europe. *Journal of Drug Issues, 32*(2), 363–378.

Bull, M. (2005). A comparative review of best practice guidelines for the diversion of drug related offenders. *International Journal of Drug Policy, 16*(4), 223–234.

Bureau of Justice Statistics. (2000). *Special report: Drug use, testing, and treatment in jails.* Washington, DC: U.S. Department of Justice.

Carey, S. M., & Finigan, M. W. (2004). A detailed cost analysis in a mature drug court setting. *Journal of Contemporary Criminal Justice, 20*(3), 315–338.

Carpenter, C. (2004). How do zero tolerance drunk driving laws work? *Journal of Health Economics, 23,* 61–83.

Chandler, R. K., Fletcher, B. W., & Volkow, N. D. (2009). Treating drug abuse and addiction in the criminal justice system: Improving public health and safety. *Journal of the American Medical Association, 301*(2), 183–190.

Chriqui, J. F., Pacula, R. L., McBride, D. C., Reichmann, D. A., Vanderwaal, C. J., & Terry-McElrath, Y. (2002). *Illicit drug policies: Selected laws from the 50 states.* Berrien Springs, MI: Andrews University.

Cissner, A. B., & Rempel, M. (2005). *The state of drug court research: Moving beyond "do they work?"* New York, NY: Center for Court Innovation.

Collins, J. J., Hubbard, R. L., & Rachal, J. V. (1985). Expensive drug use in illegal income: A test of explanatory hypotheses. *Criminology, 23*(4), 743–764.

Comprehensive Drug Abuse Prevention Act of 1970, 21 U.S.C. § 811 *et seq.* (1970).

Courtwright, D. T. (2004). The Controlled Substances Act: How a "big tent" reform became a punitive drug law. *Drug and Alcohol Dependence, 76,* 9–15.

Cropsey, K. L., Wexler, H., Melnick, G., Taxman, F. S., & Young, D. W. (2007). Specialized prisons and services: Results from a national survey. *The Prison Journal, 87*(1), 58–85.

De Leon, G. (2000). *The therapeutic community: Theory, model, and method.* New York, NY: Springer Publishing.

Estelle v. Gamble, 429 U.S. 97 (1976).

European Monitoring Centre for Drugs and Drug Addiction. (2003). *Treating drug users in prison – A critical area for health promotion and crime reduction policy.* Office for Official Publications of the European Union.

Farabee, D., Prendergast, M., & Anglin, M. D. (1998). The effectiveness of coerced treatment for drug-abusing offenders. *Federal Probation, 62*(1), 3–10.

Field, G. D. (2002). Historical trends of drug treatment in the criminal justice system. In C. G. Leukefeld, F. M. Tims, & D. Farabee (Eds.), *Treatment of drug offenders: Policies and issues* (pp. 9–21). New York, NY: Springer Publishing Company.

Fiscella, K., Pless, N., Meldrum, S., & Fiscella, P. (2004). Benign neglect or neglected abuse: Drug and alcohol withdrawal in U.S. jails. *Journal of Law, Medicine and Ethics, 32*(1), 129–136.

Fischer, B., Roberts, J. V., & Kirst, M. (2002). Compulsory drug treatment in Canada: Historical origins and recent developments. *European Addiction Research, 8,* 61–68.

Freeman, D. G. (2007). Drunk driving legislation and traffic fatalities: New evidence on BAC 0.08 laws. *Contemporary Economic Policy, 25*(3), 293–308.

Freeman, K. (2002). *New South Wales drug court evaluation: Health, well-being and participant satisfaction.* Sydney, NSW: New South Wales Bureau of Crime Statistics and Research.

Garcia, S. A., & Keilitz, I. (1991). Involuntary civil commitment of drug-dependent persons with special reference to pregnant women. *Mental and Physical Disability Law Reporter, 15,* 418–426.

Gerlach, R. (2002). Drug-substitution treatment in Germany: A critical overview of its history, legislation and current practice. *The Journal of Drug Issues, 32*(2), 503–522.

Greenfield, L., Burgdorf, K., Chen, X., Porowski, A., Roberts, A., & Herrell, J. (2004). Effectiveness of long-term residential substance abuse treatment for women: Findings from the three national studies. *The American Journal of Drug and Alcohol Abuse, 30*(3), 537–550.

Grichting, E., Uchtenhagen, A., & Rehm, J. (2002). Modes and impact of coercive inpatient treatment for drug-related conditions in Switzerland. *European Addiction Research, 8,* 78–83.

Harrison, P. M., & Beck, A. J. (2006). *Prisoners in 2005.* Washington, DC: U.S. Department of Justice, Bureau of Justice Statistics.

Health Insurance Portability and Accountability Act. (1996). P.L. 104–191, 42 U.S.C. 1320d.

Hiller, M. L., Knight, K., Broome, K. M., & Simpson, D. (1999). Legal pressure and treatment retention in a national sample of long-term residential programs. *Criminal Justice and Behavior, 5,* 463–481.

Hobbs, M., Krazlann, K., Ridout, S., Mai, Q., Knuiman, M., & Chapman, R. (2006). *Mortality and morbidity in prisoners after release from prison in Western Australia.* Australian Institute of Criminology Research and Public Policy Series, Nr. 71.

Huddleston, C. W., Marlowe, D. B., & Casebolt, R. (2008). *Painting the current picture: A national report card on drug courts and other problem solving court programs in the United States.* Washington, DC: Bureau of Justice Assistance, U.S. Department of Justice.

Inciardi, J. A., Martin, S. S., & Butzin, C. A. (2004). Five-year outcomes of therapeutic community treatment of drug-involved offenders after release from prison. *Crime and Delinquency, 50*(1), 88–107.

Inciardi, J. A., Martin, S. S., Butzin, C. A., Hooper, R. M., & Harrison, L. D. (1997). An effective model of prison-based treatment for drug-involved offenders. *Journal of Drug Issues, 27,* 261–278.

Insurance Institute on Highway Safety (IIHS). (2008). DUI/DWI laws. Available at <http://www.iihs.org/laws/dui.aspx/> .

Karberg, J. D., & James, D. J. (2005). *Substance dependence, abuse, and treatment of jail inmates, 2002 Special report.* Washington. DC: U.S. Department of Justice, Office of Justice Programs, Bureau of Justice Statistics.

Kildal, N., & Kuhnle, S. (Eds.), (2005). *Normative Foundations of the Welfare State: The Nordic Experience.* London, UK: Routledge.

Kinnunen, A., & Nilson, M. (1999). Recent trends in drug treatment in Europe. *European Addiction Research, 5*(3), 145–152.

Kitzmann, J. (1997). A survey of statutes allowing involuntary commitment for drug and alcohol dependent persons. *Developments in Mental Health Law, 16*(1), 1–19.

Knight, K., Simpson, D. D., & Hiller, M. L. (1999). Three-year reincarceration outcomes for in-prison therapeutic community treatment in Texas. *Prison Journal, 79*(3), 337–351.

Koerner, H. H. (2002). The efficacy of forced treatment. *Journal of Drug Issues, 32*(2), 543–552.

Kothary, G., Marsden, J., & Strang, J. (2002). Opportunities and obstacles for effective treatment of drug misusers in the criminal justice system in England and Wales. *British Journal of Criminology, 42,* 412–432.

Krongard, M. L. (2002). A population at risk: Civil commitment of substance abusers after *Kansas v. Hendricks. California Law Review, 90*(1), 111–163.

Langan, P. A., & Levin, D. J. (2002). *Recidivism of Prisoners Released in 1994.* Washington, DC: U.S. Department of Justice, Office of Justice Programs, Bureau of Justice Statistics.

Leukefeld, C. G., Logan, T. K., Martin, S. S., Purvis, R. T., & Farabee, D. (1998). A health services use framework for drug-abusing offenders. *American Behavioral Scientist, 41*(8), 1123–1135.

Marlowe, D. B., DeMatteo, D.S., & Festinger, D. S. (2003). A sober assessment of drug courts. *Federal Sentencing Reporter, 16*(1),113–128.

Martin, S., Butzin, C. A., Saum, C. A., & Inciardi, J. A. (1999). Three-year outcomes of therapeutic community treatment for drug-involved offenders in Delaware: From prison to work release to aftercare. *The Prison Journal, 79*(3), 294–320.

McCartt, A. T., & Northrup, V. S. (2004). Effects of enhanced sanctions for high-BAC DWI offenders on case dispositions and rates of recidivism. *Traffic Injury Prevention, 5,* 270–277.

McCollister, K. E., French, M. T., Inciardi, J. A., Butzin, C. A., Martin, S. S., & Hooper, R. M. (2003). Post-release substance abuse treatment for criminal offenders: A cost-effectiveness analysis. *Journal of Quantitative Criminology, 19*(4), 389–407.

McSweeney, T., Turnbull, P. J., & Hough, M. (2004). A review of criminal justice interventions for drug users in other countries. In: *The drug treatment and testing order: Early Lessons.* London, UK: National Audit Office.

McSweeney, T., Stevens, A., & Hunt, N. (2006). *The quasi-compulsory treatment of drug-dependent offenders in Europe: Final national report.* England, UK: Institute for Criminal Policy Research.

McSweeney, T., Turnbull, P. J., & Hough, M. (2008). *The treatment and supervision of drug-dependent offenders.* King's College London, UK: Institute for Criminal Policy Research.

Meier, P. (2005). *A national survey of retention in residential rehabilitation services. Research briefing 10.* London, UK: National Treatment Agency for Substance Misuse.

Michels, I., Stoever, H., & Gerlach, R. (2007). Substitution treatment for opioid addicts in Germany. *Harm Reduction Journal, 4*(5), 1–13.

Mueser, K. T., Noordsy, D. L., Drake, R. E., & Fox, L. (2003). Integrated treatment for dual disorders. New York, NY: Guilford Publications.

Nace, E. P., Birkmayer, F., Sullivan, M. A., Galanter, M., Fromson, J. A., Frances, R. J., Levin, F. R., Lewis, C., Suchinsky, R. T., Tamerin, J. S., & Westermeyer, J. (2007). Socially sanctioned coercion mechanisms for addiction treatment. *American Journal on Addictions, 16*(1), 15–23.

National Association of Drug Court Professionals. (1997). *Defining drug courts: The key components.* Washington, DC: Bureau of Justice Assistance, U.S. Department of Justice.

National Association of Drug Court Professionals. (2008). *Talking Points/Statistics on Drug Courts.* Retrieved from <http://www.nadcp.org/whatis/generalTalkingPoints.html/> .

National Center on Addiction and Substance Abuse. (2001). *Shoveling up: The impact of substance abuse on state budgets.* New York, NY: Columbia University.

National GAINS Center for People with Co-Occurring Disorders in the Justice System. (2004). *The prevalence of co-occurring mental illness and substance use disorders in jails.* Fact Sheet Series. Delmar, NY: GAINS.

National Institute of Justice. (2000). *1999 Annual report on drug use among adult and juvenile arrestees: Arrestee drug abuse monitoring program.* Washington, DC: U.S. Department of Justice.

National Institute on Drug Abuse. (2006). *Principles of drug abuse treatment for criminal justice populations: A research-based guide* (NIH Publication No, 06, 5316). Bethesda, MD: National Institute on Drug Abuse.

NCCHC. (2008a). *Standards for health services in jails.* Chicago, IL: National Commission on Correctional Health Care.

NCCHC. (2008b). *Standards for health services in prisons.* Chicago, IL: National Commission on Correctional Health Care.

NCSL. (2008). *Criminal Status of State Drunk Driving Laws.* National Conference of State Legislatures. Available at: <http://www.ncsl.org/print/transportation/drunkdrivecriminal.pdf/>.

National Highway Safety Administration (NHTSA). (2008a). *Traffic Safety Facts: Laws.* Available at: <http://www.nhtsa.dot.gov/staticfiles/DOT/NHTSA/Communication%20&%20Consumer%20Information/Articles/Associated%20Files/810883.pdf/>.

National Highway Safety Administration (NHTSA). (2008b). *The Facts: Zero Tolerance.* Available at: <http://www.nhtsa.dot.gov/people/outreach/safesobr/13qp/facts/factzero.html/>.

Office of National Drug Control Policy. (2001). *Drug treatment in the criminal justice system.* Washington, DC: ONDCP Drug Policy Information Clearinghouse.

Office of National Drug Control Policy. (2008). *Drug Courts.* Retrieved from <http://www.white-housedrugpolicy.gov/enforce/drugcourt.html/>.

Palm, J., & Stenius, K. (2002). Sweden: Integrated compulsory treatment. *European Addiction Research, 8*(2), 69–77.

Pearson, F. S., & Lipton, D. S. (1999). A meta-analytic review of the effectiveness of corrections-based treatments for drug abuse. *The Prison Journal, 79*(4), 384–410.

Peters, R. H., & Bekman, N. M. (2007). Treatment and reentry approaches for offenders with co-occurring disorders. In R. B. Greifinger, J. Bick, & J. Goldenson (Eds.), *Public health behind bars: From prisons to communities* (pp. 368–384). New York, NY: Springer Publishers.

Peters, R. H., & Wexler, H. K. (Eds.). (2005). *Substance Abuse Treatment for Adults in the Criminal Justice System.* Treatment Improvement Protocol (TIP) #44. Rockville, MD: Substance Abuse and Mental Health Services Administration, Center for Substance Abuse Treatment.

Peters, R. H., Matthews, C. O., & Dvoskin, J. A. (2005). Treatment in prisons and jails. In J. H. Lowinson, P. Ruiz, R. B. Millman, & J. G. Langrod (Eds.), *Substance abuse: A comprehensive textbook* (4th ed.) (pp. 707–722). Baltimore, MD: Williams and Wilkins Publishers.

Prendergast, M. L., Hall, E. A., Wexler, H. K., Melnick, G., & Cao, Y. (2004). Amity prison-based therapeutic community: 5-year outcomes. *The Prison Journal, 84*(1), 36–59.

Rempel, M., Fox-Kralstein, D., Cissner, A., Cohen, R., Labriola, M., Farole, D., Bader, A., & Magnani, M. (2003). *The New York State adult drug court evaluation: Policies, participants and impacts.* New York, NY: Center for Court Innovation.

Robinson v. California, 370 U.S. 660. (1962).

Roman, J., Townsend, W., & Bhati, A. (2003). *National estimates of drug court recidivism rates.* Washington, DC: National Institute of Justice, U.S. Department of Justice.

Sacks, S., Sacks, J. Y., McKendrick, K., Banks, S., & Stommel, J. (2004). Modified TC for MICA offenders: Crime outcomes. *Behavioral Sciences and the Law, 22*, 477–501.

Savage, M. A., Sundeen, M., & Tiegen, A. (2007). Traffic safety and public health: State legislative action 2007. *National Conference of State Legislatures Transportation Series, 27*.

Sheldon, R. G. (2004). The imprisonment crisis in America: Introduction. *Review of Policy Research, 21*(1), 5–12.

Simpler, A. H., & Langhinrichsen-Rohling, J. (2005). Substance use in prison: How much occurs and is it associated with psychopathology? *Addiction Research and Theory, 13*(5), 503–511.

Simpson, D., & Joe, G. W (2004). A longitudinal evaluation of treatment engagement and recovery stages. *Journal of Substance Abuse Treatment, 27*, 89–97.

Stevens, A., Berto, D., Heckmann, W., Kerschl, V., Oeuvray, K., Ooyen van, M., Steffan, E., & Uchtenhagen, A. (2005). Quasi-compulsory treatment of drug dependent offenders: An international literature review. *Substance Use and Misuse, 40*(3), 269–283.

Stevens, A., Berto, D., Kerschl, V., Oeuvray, K., Ooyen van, M., Steffan, E., Heckmann, W., & Uchtenhagen, A. (2003). *Summary literature review: The international literature on drugs, crime and treatment*. University of Kent, UK: QCT Europe Project.

Stoever, H. (2001). *An overview study: Assistance to drug users in European union prisons*. Lisbon: European Monitoring Centre for Drugs and Drug Addiction.

Stoever, H. (2002). Drug substitution treatment and needle exchange programs in German and European prisons. *Journal of Drug Issues, 32*(2), 597–606.

Substance Abuse and Mental Health Services Administration (SAMHSA). (2002). *Substance abuse treatment and staffing in adult correctional facilities*. Rockville, MD: SAMHSA Also available at: http://www.sanhsa.gov/oas/2k2/justice/justice.

Taxman, F. S., Perdoni, M. L., & Harrison, L. D. (2007). Drug treatment services for adult offenders: The state of the state. *Journal of Substance Abuse Treatment, 32*(3).

UCR/FBI. (2003). *Crime in America: FBI Uniform crime reports 2002*. Washington, DC: U.S. Government Printing Office (Online) Available at http://www.fbi.gov/ucr/cius_02/02preliminannual.pdf.

U.S. Code of Federal Regulations, Title 42, Volume 1, Part 2. (1995). *Confidentiality of Alcohol and Drug Abuse Patient Records*. Washington, DC: U.S. Government Printing Office.

Victorian State Government. (2008). *Victorian government response to the DCPC inquiry into misuse/abuse of benzodiazepines and other pharmaceutical drugs*. Melbourne, Victoria: Victorian State Government.

Wagenaar, A. C., Maldonado-Molina, M. M., Erickson, D. J., Ma, L., Tobler, A. L., & Komro, K. A. (2007). General deterrence effects of U.S. statutory DUI fine and jail penalties: Long-term follow-up in 32 states. *Accident Analysis and Prevention, 39*, 982–994.

Walker, J. (2001). *International experience of drug courts*. Edinburgh, UK: The Scottish Executive Central Research Unit.

Walmsley, R. (2007). *World prison population list* (7th ed.). London, UK: International Centre for Prison Studies.

Warren, J. (2008). *One in 100: Behind bars in America 2008* Pew Center of the Streets and the Public Safety Performance Project. Philadelphia, PA: The Pew Charitable Trusts.

Weinman, B. A., & Dignam, J. T. (2002). Drug-abuse treatment programs in the federal bureau of prisons: Past, present, and future directions. In C. G. Leukefeld, F. M. Tims, & D. Farabee (Eds.), *Treatment of drug offenders: Policies and issues* (pp. 91–104). New York, NY: Springer Publishing.

Werdenich, W., Waidner, G., & Trinkl, B. (2004). Quasi-compulsory treatment of drug-dependent offenders – A description of existing systems. *Verhaltenstherapie and Verhaltensmedizin, 25*, 71–78.

Wexler, H., Melnick, G., Lowe, L., & Peters, J. (1999). Three-year reincarceration outcomes for Amity in-prison therapeutic community and aftercare in California. *The Prison Journal, 79*(3), 321–336.

Wilson, D. J. (2000). *Drug use, testing, and treatment in jails*. In Bureau of Justice Statistics Special Report (May) (Online). Available at: <http://www.ojp.usdoj.gov/bjs/pub/pdf/duttj.pdf/> (NIJ 179999).

Wilson, D., Mitchell, O., & MacKenzie, D. (2006). A systematic review of drug court effects on recidivism. *Journal of Experimental Criminology, 2*(4), 459–487.

Chapter 17

Legal Authority, Medical Basis and Public Policy for Controlling and Scheduling Controlled Substances

Norman S. Miller, JD, MD, PLLC
Department of Medicine, College of Human Medicine, Michigan State University, East Lansing, MI, USA

OVERVIEW OF CONTROLLING AND SCHEDULING DRUGS AND OTHER SUBSTANCES

The impetus for controlling and scheduling of drugs and other substances was derived from the concept of their abuse potential, which in turn was determined by balancing legal, medical and public policy considerations (21 U.S.C. § 301 (2001); 21 U.S.C. § 801(a) (2001)). Consequently, the controlled substance laws themselves were based on medical and legal policies for public safety and individual welfare, to minimize the abuse potential of controlled substances (21 U.S.C. § 801 (2002)). For the purposes of controlling and scheduling drugs and other substances, their abuse potential pertains principally to the risks of these drugs and other substances being used abnormally to the legal detriment of society, with adverse effects on the health of individuals (21 U.S.C. § 821 (2001); Comprehensive Drug Abuse Prevention and Control Act of 1970, Pub. L. No. 91–513, 84 Stat. 1236 (1970) (codified in 21 U.S.C. § 801)).

The protocols for controlling drugs and estimates of United States medical requirements for scheduling drugs arose from the Controlled Substance Act (CSA, 1970) (21 U.S.C. § 811 (1994)). Moreover, the principal purpose of this statute was to meet in a comprehensive way the enormous problem of drug abuse (21 USCS §§ 801 *et seq.*). The overall process for controlling and scheduling drugs was balanced on comparing approved medical use to their relative potential for abuse and dependence liability (21 U.S.C. § 812 (1994)).

Within the meaning of the Controlled Substance Act, "control" means to add a drug or substance, or immediate precursor, to a schedule whether by

277

transfer from another schedule or otherwise under part B, Authority to Control; Standards and Schedules, Section 811 (21 U.S.C. § 811). Moreover, the term "controlled substance" means a drug or other substance, or immediate precursor, included in schedule I, II, III, IV, or V established by section 812 under part B (21 U.S.C. § 812).

Importantly, the term does not include distilled spirits, wine, malt beverages, or tobacco, as those terms are defined or used in subtitle E of the Internal Revenue Code of 1986. The term "drug" has meaning given by section 321(g)(1), 21 USC, Section 802 (21 U.S.C. § 802 (2002)). A "medicine" is any substance or preparation used in treating disease (§ 802; *State v. Baker*, 1948). A state statute as a written request has defined a "prescription" for drug or therapeutic aid issued by a licensed physician, dentist, veterinarian, osteopath, or podiatrist for legitimate purpose (*State v. Brown*, 1979).

The Controlled Substance Act (CSA) requires an eight-factor analysis for determining the potential for abuse as required by the CSA (21 U.S.C. § 811). These factors pertain to the medical, social and individual effects of the drug or substance on health, based on the actual and potential for abuse (including addictive use), pharmacology, other current scientific knowledge, history and current pattern of abuse, scope, duration and significance of abuse, psychic or physiological dependence liability, and if the drug is an immediate precursor of a controlled substance (§ 811; 21 U.S.C. § 812).

The responsibility for controlling and scheduling drugs and other substances is jointly shared by the Drug Enforcement Agency (DEA) expressed through the United States attorney general, and the Food and Drug Administration (FDA) within the Department of Health and Human Services (21 U.S.C. § 821; 20 U.S.C. § 3508 (2002)). In its role, the FDA assesses the abuse potential through a risk assessment and labeling of abuse/dependence risks, but has no control at the level of prescriber, dispenser, or patient (21 U.S.C. § 821). The DEA issues licenses for controlled substances and manufacturers, sets quotas and licenses prescribers, and provides law enforcement. Jointly, the FDA and the DEA classify controlled substances according to schedules based on abuse potential, ranging from the highest, Class I to the lowest, Class V (§ 821; 20 U.S.C. § 3508).

LEGAL AUTHORITY TO CONTROL SUBSTANCES: STANDARDS AND SCHEDULES

Federal Rules and Regulations for Controlled Substances

The legal authority and criteria for the classifications of substances are derived from Part B Authority to Control: Standards and Schedules in the Section 811: subsection (a) the attorney general shall determine the scheduling of substances pursuant to rules and regulations in subsection (a), except as provided in subsections (d) for international treaties and (e) for immediate precursors in Section 811 (21 U.S.C. § 811). The attorney general may (1) add to such a schedule or transfer between such schedules any drug or other substance if he: (A) finds that such drug or other substance has a potential for abuse; and (B) makes with respect to such drug or other substance the findings prescribed by subsection (b) of section 812 of this title for the schedule in which such drug is to be placed (21 U.S.C. § 812); or (2) remove any drug or other substance from the schedules if he finds that the drug or other substance does not meet the requirements for inclusion in any schedule (21 U.S.C. § 811).

In addition, the Food and Drug Administration (FDA) approves drugs and medications for medical use and commercial marketing under the Federal Food, Drug and Cosmetic Act of 1962. However, the determination of abuse potential and labeling in the drug abuse and dependence section originated under the FD&C Act, 1938. Consequently, federal rules and regulations directly and indirectly govern the manufacture, distribution and use of controlled drugs and other substances, which are either illicit to the general public or legally prescribed by physician for medical indications in patient populations (21 U.S.C. § 301 (2001)).

State Statutes and Regulations for Controlled Substances

Correspondingly, the states have the authority to regulate further the use and distribution of substances controlled by the CSA in medical practice, based on their broad police power to protect the public morals, health and safety afforded to the states in the United States Constitution (21 U.S.C. § 873 (1986); *Minnesota ex rel. Whipple v. Martinson*, 1921). A state may regulate the administration of drugs by health professions (*Pharmaceutical Soc. of New York, Inc. v. Lefkowitz*, 1978) and a state legislation, in the exercise of its police power, has the right to reasonably regulate the administration of drugs for the protection of the lives, health, safety and welfare of the people (*McCurley v. State*, 1980). In this regard, the purpose of the state controlled substance act has been to establish a scheme to identify and protect legitimate purposes for drugs, and to prohibit illicit drug use (*State v. Mann*, 1978).

The Uniform Controlled Substance Act was drafted to maintain uniformity between the laws of the states and federal government, and to complement the federal law to enable government at all levels to control the drug abuse problem more effectively (Uniform Controlled Substance Act (1994) § 201(a)).

In the state of Michigan, the statute for the Official Prescription Program was instituted to prevent illicit use of schedule II controlled substances, and decrease the potential for diversion and addictive use of these controlled prescription medications. Prescription monitoring programs were established to prevent diversion of prescription medication to illicit use and to decrease the potential for prescribing for addictive use in patients. The utility of these regulatory programs was based on detecting patterns and practices of prescribing of schedule II medications. Accordingly, the state of Michigan established the Triplicate Prescription Program (TPP) and the Michigan Controlled Substance

Advisory Commission. In 1993, the legislature changed the TPP to the Official Prescription Program (OPP) (Michigan Department of Consumer and Industry Services, 1997) (Mich. Pub. Health Code Article 7, § 333.7333 (2001); Article 15, § 333.7333; Article 15, § 333.16315; Article 7, § 333.7104).

The OPP requires all schedule II drugs to be written on an official prescription form. The OPP mandates a single prescription and allows for electronic transmission of prescription information from the pharmacy to the OPP. The diversion of schedule II drugs is monitored by drug abuse warning network (DAWN) data, the Michigan state police diversion unit (DIU) and the automation of reports and consolidated orders system (ARCOS) (Michigan Department of Consumer and Industry Services, 1997).

Drug Enforcement Administration and Food and Drug Administration

Together, the Drug Enforcement Administration and the Food and Drug Administration establish legal procedures and scheduling, based on scientifically verified and legally defensible data (21 U.S.C. § 811). Drug classes subject to regulation under the CSA are opioids, central nervous system depressants and stimulants, hallucinogens, cannabinoids and anabolic steroids (§ 811; 21 U.S.C. § 812).

Proceedings to control a substance are initiated by the attorney general or at the request of the secretary of Health and Human Services, or on the petition of an interested party. Administratively, the secretary of DHHS delegates to the FDA 21 USC 5.10, the attorney general delegates authority under the Controlled Substance Act to the Administrator of the Drug Enforcement Agency (DEA) under 28 CFR § 0.1000 (b), and such authority includes the authority to schedule controlled drugs pursuant to 21 USCS § 811 (21 U.S.C. § 811; *United States v. Lippner*, 1982; 10 Fed. R. Evid. Serv. 836). In addition, the validity of the delegation to Drug Enforcement of authority to schedule or reschedule drugs is subject to the Controlled Substance Act (21 U.S.C.S. §§ 801 *et seq.*) (McDaniel, 1980).

Immediate Precursors

Under subsection (e), the attorney general may, without regard to the findings by subsections (a) and (b), place an immediate precursor in the same schedule as the controlled substance for that precursor or a higher numerical schedule. However, other precursors are not automatically placed in higher designations (21 U.S.C. § 811).

Temporary Scheduling to Avoid Imminent Hazards to Public Safety

Under section (h)(1), the attorney general may place a substance in schedule I on a temporary basis as necessary to avoid an imminent hazard to the public safety, and may order without regard to subsection (b) (§ 811).

Abuse Potential

Under section (f), if at the time a new drug application is submitted to the secretary for any drug having a stimulant, depressant, or hallucinogenic effect on the central nervous system, it appears that such a drug has an abuse potential, such information is forwarded by the secretary to the attorney general (§ 811).

Under subsection (g) (1) requires the attorney general to exclude any non-narcotic substance from a schedule if the substance may be sold over the counter without a prescription under the Federal Food, Drug and Cosmetic Act, unless subsequently controlled after the enactment of Part B pursuant to provisions of section 811 (§ 811). However, this subsection is not intended to prevent control of the drug in the future should an abuse potential be found (§ 811).

Evaluation of Drugs and Other Substances

The DHHS and FDA must perform scientific assessment and recommend initial schedule or change to the DEA. Subsequently, the DEA schedules drugs through rule-making (§ 811). Moreover, schedule changes can be initiated by DEA, FDA, Congress and by citizen or sponsor petitions, and must be in compliance with International Treaties (§ 811; Comprehensive Drug Abuse Prevention and Control Act of 1970, Pub. L. No. 91–513, 84 Stat. 1236 (1970) (codified in 21 U.S.C. § 801)). Subsection (b) requires that, before modification of the classification of a substance, the attorney general, "after gathering the necessary data," will request from the secretary of Health and Human Services a scientific and medical evaluation with recommendations as to whether or not a substance should be added, deleted or rescheduled as a controlled substance (21 U.S.C. § 811; Comprehensive Drug Abuse Prevention and Control Act, 84 Stat. at 4599). The attorney general is not intended to be authorized to undertake or support medical and scientific research for the purpose, which is within the competence of the secretary, or to limit the secretary's evaluation to data submitted by the attorney general. Moreover, the phrase "gathering necessary data" does envision utilization of laboratory facilities within the United States government for chemical analysis, especially of substances being "abused" in the street, which require identification (21 U.S.C. § 811; Comprehensive Drug Abuse Prevention and Control Act, 84 Stat. at 4600).

Further, subsection (a) provides that the secretary's evaluations and recommendations shall be in writing and shall be submitted to the attorney general within a reasonable time, and shall be binding pertaining to scientific and medical matters. In addition, the attorney general may not control a drug or substance if the secretary recommends against it. However, if the attorney general determines that these facts and all other relevant data constitute substantial evidence of potential for abuse such as to warrant control, or substantial evidence that the drug or other substance should be removed entirely from the schedules, he shall initiate proceedings for control or removal under subsection (a). If the attorney general finds that all the relevant data constitutes substantial evidence

of a potential for abuse, he or she may proceed under the rulemaking procedures of the Administrative Procedure Act to control the substance (21 U.S.C.
§ 811; 21 C.F.R. § 1308 (2000)).

Factors Determinative of Control or Removal from Schedules

According to subsection (c) of § 811, the attorney general shall consider a
number of factors with respect to each drug or substance proposed to be controlled or removed from the schedules, and must consider any findings under
subsection (a), or under subsection (b) of section 812 (21 U.S.C. § 811; 21
U.S.C. § 812).

In determining whether a drug or substance should be scheduled and at
which level, the following factors are required to be considered, although specific findings are not required for each factor. These factors are listed in Section
201 (c), (21 U.S.C. 811 (c)), of the CSA (21 U.S.C. § 811; § 811):

1. The drug's actual or relative potential for abuse.
2. Scientific evidence of the drug's pharmacological effects. A major consideration is the state of knowledge with respect to the effects of a specific drug,
   e.g., is the drug hallucinogenic. The best available pharmacological knowledge will be considered in these determinations.
3. The state of current scientific knowledge regarding the substance. The
   information is primarily concerned with scientific knowledge in addition to
   the pharmacological effects, e.g., medical effects.
4. Its history and current pattern of abuse. It is important to know the pattern
   of abuse of the substance, including the socioeconomic characteristics of
   the segments of the population involved in such abuse.
5. The scope, duration and significance of abuse. In evaluating existing abuse,
   the administrator must know not only the pattern of abuse, but whether it is
   widespread. In considering its range of abuse, economics of regulation and
   enforcement and social significance, especially impact on young people, are
   included in decisions regarding scheduling of a drug or substance.
6. What, if any, risk there is to the public. If a drug creates dangers to the public health, in addition to or because of its abuse potential, then these dangers
   must also be considered.
7. The drug's psychic or physiological dependence liability. An assessment of
   the extent to which a drug is physically addictive or psychologically habit-
   forming, if such information is known, is performed.
8. Whether the substance is an immediate precursor of a substance already
   controlled. The CSA includes immediate precursors on this basis alone in
   the appropriate schedule, and thus provides safeguards against the possibilities of clandestine manufacture.

As presented above, a key criterion for controlling a substance, and the one
which will be used most often, is the substance's potential for abuse. If the

attorney general determines that the data gathered and the evaluations and recommendations from the secretary constitute substantial evidence of potential for abuse, she or he may initiate control proceedings under this section. Final control by the attorney general will be based on findings as to the substance's abuse for potential (§ 811; 21 U.S.C. § 812).

Legislative Intent for Potential for Abuse

The term "potential for abuse" is not defined in the CSA, although discussion of its meaning is contained in the legislative history of the act. The basis for "potential for abuse" is found in the definition of a "depressant or stimulant drug" contained in section (v) of the Federal, Drug and Cosmetic Act, and is characterized further in the regulations promulgated under that section (21 C.F.R. § 166.2(e) (2000)).

The "director" (FDA/HHS) may determine that a substance has a potential for abuse because of its depressant effect on the central nervous system or its hallucinogenic effect if (Comprehensive Drug Abuse Prevention and Control Act, 84 Stat. at 4601):

1. The drug or substance is taken in amounts sufficient to create a hazard to the health or safety of other individuals or to the community; or
2. The drug or substance is sufficiently diverted from legitimate drug channels, e.g., physicians, pharmacies, hospitals; or
3. Use of the drug or substance is initiated by individuals, and not on the advice from practitioners licensed by law to administer such drugs; or
4. The drug or substance is so new or related to other drugs or substances with known potential of abuse to make it reasonable to assume there will be significant diversions from legitimate channels, use contrary or without medical advice, or substantial capability to create hazards to the health of users or to the safety of the community. Of importance is that actual abuse of a substance is indicative that a drug has a potential for abuse or addiction.

These regulations follow and extend the suggestions contained in the report of this committee accompanying H.R. 2, 89th Congress, which became the Drug Abuse Control Amendments of 1965 (House Report No. 130, 89th Congress, first session, (1965)) (Comprehensive Drug Abuse Prevention and Control Act, 84 Stat. at 4602). The report discussed further the "potential" aspect of the term abuse. It stated that it did not intend that potential for abuse be determined on the basis of: "isolated or occasional nontherapeutic purposes." The committee felt that there must exist: "a substantial potential for the occurrence of significant diversions from legitimate channels, significant use by individuals contrary to professional advice, or substantial capability of creating hazards to the health of the user or the safety of the community" (*Idem* at 4602).

With respect to the question of the extent to which actual, as distinguished from potential, abuse was required to be established, that report stated that "the secretary of health should not be required to wait until a number of lives have been destroyed or substantial problems have already arisen before designating a drug as subject to controls of the bill" (*Idem* at 4602).

The term "substantial" potential means more than a mere scintilla of isolated abuse, but less than a preponderance of abuse. Therefore, documentation that say, several hundred thousand dosage units of a drug has been diverted, would be "substantial" evidence of abuse despite tens of millions of dosage units of that drug being used legitimately in the same time period. Normally, diversion is demonstrated by accountability audits of the legitimate sources of distribution, such as manufacturers, wholesalers, pharmacies and doctors (*Idem* at 4602). Moreover, misuse of a drug in suicides and attempted suicides, in addition to injuries from unsupervised use, are regarded as indicative of the drug's potential for abuse (*Idem* at 4602).

The general philosophy of the Commission that drafted the Drug Control Act can be stated in three parts (H.R. 18583, Title I, Drug Control Act; *Idem* at 4575):

1. The illegal traffic in drugs should be attacked with the full power of the federal government. The price for participation in this traffic should be prohibitive. It should be made too dangerous to be attractive (*Idem* at 4575).
2. The individual abuser should be rehabilitated. Every possible effort should be exerted by all governments – federal, state and local – and by every community toward this end. Where necessary to protect society, this may have to be done at times against the abuser's will. Pertinent to all, the causes of drug abuse must be found and eradicated (*Idem* at 4575).
3. Drug abusers who violate the law by small purchases or sales should be made to recognize what society demands of them. In these instances, penalties should be applied according to the principles of our present code of justice. When the penalties involve imprisonment, however, the rehabilitation of the individual, rather than retributive punishment should be the major objective (*Idem* at 4575).

Levels of Drug Control and Scheduling

The levels of drug control consist of five classes or schedules under the CSA. Schedule I drug is not approved for use in the United States, and has high abuse potential (most restrictive). A special DEA license for research is required. Schedule II–V drugs are approved for medical use in the United States, and have high abuse potential and dependence liability (C–II/III) to limited abuse potential physical or psychological dependence liability (C–IV/V) (21 U.S.C. § 812(b) (1994)).

Subsection (a) establishes five schedules, and provides that these schedules initially consist of the substances listed in § 812. Moreover, the subsection provides for a semi-annual updating and republishing of the schedules during the two year period beginning one year after the date of enactment of title II of the act. After the expiration of the two year period, the schedules are to be updated and republished on an annual basis (21 U.S.C. § 812).

Subsection (b) sets out the criteria for each schedule of controlled drugs. However, findings for these criteria are not required for placement of a substance in a schedule except where control is required by United States obligations under an international treaty, convention, or protocol, in effect on 27 October 1970, and except in the case of an immediate precursor, a drug or other substance may not be placed in any schedule unless the findings required for such schedule are made with respect to such drug or other substance. The criteria required for each of the schedules are as follows (21 U.S.C. § 829 (1990)):

Schedule I Drug or Substance

1. The drug or other substance has a high potential for abuse.
2. The drug or other substance has no currently accepted medical use in treatment in the United States.
3. There is a lack of accepted safety for use of the drug or other substance under medical supervision (21 U.S.C. § 829).

Examples of Class I substances included heroin, LSD and marijuana (21 C.F.R. § 1308.11 (2000)).

Schedule II Drug or Substance

1. The drug or other substance has a high potential for abuse.
2. The drug or other substance has a currently accepted medical use in treatment in the United States, or currently accepted medical use with severe restrictions.
3. Abuse of the drug or other substance may lead to severe psychological or physical dependence.
4. Schedule II substances include morphine, phencyclidine, methadone and methamphetamine (21 U.S.C. § 829).

Examples of Class II substances include cocaine, morphine, opium and oxycodone (21 C.F.R. § 1308.12 (2000)).

Schedule III Drug or Substance

1. The drug or other substance has a potential for abuse less than the drugs or other substances in Schedules I and II.
2. The drug or other substance has a currently accepted medical use in treatment in the United States.
3. Abuse of the drug or other substance may lead to moderate or low physical dependence or high psychological dependence.
4. Anabolic steroid, codeine and hydrocodone with aspirin or Tylenol, and some barbiturates are Schedule III substances (21 U.S.C. § 829).

Examples of Class III substances include amphetamines, methylphenidate and hydrocodone (21 C.F.R. § 1308.13 (2000)).

Schedule IV Drug or Substance

1. The drug or other substance has a low potential for abuse relative to the drugs or other substances in Schedule III.
2. The drug or other substance has a currently accepted medical use in treatment in the United States.
3. Abuse of the drug or substance may lead to limited physical dependence or psychological dependence relative to the drug or other substances in Schedule III (21 U.S.C. § 829).

Examples of Class IV drugs are propoxyphene, diazepam alprazolam (21 C.F.R. § 1308.14 (2000)).

Schedule V Drug or Substance

1. The drug or other substance has a low potential for abuse relative to the drugs or other substances in Schedule IV.
2. The drug or other substance has a currently accepted medical use in treatment in the United States.
3. Abuse of the drug or other substance may lead to limited physical dependence or psychological dependence relative to the drugs or other substances in Schedule IV (21 U.S.C. § 829).

Examples of Class V substances include codeine and opium (dose dependent) (21 C.F.R. § 1308.15 (2000)).

For drugs providing serious addiction or abuse problems (those listed in Schedules I and II), tighter legal controls are provided (21 U.S.C. § 812). These controls include the establishment of quotas for imports and for domestic manufacture. In addition, transfers of these drugs may only be made through the use of officially prescribed order forms, with a copy furnished to the attorney general (§ 812; 21 U.S.C. § 811). All persons in the distribution chain must be registered and, with certain exceptions, must keep records with respect to all transfers of controlled drugs (§ 811; 21 U.S.C. § 812). Practicing physicians are required to keep records of Schedule I substances and narcotic drugs in other schedules which they dispense, as distinguished from prescribing or administering to patients (§ 812; 21 U.S.C. § 811; 21 U.S.C. § 801(a) (2001)).

The laws provide for control and enforcement by the Justice Department of problems related to drug abuse through registration of manufactures, wholesalers, retailers and all others in the legitimate distribution chain, and makes transactions outside the legitimate distribution chain illegal (21 U.S.C. § 801(a); 21 U.S.C. § 811; 21 U.S.C. § 812).

MEDICAL BASIS FOR POTENTIAL OF ABUSE

FDA Role

New Drug Application (NDA) Requirements

For new drug applications, if the potential for abuse exists, all data pertinent to the abuse of the drug, particularly data on overdose, and a proposal for scheduling under the CSA must be included (21 CFR § 314.50(5)(vii) (2000)). "If, at the time a new drug application is submitted to the secretary for any drug having a stimulant, depressant, or hallucinogenic effect on the central nervous system, it appears that such drug has an abuse potential, such information shall be forwarded by the secretary to the attorney general" (21 U.S.C. § 811).

The medical basis for scheduling medications is a complex process that focuses on balancing the therapeutic value against the abuse potential of the medications as indicated by the numbered class (CI–V) assigned to the drugs and other substances (21 U.S.C. § 355 (2001)). These seemingly diametrically opposed major determinants are evaluated during the phases of drug development and postapproval phase, when the drug is actually being used in clinical practices (21 C.F.R. § 314.50(5)(vii)). During the phases of drug development, including pre-investigational drug phase (pre-IND), investigational drug phase (IND) and new drug application phase (NDA), the abuse potential of the drug is evaluated from all data acquired during the "abuse liability assessment" conducted and overseen by the FDA (21 C.F.R. § 314.50(5)(vii)).

Evaluation of all data is based on characteristics of the drug, which include chemistry, pharmacology (animal and human), pharmacokinetics and pharmacodynamics, and adverse events reported in clinical trials. Of importance is that the drug considered for scheduling is compared to other drugs, particularly those already scheduled as controlled substances. In addition, the abuse potential of a particular drug can be suspected by the chemical structure, e.g., if it is similar to a morphine structure. Also, the pharmaceutical characteristics such as ease of synthesis, extractability and solubility are important in considering how the drug might be used or altered (21 C.F.R. § 314.50(5)(vii)), (Gold & Johnson, 1998; Walker & Zacny, 1998; Schuckit, 2000).

The abuse liability assessment for a NDA includes the preclinical pharmacology, human pharmacology, clinical trial data, CSA scheduling proposal and data on overdose (21 C.F.R. § 314.50(5)(vii)). The preclinical evaluations depend on neuropharmacological characterizations, such as identifying the brain sites for drug action and receptor binding within these brain sites, e.g., those brain sites responsible for abuse, addiction and dependence. Within the CNS, the receptor sites for drug action and the consequent behavioral effects are evaluated, e.g., morphine-like substances that act at mu receptors in the brain to produce analgesia and dependence (21 C.F.R. § 314.50(5)(vii)) (King & Miller, 1998; Gutstein & Alcil, 2001).

Studies of animal behavior under the influence of the drugs focus on fundamental aspects of the abuse potential of drugs, namely, the reinforcing effects through self-administering of the drug by the animal. For instance, does the animal self-administer the drug in patterns comparable to other drugs, such as morphine and cocaine self-administered in other animals? Also, in animals evaluating the discriminative effects through drug discrimination trials is important in identifying and characterizing specific effects of the drug. The drug is tested for its capacity to induce physical dependence or withdrawal following cessation of the drug, particularly after repetitive use over time. Correspondingly, the drug is tested for its ability to produce tolerance to increasing doses, or losing effects at particular doses of the drug. Importantly, tolerance and dependence are commonly associated with drugs which possess a potential for abuse, and frequently accompany each other (21 C.F.R. § 314.50(5)(vii)) (Swift et al., 1998; Walker & Zacny, 1998).

Evaluation of pharmacology is conducted in humans based on characteristics believed to be associated with potential for abuse, namely, toxicity and impairment in performance from the drug, and tolerance and dependence to the drug as in animals. Also, self-administration studies are performed in humans to demonstrate subjective effects of drug liking, and actual patterns of drug use suggestive of addiction to these drugs (21 C.F.R. § 314.50(5)(vii)).

PUBLIC POLICY FOR CONTROLLING AND SCHEDULING SUBSTANCES

Controlled substance laws contain three sources of policy framework to regulate the production and distribution of controlled substances: international treaties; federal laws and regulations; and state laws and regulations (Joranson & Gilson, 1994). In addition, a drugs scheduling level (I –V) is based on its medical use, potential for abuse, addiction and safety (21 U.S.C. § 812). The Controlled Substance Act (21 U.S.C. § 811) provides a mechanism for drugs to be controlled, decontrolled, or rescheduled (21 U.S.C. § 811).

The current policy for drug control is a mixture of law and medicine more clearly articulated for the legal means for controlled drugs and other substances than skilled and focused medical management. Consequently, the current drug control policy balances the availability for medical use against the prohibition to reduce actual and potential abuse from scheduled medications (21 U.S.C. § 812; 21 U.S.C. § 802) (Joranson & Gilson, 1994). Moreover, the primary methods of reducing the misuse of controlled substances include increased monitoring and restrictions on availability of obtaining controlled substances through illicit and fraudulent means. While the use of controlled substances is permitted for legitimate medical purposes, diversions from sources such as physicians and pharmacists are also common occurrences (Wesson & Smith, 1990).

The CSA was derived from public policy concerns for adverse effects from the actual and potential abuse of controlled substances (Comprehensive Drug Abuse Prevention and Control Act, 84 Stat. 1236). Thus, the attorney general is authorized to carry out educational and research programs directly related to enforcement of the laws under its jurisdiction concerning drugs or other substances, which are or may be subject to the control (21 U.S.C. § 872 (1988)) (Scott, 2000). These programs include educational and training programs on drug abuse and controlled substances law enforcement (21 U.S.C. § 872 (1986)). In addition the attorney general shall cooperate with local, state and federal agencies concerning traffic in controlled substance and in suppressing the abuse of controlled substances (21 U.S.C. § 873 (1986)).

The assessment of actual and potential for abuse of controlled substances is based on a composite of a review of the chemistry, pharmacology, clinical considerations and the public health risks following the introduction of the drug to the general population (Adams, 1991; Lurie & Lee, 1991). For drugs with medical and therapeutic value, the abuse and dependence potential poses risks which require management and control at multiple levels, particularly by physicians who prescribe these drugs in clinical practice (Warner et al., 1995; Fe Caces et al., 1998).

However, labeling and drug scheduling alone have substantial impact, but cannot replace the medical judgment of skilled physicians who prescribe controlled substances. Unfortunately, the current state of knowledge and skill possessed by physicians is generally insufficient to meet the expected demands implicit within the controlled substance laws (Center on Addiction and Substance Abuse, 2000; Miller et al., 2001). While the scheduling of drugs provides specific guidance for the risk potential for abuse, physicians typically still do not adequately evaluate their prescribing controlled substances to patients according to the meaning and intent of the CSA (Center on Addiction and Substance Abuse, 2000; Miller et al., 2001). Overcoming these deficiencies through education and training in medical schools and residencies and continuing medical education will provide physicians with the knowledge and skill to protect their patients, and protect the public at large from the actual and potential abuse of controlled substances (Center on Addiction and Substance Abuse, 2000; Miller et al., 2001).

The prevalence of prescription addiction continues to grow among those who already have an identifiable alcohol and drug disorder, as would be expected in populations of addicts who are vulnerable to developing addiction to drugs in general. After cannabis, non-medical use of psychotherapeutic drugs represents the second largest drug problem in the United States. According to recent surveys, 37% of the United States population has tried an illicit and therapeutic drug and 16% report current use of these drugs, including narcotic medications (Miller et al., 2001).

Therefore, legal intervention through regulation and monitoring continues to be necessary, because of the potential for abuse and the addictive nature of controlled substances (21 U.S.C. § 811; 21 U.S.C. § 812). Thus, the current lack of knowledge and skill possessed by physicians in prescribing these medications, in addition to the potential for illicit diversion, warrant continued monitoring and scheduling for control of abusive use (Center on Addiction and Substance

Abuse, 2000; Miller et al., 2001). Important targets for reducing morbidity and mortality from these controlled substances consist of a combination of improved undergraduate, graduate and continuing medical education, and increased public awareness of the public health issues pertaining to narcotic medications (Center on Addiction and Substance Abuse, 2000; Miller et al., 2001).

REFERENCES

Adams, E. H. (1991). Prevalence of prescription drug abuse: data from the National Institutes on Drug Abuse. *New York State Journal of Medicine*, *91*(11 Suppl), 32S–36S.

Center on Addiction and Substance Abuse (CASA). (2000). *Missed Opportunity: National Survey of Primary Care Physicians and Patients on Substances Abuse*. New York, NY: CASA.

Fe Caces, M., Harford, T. C., & Aitken, S. S. (1998). Prescription and non-prescription drug use: a longitudinal study. *Journal of Substance Abuse*, *10*(2), 115–126.

Gold, M. S., & Johnson, C. R. (1998). Psychological and psychiatric consequences of opiates. In R. E. Tartar., R. T. Ammerman., & P. J. Ott (Eds.), *Handbook of Substances: Neurobehavioral Pharmacology*. New York, NY: Plenum Press.

Gutstein, H. B., & Alcil, H. (2001). In J. G. Hardman & L. B. Limberd (Eds.), *Goodman and Gilman's The Pharmacological Bases of Therapeutics* (tenth ed.). New York, NY: McGraw-Hill.

Joranson, D. E., & Gilson, A. M. (1994). Controlled substances, medical practice and the law Available at http://www.medsch.wisc.edu/painpolicy/publicat/94appcs.htm. In H. I. Schwartz (Ed.), *Psychiatric Practice Under Fire: The Influence of Government, The Media and Special Interests on Somatic Therapies* (pp. 173–194). Arlington, VA: American Psychiatric Press, Inc.

King, A. C., & Miller, N. S. (1998). Medications of abuse: opioids. In R. E. Tartar., R. T. Ammerman., & P. J. Ott (Eds.), *Handbook of Substances: Neurobehavioral Pharmacology*. New York, NY: Plenum Press.

Lurie, P., & Lee, P. R. (1991). Fifteen solutions to the problems of prescription drug abuse. *Journal of Psychoactive Drugs*, *23*(4), 349–357.

McCurley v. State, 390 So.2d 15 (Ala. Crim. App. 1980).

McDaniel, B. I. (1980). *Validity of Delegation to Drug Enforcement Administration of Authority to Schedule or Reschedule Drugs Subject to Controlled Substances Act*, (Annotation), (21 U.S.C.A. §§ 801 *et seq.*), 47 A.L.R. Fed. 869.

Michigan Department of Consumer and Industry Services. (1997). *Michigan Official Prescription Program Evaluation Report*. Michigan Department of Consumer and Industry Services, Office of Health Services, and Michigan Controlled Substances Advisory Commission.

Miller, N. S., Sheppard, L. M., Colenda, C. C., & Magen, J. (2001). Why physicians are unprepared to treat patients who have alcohol and drug-related disorders. *Academic Medicine*, *76*(5), 410–418.

Minnesota ex rel. Whipple v. Martinson, 256 U.S. 41, 41 S. Ct. 425, 65 L. Ed. 819 (1921).

Pharmaceutical Soc. of New York, Inc. v. Lefkowitz, 454 F.Supp. 1175 (S.D.N.Y. 1978), aff'd, 586 F.2d 953 (C.A.N.Y. 1978).

Schuckit, M. A. (2000). *Drug and Alcohol Abuse A Clinical Guide to Diagnosis and Treatment* (fifth ed.). New York, NY: Kluwer Academic/Plenum Publishers.

Scott, L. (2000). The pleasure principle: a critical examination of federal scheduling of controlled substances. *Southwestern University Law Review*, *29*, 447.

State v. Baker, 48 S.E. 2d 61, 73 (N.C. 1948).

State v. Brown, 366 So. 2d 550 (La. 1979).

State v. Mann, 382 A.2d 1319 (R.I. 1978).

Swift, R. M., Griffiths, W., & Camara, P. (1998). Addictive disorders. In L. S. Goldman., T. N. Wise., & D. S. Brody (Eds.), *Psychiatry for Primary Care Physicians*. Chicago, IL: American Medical Association.

United States v. Lippner, 676 F.2d 456 (C.A.Ga. 1982).

Walker, E. A., & Zacny, J. P. (1998). Behavioral pharmacology of opiates. In R. E. Tartar., R. T. Ammerman., & P. J. Ott (Eds.), *Handbook of Substances: Neurobehavioral Pharmacology*. New York, NY: Plenum Press.

Warner, L. A., Kessler, R. C., Hughes, M., Anthony, J. C., & Nelson, C. B. (1995). Prevalence and correlation of drug use and dependence in the United States. *Archives of General Psychiatry*, *52*(3), 219–229.

Wesson, D. R., & Smith, D. E. (1990). Prescription drug abuse, patient, physician, and cultural responsibilities. *The Western Journal of Medicine*, *152*(5), 613–616.

Chapter 18

Use of Addictive Medications and Drugs in Athletics

Woodburne O. Levy, MD
Department of Mental Health and Behavioral Sciences, University of South Florida College of Medicine, James A Haley Veteran Affairs Medical Center, Tampa, FL, USA

Kavita Kalidas, MD
Department of Neurology, University of South Florida College of Medicine, FL, USA

INTRODUCTION

Doping is probably derived from the Dutch word dop, an alcoholic drink made from grape skins by Zulu warriors to enhance their battle prowess. The actual term doping became more widely used at the turn of the twentieth century in association with the administration of illegal substances to racehorses to decrease performance, although today the term is associated with increasing performance (Fraser, 2004). Drug use has been prevalent in sports since the initiation of competitive games. In ancient times, West Africans used Cola acuminita and Cola nitida for running competitions. The Greeks ingested hallucinogenic mushrooms and sesame seeds to enhance performance, at the risk of becoming psychotic, while the Roman gladiators were known to abuse stimulants to overcome fatigue and injury (Yesalis, 2000).

The birth of modern drug testing in the international setting began at the Pan American Games in 1983 after Manfred Donike, a German biochemist and leading international expert on doping of the era, introduced his newly-developed procedure capable of accurate detection of banned substances and their metabolites. Early in the games, after 11 weightlifters tested positive for anabolic substances, 13 United States athletes flew home from Caracas, Venezuela before the start of competition in their respective events. Sports commentators portrayed the track and field athletes as cheats, although they had not failed a drug test. Overall, 19 individuals from various countries around the world tested positive for using anabolic steroids at the tournament, while many others returned to their home countries for undisclosed reasons, fell "injured," or performed poorly in order to finish badly and avoid being tested (Todd, 1987).

The repercussions of the doping scandal shook the sports industry to its core. Weeks after the incident, the American media continued to probe the United States Olympic Committee (USOC) about the members of the American squad who left Caracas without being tested. Journalists investigated the amateur and professional sports practices of drug testing, and concluded that administrators of their respective sports were indifferent to the issue for decades. Society was now getting its first glimpse into the widespread doping practices of competitive athletes. Donike's improved detection technique, revealing athletes hidden use of performance-enhancing substances, warped society's perception of the modern-day athlete as an individual who would resort to unethical tactics to "win at all costs."

The surge of positive steroid tests in the 1980s and 1990s continued to herald athletes' misuse of drugs. Major League Baseball's (MLB) Mark McGuire and Sammy Sosa, suspected of using anabolic steroids during the famous home run derby of 1998, likely used these substances for no different reasons than the athletes of early history. Female athletes are also susceptible to the use of performance-enhancing drugs to circumvent the rules of "fair play," as exemplified by former track and field superstar Marion Jones, who was stripped of her five Olympic Gold Medals by the International Olympic Committee on 7 October 2007. Monitoring of one's diet, the diligent use of supplements, engaging in intense, scientifically-based workouts, and allowing time for adequate rest to rebuild muscle cannot match the "edge" performance-enhancing drugs affords athletes. As described by Jose Canseco, the infamous "black-eye" of the MLB in his first book, *Juiced: Wild Times, Rampant 'Roids, Smash Hits, and How Baseball Got Big*, even if a competitor uses the most expensive and high-tech non-illegal methods to improve performance, they will never be able to achieve the same results as an athlete injecting themselves with new designer drugs that are almost undetectable by current laboratory techniques. In addition to the use of injectable steroids, Canseco also details the rampant use of recreational drugs by athletes in order to cope with their grueling lifestyles.

Cocaine, marijuana, alcohol, narcotics, muscle relaxants and other substances of abuse are used by athletes at rates greater than or equal to the general public (Martens et al., 2006; Wetherill & Fromme, 2007), as personified when individual cases of popular sports figures' exploits are cover stories for national publications. Infamous examples include for MLB pitcher Dwight Gooden's struggles with cocaine, the death of potential National Basket Ball Association (NBA)-star Len Bias by cocaine overdose and former National Football League (NFL) linebacker Lawrence "LT" Taylor's struggles to maintain sobriety to prolong his football career. Although the consumption of these substances provides no "true" added benefit to athletes on the playing field, they are used as a mechanism to cope with the high stress environment of competitive sport. The person tends to rely on this crutch and requires increasing amounts of drugs to function on a daily basis, which can then turn into an addiction.

According to Shaffer (1986, 1997), addiction is an insidious process that an individual is powerless to control, propelling the affected to act in ways contrary to society's values and beliefs, and possibly progressing to obsession and maladaptive action. The three characteristics of addition are: (1) behavior that is motivated by emotions ranging from craving to compulsion (mild desire to powerful repeating pattern of action due to an overpowering impulse); (2) continued involvement with the drug in spite of adverse social, psychological, or biological consequences; and (3) loss of control (a subjective sense that one can no longer control one's behavior). Furthermore, addictive behaviors have a tendency to be ego–syntonic, where the actions are experienced as consistent with a sense of self, and are not perceived to be the cause of personal problems. However, psychiatric illnesses are likely to be experienced as ego–dystonic or ego–alien, as if the alterego of oneself were taking control against one's will, or directing behaviors toward undesirable ends. Nonetheless, an addict can become so engrossed in their self-damaging behavior that their actions may lead to legal problems.

The legal ramifications of having a positive drug test or being arrested by the local authorities for drug charges vary according to individual sport regulating bodies and state laws. However, the inconsistencies of the judicial process raise concerns about whether professional athletes receive preferential treatment when found to be using. Whether this is caused by a lack of oversight by the self-regulatory groups is highly debatable. The International Olympic Committee formed the World Anti-Doping Agency (WADA) to counter claims that its drug policies were designed for self-preservation (Roberts, 2005). Some professional leagues, such as Major League Soccer (MLS) and the NFL, already have relatively stringent drug and doping policies in effect. However, others, especially the MLB, are designing stricter policies against use of illicit drugs and doping, but there still remain major loopholes due to ongoing negotiations between the league and the player's unions. Doping regulation is mired by legitimate legal concerns by the athletes, including the concepts of athlete rights, burden of proof and due process. With the infamous and biased 2007 Mitchell Report, the 409-page report written by former senator George Mitchell after investigating the involvement of steroids in the MLB, and the Senate's continued involvement in prominent steroid cases, the United States government has tried to take a lead role in mitigating the perceived substance abuse epidemic in sports by attempting to legislate new laws addressing the issue.

The prospect of fame and fortune are among the leading factors that influence athletes to use substances. These factors usually override both legal and medical pitfalls that may arise while an athlete is using performance-enhancing drugs. The actual or perceived benefits drive the athlete to continue their drug habits, often to the detriment of their health. With fortunes to be made in supplying athletes with substances, both illicit and for doping, it is no surprise that trafficking and distribution of substances is dominated by organized crime, multinational pharmaceutical companies, both legitimate (e.g., BALCO) and clandestine, and even rogue governments; with physicians, pharmacists, other athletes and the Internet playing a major role in athletes' relative ease of access to these substances. With new developments in masking techniques for steroid users, gene doping and designer street drugs, all parties involved, including lawyers, physicians and administrators, must continue to increase their knowledge base to be effective in their endeavors to control substance use in athletes. This chapter will discuss the historical perspective of drug use among athletes, elaborate on the reasons athletes use substances, and detail both specific performance-enhancing and recreational drugs.

HISTORICAL PERSPECTIVE

As chronicled by the famous Greek physician and writer, Galen, ancient Olympic participants ate sheep's testicles, a source of testosterone, to boost strength and increase aggression. The athletes of the classical era also used substances derived from plants including hemp, kava, opium, ginseng root, "ma huang" (ephedra), *Strychnos nux vomica* (strychnine tree), and hallucinogenic mushrooms. Athletes would eat and drink almost any concoction believed to augment their prowess, often in spite of not knowing if the product had only a placebo effect or was potentially toxic. The prohibition of paganism, decreed by the Roman emperor Theodosius I, after declaring Christianity the imperial religion in 380 AD, terminated the "hedonistic" Olympic Games following the 393 AD tournament (Buti & Fridman, 2001).

As antiquity advanced towards the contemporary era, the near simultaneous birth of modern science and sport ushered in more sophisticated, progressive forms of doping. During the eighteenth and nineteenth centuries, the Industrial Revolution with its mass production increased the amount of leisure time available for the expanding middle class. Spectator sports became an inexpensive form of entertainment for the masses. With the rebirth of competitive sport, including the restart of the modern day Summer Olympics in 1896, the desire to win at all costs underwent a resurgence. At the Third Olympic Games in St. Louis in 1904, Thomas J. Hicks was given multiple doses of strychnine mixed with brandy by his assistants after he was found trailing in the marathon race. He rallied to win the gold medal, but collapsed soon after completing the race. Had physicians not been present at the finish line, he may not have lived (Martin & Gynn, 2000). The intensification of stimulant development and utilization preceded World War II, with the European powers manufacturing drugs used by military personnel to increase or maintain alertness, counteract fatigue, boost endurance, increase productivity and to cause euphoria. Synthetic amphetamines permeated the competitive realm in the 1940s and 1950s, especially in endurance sports, such as cycling and track events. It was not until the "Golden Age of Steroid Chemistry" that athletes turned to the use of synthetic forms of testosterone to increase muscle mass, strength and endurance

(Schwarz et al., 1999). Although it was rumored German athletes used partially-synthetic steroid preparations for the 1936 Olympics (Francis & Coplon, 1990), Soviet Union competitors, most notably their weightlifting teams, had began using anabolic steroids systematically following World War II. Once the United States weightlifting team physician, Dr John Ziegler, was notified of his opponent's use of synthetic testosterone, he decided to study its effects on his team. Ziegler gave the first mass-produced anabolic steroid, methandrostenalone, to the entire team in preparation of the 1960 Rome Olympic Games. Nonetheless, his team lost to the Soviets, as their program had trumped the United States by using the next generation of anabolic performance enhancers (Verroken, 2000).

In order to preserve the integrity of competitive sport, futile attempts to prohibit the use of performance-enhancing drugs were made by the formation of international sport syndicates, such as the International Association of Athletic Federation (IAAF: formerly known as International Amateur Athletic Federation) in 1928 (Buti & Fridman, 2001). The federations declared bans on specific substances, but had no method of detecting if an athlete was using them. Unsophisticated urine drug testing began in the 1950s, but the dishonest athlete could easily calculate clearance times of the exogenous substance's metabolites and discontinue their use prior to the specific competition's testing schedule (typically immediately before or after the event). The amphetamine-precipitated deaths of two cyclists in the heat of competition, Knut Jensen (1960 Olympic Games) and Tom Simpson (1967 Tour de France), galvanized the international sports organizations to institute more specific bylaws, improve testing and sanction those who used banned substances.

Among the first to introduce mandated drug testing was the International Olympic Committee (IOC) in both the winter and summer Olympics of 1968. During the aforementioned Summer Games in Mexico City, Hans-Gunnar Liljenwall, a Swedish modern pentathlete, was forced to return his bronze medal after an elevated blood alcohol reading following his drinking of "two beers" prior to the pistol shooting competition. The IOC initiated comprehensive testing, where every athlete was examined, substituting the previous testing of only random athletes in every event, and finally added steroids to the list of banned substances in 1972 and 1976, respectively. The IOC and other federations were aware of the apparent anabolic steroid use in sport prior to the mid-1970s; however, reliable testing was not developed until 1976 by Manfred Donike. Despite the bans and refined steroid testing, the East German Olympic Team's steroid use, typified by the masculinization of their triumphant women's swim team (also known as the "Wonder Girls"), went undetected in the 1970s and 1980s. Under "State Plan 14.25," athletes were surreptitiously administered high doses of a steroid, Oral Turinabol, by their coaches and trainers. Following the reunification of Germany in 1990, the East German clandestine government plan was discovered. The comprehensiveness of the project included research into timing the administration of the steroid and other

TABLE 18.1 The 2009 Prohibited List per the World Anti-Doping Agency

Alcohol	Banned
Anabolic steroids/agents	Banned
Cannabinoids	Banned
Hormone modulators such as growth hormone, EPO, aromatase inhibitors	Banned
Beta blockers	Banned
Beta-2 agonists	Banned
Dietary supplements	Most banned
Diuretics and other masking agents	Banned
Glucocorticoids	Banned
Narcotics	Banned
Prohibited methods (blood doping, gene therapy)	Banned
Stimulants	Banned

various techniques to have their athletes illegitimately pass drug tests (Ungerleider, 2001).

The infamous 1988 Olympic doping scandal involving Canadian Ben Johnson's use of the anabolic steroid stanozolol prior to his 100 meter race victory over American Carl Lewis, and the unraveling of Eastern Germany's plan, were the impetuses in the design of the 1994 Lausanne Agreement, a statement of intention to consolidate the divided sports organizations (De Rose, 2008). It was not until after the 1998 Tour de France debacle, where French police officers found anabolic steroids, erythropoietin and other doping paraphernalia in the car of the Festina Cycling Team, that the different sports, sports federations, governments and the IOC reconvened at Lausanne, Switzerland, to draft a proposal to form the World Anti-Doping Agency (WADA). This private, non-governmental organization was established on 10 November 1999 to centralize, standardize and unify the anti-doping efforts across sports and countries. Table 18.1 details the WADA's list of prohibited substances as of 2009. In preparation for the Summer Olympics return to Athens, Greece, the following year, in 2003, WADA enacted the "World Anti-Doping Code," with: "the purpose to protect the athlete's fundamental right to participate in doping-free sport," and: "to ensure harmonized, coordinated and effective anti-doping programs at the international and national level with regard to detection, deterrence and prevention of doping" (WADA, 2003).

OVERVIEW

Since the advent of competitive sports, athletes have tried to gain an advantage over their competitors. One such advantage included the use of performance-enhancing drugs to allow athletes to extend their skills beyond their natural capabilities. In modern times, when the use of such exogenous substances has been made illegal, many athletes often make headline news on either the confession of or the determination of using performance-enhancing drugs through laboratory testing, which can cause professional disgrace. Because of the arguably controversial nature of performance-enhancing drugs, its effects on using and non-using athletes, and its meaning to sports and medicine in and of themselves, this topic is significant.

FACTORS INFLUENCING ATHLETES USE OF SUBSTANCES

The financial incentives for taking performance-enhancing drugs are significant and enticing. Despite never having publicly admitted to taking exogenous substances, it is rumored that Mark McGwire, a former Major League Baseball player, used human growth hormone, a performance enhancer. His salary increased as his batting average grew, with a salary starting at $60,000 in 1986 (and a batting average of 0.189) to $11 million in 2001 (and a batting average of 0.305 the previous year). Likewise, Terry Bolea, more famously known as Hulk Hogan, admitted to steroid use in 1993 when it was still legal. He earned a reported $2 to $3 million per year with the World Wrestling Federation in the 1980s, $4 to $12 million per year with World Championship Wrestling in the 1990s and approximately $250,000 for each television appearance.

Beside the conspicuous nature of an increasing salary, the benefits of performance-enhancing drugs also spill over into the psychological realm. The competitive nature inherent in sports can influence individual peak performance, more commonly referred to as "being in the flow." Activation, concentration, confidence, motivation and preparation are all psychological components of this flow state. Activation involves psychological arousal that naturally enhances performance. Just as too much activation can be detrimental to the flow state when it crosses into anxiety, apathy can negatively impact peak performance, as well. Concentration, or focusing on the task at hand, comprises sustaining alertness, flexibility to shifting stimuli or internal cues, and prioritizing the steps required to win. Both the desire for success and the fear of failure affect confidence and motivation. Also, athletes can improve their performance by being prepared, which encompasses a variety of tasks, such as developing game plans or taking care of their health (Kirker, 2000).

In his 1992 book, *Death in the Locker Room II: Drugs and Sports*, Robert Goldman's often-cited survey (although never submitted to a peer review), demonstrates athletes drive to win. In the survey Goldman asked two questions of aspiring Olympians. First, "if you were offered a banned performance-enhancing drug that guarantees that you would win an Olympic medal and you would not be caught, would you take it?" Incredibly 195 out of 198 athletes said "yes." Second, "would you take a performance-enhancing drug with a guarantee that you will not be caught, you will win every competition for the next five years, but will then die from the adverse effects of the substance?" Still 103 out of 198 athletes said "yes" (Calfee & Fadale, 2006).

Athletes, as a group, function in a position of social privilege and/or higher social status, therefore undergoing more intense scrutiny by the public and also a degree of segregation and resulting isolation (Harvey, 1999). College athletes, mostly due to the time constraints placed on them of the need to maintain their GPA's and excel in the intense physical demands of their sport, are less likely to be involved in nonathletic activities and therefore their primary social support network is compromised of others in sport, such as coaches, staff and fellow athletes. Balancing this set of demands of being a student and athlete while growing and trying to figure out one's life partly results in excessive stress and anxiety. There are no studies specifically proving this theory, but it would seem logical for athletes to participate in some form of stress relief and subsequent coping behavior.

Athletes at any level are not exempt from succumbing to the risks of alcohol and other related problems similar to those of general public, such as being male, belonging to a fraternity or sorority, strong family history of alcohol abuse/dependence, peer influence (Martens et al., 2006). McDuff and Baron (2005) correctly point out that the reasons for athletes to begin use of drugs such as alcohol, cocaine, marijuana and other club drugs may be to "fit in" or boost self-confidence, produce pleasure or simply "escape," however, their continued use may be the product of psychological and/or physiological dependence. There is little definitive data available regarding whether the use of performance-enhancing steroids at doses between 2 and 100 times the physiological dose has typical motivation for continued use, such as persistent physical benefits of endurance and increased muscle mass, or other psychological effects not yet identified. Little reliable knowledge exists related to the unique role of the athlete and the surrounding athletic world and its contribution to athlete substance abuse, making this an arena in great need of exploration with well-designed studies.

PERFORMANCE-ENHANCING DRUGS

In order to understand the appeal of performance-enhancing drugs, it is necessary to describe the pharmacology and physiology of these substances, including their detrimental effects, both physically and psychologically.

Anabolic Steroids

Anabolic androgenic steroids (AAS) are synthetic derivatives, similar to testosterone, that have two main effects through two different pathways; the anabolic pathway, affecting muscle mass; and the androgenic pathway, impacting male traits. The anabolic pathway results in the generation of increased muscle mass, decreased body fat and increased size of the organs involved in oxygenation and energy metabolism, such as the heart, liver and kidneys. The androgenic properties result in development and enhancement of male traits, such as distribution of male body hair, changes in testicular size and deepening of the voice (Hall & Hall, 2005). The theoretical mechanisms of action of anabolic steroids involve alteration of gene transcription at the androgen receptors of skeletal muscle, which in conjunction with exercise may result in increased muscle growth, stimulation of growth hormone insulin like growth factor (IGF-1) (also important in muscle growth), and inhibition of catabolic activity by displacing cortisol from glucocorticoid receptors (Evans, 2004; Hall & Hall, 2005).

The cognitive and behavioral effects of AAS (described in the past by Brown Sequard as "increased intellect," now better known as the "steroid rush"), comprise enhanced mood with increased euphoria, aggressiveness and a feeling of quicker recovery and increased level of intensity while on the drug (Hall & Hall, 2005). The main current therapeutic indications for AAS include male endocrine and hypothalamic–pituitary–gonadal dysfunction, such as male hypogonadism and growth retardation. AAS have also been used in muscle wasting syndromes like HIV (Evans, 2004; Pagonis et al., 2006). Anabolic steroids have multiple modes of administration, including topical gels and patches applied to the skin, oral agents, intramuscular or subcutaneous injection and pellet implantation under the skin (Drug Enforcement Agency, 2004). According to recent surveys, the injectable intramuscular mode of admistration is the preferred method, as up to 96% of AAS users report this method of administration (Evans, 2004). However, in reality, the majority of athletes who use AAS use more than one type of steroid at any given time, typically an oral and an injectable form; a method defined as stacking (Maravelias et al., 2005). The theoretical goal of stacking is to target multiple steroid receptor sites and maximize AAS steroid receptor binding (Hall & Hall, 2005).

The difference between the use of anabolic steroids for therapeutic purposes and recreational abuse or performance enhancement is the dosage and frequency of administration, where enhancers may use anywhere from two (sprinters) to 100 (weightlifters) times the physiological dose and may participate in drug free periods or "holidays" to limit side-effects (Hall & Hall, 2005; Drug Enforcement Agency, 2004). AAS are used in cycles of 6–12 weeks in duration with a rest period between cycles and a typically about 2–3 cycles per year of use, believed to reduce tolerance, adverse effects and detection. Another method believed to give optimal effects from AAS, while decreasing the likelihood of detection, is known as "stacking the pyramid." This method involves a progressive increase in doses and types of AAS early in the cycle, with a gradual reduction of both doses and types of AAS in the latter part of the cycle (Mottram & George, 2000; Drug Enforcement Agency, 2004). AAS use has recently filtered through to "recreational street drug" users, usually taken

TABLE 18.2 Known Side-Effects of Anabolic-Androgenic Steroids

Male Predominance	Female Predominance
Testicular atrophy	Voice deepening
Decreased spermatogenesis	Hirsuitism
Gynecomastia	Clitoral hypertrophy Male pattern baldness Amenorrhea
Psychiatric	**Reproductive**
Dependence/addiction	Decreased LH
Mood lability	Decreased FSH
Increased aggressiveness	
Dermatologic	**Hepatic**
Sebaceous cysts	Elevated AST/ALT
Alopecia	Liver masses/cancer
Acne	
Cardiac	
Hypertension	
Hypercholesterolemia	
Arrythmias	
Thrombosis	
Cardiac hypertrophy	

to counteract the anorexic and cachectic effects of some illicit drugs. AAS represents the largest growth of drugs in this class. Although there is increased support for the AAS user, it is still not considered a major psychiatric condition by the medical profession, despite AAS well-documented adverse effects and potential dangers (Graham et al., 2008).

Epidemiology

Studies estimate as many as three million Americans use AAS. A survey of community weight trainers at gyms and health clubs revealed up to 30% of participants use AAS (Evans, 1997, 2004). Many in this arena use AAS for cosmetic purposes rather than performance enhancement. "Monitoring the Future," a study sponsored by the National Institute on Drug Abuse conducted by the

University of Michigan suggests that between 1999 and 2001 anabolic steroid use reached its peak for male students from the eighth to the twelfth grades. Recent data from 2008 suggest that since the peak between 1999 and 2001, there has been a decrease in annual prevalence of use between 30% and 50%. Among eighth grader's, the prevalence is 1.2%, tenth grader's 1.4% and twelfth grader's 2.5% (www.monitoringthefuture.org). Females have an overall lower prevalence rate of use and their trend mirrors that of their male counterparts.

The 2001 NCAA study of substance abuse in college athletes, as cited by McDuff and Baron (2005), revealed an average rate of use at 1.4%, with highest rates among water polo athletes at 5%, followed football players at 3.0% and baseball players at 2.3%. In 2003 there was a 5% to 7% positive rate of urine surveys for steroids. It remains questionable as to whether this figure is an underestimation, because of the methodology of testing which included testing only once during the entire season (McDuff & Baron, 2005).

Adverse Effects

The use of multiple anabolic steroids at supraphysiological doses has potential for multiple adverse effects, some benign like acne and gynecomastia, and others more serious, such as myocardial infarction and hepatocellular damage. The most common adverse effects are gynecomastia in men, masculinization in women and reduced fertility in both. Other adverse effects include inflammatory reaction, bacterial and fungal infections at injection site, jaundice, elevation in liver enzymes, liver structural changes (such as masses), cardiac toxicity with hypertension, accelerated artherosclerosis, changes in blood clotting, and behavioral and psychiatric disturbances. Table 18.2 lists known adverse effects of anabolic androgenic steroids. Much of the knowledge regarding adverse effects is anecdotal and based on experience using AAS for therapeutic purposes. Ethical concerns limit the feasibility of trials with high doses of steroids. Since most AAS use is illegal, it is difficult to get a precise correlation between any particular AAS at any particular dose or method and corresponding adverse effects.

Hepatic Effects

Hepatic enzyme elevations (aspartate aminotransferase, alanine aminotransferase, lactate dehydrogenase) and changes in hepatic structure are commonly reported with use of the oral 17-alkylated AAS (Hall & Hall, 2005; Maravelias et al., 2005). Cholestatic jaundice, hepatocellular adenoma, hepatocellular carcinoma and peliosis hepatis (a rare form of hepatitis that has multiple blood-filled cysts which may rupture and be fatal) are other recorded complications. Elevations in hepatic enzymes and the development of cholestatic jaundice are dose-dependent, and cessation of drug use may result in regression and resolution of both including some hepatic masses. Maravelias et al. (2005) report that cholestatic jaundice may resolve within three months of cessation of AAS, and hepatic adverse effects may be decreased by engaging in drug free periods or "holidays" and avoiding 17-alkylated AAS. Death related to AAS-induced hepatotoxicity is rare.

Cardiac Effects

The adverse effects of long-term AAS are likely most severe on the cardiac system. Cardiac adverse effects of AAS are precipitated through multiple mechanisms, including alterations in lipid profile predisposing to premature artherosclerosis, alterations of the blood clotting cascade predisposing to thrombus formation and hypertension which may lead to myocardial infarction, left ventricular hypertrophy and arrythmias, and sudden death.

Lipid alterations are predominantly increases in low density liproprotein (LDL) levels and decreases in high density lipoprotein (HDL) levels, which are not dependent on dose, but instead are dependent on duration of use. Some authors report that the most significant effect of decreased HDL is noted within one week of iniation of AAS use and may recover within weeks to months of cessation of steroid use (Kutscher et al., 2002; Hartgens & Kuipers, 2004). The increased LDL levels may contribute to accelerated coronary artherosclerosis with long-term use (Sullivan et al., 1998).

Anabolic steroids, specifically 17-alpha alkylated steroids, may predispose to thrombus formation by increasing procoagulant factors such as antithrombin III, protein C and plasminogen activator levels (Sullivan et al., 1998). Platelet aggregation increase was demonstrated in elderly patients who were found to have multiple thrombi during cardiac catheterization for myocardial infarction while being treated for aplastic anemia with AAS. Other cases involve athletes as young as a 22-year-old power lifter with AAS use, who had hyperlipidemia and a myocardial infarction, with alterations in his platelet aggregation levels (Sullivan et al., 1998). This combination of increased plaque formation with decreased HDL and increased LDL, enhanced platelet aggregation and increased procoagulant factors, may precipitate coronary thrombus formation and subsequent myocardial ischemia.

Hypertension is theorized to be a result of increased blood volume and fluid retention. The evidence is essentially inconclusive as to how AAS directly increases blood pressure and in some studies the elevation is minimal to nonexistent.

Reproductive adverse effects include decreased libido and changes in fertility. Libido in both males and females is thought to be influenced in part by testosterone. High levels of circulating anabolic steroids result in decreased natural testosterone secretion and therefore reduced libido (Mottram & George, 2000). With chronic high dose anabolic steroid use decreased sperm counts and even azoospermia have been documented.

Gynecomastia occurs in male athletes due to the development of mammary tissue. The most common cause of gynecomastia development is due to the fact that anabolic steroids are converted by hepatic aromatase enzymes to estradiol, which then contributes to the development of mammary tissue (Mottram & George, 2000).

Psychiatric Effects

The most prominent psychiatric features noted in a study performed by Pope and Katz (1999) after use of supraphysiological doses (greater than 1,000 mg/week), included manic-like presentations with irritability, aggressiveness, euphoria, grandiose beliefs, hyperactivity, impulsivity and reckless behavior. Other known psychiatric symptoms include: acute psychoses; exacerbation of tics; and the development of acute confusional states (Hall & Hall, 2005). The overall theory remains that the occurrence and seriousness of mood disturbances are dose-dependent (Hartgens & Kuipers, 2004). AAS dependency and withdrawal may develop with continued use (although still not considered a major psychiatric disorder classified in the *Diagnostic and Statistical Manual of Mental Disorders IV–TR*). Acute anabolic steroid withdrawal symptoms may include anxiety, irritability, insomnia, hot flushes, sweats, chills, anorexia, myalgia, nausea, committing, pilorection, tachycardia and hypertension (Maravelias et al., 2005). Other studies suggest that depression, anhedonia, impaired concentration and even suicidal tendencies may occur during the acute withdrawal period (Hall et al., 2005).

Central Nervous System Stimulants

Central nervous system (CNS) stimulants have been used for thousands of years to combat fatigue and alter mood, as exemplified by the Incas of South American, who chewed the leaves of the coca plant whose extract is used to produce cocaine. In 1884 Sigmund Freud in *"Über Coca,"* wrote that cocaine causes: "exhilaration and lasting euphoria, which in no way differs from the normal euphoria of the healthy person ... You perceive an increase of self-control and possess more vitality and capacity for work" (Freud, 1884). Athletes possess a perceived benefit of increased alertness, awareness, responsiveness and overall ability to function under the influence of ergogenic substances like cocaine, caffeine, ephedra and amphetamines.

Cocaine

Cocaine is a highly addictive and potent CNS stimulant. Its recreational use is widespread and its addictive potential is mediated through dopamine release, stimulating the mesocortical and mesolimbic systems; the so-called pleasure and reward centers of the brain (George, 2000). Cocaine's most potent known action is inhibition of reuptake of dopamine into the presynaptic terminals of dopamine releasing neurons. Cocaine may be snorted, smoked or injected. The most popular route of administration is snorting which produces peak effect in 5–15 minutes, lasting for as long as an hour (George, 2000), but smoking cocaine has gained popularity, due to its relatively inexpensive, rapid, short (minutes), euphoric effect. Typical physiologic effects of cocaine include constricted blood vessels, dilated pupils, increased temperature, heart rate and blood pressure. It also increases motor activity and is a potent inducer of euphoria. For the athlete, studies have shown that cocaine does not enhance performance. In particular, cocaine has no effect on running times at doses lower than 12.5 mg/kg, and above this dose actually decreases running time. The theory regarding cocaine's effects of impaired endurance as seen with runners is theorized to be due to increased glycogen degradation, and increased lactate production without consistent increased catecholamines, resulting in early fatigue (George, 2000; Avois et al., 2006). In addition, cocaine may induce skeletal muscle vasoconstriction, reducing oxygen delivery, metabolism, strength, reaction time and stimulating glycogen breakdown (George, 2000; Avois et al., 2006). Despite clear evidence that there is no improvement in endurance performance cocaine continues to be misused in sport. It may be likely that cocaine is beneficial in settings where short duration, high intensity activities are performed. Athletes likely continue to use cocaine despite its detrimental effects due to its cognitive effects of heightened arousal and increased alertness.

Adverse effects associated with cocaine use include tolerance, requiring athletes to use increasingly higher doses and resulting in cognitive symptoms of irritability, restlessness, anxiety, paranoia and psychosis. Some athletes complain of reduced athletic performance due to perceptual misjudgments and time disorientation (Avois, 2006). Other fatal adverse effects include arrythmias and hypertension, which result in myocardial infarction and cerebral vasospasm causing stroke, cerebral vascular spasm or rupture, with subsequent permanent neurological deficits such as weakness and seizures. The combination of alcohol and/or other drugs and cocaine, used to treat the withdrawal syndrome (dysphoric mood, fatigue, vivid, unpleasant dreams, insomnia or hypersomnia, increased appetite, psychomotor agitation or retardation) associated with cocaine may have lethal cardiac and respiratory consequences (American Psychiatric Association. (2000). Substance Related Disorders. Diagnostic and Statistical Manual of Mental Disorders (4th ed. text revision). Washington, D.C.).

Caffeine

Caffeine (1,3,7-trimethyxanthine) produces CNS stimulation by blocking adenosine activity at the receptors, speeding up activity. The effects of caffeine in reducing fatigue and increasing wakefulness and alertness have been recognized for many centuries and hold a worldwide social acceptance that does not carry the stigma branded to similar other supplements and ergogenic aids. It is found naturally in coffee beans, tea, cocoa beans and cola nuts. The level of caffeine in foods varies greatly depending on preparation. Caffeine has no documented nutritional value; however, it is valued for its ergogenic effectiveness. Caffeine's systemic effects include bronchodilation of alveoli, vasodilation of blood vessels, neural activation of muscle contraction, increased blood filtration in the kidneys, catecholamine secretion and lypolysis (Sokmen et al., 2008). In trained and untrained individuals, caffeine also increases oxygen uptake, cardiac output, ventilation, circulating levels of epinephrine, metabolic rate and fat oxidation (Sokmen et al., 2008; Juhn, 2003).

The cognitive and mood effects of caffeine include increased mental alertness, decreased tiredness and energetic arousal, which may provide a competitive edge in sports performance. The most attractive route of administration is caffeine capsules. The literature remains limited at this time regarding the ergogenic effective of other forms of caffeine (Sokmen et al., 2008). The evidence of the ergogenic benefits of caffeine are pronounced for aerobic exercise. In a double-bind cross-over study where male triathletes and cyclists in a one-hour cycling time trial consumed three different doses of caffeine: 2.1 mg/kg, 3.2 mg/kg and 4.5 mg/kg, improvement was noted in time trial performance with all doses. Of note, the highest dose was no more efficacious than the middle dose (Kovacs et al., 1998; Juhn, 2003). This is likely a result of the "inverted U" dose–response curve identified for the ergogenic and cognitive benefits. Sokmen et al. (2008) suggest that peak effects of ergogenic symptoms may be reached over a range of doses, rather than at a single dose, and after reaching doses higher than the peak range may have negative effects on cognition and mood.

Overall, Sokmen et al. (2008) reveal that caffeine use sustains exercise intensity during heavy and intense endurance training, helps the athlete remain mentally focused, improves visual vigilance, improve reaction time and self-reported fatigue, along with lowering pain perception. However, these benefits appear to depend on the quantity of acute caffeine intake, tolerance to caffeine and cessation from caffeine. Adverse effects associated with caffeine include: mild acute effects such as nervousness; irritability; insomnia; gastrointestinal distress; and difficulty concentrating (George, 2000). The main symptom of caffeine withdrawal, which typically begins within 12 hours of the last dose, is a severe headache, theoretically the result of vasodilatation of cerebral blood vessels. Performance may decrease during withdrawal. Caffeine reaches its peak at 30 to 75 minutes after ingestion and has a half-life of four to five hours. The greatest benefit is seen if caffeine is ingested at the latest three hours before power sprint and short endurance events, and one hour before prolonged endurance events. Disqualification limits by the Internal Olympic Committee are a urinary caffeine level exceeding 12 micrograms/ml and in the United States-based National Collegiate Athletic Association 15 microgram/ml.

Ephedrine and Pseudoephedrine

Ephedra alkaloids are naturally occurring CNS stimulants obtained from several Ephedra species, and are popular components of nutritional supplements. The Chinese have used Ephedra species, also known as ma huang, for over 5,000 years and the Han Dynasty (207 BC–220 AD) documented the use of ma huang as a stimulant and an antiasthmatic (Abourashed et al., 2003). Purified forms of the ephedra species include ephedrine, pseudoephedrine, norephedrine, methylephedrine, norpseudoephedrine and methylpseudoephedrine (Avois et al., 2006).

Ephedrine is a sympathomimetic agonist, enhancing the release of noradrenaline stimulating the nonselective alpha and beta adrenergic receptors (Abourashed et al., 2003; Avois et al., 2006). The systemic effects of alpha and beta adrenergic stimulation include increased heart rate and cardiac output, peripheral vasoconstriction, bronchodilation, appetite suppression and increase in metabolic rate of adipose tissue. The central nervous system effects are due to its stimulant properties decreasing fatigue and allowing for improved performance in a fatigued state (Lombardo, 2004). Pseudoephedrine's most popular use is to relieve nasal decongestion due to its vasoactive properties. Previously available supplements include Metabolife 356 and Ripped Fuel, now banned since 2004. The stimulant and sympathomimetic effects of ephedrine alkaloids have an attractive ergogenic potential.

Ephedrine has typically been used by athletes to provide increased energy and aid in weight loss, improving both appearance and performance. Bell et al. (2001) and Juhn (2003) hypothesized that ephedrine improved anaerobic performance due to increased arousal, as opposed to increased muscle metabolism. However, the greatest benefit is seen with a combination of ephedrine and caffeine, where athletes seek to enhance acute intense exercise (Bell et al., 2001). Other studies evaluating the use of ephedrine, pseudoephedrine and phenylpropanolamine alone at usual doses have inconsistent performance-enhancing benefits (Avois et al., 2006). The use of ephedrine and pseudoephedrine for purposes of performance enhancement is demonstrated in the study by Bents and Marsh (2006), where over half of the hockey athletes (51.8%) confirmed stimulant use before a hockey game or practice, and about half of the respondents (48.5%) reported having used ephedra at least once to improve athletic performance. Additionally, 17.4% reported using pseudoephedrine to improve performance in the 30 days prior to the administration of the survey. National Collegiate Athletic Association (NCAA) data from 2001 suggests a 3.9% incidence of ephedrine use in the past 12 months (Green et al., 2001).

Common side-effects of ephedrine are headache, hypertension, palpitations, tachycardia, dizziness, irritability, anxiety, tremor and psychosis. At doses ranging from 20 to 60 mg per day, within the range of many over-the-counter products, related adverse effects in a 22-month review primarily included cardiovascular events with arrythmias, myocardial infarction, sustained hypertension and stroke resulting in permanent disability and death (Haller & Benowitz 2000). The joint use of ephedrine and caffeine can augment adverse cardiovascular and CNS effects.

There are significant concerns regarding the use of food and nutritional supplements containing ephedra alkaloids, since their over-the-counter status subjects them to fewer regulations and they have the potential for serious side-effects. The medical use of ephedrine is tolerated by the World Anti-Doping Agency (WADA) and the International Olympic Committee (IOC) at therapeutic levels, however urine concentrations greater than 10 micrograms/ml are considered positive (Avois et al., 2006; WADA Code, 2009).

The use of a new class of stimulants known as Modafinal and Adrafinil, designed initially for the treatment of narcolepsy and hypersomnia, has increased. Compared with amphetamines, modafanil is thought to have a low abuse liability and fewer side-effects such as insomnia, anxiety and agitation, due it's mechanism of action. Modafinil acts by its dopamine-releasing action in the nucleus accumbens, and although weak and dose-dependent, it still carries an abuse potential. Modafinil's arousal properties are due to the inhibition of the reuptake of noradrenaline by the noradrenergic terminals on sleep-promoting neurons of the ventrolateral preoptic nucleus.

Creatine

Creatine is an amino acid composed of glycine, arginine and methionine. Creatine is acquired through a diet of meat and fish, and is naturally produced in the liver, kidney and pancreas. Up to 95% of the body's creatine is stored in skeletal muscle. Daily creatine requirement is two grams, half acquired through diet and the other half through *in vivo* production (Metzel et al., 2001). During short-burst, high-intensity activity, adenosine triphosphate (ATP), the main source of energy for muscles, loses a phosphate becoming adenosine diphosphate (ADP). The phosphate required to return to ATP is stored in muscle as creatine phosphate. The availability of creatine phosphate is the rate-limiting step in short, high-intensity activities. The more creatine in the muscle, the more creatine phosphate is present, and therefore the more efficient the regeneration of ATP from ADP, resulting in more energy (Metzel et al., 2001).

Theoretically, increased creatine would result in improved performance in repetitive, short-burst high-intensity activity. Creatine does not improve endurance related activities, because ATP required for energy is available from creatine phosphate for only the first 10 seconds from initiation of exercise. Following the first 10 seconds of exercise, the body depends on glycolysis and glycogenolysis for ATP (Brudnak, 2004; Calfee & Fadale, 2006). Creatine dosing regimens include 20 grams per day for one week, then a maintenance dose of 2 to 5 g per day. The benefits of creatine are ergogenic for repetitive bouts of high-intensity anaerobic exercise which is not mass-dependent and limited single repetition strength training. Its effect is highly variable between individuals, with up to 30% of nonresponders (Calfee & Fadale, 2006). In a well-controlled setting, Volek et al. revealed that after 12 weeks of creatine use in recreational weightlifters, those athletes who were taking creatine had significant increases in fat-free body mass, bench press maximal lift and peak power production in sets of repeated jump squats (Volek et al., 1999; Calfee & Fadale, 2006). In collegiate creatine users, the most common effects athletes experienced were increased strength and muscle size (LaBotz & Smith, 1999). A summary of 31 studies on sprint performance showed that creatine may improve athletic performance in laboratory settings, but most findings indicated no benefit on the field (Ahrent, 2001). Creatine research generally shows a positive benefit on performance, with the greatest benefits seen in increasing strength and outcomes in short duration, anaerobic events.

Creatine was introduced in 1992 and since then has become one of the most popular nutritional supplements on the market. In 2000, estimated sales were more than \$300 million in the United States (Tokish et al., 2004). Several prevalence studies of its use among college athletes quote usage of 41% to 48% among men compared to 4% among women (LaBotz & Smith, 1999; Tokish et al., 2004). Of all the athletes who had used creatine, 30% had first used it in high school (LaBotz & Smith, 1999). Metzel et al. (2001) report creatine use among young athletes from sixth to twelfth grade at 5.6%, also defining an increasing trend of use with each grade level so that a twelfth grader's use almost parallels that of college athletes, at about 44%.

Adverse effects include diarrhea, nausea, vomiting, muscle cramps and weight gain. Calfee & Fadale (2006) report that weight gain of 1.6 to 2.4 kg may be experienced. Creatine is commonly thought to lead to dehydration, but there have been no studies that have demonstrated this side-effect (Tokish et al., 2004). Concerns regarding adverse renal effects remain unsubstantiated at this time after researchers examined renal function of patients who had been using creatine for as long as five years and found no detrimental effects (Poortmans & Francaux, 1999; Ahrent, 2001). There is insufficient data available regarding the long-term effects of creatine, since most research to date has examined creatine use over three months or less and research regarding creatine supplementation effects in other tissues, such as the brain and cardiac muscle where it is stored, is lacking (Juhn, 2003; Tokish et al., 2004).

Creatine remains a legal nutritional supplement in amateur and professional sports. Trainers, physicians, parents and athletes less than 18-years-old should be advised not to use creatine supplementation. The short-term and particularly the long-term health risks in adolescents and preadolescents are unknown.

Growth Hormone and Insulin-Like Growth Factor-1

Human growth hormone (hGH) is an endogenous compound produced by the anterior pituitary. It is generally known to have anabolic functions, increasing protein synthesis and increasing lipid metabolism and bone growth. Patients deficient in growth hormone are short in stature, whereas those with excess in growth hormone have gigantism or acromegaly. Current therapeutic indications for hGH use include Turner Syndrome and Adult Growth Hormone Deficiency syndrome. Due to its potential for enhanced growth, growth hormone has become attractive to athletes as a potential ergogenic aid.

Human growth hormone is a 191-residue, 22 kDa peptide released from the anterior pituitary. For many years, hGH isolated from human pituitaries was used as therapy for growth-hormone deficient patients. However, since the advent of recombinant growth hormone (rhGH), it has now become the major source of the hormone. Factors influencing release of hGH include exercise, stress, growth-hormone releasing hormone and sleep (Tokish et al., 2004; Holt & Sönksen, 2008). The half-life of growth hormone is about thirteen minutes. Recombinant human growth hormone (rhGH) is administered intermittently via subcutaneous injection. The estimated bioavailability of rhGH is 50–70% because of degradation at the site of injection (Holt & Sönksen, 2008). There is quicker clearance of rhGH in women, due to a higher body fat content, which has higher numbers of growth hormone receptors (Vahl et al., 1997). It is believed that athletes are using doses that are up to 10 times those used for therapeutic purposes (Holt & Sönksen, 2008).

GH remains attractive to athletes because of its potential for increased skeletal muscle and concomitant loss of fat. Studies in patients with hypopitutiarism and growth hormone deficiency who receive rhGH have repeatedly had a normalization of body composition, with increased lean body mass. This improved body composition results in a feeling of "increased energy" and performance (Cuneo et al., 1992; Holt & Sönksen, 2008). It however remains controversial as to whether growth hormone administration enhances performance for a normal healthy adult. In acromegalic states, there is typically increased strength in the first few years; however, subsequently there is development of myopathy. In reality, most abusers of growth hormone likely also use insulin and anabolic steroids in addition to growth hormone, making it difficult to determine which effects are related to which drug. Growth hormone exerts most of its anabolic actions through the generation of circulating IGF-1, predominantly produced in the liver (Le Roith et al., 2001). Anabolic effects are on protein metabolism inhibiting whole body protein breakdown and stimulating protein synthesis. These effects are mediated through serum insulin and adequate amino acids, and having adequate amino acid supply. In insulin-deficient states there is increased rate of protein degradation in cardiac and skeletal muscle.

The clinical knowledge regarding side-effects growth hormone is well-known from its therapeutic use in growth hormone deficient patients and in the setting of acromegaly. Side-effects include the development of insulin resistance, cardiomyopathy related to increased intracellular calcium and alteration of cardiomyocytes, arrythmias and increased sodium absorption resulting in fluid retention contributing to hypertension (Lombardi et al., 2006).

Cannabis

Products of *Cannabis sativa*, such as marijuana, hashish and sensemilla, each obtained from a different part of the plant, are among the most popular illicit drugs throughout the world. The psychoactive properties of cannabinoids are due to delta-9-tetrahydrocannbinal (THC) (Campos et al., 2003). A synthetic derivative of THC, Dronabinol, prescribed in a capsulated form as Marinol, has been proven to treat anorexia and weight loss associated with AIDS, and nausea and vomiting associated with cancer therapy, with very good results (Campos et al., 2003).

The rate of absorption of THC by the lungs is very high and maximal blood concentration may be reached within 3–8 minutes after smoking a marijuana cigarette. The onset of action in the CNS is 20 minutes and peak effect is 2–4 hours with 4–6 hour's duration of action for psychoactive effects (Campos et al., 2003). THC is biotransformed in the liver to 11-OH-THC and carboxy-THC, the main metabolite found in urine.

The recreational features for which cannabis is used are its induction of a feeling of euphoria with decreased anxiety, increased sociability and resulting alleviation of stress. The physical and psychological effects of cannabis vary, with lower doses inducing mild intoxication, sedation and drowsiness, reduced inhibition, slower reaction time and memory problems. At high doses, amnesia, hallucinations, alteration of perception and reality and marked reduction in concentration may occur. Other effects include anxiety, asthenia, facial flushing, palpitations and tachycardia (Ashton, 2001; Campos et al., 2003; Saugy et al., 2006). Users have the potential for elevation of mood, but may also experience a dysphoric reaction, becoming stressed, anxious, depressed, paranoid and psychotic (Ashton, 2001). Due to the CNS and physical side-effects or sedation and decreased reaction time, cannabis will not enhance performance and is considered ergolytic (has a detrimental effect on physical performance) rather than ergogenic. Eichner (1993) documents the decrease in psychomotor skills, reaction time and standing steadiness in cyclists and athletes who were given 215 mg/kg of THC orally.

There is potential that cannabis use may indirectly improve performance by decreasing anxiety and therefore cannabis may be considered a doping agent, although most of the effects of cannabis use are absolutely incompatible with athletic activities (Saugy et al., 2006). Lorente et al. (2005) evaluated the use of cannabis among French university students in relation to athletic activity and non-sporting events. They reveal that the relaxing properties of cannabis were used to enhance performance, particularly in athletes involved in "sliding sports" like windsurfing, sailing, snowboarding, skiing and surfing. Sliding sports and drug use may be motivated by the same sensation-seeking behavior where athletes desire a thrill or a feeling of exhilaration and the psychoactive effects of cannabis may enhance the exhilarating experience during sliding sport performance.

Lorente et al. (2005) and Chen and Kandel (1998) suggest that cannabis use for performance enhancement was more frequent among respondents whose main motive was relaxing or forgetting problems, and less frequent among those for whom the main motive was recreational suggesting that the relaxing properties of cannabis could frequently be used to enhance performance.

Cannabis, when used regularly, may be habit forming and symptoms of withdrawal including feeling weak or tired, hypersomnia, yawning, psychomotor retardation, restlessness and depressed mood (Hasin et al., 2008). Particular care should be taken in monitoring for signs and symptoms of dependence in vulnerable players with poor support networks, high stress and anxiety related to performance, and players with prolonged or repeated injuries. Cannabis use was banned by the IOC in 1989 and a urine level in excess of 15 micrograms/L is considered positive.

Cannabis products are illegal in most countries; however, their recreational use remains highly extensive. The intent to use them for performance-enhancement will likely be of limited benefit considering the adverse CNS and other physical side-effects.

Erythropoietin and Blood Doping

Blood doping, popular since the 1960s, involves autologous transfusion of previously donated blood after a period of hematocrit recovery or through homologous transfusion from a cross-matched donor. These transfusions artificially increase the oxygen carrying capacity through increased hematocrit which provides a tremendous aerobic advantage (Tokish et al., 2004). Recombinant human erythropoietin (rEPO) has replaced blood doping. Erythropoietin (EPO) is produced naturally by the kidneys to regulate red blood cell production. It has therapeutic indications in chronic renal failure and certain anemias. rEPO is administered via a subcutaneous injection, not requiring the donation of blood and avoiding the potential risks of transfusion to achieve increased hematocrit. EPO's effect of increasing hemoglobin and therefore the body's oxygen carrying capacity makes it an attractive ergogenic aid for athletes desiring to increase endurance and enhance oxygen supply to heart and muscles.

Adverse effects are serious and sometimes fatal, including myocardial infarction, pulmonary embolism, cerebrovascular disease and thromboembolic events such as cerebral sinus thrombosis due to the increased packed red blood cell count and viscosity (Juhn, 2003; Sjöqvist et al., 2008). Other adverse effects associated with blood transfusions include infections with such pathogens like HIV and hepatitis, injection site reactions and transfusion reactions. EPO is only available under physician prescription. It is banned in all sports.

Detection Methods

A test based on the blood urine matrix (blood test performed first and confirmed by a urine test) to detect possible rEPO use was developed and introduced at the 2000 Summer Olympic Games in Sydney, Australia. In 2003 urine tests alone became the accepted procedure for detection of rEPO and other new erythropoiesis stimulating agents. Currently there are tests for homologous blood doping (blood from a compatible donor), but none for autologous blood doping (athletes own blood). WADA's current anti-doping strategy, called the "Athlete Passport," is based on following an individual athletes biological blood variables longitudinally, to detect abnormal variations of determined biological variables, in addition to traditional testing (WADA, n.d.).

Alcohol

Alcohol crosses the blood–brain barrier easily, affecting judgment, reaction time and level of alertness through brain centers of control located in the cerebellum. The motivation by athletes for alcohol consumption includes social interaction, coping and performance categories (McDuff & Baron, 2005) and differs by sport. The NCAA 2001 study shows that college athletes drink usually in a social setting for social reasons (83.9%) followed by for positive emotional impact (12.9%), coping (3%) and performance (0.2%) (NCAA, 2001). Despite the high rates of alcohol abuse by athletes and higher rates of binge drinking in athletes at 25 to 50% compared with non-athletes at 16 to 43% (Ford, 2007; NCAA, 2001), alcohol largely adversely impacts athletic performance by decreasing aerobic performance, causing higher rates of injuries, dehydration, mood instability and sensory motor system dysfunction. These symptoms are classically described as part of the "hangover effect" (Wechsler, 1998). There are a number of factors that may potentially explain the higher level of alcohol use among college athletes. Athletes are viewed as a "special population" who fulfill roles of both students and athletes. They are faced with different stressors, including balancing academic, social and sports life in addition to career concerns, social isolation, and injuries, which serve as major physical and psychological stressors, as well as having to manage success or lack of success (Wechsler et al., 1997; Ford, 2007).

CONCLUSION

Drug use to enhance performance is an undeniable complex phenomenon present in sport since the early Olympians remaining prominent today in the 21st century. Despite increasing attention and criticism of doping, the practice continues. The 'win at all costs' mentality embedded in the philosophy of athletes along with desire for social adoration and financial success it embodies are potent motivators. With increasing social scrutiny and skepticism regarding the impact of ergogenic aids on performance, a new era is emerging, where fairness, integrity, honesty and success based on hard work is in the making. The ultimate question remains as to whether doping and its associated perceived rewards of record breaking performances for the history books and it's significant monetary gain and social stature are worth the known potential pitfalls. Some opponents to the anti-doping movement suggest that nature is "not fair" and the use of performance enhancing drugs may create a level playing field. After all, inherent within the human spirit is the desire to succeed. Therefore, as long as the combination of the human spirit and the desire for fame and fortune persists, doping will likely continue. In order to maximize the potential of achieving the goal of dope free sports, there needs to be continued education of young athletes through open communication involving coaches, athletic trainers and physician emphasizing the "true spirit of sport," the importance of healthy behaviors, potential adverse effects of ergogenic aids and on developing more sophisticated methods of drug testing with a uniform anti-doping policy.

REFERENCES

(2003). *British Journal of Sports Medicine*, 37:335–338© 2003 BMJ Publishing Group Ltd. & British Association of Sport and Exercise Medicine

Abourashed, E. A., El-Alfy, A. T., Khan, I. A., & Walker, L. (2003). Ephedra in perspective – a current review. *Phytotherapy Research*, *17*, 703–712.

Ahrent, D. M. (2001). Erogenic aids: counseling the athlete. *American Family Physician*, *63*(5), 913–922.

Albert, T. (2002). Philadelphia Flyers hockey player sues team, doctor over care of injury, (May 20). Retrieved 10 April 2009 from <http://www.amaassn.org/amednews/2002/05/20/prse0520.htm/>

American College of Sports Medicine (ACSM). (1982). The use of alcohol in sports. Retrieved from http://www.acsm-msse.org/pt/pt-core/template-journal/msse/media/0682.pdf. *Medicine & Science in Sports & Exercise*, *14*(6), ix–xi.

American College of Sports Medicine (ACSM). (1987). The use of anabolic androgenic steroids in sports. Retrieved from http://www.acsm-msse.org/pt/pt-core/template-journal/msse/media/0587.pdf. *Medicine & Science in Sports & Exercise*, *19*(5), 534–539.

American College of Sports Medicine (ACSM). (2007). *About ACSM.* Retrieved 12 May 2009 from <http://www.acsm.org/AM/Template.cfm?Section=About_ACSM/>

American Medical Association. (2001). *Principles of Medical Ethics.* Retrieved 10 April 2009 from <http://www.ama-assn.org/ama1/pub/upload/mm/Code_of_Med_Eth/principles.html/>

American Psychiatric Association. (2000). *Diagnostic and Statistical Manual of Mental Disorders.* Washington, DC: American Psychiatric Association (4th ed., text revision).

Ashton, C. H. (2001). Pharmacology and effects of cannabis: a brief review. *British Journal of Psychiatry*, *178*, 101–106.

Associated Press. (2007). Hunter suspended after testing positive for phentermine, (March 8). Retrieved 12 May 2009 from <http://sports.espn.go.com/nba/news/story?id=2791107/>

Associated Press. (2007). Ex-olympian Tim Montgomery pleads guilty in multimillion dollar fraud scheme, (April 10). Retrieved 10 April 2009 from <http://www.foxnews.com/story/0,2933,264956,00.html/>

Associated Press. (2007). Olympic medallist Gatlin at Buccaneers minicamp, (May 5). Retrieved 11 April 2009 from <http://sports.espn.go.com/nfl/news/story?id=2861190/>

Associated Press. (2007). Sylvester Stallone convicted of bringing banned hormone into Australia, (May 20). Retrieved 4 April 2009 from <http://www.foxnews.com/story/0,2933,274141,00.html/>

Associated Press. (2008). Graham banned for life for role in assisting athletes with steroids, (July 15). Retrieved 11 April 2009 from <http://www.usdoj.gov/dea/agency/penalties.htm/>

Associated Press. (2008). Graham banned for life for role in assisting athletes with steroids, (July 15). Retrieved 11 April 2009, from <http://sports.espn.go.com/oly/trackandfield/news/story?id=3490949/>

Associated Press. (2009). NFL to test for more performance-enhancing drugs. Retrieved 12 May 2009 from <http://sports.espn.go.com/nfl/news/story?id=2741136/>

Audran, M., Gareau, R., Matecki, S., Durand, F., Chenard, C., Sicart, M. T., Marion, B., & Bressolle, F. (1999). Effects of erythropoietin administration in training athletes and possible indirect detection in doping control. *Medicine and Science in Sports and Exercise*, *31*(5), 639–645.

Avois, L., Robinson, N., Saudan, C., Baume, N., Mangin, P., & Saugy, M. (2006). Central nervous system stimulants and sport practice. *British Journal of Sports Medicine*, *40*(1), 16–20.

Bahrke, M. S. (1994). Internal conference on abuse and trafficking of anabolic steroids. Retrieved from http://www.drugtext.org/library/articles/945105.htm. *The Internal Journal of Drug Policy, 5*(1).

Bahrke, M. S., Yesalis, C. E., Kopstein, A. N., & Stephens, J. A. (2000). Risk factors associated with anabolic-androgenic steroid use among adolescents. *Sports Medicine, 29*(6), 397–405.

Bell, D. G., Jacobs, I., & Ellerington, K. (2001). Effect of caffeine and ephedrine ingestion on anaerobic exercise performance. *Medicine and Science in Sports and Exercise, 33*(8), 1399–1403.

Bowers, L. (2002). Abuse of performance enhancing drugs in sport. *Therapeutic Drug Monitoring, 24*(1), 178–181.

Bents, R. T., & Marsh, E. (2006). Patterns of ephedra and other stimulant use in collegiate hockey athletes. *International Journal of Sport Nutrition and Exercise Metabolism, 16*(6), 636–643.

Brown, D. K. (1986) Anti-Drug Abuse Act (1986). Retrieved 10 April 2009, from <http://www.enotes.com/major-acts-congress/anti-drug-abuse-act/>

Brudnak, M. A. (2004). Creatine: are the benefits worth the risk?. *Toxicology Letters, 150*, 123–130.

Buckley, W. E., Yesalis, C. E., Friedl, K. E., Anderson, W. A., Streit, A. L., & Wright, J. E. (1988). Estimated prevalence of anabolic steroid use among male high school seniors. *Journal of the American Medical Association, 260*, 3441–3445.

Buti, A., & Fridman, S. (2001). *Drugs, Sport and the Law*. Mudgeeraba, Qld: Scribblers Publishing.

Calfee, R., & Fadale, P. (2006). Popular ergogenic drugs and supplements in young athletes. *Pediatrics, 117*(3), 577–589. doi:10.1542/peds.2005-1429.

Campos, D. R., Yonamine, M., & de Morares Moreau, R. L. (2003). Marijuana as doping in sports. *Sports Medicine, 33*(6), 395–399.

Catlin, D. H., Fitch, K. D., & Ljungqvist, A. (2008). Medicine and science in the fight against doping in sport. *Journal of Internal Medicine, 264*(2), 99–114.

Chen, K., & Kandel, D. B. (1998). Predictors of cessation of marijuana use: an event history analysis. *Drug and Alcohol Dependence, 50*, 109–121.

Cooper, D. L. (1972). Drugs and the athlete. *Journal of the American Medical Association, 221*(9), 1007–1011.

Cuneo, R. C., Salomon, F., McGauley, G. A., & Sönksen, P. H. (1992). The growth hormone deficiency syndrome in adults. *Clinical Endocrinology, 37*, 387–397.

De Rose, E. (2008). Doping in athletes – an update. *Clinics in Sports Medicine, 27*(1), 107–130. viii–ix.

Donati, A. (2007). World traffic in doping substances. Retrieved 2 April 2009 from <http://www.wada-ama.org/rtecontent/document/Donati_Report_Trafficking_2007-03_06.pdf/>

Drug Enforcement Administration – Office of Diversion. (2005). *Rules 2005*. Retrieved 11 April 2009 from <http://www.deadiversion.usdoj.gov/fed_regs/rules/2005/fr1216.htm/>

Drug Enforcement Administration. (a). *DEA history 1970–1975*. Retrieved 12 April 2009 from <http://www.usdoj.gov/dea/pubs/history/1970-1975.pdf/>

Drug Enforcement Administration. (b). *DEA history 1990–1994*. Retrieved 10 April 2009 from <http://www.usdoj.gov/dea/pubs/history/1990-1994.pdf/>

Drug Enforcement Administration. (c). *DEA history 2003–2008*. Retrieved 12 April 2009 from <http://www.usdoj.gov/dea/pubs/history/2003-2008.pdf/>

Drug Enforcement Administration. (d). *Federal trafficking penalties*. Available at <http://www.usdoj.gov/dea/agency/penalties.htm/>

Drug Enforcement Agency, Office of Diversion Control. (2004). *Steroid abuse in today's society: a guide for understanding steroids and related substances*. Retrieved 17 May 2009 <http://www.deadiversion.usdoj.gov/pubs/brochures/steroids/professionals/index.html/>

Drug Enforcement Agency, Office of Diversion Control. (2009). *Cases against doctors*. Retrieved 12 April 2009 from <http://www.deadiversion.usdoj.gov/crim_admin_actions/index.html/>

Dublin, C. L. (1990). *Commision of Inquiry into the Use of Drugs and Banned Practices Intended to Increase Athletic Performance.* Ottowa, Canada: Canadian Government Publishing Centre.

Eichner, E. R. (1993). Ergolytic drugs in medicine and sports. *American Journal of Medicine, 94*(2), 205–211.

Elliott, V. S. (2001). Anti-doping effort looks at sports doctors. Retrieved 10 March 2009 from <http://www.ama-assn.org/amednews/2001/08/20/hlsc0820.htm/>

Epstein, R. (1995). Cases and Materials on Torts. New York, NY: Aspen Publishers, Inc.

ESPN.com News Services. (2008). Gatlin banned, won't be eligible to defend Olympic 100-meter title, (January 1). Retrieved 11 April 2009 from <http://sports.espn.go.com/oly/trackandfield/news/story?id=3176064/>

Evans, N. A. (1997). Gym and tonic: a profile of 100 male steroid users. *British Journal of Sports Medicine, 31*, 54–58.

Evans, N. A. (2004). Current concepts in anabolic-androgenic steroids. *American Journal of Sports Medicine, 32*, 534–541.

Faigenbaum, A. D., Zaichkowsky, L. D., Gardner, D. E., & Micheli, L. J. (1998). Anabolic steroid use by male and female middle school students. *Pediatrics, 101*(5), 6–12.

Food and Drug Administration. The 1938 Food, Drug, and Cosmetic Act. Retrieved 13 May 2009 from <http://www.fda.gov/oc/history/historyoffda/section2.html/>

Ford, J. A. (2007). Alcohol use among college students: a comparison of athletes and nonathletes *Substance Use & Misuse, 42*(9), 1367–1377. doi:10.1080/10826080701212402.

Francis, C., & Coplon, J. (1990). *Speed Trap: Inside the biggest scandal in olympic history.* New York, NY: St. Martin's Press (1st U.S. ed.).

Fraser, A. D. (2004). Doping control from a global and national perspective. *Therapeutic Drug Monitoring, 26*, 171–174.

Freud, S. (1884). "Über Coca," Centralblatt für die ges *Therapie, 2*, 289–314. http://www.heretical.com/freudian/coca1884.html.

Gaffney, G. (2007). Steroid nation: NBA's performance drugs policy allows quick resolution of problems, (March 11). Retrieved 12 May 2009 from <http://grg51.typepad.com/steroid_nation/2007/03/nbas_performanc.html/>

Gallup, E. M. (1995). *Law and the Team Physician.* Champaign, IL: Human Kinetics Books (pp. 80–81, *supra* note 5).

Garber, D. P. (2005). Written statement of Donald P. Garber. Commissioner major league soccer, before the House Energy and Commerce Subcommittee on Commerce, Trade and Consumer Protection on H. R, (May 18). The drug free sports act. Retrieved 13 May 2009 from <http://archives.energycommerce.house.gov/reparchives/108/Hearings/05192005hearing1507/Garber.pdf/>

George, A. J. (2000). Central nervous system stimulants. *Bailliere's Clinical Endocrinology and Metabolism, 14*, 1479–1488.

Govtrack.us. (2006). S. 3546 [109th] – summary: Dietary Supplement and Nonprescription Drug Consumer Protection Act. Retrieved 13 May 2009 from <http://www.govtrack.us/congress/bill.xpd?bill=s109-3546&tab=summary/>

Govtrack.us. (2009). *A Civic Project to Track Congress.* Text of H.R. 6344 [109th]: Office of national drug control policy reauthorization act of 2006. Retrieved 11 April 2009 from <http://www.govtrack.us/congress/billtext.xpd?bill=h109-6344/>

Graham, M. R., Davies, B., Grace, F. M., Kicman, A., & Baker, J. S. (2008). Anabolic steroid use: patterns of use and detection of doping. *Sports Medicine, 38*(6), 505–525.

Green, G. (2006). Doping control for the team physician: a review of drug testing procedures in sport. *The American Journal of Sports Medicine, 34*, 1690–1698.

Green, G. A., Urvasz, F. D., Petr, T. A., & Bray, C. D. (2001). NCAA study of substance use and abuse habits of college student-athletes. *Clinical Journal of Sport Medicine, 11*(1), 51–56.

Hall, R. C. W., & Hall, R. C. W. (2005). Abuse of supraphysiologic doses of anabolic steroids. *Southern Medical Association, 98*(5), 550–555.

Hall, R. C. W., Hall, R. C. W., & Chapman, M. J. (2005). Psychiatric complications of anabolic steroid abuse. *Psychosomatics, 46*(4), 285–290.

Haller, C. A., & Benowitz, N. L. (2000). Adverse cardiovascular and central nervous system events associated with dietary supplements containing ephedra alkaloids. *The New England Journal of Medicine, 343*(25), 1833–1838.

Hartgens, F., & Kuipers, H. (2004). Effects of anabolic androgenic steroids in athletes. *Sports medicine, 34*(8), 513–554.

Harvey, S. J. (1999). Hegemonic, masculinity, friendship and group formation in an athletic subculture. *Journal of Men's Studies, 8*, 91–125.

Hasin, D. S., Keyes, K. M., Alderson, D., Wang, S., Aharonovich, E., & Grant, B. F. (2008). Cannabis withdrawal in the United States: results from NESARC. *The Journal of Clinical Psychiatry, 69*(9), 1354–1363.

Hiltzik, M. B. (2009). Manny's ban might revive big debate, (May 8). <Dailypress.Com/>, Retrieved from <http://www.dailypress.com/sports/dp-spt_manny_0508may08,0,4947343.story/>

Hoberman, J. (2002). Sports physicians and the doping crisis in elite sport. *Clinical Journal of Sports Medicine, 12*(4), 203–208.

Hohler, B. (2005). *NBA slammed by Lynch for steroid policy, May 20.* Boston, MA: The Boston Globe.

Holt, R. I. G., & Sönksen, P. H. (2008). Growth hormone, IGF-I and insulin and their abuse in sport. *British Journal of Pharmacology, 154*(3), 542–556. doi:10.1038/bjp.2008.99

Howard, B., & Gillis, J. (2009). High school sports participation increases again; boys, girls and overall participation reach all-time highs. Retrieved 23 April 2009 from <www.nfhs.org/web/2008/09/high_school_sports_participation.aspx/>

International Olympic Committee. (1999). Lausanne declaration on doping in sport, (February 4). Retrieved 3 May 2009, from <http://www.sportunterricht.de/lksport/Declaration_e.html/>

IOC. (2009). History and Mission of the International Olympic Committee Medical Commission. London, UK: BMJ Publishing. Retrieved 30 March 2009 from <http://www.olympic.org/uk/organisation/commissions/medical/index_uk.asp/>

Janofsky, M. (2002). In Phoenix, a drug theft may have led to murder. *New York Times*, 23 January. Retrieved 3 April 2009 from <http://www.nytimes.com/2002/01/23/us/in-phoenix-a-drug-theft-may-have-led-to-murder.html?sec=health/>

Johnston, L. D., O'Malley, P. M., Bachman, J. G., & Schulenberg, J. E. (2009). *Monitoring the Future National Results on Adolescent Drug Use: Overview of Key Findings, 2008.* Bethesda, MD: National Institute on Drug Abuse (NIH Publication No. 09–7401).

Juhn, M. S. (2003). Popular sports supplements and ergogenic aids. *Sports Medicine, 33*(12), 921–939.

Kiely, K. (2005). Focus on NBA, NHL to improve drug-testing policies, (November 15), <USATODAY.com/>. Retrieved 12 May 2009 from <http://www.usatoday.com/sports/basketball/nba/2005-11-15-nhl-nba-drug-testing-sidebar_x.htm/>

King, J. H. (1981). *The Duty and Standard of Care for Team Physicians* 18 Hous. L. Rev., *supra* note 7, (p. 664), citing Prosser and Keeton, *The Law of Torts* (p. 324) (4th ed.) (1971). St. Paul, MN: West Publishing Company.

Kirker, B. (2000). Special Problems Psychology and the Athlete. In Sherry, E. & Wilson, S. (Eds), Oxford Handbook of Sports Medicine. Oxford University Press.

Kohn, S. M., & Quinn, C. E. (2002). The new sports injury – injuries related to ephedrine alkaloid containing dietary supplements, (April). Retrieved 13 May 2009 from <http://www.iadclaw .org/pdfs/ddbIssue4April.pdf/>

Kovacs, E. M. R., Stegen, J. H. C. H., & Brouns, F. (1998). Effect of caffeinated drinks on substrate metabolism, caffeine excretion, and performance. *Journal of Applied Phycology*, *85*(2), 709–715.

Kriebitzsch-Lejeune, A. (2000). Retail pharmacists and doping in sports: knowledge and attitudes. a national survey in france. *Science & Sports*, *15*(3), 141–146.

Kutscher, E. C., Lund, B. C., & Perry, P. J. (2002). Anabolic steroids: review for the clinician. *Sports Medicine*, *32*(5), 285–296.

LaBotz, M., & Smith, B. W. (1999). Creatine supplement use in NCAA Division I athletic program. *Clinical Journal of Sport Medicine*, *9*, 167–169.

Landis, M. (2003). The team physician: an analysis of the causes of action, conflicts, defenses and improvements. *Journal of Sports Law and Contemporary Problems*, *1*, 139–158.

Laure, P., Binsinger, C., & Lecerf, T. (2003). General practitioners and doping in sport: attitudes and experience. *British Journal of Sports Medicine*, *37*, 335–338. doi:10.1136/bjsm. 37.4.335.

Le Roith, D., Scavo, L., & Butler, A. (2001). What is the role of circulation IGF-1? *Trends in Endocrinology and Metabolism*, *12*(2), 48–52.

Leichliter, J. S., Meilman, P. W., Presley, C. A., & Cashin, J. R. (1998). Alcohol use and related consequences among students with varying levels of involvement in college athletics. *Journal of American College Health*, *46*, 257–262.

Lombardi, G., Galdiero, M., Aurlemm, R. S., Pivonello, R., & Coalo, A. (2006). Acromegaly and cardiovascular system. *Neuroendocrinology*, *83*, 211–217.

Lombardo, J. A. (2004). Supplements and athletes. *Southern Medical Journal*, *97*(9), 877–879.

Lorente, F. O., Peretti-Watel, P., & Grelot, L. (2005). Cannabis use to enhance sportive and non-sportive performance among French athletes. *Addictive Behaviors*, *30*, 1382–1391.

Mackay, D. (2006). Gatlin turns into the fastest falling hero in the world, (July 31) Retrieved from http://www.guardian.co.uk/sport/2006/jul/31/athletics.sport. *The Guardian*.

Major League Soccer. (1 December 2004 to 31 January 2010). Collective bargaining agreement between major league soccer and the major league soccer players union. Retrieved 13 May 2009 from <http://www.mlsplayers.org/files/collective_bargaining_agreement__final.pdf/>

Maravelias, C., Dona, A., Stefanidou, M., & Spiliopoulou, C. (2005). Adverse effects of anabolic steroids in athletes. A constant threat. *Toxicology Letters*, *158*, 167–175.

Martens, M. P., Dams-O'Connor, K., & Beck, N. C. (2006). A systematic review of college student-athlete drinking: prevalence rates, sport-related factors, and interventions. *Journal of Substance Abuse Treatment*, *31*(3), 305–316.

Martin, D. E., & Gynn, R. W. H. (2000). *The Olympic Marathon*. Champaign, IL: Human Kinetics.

Matheson, G. O. (2001). Maintaining professionalism in the athletic environment. *Physician and Sports Medicine*, *29*(2), 1.

McDuff, D. R., & Baron, D. (2005). Substance use in athletics: a sports psychiatry perspective. *Clinics Sports Medicine*, *24*, 885–897.

Metzel, J. D., Levine, S. R., & Gershel, J. C. (2001). Creatine use among young athletes. *Pediatrics*, *108*, 421–425.

Mitten, M. J. (1993). Team physicians and competitive athletes: allocating legal responsibility for athletic injuries. *supra* note 17, 144–145. *U Pitt Legal Rev.*, *55*(1), 129–169.

MLB.com: News. *Drug policy coverage*. Retrieved 12 May 2009, from <http://mlb.mlb.com/mlb/ news/drug_policy.jsp?content=/>

Modafinil. (2009). Referenced 22 April from

Mottram, D. R., & George, A. J. (2000). Anabolic steroids. *Bailliere's Clinical Endocrinology and Metabolism, 14*(1), 5–69.

National Basketball Players Association. *Anti-drug program.* Retrieved 12 May 2009 from <http://www.nbpa.com/cba_articles/article-XXXIII.php#section9/>

National Collegiate Athletic Association. (2001). *NCAA Study of Substance Use Habits of College Student-Athletes.* Retrieved 3 January 2010 from <http://nacc.org/wps/wcm/connect/57986c804e0b8a4e9a8efa1ad6fc8b25/NCAADrugUseStudy2001.pdf?MOD=AJPERES&CACHEID=57986c804e0b8a4e9a8efa1ad6fc8b25>

National Collegiate Athletic Association. (2005). Government relations report, (December). Retrieved 11 April 2009 from <http://www.ncaa.org/wps/ncaa?ContentID=7565/>

National Collegiate Athletic Association. (2009). *1981–1982 – 2007–2008 NCAA sports sponsorship and participation rates.* Retrieved 22 April 2009 from <http://www.ncaapublications.com/Uploads/PDF/ParticipationRates2009c2f40573-60aa-4a08-874d-1aff4192c5e4.pdf/>

National Collegiate Athletic Association. (2009). Drug testing program 2008–2009. Retrieved 22 April from <http://www.ncaapublications.com/Uploads/PDF/DT%20Program%20Book%202008-098066e117-09c3-4244-a00f-fa68a2c6c96c.pdf/>

National Collegiate Athletic Association. (2009). *Official web site of the NCAA.* Retrieved 12 May 2009 from <http://www.ncaa.org/wps/ncaa?ContentID=7565/>

National Federation of High Schools. (2009). *Drug testing - what are the legal issues?* Retrieved 22 April 2009 from <www.nfhs.org/web/2004/04/drug_testing__what_are_the_legal_issues.aspx/>

National Federation of High Schools. (2009). *NFHS steroids awareness.* Retrieved 22 April 2009 from <www.nfhs.org/web/2006/09/nfhs_steroids_awareness.aspx/>

National Football League. (2008a). *National football league policy and program for substances of abuse 2008.* Retrieved 13 May 2009 from <http://www.nflplayers.com/images/fck/2008%20Substances%20of%20Abuse%20Policy%20(FINAL).pdf/>

National Football League. (2008b). *National football league policy on anabolic steroids and related substances 2008.* Retrieved 13 May 2009 from <http://www.nflplayers.com/images/fck/2008%20Steroid%20Policy%20_Final%20Version_.pdf/>

National Hockey League Player's Association. (2005). Collective bargaining agreement, (July 22), <NHL.com/>. Retrieved 12 May 2009 from <http://www.nhl.com/nhlhq/cba/drug_testing072205.html/>

National Hockey League Players' Association. (2009). *About the NHLPA.* Retrieved 12 May 2009 from <http://www.nhlpa.com/CBA/index.asp/>

Nilsson, S., Baigi, A., Marklund, B., & Fridlund, B. (2001). The prevalence of the use of androgenic anabolic steroids by adolescents in a county of Sweden. *European Journal of Public Health, 11*(2), 195–197. doi:10.1093/eurpub/11.2.195.

Office of National Drug Control Policy. (2009). *About the Office of National Drug Control Policy.* Retrieved 10 April 2009, from <http://www.whitehousedrugpolicy.gov/about/index.html/>

Office of National Drug Control Policy. (2009). *Office of National Drug Control Policy: Steroids Facts and Figures.* Retrieved 2 April 2009 from <http://www.whitehousedrugpolicy.gov/drugfact/steroids/steroids_ff.html/>

Pagonis, T. A., Angelopoulos, N. V., Koukoulis, G. N., & Hadjichristodoulou, C. S. (2006). Psychiatric side effects induced by supraphysiological doses of combinations of anabolic steroids correlate to the severity of abuse. *European Psychiatry, 21*, 551–562.

Pasquarelli, L. (2007). Williams starting process to return to NFL, (March 31). Retrieved 12 May 2009 from <http://sports.espn.go.com/nfl/news/story?id=2820270/>

Poortmans, J. R., & Francaux, M. (1999). Long-term creatine supplementation does not impair renal function in healthy athletes. *Medicine and Science in Sports and Exercise, 31,* 1108–1110.

Pope, H. G., & Katz, D. L. (1999). Psychiatric effects of anabolic steroids. *Psychiatric Annals, 22,* 24–29.

Rickert, V. I., Pawlak-Morello, C., Sheppard, V., & Jay, S. M. (1992). Human growth hormone: a new substance of abuse among adolescents? *Clinical Pediatrics, 31*(12), 723–726. doi:10.1177/000992289203101206.

Roberts, S. (2005). *Steroid Laws: Punishment and Justice For all.* The New York Times.

Saugy, M., Avois, L., Sudan, C., Robinson, N., Giroud, C., Mangin, P., & Dvorak, J. (2006). Cannabis and sport. *British Journal of Sports Medicine, 40,* 13–15.

Sawka, M. N., Joyner, M. J., Miles, D. S., Robertson, R. S., Spriet, L. L., & Yound, A. J. (1996). The use of blood doping as an ergogenic aid. *Medicine & Science in Sports & Exercise,* 1 June, i–viii. <http://www.acsm-msse.org/pt/pt-core/template-journal/msse/media/0696a.pdf/>

Schwarz, S., Onken, D., & Schubert, A. (1999). The steroid story of Jenapharm: from the late 1940s to the early 1970s. *Steroids, 64*(7), 439–445.

Selig, A. H. (2008). Statement of Commissioner Allan H. Selig before the house committee on oversight and government reform, (January 15), MLB.com: News. Retrieved 12 May 2009 from <http://mlb. mlb.com/news/article.jsp?ymd=20080115&content_id=2346206&vkey=news_mlb&fext=. jsp&c_id=mlb/>

Shaffer, H. J. (1986). Conceptual crises and the addictions: a philosophy of science perspective. *Journal of Substance Abuse Treatment, 3*(4), 285–296.

Shaffer, H. J. (1997). The most important unresolved issue in the addictions: conceptual chaos. *Substance Use & Misuse, 32*(11), 1573–1580.

Silver, M. D. (2001). Use of ergogenic aids by athletes. *Journal of the America Academy of Orthopedic Surgeons, 9,* 61–70.

Sjöqvist, F., Garle, M., & Rane, A. (2008). Use of doping agents, particularly anabolic steroids, in sports and society. *Lancet, 71,* 1872–1882.

Smith, R. A. (1981). Harvard and Columbia and a reconsideration of the 1905–1906 football crisis. *Journal of Sport History, 8*(3), 5–19.

Sokmen, B., Armstrong, L. E., Kraemer, W. J., Casa, D. J., Dias, J. C., Judelson, D. A., & Maresh, C. M. (2008). Caffeine use in sports: considerations for the athlete. *Journal of Strength and Conditioning Research, 22*(3), 978–986.

Sturmi, J. E., & Diorio, D. J. (1998). Anabolic agents. *Clinics in Sports Medicine, 17,* 261–282.

Sullivan, M. L., Martinez, C. M., Gennis, P., & Gallagher, E. J. (1998). The cardiac toxicity of anabolic steroids. *Progress in Cardiovascular Diseases, 41*(1), 1–15.

Todd, T. (1987). Anabolic steroids: the gremlins of sport. *Journal of Sport History, 14*(1), 87–107.

Tokish, J. M., Kocher, M. S., & Hawkins, R. J. (2004). Ergogenic aids: a review of basic science, performance, side effects and status in sports. *American Journal of Sports Medicine, 32,* 1543–1553.

Tynes, J. R. (2006). Performance enhancing substances; effects, regulations and the pervasive efforts to control doping in major league baseball. *The Journal of Legal Medicine, 27*(4), 493–509. doi:10.1080/01947640601021113.

Ungerleider, S. (2001). *Faust's Gold: Inside the East German Doping Machine* (First ed.). New York, NY: Thomas Dunne Books/St. Martin's Press.

United States Anti-Doping Agency. (2007). Marion Jones accepts sanction for doping violation; hands over Olympic medal, (October 8). Retrieved 11 April 2009, from <http://www.

usantidoping.org/files/active/resources/press_releases/press%20release%20-%20jones%20-%20october%202007.pdf/>

United States Anti-Doping Agency. (2008). *USADA – who we are: USADA history.* Retrieved 12 May 2009 from <http://www.usantidoping.org/who/history.html/>

United States Immigrations and Customs Enforcement. (2008). Former Olympic champion Marion Jones-Thompson, sentenced to 6 months in prison for making false statements in two federal criminal investigations, (January 14). Retrieved 11 April 2009 from <http://www.ice.gov/pi/news/newsreleases/articles/080111newyork.htm/>

Vahl, N., Moler, N., Lauritzen, T., Christiansen, J. S., & Jorgensen, J. O. (1997). Metabolic effects and pharmacokinetics of a growth hormone pulse in healthy adults: relation to age, sex and body composition. *Journal of Clinical Endocrinology and Metabolism, 82,* 3612–3618.

Verroken, M. (2000). Drug use and abuse in sport. *Baillieres Best Practice Research Clinical Endocrinology and Metabolism, 14*(1), 1–23.

Volek, J. S., Duncan, N. D., Mazzetti, S. A., Staron, R. S., Putukian, M., Gómez, A. L., Pearson, D. R., Fink, W. J., & Kraemer, W. J. (1999). Performance and muscle fiber adaptations to creatine supplementation and heavy resistance training. *Medicine and Science in Sports and Exercise, 31,* 1147–1156.

Wechsler, H., Davenport, A. E., Dowdell, G. W., Grossman, S. J., & Zanakos, S. I. (1997). Binge drinking, tobacco, and illicit drug use and involvement in athletics: A survey of students at 140 American colleges. *Journal of the American College of Health, 45,* 195–200.

Weiler, P. C., & Roberts, G. R. (1998). Sports and the Law. Berkeley, CA: West Group.

Wetherill, R. R., & Fromme, K. (2007). Alcohol use, sexual activity, and perceived risk in high school athletes and non-athletes. *Journal of Adolescent Health, 41*(3), 294–301.

Williams, L., & Fainaru-Wada, M. (2005). *House steroid panel sets new target: NFL / NBA, NCAA and others also likely to be scrutinized.* San Francisco Chronicle, April 5.

Wilson, G. S., Pritchard, M. E., & Schaffer, J. (2004). Athletic status and drinking behavior in college students: the influence of gender and coping styles. *Journal of American College Health, 52,* 269–273.

World Anti-Doping Agency. (2003). *World Anti-Doping Code, Introduction.* Montreal, Canada: World Anti-Doping Agency (p. 1).

World Anti-Doping Agency. (2003). *A brief history of anti-doping.* Retrieved 30 March 2009 from <http://www.wada-ama.org/en/dynamic.ch2?pageCategory.id=312/>

World Anti-Doping Agency. (2009). *Anti-doping development.* Retrieved 2 April 2009 from <http://www.wada-ama.org/en/dynamic.ch2?pageCategory.id=437/>

World Anti-Doping Agency. (2009). *Science & Medicine: Blood Doping.* Retrieved 18 May from <http://www.wadaama.org/en/dynamic.ch2?pageCategory.id=626/>

World Anti-Doping Agency. (2009a). *Therapeutic use exemption.* Retrieved 31 March 2009 from <http://www.wada-ama.org/en/dynamic.ch2?pageCategory.id=373/>

World Anti-Doping Agency. (2009b). *World anti-doping code.* Retrieved 30 March 2009 from <www.wada-ama.org/rtecontent/document/code_v2009_En.pdf/>

World Anti-Doping Agency. (n.d.). *Blood Doping. Questions and Answers on Blood Doping.* Retrieved 3 January 2010 from <http://www.wada-ama.org/en/Resources1/Q-and-A/Q-A-Blood-Doping/>

Yesalis, C. (2000). *Anabolic Steroids in Sport and Exercise* (2nd ed.). Champaign, IL: Human Kinetics.

Yesalis, C. E., & Bahrke, M. S. (2000). Doping among adolescent athletes. *Best Practice & Research Clinical Endocrinology & Metabolism, 14*(1), 25–35.

Chapter 19

Class Action to Protect Against Discrimination of Individuals with Alcohol and Drug Addictions

Norman S. Miller, MD, JD, PLLC
Department of Medicine, College of Human Medicine, Michigan State University, East Lansing, MI, USA

INTRODUCTION

Class Action as a Thesis to Promote Change for Discriminated Members

Overall, class actions show promise as a legal procedural device to protect the "picked on, little people" with "small claims" who are vulnerable to discriminatory practices (Garner, 2001) and outmatched by more financially resourceful and politically powerful forces (Conte & Newberg, 2002) (*Achem Prods. v. Windsor*, 1997, quoting *Mace v. Van Ru Credit Corp.*, 1997, "the policy at the very core of the class action mechanism is to overcome the problem that small recoveries do not provide the incentive for any individual to bring a solo action prosecuting his or her rights. A class action solves this problem, by aggregating the relatively paltry potential recoveries into something worth someone's (usually an attorney's) labor"). To even the playing field, a stigmatized class of alcoholics and drug addicts might band together for collective strength to claim damages from fraudulent and negligent practices by producers of addicting alcohol and other drugs (*Grace v. City of Detroit*, 1992, "one major advantage of class actions to the courts, attorneys, and litigants is the judicial economy and efficiency they can achieve"). Importantly, the class members can pursue their rights against unjust and discriminatory state and federal laws that exploit their vulnerable status as alcoholics and drug addicts (class actions deter mass wrongs and fraud and fulfill legislative policy (*Midwest Motor Freight Bureau v. U.S.*, 1970). They enforce constitutional rights of broad classes of persons).

Specifically, discrimination is the effect of a law or established practice that confers privileges on a certain class, or that denies privileges to a certain class because of race, age, sex or handicap (Garner, 2001, *supra* note 2). *De facto* discrimination is a form of discriminatory administration, by showing circumstantial evidence of a discriminatory purpose. This occurs when a statute or practice is not facially discriminatory, but has such an effect that purposeful discrimination can be inferred (in *Rogers v. Lodge*, 1982, the Supreme Court declared unconstitutional an at-large voting system by finding intentional discrimination based on evidence of past discrimination in voting and schooling, limited black participation in the political process, and the failure of any black to be elected to the city council). Thus, a major purpose of class action is proposed to overcome past, present and future discriminatory practices against alcoholics and drug addicts on the basis of negative stereotypes which intentionally or unintentionally result in harmful consequences (Miller et al., 2001).

In forming a class, the core thesis is that these vulnerable individuals are unfairly discriminated against based on stigma and moral judgments, although they suffer from a disease process that originates in the brain, for which the afflicted individual is not at fault (Miller & Chappel, 1991). Despite abundant scientific evidence that addiction is a medical disorder, the majority's prejudicial practices, similar to those held against other discriminated classes, continue to deny alcoholics and drug addicts equal and fair treatment in medical care and legal actions (Miller & Swift, 1997, p. 415, "alcohol and drug disorders and the individuals who suffer from them have long been stigmatized and marginalized").

Central to discrimination is the perception that alcoholics and drug addicts self-inflict their woes, and contribute to or even alone cause their damages. Thus, the tolerance level is low for their claims, because of the view that they exercise a "personal choice" to use alcohol and addictive prescription medication, requiring a showing of fraudulent practice in order to overcome the stigma that alcoholics and drug addicts deserve their plight (Miller et al., 1991), *supra* note 9, at 196–197. "Alcoholism has followed, but suffered from the belief that has also plagued psychiatric disorders, although not as severely. That belief is the moral explanation for drinking and other drug use"). An alcoholic or drug addict's qualifying as a full-fledged victim in a medical sense is a "tough" sell to courts and juries, and to the public as a whole.

History of Mixed Success in Class Action Litigation for Addictions

These special barriers based on discrimination and economic gain make traditional case-by-case methods daunting for a single or small number of litigants who are seeking damages for wrongs committed against them. Overcoming the surrounding moral cloak may require classes of alcoholics and addicted individuals whose power lies collectively in numbers, and legal actions with large impact on defendants to change discriminatory polices. Otherwise the legal pitfalls in class action litigations are similar to class actions in medically-related claims, namely, achieving class certification and engineering settlement or trying a class action case with complex medical and legal issues (Rossman & Edelman, 2002, 1.1. "Instead of sending such clients to small claims courts on their own, an attorney can bring a class action which better protects not only the individual clients, but also numerous other consumers victimized by the same practice").

At what point is class action useful and when should it be initiated, and is it superior to individual, traditional trial actions? The answer to this question is on a case-by-case basis, but class action is indicated and advantageous for proposed classes of addicted individuals who are discriminated against to protect their rights and remedy their damages from drugs and alcohol against powerful foes and unlikely odds (in *Phillips Petroleum Co. v. Shutts*, 1985, the Supreme Court emphasized that a major advantage of permitting class action was to afford access to judicial relief for similar persons who had small individual claims, and who could not otherwise finance individual litigation).

UNFAIR AND LETHAL DISCRIMINATION AGAINST CLASSES OF ADDICTED INDIVIDUALS EVIDENT IN GOVERNMENT POLICY

Discriminatory Policies and Laws against Cigarette Smokers

Inexplicably, the tobacco settlement does not stipulate that the states must use funds to treat and reduce health-related consequences from smoking, despite litigation based on damages to cigarette smokers. Similarly, states can determine how much to tax, and how to spend the tax revenue from cigarette sales, without having to apply tax revenue to tobacco-related issues (Daynard et al., 2001).

Consequently, because the terms of the tobacco settlement and tax revenue are dependent on sales of tobacco products, the incentive for states is to implicitly encourage cigarette consumption by people at any age, particularly young people. For the state to do otherwise would mean tax revenues would decline correspondingly (Gross et al., 2002). Across states, an average of only 6% of the tobacco settlement funding is dedicated to health-related consequences from tobacco consumption and prevention and treatment of nicotine addiction. Moreover, the State of Michigan dedicates less than 20% of tobacco tax revenue to cigarette health-related consequences and prevention, and applies tobacco tax revenue mostly to nonhealth expenditures, e.g., education and general government operating expenses (Office of Revenue and Tax Analysis, Michigan, 2002).

Given that 440,000 persons die annually from tobacco-related use, only discriminatory practices by states could explain using settlement and tax money to fund government activities totally unrelated to the health and welfare of those already addicted to cigarettes or at risk of becoming addicted (Centers

for Disease Control and Prevention, 2003). However, there is no other condition, medical or otherwise, where public policy and public health and safety
condone such a magnitude of self-destruction in the United States.

Thus, a question remains whether class action litigation for tobacco settlement was to remedy healthcare practices, or just to perpetuate the discrimination against afflicted, powerless, addicted individuals by exploiting a funding
source to support state governments. The answers are mixed from the history
of class action litigation for addictions until now, as courts have been reluctant
to fully endorse class action as a superior method to traditional litigation, and
find common questions predominant among individuals with drug and alcohol
addictions.

ADDICTION

Addiction is a legal and medical disease where personal choice is overcome by
changes in brain chemistry that compel victims to use alcohol and addicting
medications destructively.

Addiction is a Disease Defined as a Medical Disorder and by Legal Status

Addiction is a disease as defined by a preoccupation with acquiring alcohol
and drugs, and compulsive use and a pattern of relapse despite adverse consequences (Miller, 2001). Preoccupation is demonstrated by a high priority
of use, as illustrated by continuing to purchase cigarettes despite escalating
taxes; compulsive use is evident in continued use despite an annual mortality rate of over 400,000 and relapse manifested by unsuccessful attempts to
remain abstinent from cigarettes despite these fatal consequences (McGinnis
& Foege, 1993). Pervasive to these behaviors is a loss of control over drug
use seen in excessive use over time, despite accumulation of morbidity and
mortality (Miller et al., 1987). The loss of control is largely unconscious and
persistent, and is similar to drive states such as hunger and sex. As with drive
states, conscious control is possible, but the untreated drive state to smoke
is expressed ultimately in compulsive and repetitive drug use (Miller &
Lyon, 1997).

Court decisions generally hold that addiction to alcohol and drugs is not
willful misconduct. In addition, being a drug addict or alcoholic is a status and
not a crime (*Robinson v. California*, 1962, Robinson was arrested in violation
of a state law making it criminal to be an opiate or drug addict. The Supreme
Court held that the state could not make "being" a drug addict a crime). The
Supreme Court ruled that the Calfornia law against being a drug addict, making it a crime, was unconstitutional. As such, the court held a law could not
make "status" a crime, and the treatment for addiction represented a different
goal than punishment for a crime (*Idem* at 662). Moreover, in *Powell v. State*

of Texas, (1961) the Supreme Court held that while public drunkenness was a crime, being an alcoholic was not; rather it was a status (Powell could be arrested for public intoxication, but not for "being" an alcoholic).

Addiction as a Medical Disease

Scientific evidence demonstrates that there are centers in the brain responsible for the addictive use of alcohol and other drugs. These addictive brain centers are similar to those responsible for other drive states in the phylogenetically older portions of the brain responsible for instincts and basic drive states, such as hunger and sex (Miller & Goldsmith, 2001). Addictive drugs, including nicotine and alcohol, act on specific neuronal circuitry to stimulate reinforced use and ultimately compulsive, pathological use. Once loss of control develops, which is the cardinal manifestation of addictive disease; it remains indefinitely (Miller & Gold, 1994).

The addicted individual is responsible for the consequences of their actions while under the influence of addicting drugs through out of control use. However, they do not use addicting drugs intentionally in a pathological pattern, and often commit acts against their will, or at least unintentionally. Courts often mitigate charges and sentencing for alcoholics and drug addicts, recognizing their lack of *mens rea* for their actions, due to the influence of addictive disease (Miller, 2000, 2001).

CLASS ACTIONS

Class actions protect a discriminated class where joinder is impractical and traditional legal means will not suffice, such as individual trials.

Class Action Litigation is an Effective Strategy to Protect against Discriminatory Policy and Laws

Over the last decade, class action suits grew increasingly successful in obtaining large settlements for individuals who were historically disadvantaged, such as those afflicted by tobacco addiction and discrimination of civil rights (Conte & Newberg, 2002, *supra* note 3, Employment Discrimination Class Action, § 24:1, § 24.2). Correspondingly, class action litigation can be effective and far-reaching for plaintiffs for criminal and civil wrongs committed against them. In many instances, class action provides a means of enabling litigation that could not be practically brought for small claims on an individual basis against more resourceful adversaries (Rossman & Edelman, 2002, *supra* note 12 § 1.1.4, 6–7). Specifically, forming large classes promotes pursuit of larger societal goals, such as deterring unsafe health practices and enforcing government regulations, than the limited effects of individual legal actions (Conte & Newberg, 2002, *supra* note 3, § 5:49, § 5:51).

History of Tobacco Cases Demonstrate Powerful and Unethical Forces against Traditional Litigation

The tobacco cases originated in 1954, and 100–150 cases were filed over the next 20 years (Gostin, 2000). Very few cases came to trial, and there was no verdict in the plaintiff's favor over the tobacco industry. These early cases failed under the theories of negligence, breach of warranty and misrepresentation, despite the fact that plaintiffs started smoking without knowledge of the harmful effects of smoking and misrepresentation by the tobacco industry that smoking was safe. The scientific basis for the harmful effects of smoking did not emerge with certainty until later (*Idem* at 295–296).

Subsequently, cigarette smoking lost its glamor and became a predictable symbol of weak character and lower social class. Progressively, the public became more health conscious as cigarettes were increasingly viewed as dangerous products. With better scientific studies problems with causation were reduced, but plaintiffs could no longer claim ignorance of the health risks (*Idem* at 294). Moreover, defense counsels took advantage by portraying plaintiffs as morally responsible for their own illnesses, because they chose to smoke in the first place. Defense counsel could also point to the warnings on cigarette packs required by the Cigarette Labeling and Advertising Act, enacted in 1965 (15 U.S.C. §§ 1331–1340 (1965). The Cigarette Labeling and Advertising Act of 1965, as amended in 1969, 15 U.S.C. 331–1340 (1969) pre-empts state regulation based on "smoking and health").

It was not until 1990 that a New Jersey jury awarded damages of $400,000 to a smoker, Rose Cipollone, who died of cancer at the age of 58. Despite being overturned on appeal, it was the first plaintiff verdict in the extensive tobacco litigation (505 U.S. 504 (1992)). Justice John Paul Stevens, in a plurality decision, held that the 1969 act pre-empts tort claims based on "failure to warn and the neutralization of federally mandated warnings to the extent that those claims rely on omissions or inclusions in the manufacturers' advertising or promotions. However, the act does not pre-empt tort claims based on express warranty, intentional fraud and misrepresentation, or conspiracy (*Idem* at 530–531). Importantly, the legal success of tobacco defendants prior to this litigation related to their resisting all discovery in requiring a hearing before plaintiffs could obtain the most basic discovery, by obtaining confidentiality orders to prevent plaintiff sharing of discovery material, and by taking exceedingly lengthy depositions and naming multiple experts of their own specialties, taking dozens and dozens of oral depositions across the country of trivial fact witnesses (Gostin et al., 1991).

These aggressive and obstructionistic tactics created extremely burdensome and expensive litigation for the plaintiffs, forcing plaintiffs to exhaust their resources, principally, money (*Idem*). Many of the plaintiff's lawyers were situated in small law firms, practicing on a contingency basis, and could not cope with these large expenses to fight cases to the bitter end. For instance, the Cipollene case produced 12 federal opinions and a cost to the plaintiffs of roughly $4 million. In addition, the tobacco industry adopted a "no-holds-barred" defense by probing the moral habits of the plaintiff, urging juries to find personal blameworthiness (Arno et al., 1996). The strategy was to create doubt about the health charge without actually denying it, and advocating the right of the public to smoke without actually urging them to take up the practice (Janson, 1988).

Eventually, evidence emerged that the tobacco industry knew and understood the health effects of smoking, the addictive quality of nicotine and the toxicity of pesticides contained in cigarettes (Hurt & Robertson, 1998). In addition, the tobacco industry manipulated the nicotine content of cigarettes and marketed their products to young people to increase rates of use and addiction (Hilts & Collins, 1995). Medical cost reimbursement became a dominant theme as state attorneys general filed direct claims against the tobacco industry for reimbursement of public money that had been spent to pay for tobacco-related illness. On 20 June 1997, the tobacco industry and the attorneys general ended their negotiations and presented a settlement that required Congress to grant the industry immunity from certain forms of litigation. In exchange, the state would receive $368 billion over 25 years (Gostin, 2000, *supra* note 36, at 3180).

Class action litigation has become a key strategy adopted by the plaintiffs in further tobacco litigation. In 1994, nonsmoking flight attendants filed class action against the tobacco industry, alleging injuries sustained by inhalation of second-hand smoke in airplane cabins. In addition to certifying the class, the court approved a settlement from a $300 million medical foundation, allowing individual lawsuits. In 2000, a jury awarded compensatory damages to three Florida smokers in the first class action verdict (*Engle v. R. J. Reynolds Co.*, 2000).

FORM A DISCRIMINATED CLASS OF HARMED INDIVIDUALS WITH SMALL CLAIMS TO MAKE CLASS TIGHT AND CLASS ACTION SUPERIOR

Public Support for a Class Consisting of Alcoholics and Drug Addicts Suffering from a Disease

In surveys of the general public, 90% of respondents supported the idea that alcoholism was a disease, and 75% felt alcoholism was a "progressive physical disease" (Caetano, 1987). Moreover, the concept of loss of control was strongly supported; 85% endorsed that alcoholics were addicted to alcohol and that without help, problems from drinking worsened. Unfortunately, the moral stigma was not lost, as 20% of those endorsing alcoholism as a disease simultaneously considered it a moral weakness. Moreover, 44% of those rejecting the disease concept considered it a moral weakness.

Despite apparent favorable views, some studies revealed that alcoholics were perceived more unfavorably than persons with other diseases such as epilepsy, and attitudes towards alcoholics were generally negative (Dean & Poremba, 1983). Perhaps the relevant variable was the notion of responsibility. Correspondingly, alcoholics were perceived as responsible for their drinking behavior by the majority of the United States population (Caetano, 1987, *supra* note 40, at 155). By contrast, a disease state implies the absence of responsibility for causing one's malady, thus, a key characteristic of the "sick role". However, addictive disorders are similar to other chronic diseases, such as diabetes mellitus, epilepsy and hypertension. In these disorders, personal responsibility is often implicated in their origin and ultimately determines the success or failure of treatment (Vaillant, 1983).

Class Defined

Nature and Extent for Those Who Consume Alcohol and Other Addicting Drugs

Class definition determines who is entitled to relief, bound by decision, receives notice, and to ascertain members and future members. In addition, class definition is central to class certification, which is the most important aspect in class action litigation (*General Telephone Co. of the Southwest v. Mariano S. Falcon*, 1982; the Supreme Court held the district court erred in permitting plaintiff to maintain a class action on behalf of all Mexican–American applicants for employment whom employer did not hire without any specific presentation identifying the questions of law or fact that were common to claims of employee and of class members the plaintiff sought to represent. The mere fact a complaint alleges racial or ethnic discrimination does not in itself ensure that the party who has brought the lawsuit will be an adequate representative of those who may have been the real victims of discrimination (Fed. Rules Civ. Proc. Rule 23(a), 28 U.S.C.A.). Further, class certification defines the class, determines the members of the class, and who is entitled to relief in the class action suit). Although class representatives must have the same interests and injuries and not be moot, a class can continue even if the representative's claim is moot after class certification (*United States Parole Comm'n v. Geraghty*, 1980; a class action does not become moot upon expiration of the named plaintiff's substantive claim, even though class certification was denied and the named plaintiff was a proper representative for the purpose of appealing the ruling denying class certification. In the case, the named plaintiff, a former federal prisoner, could continue to appeal the District Court's ruling denying class certification, even though he was released from prison while the appeal was pending). While not technically permissible, a court will often grant class certification if a member is perceived as being wronged, and the case has underlying merit. Also, a class is more likely to be certified if the class representative can prove liability (Hensler et al., 2000). Importantly, manageability as a superiority factor encompasses the entire suit, is often hotly contested, and goes to all the issues including individual issues of cause and effect (*Castano et al., v. The American Tobacco Company et al.*, 1996; the Court of Appeals held that multistate class would be decertified because the federal district court failed to consider how variations in state law would affect predominance and superiority, district court's predominance inquiry did not include consideration of how trial on the merits would be conducted, and class independently failed the superiority requirement). However, small claims tend to make the class tighter and class action superior to individual actions (*Kline et al., v. Coldwell Banker & Co., Realtors*, 1974; during the four-year period involved, approximately 800,000 deeds were recorded in Los Angeles County. Based on this fact defendants estimated that upwards of 400,000 sales with approximately that number of plaintiffs could well be involved in this class suit). Precise class definition for those who consume alcohol and other addicting drugs will ultimately depend on a variety of factors which can be extensively enumerated in health consequences, both large and small. For instance, morbidity for tobacco- and alcohol-related consequences cost over $100 billion per year to the affected individuals and society (Center for Disease Control and Prevention, 2002b). As stated, cigarette smoking causes death to 440,000 individuals per year and alcohol causes death to 100,000 individuals per year (McGinnis & Foege, 1993, *supra* note 19, at 2270). In addition, there *are* staggering costs to private health insurance, medicaid and medicare from tobacco- and alcohol-related healthcare costs (Warner, 2000).

Numerosity and Commonality: Prevalent Disorders

Numerosity and commonality, damages notwithstanding, will unlikely be an issue in class action suits given the high prevalence of alcohol and drug disorders (Center for Substance Drug Control Policy, 1995). (FRCP Rule 23. 13(a) Class Action; because the fundamental nature of a class action is its representative status and absent class members who share common interests, the basic structure contains prerequisites. Thus, plaintiffs as a party seeking class certification bear the burden of demonstrating that they have met the four requirements of numerosity (the class members are too numerous to make joinder practical), commonality (there must be questions of law or fact common to the class), typicality (the claims or defenses of the class representatives must be typical of the claims or defenses of the class), and adequate representation (the class representatives must fairly and adequately protect the interests of the class). Failure to satisfy any of these requirements is fatal to class certification.) These conditions are among the most prevalent illnesses in American society. In the Epidemiological Catchment Area Study, 16% of the United States population was diagnosed as alcoholic and 7% as drug dependent (Regier et al., 1990). In addition, 25% of all general hospital admissions and 50% of all psychiatric admissions are alcohol- and drug-related (Miller, 1994). Importantly, over 40% of adults reported exposure to a problem drinker in their families (Schoenborn, 1991).

DEFINE DAMAGES AND FRAUD WHERE INDIVIDUAL ISSUES DO NOT PREDOMINATE AND CLASS ACTION IS SUPERIOR TO TRADITIONAL LITIGATION FOR A DISCRIMINATED CLASS

Class action objectives include damages due to health consequences of using addictive drugs, enjoining manufacturers and prescribing physicians from fraudulent and dangerous practices where damage to victims is foreseeable, and encouraging safe marketing practices to protect the public (Conte & Newberg, 2002).

Core Legal Theories and Causality

Core legal theories often employed in health-related class action litigation include fraud and deceit, negligent misrepresentation, product liability, individual issues, violation of statutes, consumer protection and warnings, breach of express and implied warranties, and intentional torts from lying about the addictive potential of drugs (Hensler et al., 2000, *supra* note 48, at 151–153, *Roberts v. Bausch & Lomb, Inc.*; the complaint alleged that Bausch & Lomb had violated the federal Lanham Act, the RICO Act and various consumer protection acts. It also included common-law claims of misrepresentation, fraud, deceit, false statements and nondisclosures of material fact, breaches of express and implied warranties, and negligence). Liability is often joint liability, as in tobacco litigation, and strict liability for an inherently dangerous product. However, proximate cause issues are more difficult in proving health damages where individual issues may predominate over common issues (in *Zinser v. Accufix Research Institute, Inc.*, 2001, a pacemaker implantee brought class action against manufacturer of pacemaker lead and related corporations, asserting claims for negligence, products liability, negligent misrepresentation, fraud and deceit, breach of express and implied warranties, and infliction of emotional distress. "Certainly, there may be common issues in this case, such as those relating to liability to the extent that any alleged defect in the 854 lead may have been caused by ARI's alleged negligence." But to determine causation and damages for each of the three claims asserted here, it is inescapable that many triable individualized issues may be presented. For example, was the alleged defect in the 854 lead caused by negligent manufacturer? Was it caused by negligent shipping or handling? Was it caused by physicians or medical staff? Or was it caused by some combination of these or other factors?).

While there is scientific certainty as to whether and to what extent drug and alcohol addiction are preventable and treatable diseases, public awareness lags behind (Leshner, 1999). Because there is still a lack of their acceptance as a disease, and perceptions that drug- and alcohol-related consequences are self-inflicted, volitional and deserved, a core issue in proving liability is to show that alcohol and drug consumers are victims who have been harmed (Miller, 1994, *supra* note 20, at 105–106). On the other hand, to what extent should alcohol and drug consumers be held responsible for damages and contributing to the liability illustrates ambivalent views which must be overcome in assigning blame to manufacturers and distributors of alcohol and tobacco (*Traynor v. Turnage and McKelvy v. Turnage*, 1988. Two veterans sued the Veterans Administration for violation of the Rehabilitation Act, which prohibits discrimination against people with disabilities. The Supreme Court held that Traynor and McKelvy, who claimed that alcoholism created a disabling condition, were denied benefits: "because they engaged with some degree of willfulness in the conduct that caused them to be disabled." The decision reflects a historical dichotomy in which alcoholism is considered a disabling condition with willful misconduct).

Specific Areas of Class Action Litigation in Medically-Related Cases

There are cases already litigated in state and federal courts that are medically-related class action suits involving those who have been exposed to and become addicted to drugs and alcohol, with attendant adverse consequences (Gostin, 2000, *supra* note 27, at 290–294). As expected, plaintiffs seeking certification from the court and remedies from manufacturers experienced varying degrees of success and failure (*Idem.* "The Tobacco Wars: A Case Study." The first tobacco lawsuit was filed in 1954, initiating what torts-scholar Robert Rabin called the first wave of tobacco litigation. During this wave from 1954 to 1973, approximately 100–150 cases were filed; very few of these cases ever came to trial, and in no case did a plaintiff prevail over tobacco industry ... It was not until 1990 that a New Jersey jury awarded damages of $400,000 to the estate of Rose Cipollone, a smoker who died of cancer at the age of 58. The jury verdict (which was overturned on appeal) was the first in the history of the extensive tobacco litigation in which a plaintiff was awarded damages). Thus, the critical step in this class action litigation, as in general, is class certification where courts frequently decide the fate of a class before the merits of the claims are even argued (*Northern District of California, Dalkon Shield IUD Products Liability Litigation v. A. H. Robins Co., et al.*, 1982; in an action brought by plaintiffs claiming to have been injured by an intrauterine device, the United States District Court for the Northern District of California, 521 F.Supp. 1188, conditionally certified plaintiff's claims as a nationwide class on issue of punitive damages and a statewide California class on issue of liability. The Court of Appeals held that: (1) it was error to certify nationwide class of punitive damages claimants; and (2) California liability class did not satisfy typicality requirement or requirement that class action be superior to other means of adjudication).

Liability for Fraudulent Marketing of Controlled Substances: Litigation against Purdue Pharma

As manufacturers liable for their acts, pharmaceutical companies can be held to the established legal standards for product liability, expressed and implied warranties, negligence and fraud (Matthew Bender & Co., 2004). (As of May 2002, 75 lawsuits were filed against the manufacturer and distributor, claiming that the companies failed to warn of the highly addictive nature of OxyContin® (*Ohler v. Purdue Pharma*, 2002; *Little v. Purdue Pharma*, 2002; *Ewing v. Purdue Pharma*, 2002)). More than 12 class actions have also been filed (National L. J., 2002). The Eastern District of Kentucky denied certification of a proposed class of all persons harmed due to the addictive nature of the drug (*Foister v. Purdue Pharma*, 2002). The Southern District of Ohio denied certification of a proposed nationwide class of persons who are at risk of addiction to OxyContin but who do not presently have any personal injury claims (*Harris v. Purdue Pharma*, 2003). It also denied certification of a class of all Ohio, Kentucky, Indiana and West Virginia residents who first used OxyContin after receiving a legal prescription since 1995 (*Wethington v. Purdue Pharma*, 2003). However, an Ohio court affirmed certification of an OxyContin class action for claims against Purdue Pharma and Abbott Laboratories, subject to the trial court's modification of the class definition to exclude those who obtained the drug unlawfully (*Howland v. Purdue Pharma*, 2003). Recent cases alleging violation of these legal theories against Purdue Pharma are mounting in reaction to the growing damages from its opiate medications, particularly indiscriminate prescribing motivated by profit motives and political pressure on physicians to prescribe narcotic medications for clinical pain conditions (American Academy of Family Physicians, 2003).

Purdue Pharma denied that there was a clear indication that their marketing has led to diversion and abuse, but does admit that unfortunately prescription drug abuse has been a problem in the United States for a long time, particularly in Appalachia. Further, despite an apparent admission of a large problem of addiction to prescription opiate medication, Purdue Pharma denied a role by implying their practices did not contribute to widespread adverse consequences from manufacturing a dangerous drug (see Purdue Pharma). Unfortunately, Purdue Pharma denied a role in public health policy that would limit the danger from prescribing controlled substances, such as warning the public of OxyContin's addictive nature. Instead, it actively engaged in misinforming the public about an inherently defective or dangerous product (*Idem*).

Class Certification Upheld

In a case decided in the state court of appeals of Ohio, the trial court's judgment was affirmed in certifying a class action for the claims against the manufacturer and laboratory. The class consisted of Ohio residents who suffered addiction; physical, mental, or emotional harm; death and/or loss of consortium as a result of the use of the drug. Further, the court found evidence that the manufacturer and laboratory engaged in a common, class-wide course of conduct by not warning of the drug's addictive nature and the inappropriateness of using it for certain ailments, by distributing false and misleading promotional materials, and by promoting and selling a defectively-designed product (*Howard v. Purdue Pharma L. P.*, 2003).

Importantly, the court found properly that common questions predominated over individual questions and that a class action was the superior method of resolving the controversy. Interestingly, the appeals court did not uphold a class action against the doctor because, as to him, questions affecting only individual class members predominated over individual questions of law or fact common to class members. Importantly, the court held that his decision to prescribe the drug to any patient was based on factors that were unique to that individual (*Idem*).

Class Certification Denied

As expected in medical claims, the courts were not uniform in their opinions regarding class certification of a class defined as all persons who had been harmed by the addictive nature of the drugs (*Foister v. Purdue Pharma L. P.*, 2002). In a United States District Court in the Eastern District of Kentucky, the court denied class certification by holding that the definition was vague and called for subjective medical conclusions. Furthermore, the court held that: (1) the plaintiffs did not present evidence meeting the numerosity requirement by showing that joinder of all members would be impracticable; (2) the plaintiff's claims lacked commonality; (3) the claims of the plaintiffs were not typical of those of the putative members; and (4) the plaintiffs did not (*Idem*).

Medical Monitoring of a Class

In another United States district court for the Southern District of Ohio, the court denied class certification of all United States citizens who received a prescription for the drug and were at risk of addiction as a result, but who were not presently personal injury claims. In the decision, the court found that it was inappropriate to certify the individual's proposed medical monitoring class, because although at least a portion of the putative class had standing, having alleged the injury in-fact of increased risk of addiction, the proposed class failed to meet the commonality requirement (*Harris v. Purdue Pharma*, 2003).

CLASS ACTION IS SUPERIOR TO OTHER METHODS

Class action is superior to other methods for fair and efficient adjudication (time, effort, expense, uniformity of decision) whose members suffer discrimination as a class.

Superiority of Class Action Frequently Determines Success of Litigation

Superiority of class action suits frequently depend on the predominance of questions of law or fact common to class member issues over any questions only affecting individual members. In addition, superiority is based on individual interests controlling individual suits, the nature and extent of litigation already commenced by class, the desirability or undesirability of concentrating in a particular forum, the difficulties in calculating individual damages and small individual claims. (FRCP Rule 23 Class Actions Amendments received to 11–10–02 (b) Class Actions Maintainable (3) the court finds that the questions of law and fact common to the members of the class *predominate* over any questions affecting only individual members, and that a class action is superior to other available methods for the fair and efficient adjudication of the controversy. The matters pertinent to the findings include: (1) the interest of members of the class individually controlling the litigation concerning the controversy already commenced by or against members of the class; (2) the desirability or undesirability of concentrating the litigation of the claims in the particular forum; and (3) the difficulties likely to be encountered in the management of a class action.) Ultimately, the success of a class action frequently depends on showing superiority of nontraditional litigation as a class over individual, traditional actions, and proving predominance is often the deciding issue (417 U.S. 156; the Supreme Court held that in class action maintained in part on the basis that questions of law or fact common to members of class predominate over any questions affecting only individual members, and that class action is superior to other available methods for fair and efficient adjudication of controversy, individual notice to identifiable class members is not a discretionary consideration to be waived in a particular case, nor may notice requirement be tailored to fit the pocketbooks of particular plaintiffs). However, the class action vehicle affords the lowly, stigmatized and disadvantaged individual by allowing large numbers of plaintiffs with small claims to fight the status quo to overcome discrimination (*Idem* at 2157). The court further held that the class action is one of the few legal remedies the small claimant has against those who command the status quo. I would strengthen his hand with the view of creating a system of law that dispenses justice to the lowly, as well as to those liberally endowed with power and wealth. When the organization of a modern society, such as ours, affords the possibility of illegal behavior accompanied by widespread, diffuse consequences, some procedural means must exist to remedy – or at least deter – the conduct).

The decision in *Castano v. American Tobacco Company* in 1996 was against class certification for all nicotine-dependent smokers (*Castano v. American Tobacco Company*, 1996, *supra* note 53, at 749; the court used the district court's definition of "nicotine-dependent" as: (a) all cigarette smokers who have been diagnosed by a medical practitioner as nicotine-dependent; (b) all regular smokers who were or have been advised by a medical practitioner that smoking has had or will have adverse health consequences that thereafter do not or have not quit smoking. The definition is based upon the criteria for "dependence" set forth in the *American Psychiatric Association, Diagnostic and Statistical Manual of Mental Disorders*) in the United States, because variations in state law would render the class impracticable (*Castano v. American Tobacco Company*, 1996, *supra* note 53, at 749–750; the complexity of the choice of law inquiry makes individual adjudication superior to class treatment). Although plaintiffs' attorneys promised to initiate state-by-state class actions, some courts refused to certify state classes (*Idem* at 750; "the plaintiffs have asserted eight theories liability from every state. Prior to certification, the district court must determine whether variations in state law defeat predominance").

Superiority can be a Single Forum

A closer analysis of the decision in *Castano* will reveal pitfalls and directions for future litigation in other similarly situated areas for those suffering from damages due to drugs and alcohol. Basically the United States Court of Appeals Fifth Circuit determined that class action was premature for a single jury despite plaintiffs in other states, Florida, Oregon and California having won verdicts, and numerous individual law suits were pending (*Idem* at 751; the court held: "the collective wisdom of individual juries is necessary before this court commits the fate of an entire industry or, indeed, the fate of a class of millions, to a single jury"). To begin with, the class was perhaps the largest class action ever attempted in federal court when the district court, by entering a class certification order, embarked "on a road certainly less traveled, if ever taken at all." However, the United States Court of Appeals reversed the class certification on interlocutory appeal (*Castano v. American Tobacco Co.*, 1995, citing Edward C. Latham, *The Poetry of Robert Frost*, "The Road Not Taken" 105 (1969), and entered a class certification order for: (a) all nicotine-dependent persons in the United States … who have purchased and smoked cigarettes manufactured by the defendants; (b) the estates, representatives and administrators of these nicotine-dependent cigarette smokers; and (c) the spouses, children, relatives and "significant others" of these nicotine-dependent cigarettes smokers as their heirs or survivors. The plaintiffs limit the claims to years since 1943).

The complaint alleged the defendants fraudulently failed to inform consumers that nicotine is addictive and manipulated the level of nicotine in cigarettes to sustain their addictive nature (*Castano v. American Tobacco Co*, 1995, *supra* note 53, at 735. The plaintiffs filed this class complaint against the defendant tobacco companies and the Tobacco Institute, Inc., seeking compensation for the injury of nicotine addiction. The gravamen of their complaint is the novel and wholly untested theory that the defendants fraudulently failed to inform the consumers that nicotine is addictive and manipulated the level of nicotine in cigarettes to sustain the addictive nature). In addition, the class complaint alleged nine causes of action, fraud and deceit, negligent misrepresentation, intentional infliction of emotional distress, negligence and negligent infliction of emotional distress, violation of state consumer protection statutes, breach of express warranty, breach of implied warranty, strict product liability and redhibition pursuant to the Louisiana Civil Code (*Castano v. American Tobacco Co*, 1995, *supra* note 53, at 735. The district court refused to certify the issues of injury-in-fact, proximate cause, reliance, affirmative defenses and compensatory damages, concluding that the: "issues are so overwhelmingly replete with individual circumstances that they quickly outweigh predominance and superiority." Specifically, the court found that whether a person suffered emotional injury from addiction, whether his addiction was caused by the defendants' actions, whether he relied on the defendants' misrepresentations, and whether affirmative defenses unique to each class member precluded recovery were all individual issues).

Moreover, the plaintiffs sought compensatory and punitive damages and attorneys' fees, and equitable relief which included defendants' being financially responsible for notifying all class members of nicotine's addictive nature (*Castano v. American Tobacco Co*, 1995, *supra* note 53, at 737. The plaintiffs seek compensatory and punitive damages and attorney's fees. In addition, the plaintiffs seek equitable relief for fraud and deceit, negligent misrepresentation, violation of consumer protection statutes, and breech of express and implied warranty). Because the defendants manipulated nicotine levels with the intent to sustain the addiction of plaintiffs and class members, plaintiffs requested an order that the defendants disgorge any profits made from the sale of cigarettes, restitution of sums paid for cigarettes and establishment of a medical monitoring fund (*Castano v. American Tobacco Co*, 1995, *supra* note 53, at 738. The equitable remedies include a declaration that defendants are financially responsible for notifying all class members of nicotine's addictive nature, a declaration that the defendants manipulated nicotine levels with the intent to sustain the addiction of plaintiffs and the class members, an order that the defendants disgorge any profits made from the sale of cigarettes, restitution for sums paid for cigarettes and the establishment of a medical monitoring fund).

Predominance Requirement Depends on Individual Issues for Causes in Addiction

Of interest is that the district court found that the predominance requirement of rule 23 (b)(3) was satisfied for core liability issues. However, the court did not certify class for issues of injury-in-fact, proximate cause, reliance, affirmative defenses and compensatory damages, because the issues were so overwhelmingly replete with individual circumstances that quickly outweighed predominance and superiority (*Castano v. American Tobacco Co*, 1995, *supra* note 88, at 752. The circuit court held the district court abused its discretion by ignoring variations in state law and how a trial on the alleged causes of action would be tried. These errors cannot be corrected on remand because of the novelty of the plaintiffs' claims. Accordingly, class treatment is not superior to individual adjudication). Likely the court's failure to certify the latter issues was based on the lack of acceptance of addiction as a unity disorder caused by the use of a particular drug such as nicotine, and the view of addiction as a personal choice as in contributory negligence (*Traynor v. Turnage and McKelvy v. Turnage*, 1988, *supra* note 64, at 544).

Individual Interests in Controlling Individual Suits in Mass Tort Litigation

In particular, courts have held that a mass tort cannot be properly certified without a prior track record of trials from which the district court can draw the information necessary to make the predominance and superiority analysis required by rule 23 (*Castano v. American Tobacco Co*, 1995, *supra* note 53, at 752. The court stated "We have once before stated 'traditional ways of proceeding reflect far more than habit. They reflect the very culture of the jury trial…' " *Re Fibreboard Corp.*, 1990). Thus, courts have concluded certification of an immature tort can result in a higher than normal risk that the class action may not be superior to individual adjudication (*Idem* at 750. "State courts are more than capable of providing definitive statements of addiction-as-injury claims" *Joseph E. Seagrams & Sons v. McGuire*, 1991).

COMMON KNOWLEDGE THEORY

Common knowledge theory can be used to defeat class action to protect individuals suffering from a medical disorder. In a class action suit involving alcohol, a state court asserted that state courts were more than capable of providing definitive statements regarding the validity of addiction-as-injury claims (*Joseph E. Seagrams & Sons v. McGuire*, 1991. The Texas state court accepted "common knowledge" theory and holding no cause of action for alcohol addiction based on products liability, misrepresentations, negligence, breach of implied warranties of merchantability and fitness, violations of consumer protection statutes and conspiracy). This decision was based on the common knowledge theory that everyone knows alcohol is addictive, including alcoholics. Thus, the court rejected a claim for alcohol addiction based on products liability, misrepresentations, negligence, breach of implied warranties of merchantability and fitness, violations of consumer protection statutes and conspiracy.

Ultimately, the court revealed its bias by stating "traditional ways of proceeding reflected far more than habit but the very culture of the jury trial" (*Castano v. American Tobacco Co*, 1995, *supra* note 53, at 752). Moreover, the "collective wisdom of individual juries is necessary before this court commits the fate of an entire industry or, indeed, the fate of a class of millions, to a single jury." While the court did not come right out and say alcoholics should know better, they insinuated the same by basing its holding on the common knowledge theory (*Joseph E. Seagrams & Sons v. McGuire*, 1991, *supra* note 97). Thus, the common knowledge theory was used to reinforce the discriminatory policy against alcoholism as a medical disorder, and again circumvent holding perpetrators for inflicting damage on vulnerable individuals (Miller, 1994, *supra* note 9, at 196–197).

CONCLUSIONS FROM CLASS ACTIONS IN ADDICTION

Legacies from Tobacco, Opiate Medications and Alcohol

The tobacco litigation provides a perspective of the highs and lows of class action victories. Moreover, the tobacco wars illustrate the benefits of nontraditional class action litigation in overcoming powerful and unethical foes to defend the rights of a discriminated class (Gostin, 2000, *supra* note 36, at 3178–3179). However, it also shows that the very class the litigation sought to protect can become the victim of the class action litigation as only a fraction of the tobacco settlement funds are dedicated to tobacco control and prevention (Gross et al., 1980–1982, *supra* note 15).

On the other hand, the opiate medication litigation reveals the difficulties in meeting the requirements for class certification, particularly to establish that common questions predominate over individual issues (*Foister v. Purdue Pharma*, 2002, *supra* note 78). In particular, courts appear wary to approve the nontraditional class as a superior method to the traditional, single jury trial. Therefore, there still appears to be substantial prejudice against accepting addictions as medical disorders that involve common biological mechanisms. Rather, the courts still view addiction as individual, personal choices which often defeat the all-important predominance issues in Rule 23 (FRCP Rule 23 Class Actions Amendments, *supra* note 81).

Perhaps, the common knowledge theory is the greatest obstacle to overcome, and pervasive to the courts rationale in rejecting class certification for addiction cases. This popular view perpetuates the stereotype that everyone does or should know of the harmful, addictive effects of alcohol, tobacco and other drugs (*Joseph E. Seagrams & Sons v. McGuire*, 1991, *supra* note 97). Thus, there can be no legal theory to protect the individual who falls prey to deceptive marketing, frank denials and manipulation by manufacturers, despite the common knowledge that alcohol, tobacco and other drugs are addictive. However, it is common knowledge that surgery can result in harmful outcomes, and doctors are human, therefore, not perfect, yet they are held to a duty that protects patients from their damages caused by negligence, misrepresentation, intentional torts and other practices which result in deviations from a standard of care.

The Road Less Traveled

Ultimately, the success of class action litigation in protecting discrimination against harmful effects of addiction will depend on acceptance of addiction as a unity disorder, worthy of prevention and treatment, and a standard of care. The root of the discrimination is a persistent moral belief that addiction is a defect in character despite compelling scientific evidence to the contrary (Miller & Swift, 1997, *supra* note 10). Thus, as with other forms of discrimination, class action remains an important and potential procedural tool to correct past wrongs and to protect against future wrongs committed against stigmatized individuals. Perhaps persistent and aggressive class actions against the "mainstream" and powerful majority opinion may eventually persuade the courts in the future to choose to take "the road less traveled."

REFERENCES

Achem Prods. v. Windsor, 521 U.S. 591, 1997, quoting *Mace v. Van Ru Credit Corp.*, 109 F.3d 338 338, 344 (7th Cir. 1997).

American Academy of Family Physicians. (2003). *Pain management: Dispelling the myths.* Leawood, KA: American Academy of Family Physicians.

Arno, P. S., Brandt, A. M., Gostin, L. O., & Morgan, J. (1996). Tobacco industry strategies to oppose federal regulation. *JAMA, 275*(16), 1258–1262.

Blum, T. C., Roman, P. M., & Bennett, N. (1989). Public images of alcoholism data from a Georgia survey. *Journal of Studies on Alcohol, 50,* 5–14.

Caetano, P. (1987). Public opinions about alcoholism and its treatment. *Journal of Studies on Alcohol, 48,* 153–160.

Castano et al., v. The American Tobacco Company, et al., 84 F.3d 734 (1996).

Castano v. American Tobacco Co. 160 F.R.D. 544, 560 (1995).

Center for Disease Control and Prevention. (2002b). Annual smoking-attributable mortality, years of potential life lost, and economic costs: United States, 1995–1999. *Mortality and Morbidity Weekly Report, 51,* 300–303.

Center for Substance Drug Control Policy. (1995). Symptoms of substance dependence associated with cigarettes, alcohol, and illicit drugs – United States 1992. *MMWR Weekly, 44*(10), 830–839.

Centers for Disease Control and Prevention. (2003). Prevention of current smoking among adults and changes in prevalence of current and some day smoking: United States, 1996–2001. *Morbidity and Mortality Weekly Report, 52,* 303–307.

Conte, A., & Newberg, H. (2002). *Newberg on class actions, theory, structure and constitutionality of class action* (4th ed.). Rochester, NY: Thomson West (pp. 1–48) Supra note 3. § 1:1 Theory and procedural nature of class actions: Representative suits on behalf of others similarly situated. 6A Federal Procedures, L. Ed., Class Actions § 12:1 to 12:13 A.

Daynard, R. A., Parmet, W., Kelder, G., & Davidson, P. (2001). Implications for tobacco control of the multistate tobacco settlement. *American Journal of Public Health*, *91*(12), 1967–1971.

Dean, J. C., & Poremba, G. A. (1983). The alcoholic stigma and the disease concept. *Journal of Addictions*, *18*, 739–751.

Engle v. R. J. Reynolds Co., No. 94–08273 CA–22 (Fla. Cir. Ct. 11th April 7, 2000).

Ewing v. Purdue Pharma, L. P. (W.D.Va. April 10, 2002).

Foister v. Purdue Pharma L. P., 2002 U.S. Dist. (E.d.Ken., 2002); Lexis 8192 (Feb. 2002).

Foister v. Purdue Pharma, L. P. (E.D.Ken. Feb.26, 2002).

Garner, B. A. (2001). *Black's law dictionary*. Eagan, MN: West Group Discrimination is defined as a "differential treatment, especially a failure to treat all persons equally when no reasonable distinctions can be found between those favored and those not favored. Further, invidious discrimination is offensive or objectionable, especially if it involves prejudice or stereotyping."

General Telephone Co. of the Southwest v. Mariano S. Falcon, 102 S. Ct. 2364 (1982).

Gostin, L. O. (2000). Public health, power, duty, restraint. In *Tort Law and the Public Health*. Berkeley, CA: University of California Press (pp. 290–293).

Gostin, L. O., Brandt, A. M., & Cleary, P. D. (1991). Tobacco liability and public health policy. *JAMA*, *266*(22), 3178–3182.

Grace v. City of Detroit, 145 F.R.D. 413 (1992).

Gross, C. P., Soffer, B., Bach, P., Rajkumar, R., & Forman, H. P. (2002). State expenditures for tobacco-control programs and the tobacco settlement. *New England Journal of Medicine*, *347*(14), 1980–1982.

Harris v. Purdue Pharma, L. P., 218 F.D.R. 590, 596 (S.D. Ohio 2003).

Hensler, D. R., Moller, E. K., Giddens, B., Gross, J., & Pace, N. M. (2000). *Class Action Dilemmas: Pursuing Public Goals for Private Gain*. Santa Monica, CA: Rand Institute for Civil Justice.

Hensler, D. R., Pace, N. M., Dombey-Moore, B., Giddens, B., Gross, J., & Moller, E. K. (2000). The great big question about class action. In *Class Action Dilemmas: Pursuing Public Goals for Private Gain*. Santa Monica, CA: Rand Institute for Civil Justice.

Hilts, P. J., & Collins, G. (1995). *Records show Philip Morris studies influence of nicotine*. New York Times June 8, A1.

Howard v. Purdue Pharma L. P., 2003 Ohio 3699; Lexis 3347 (2003).

Howland v. Purdue Pharma, L. P., 2003 Ohio 3699 (2003).

Hurt, R. D., & Robertson, C. R. (1998). Prying open the door to the tobacco industry's secrets about nicotine. *JAMA*, *280*(13), 1173–1181.

Janson, D. (1988). *Data on smoking revealed at trial*. New York Times March 13, A34.

Joseph E. Seagrams & Sons v. McGuire, 814 S.W.2d 385 (1991).

Kline, et al. v. Coldwell Banker & Co., Realtors, 508 F.2d 226 (1974).

Leshner, A. I. (1999). Science-based views of drug addiction and its treatment. *JAMA*, *282*, 1314–1315.

Little v. Purdue Pharma, L. P. (S.D. Ohio September. 20, 2002).

Matthew Bender & Co. (2004). *Drug product liability. lexstate 2–15 § 15.92, chapter 15, drug litigation experience*. New York, NY: Matthew Bender & Co.

McGinnis, J. M., & Foege, W. H. (1993). Actual causes of death in the United States. Selected abstracts. *JAMA & Archives*, *270*(18), 2207.

Midwest Motor Freight Bureau v. U.S., 433 F.2d 212 (8th Cir. 1970).

Miller, N. S. & Swift, R. N. (1997). Primary care medicine and psychiatry: Addictions treatment. *Psychiatric Annals*, June, 415. "Alcohol and drug disorders and the individuals who suffer from them have long been stigmatized and marginalized."

Miller, N. S. (1994). Prevalence and treatment models for addictions in psychiatric populations. *Psychiatric Annals*, *24*, 1012–1014.

Miller, N. S. (2001). Disease orientation: Taking away blame and shame. In R. H. Coombs (Ed.), *Addiction Recovery Tools: A Practical Handbook* (pp. 99–101). London, UK: Sage Publications.

Miller, N. S. (2000, 2001). Addictions and the law. *J. of Medicine and Law*, Michigan State University-Detroit College of Law, *2*(1), 33–35.

Miller, N. S., & Chappel, J. N. (1991). History of the disease concept: The disease concept of alcoholism and drug addiction. Rarely overtly stated but clearly central to the concept of disease is the victim state. *Psychiatric Annals*, 196–197.

Miller, N. S., & Gold, M. S. (1994). Dissociation of "conscious desire" (craving) from and relapse in alcohol and cocaine dependence. *Annals of Clinical Psychiatry*, *6*(2), 99–106.

Miller, N. S., & Goldsmith, R. J. (2001). Neuroimaging and craving: Clinical and basic research. *Journal of Addictive Diseases*, *20*(3), 87–92.

Miller, N. S., & Lyon, D. (1997). Biology of opiates: Affects prevalence of addiction, options for treatment. *Psychiatric Annals*, *27*, 408–410.

Miller, N. S., Dackis, C. A., & Gold, M. S. (1987). The relationship of addiction, tolerance and depdendence to alcohol and drugs: A neurochemical approach. *Journal of Substance Abuse Treatment*, *4*(3–4), 197–207.

Miller, N. S., Sheppard, L. M., Colenda, C. C., & Magen, J. (2001). Why physicians are unprepared to treat patients who have alcohol and drug disorders. *Academy of Medicine*, *76*(5), 410–418.

Northern District of California, Dalkon Shield IUD Products Liability Litigation v. A.H. Robins Co., et al., 693 F.2d 847 (1982).

Office of Revenue and Tax Analysis, Michigan Department of Treasury. (2002). *Michigan's Cigarette and Tobacco Taxes*. 5–7.

Ohler v. Purdue Pharma, L. P. (E.D. La. Jan.22, 2002).

Phillips Petroleum Co. v. Shutts, 472 U.S. 797 (1985).

Powell v. State of Texas, 392 U.S. 514 (1961).

Purdue Pharma. Available at <http://www.pharma.com/>

Re Fibreboard Corp., 893 F.2d 706 (1990).

Regier, D. A., Farmer, M. E., Rae, D. S., Locke, B. Z., Keith, S. J., & Goodwin, F. K. (1990). Comorbidity of mental disorders with alcohol and drug abuse. *JAMA*, *368*, 1012–1014.

Robinson v. California, 370 U.S. 660 (1962).

Rogers v. Lodge, 458 U.S. 613 (1982).

Rossman, S. T., & Edelman, D. A. (2002). *Consumer Class Actions: A Practical Litigation Guide* Chapter 1 § 1.1 Whether to File as a Class Action 3 (5th ed.). Boston, MA: National Consumer Law Center.

Schoenborn, C. A. (1991). *Exposure to Alcoholism in the Family: US, 1988*. Advance Data from Vital Health Statistics, *205*. National Center for Health Statistics.

Traynor v. Turnage and McKelvy v. Turnage, 485 U.S. 539 (1988).

United States Parole Comm'n v. Geraghty, 445 U.S. 388 (1980).

Vaillant, G. E. (1983). The Natural History of Alcoholism. Cambridge, UK: Cambridge University Press.

Van Voris, R. (April 30 2002). OxyContin Maker Not Yet Feeling Much Pain. *National Law Journal*.

Warner, K. W. (2000). The economics of tobacco: Myths and realties. *Tobacco Control*, *9*(1), 78–89.

Wethington v. Purdue Pharma, L.P., 218 F.R.D. 577 (2003).

Zinser v. Accufix Research Institute, Inc., 253 F.3d 1180 (2001).

Index